Riot on Greenwood

The Total Destruction of Black Wall Street, 1921

Eddie Faye Gates

EAKIN PRESS ✠ Fort Worth, Texas

To those brave, besieged, frightened refugees of the Tulsa Race Riot of 1921. May justice be served and the survivors and their descendants, recompensed and revered by a just, honorable, and grateful nation. May the dead rest in peace, knowing that, at last, they have each been given a decent, honorable farewell.

Contents

Foreword

It has been said about the writings and ideas of Howard Thurman that for him, "Love is synonymous with reconciliation and expresses the 'intent' of God." In this sense, Eddie Faye Gates has now provided us with a third book that transforms her hard work, scholarship, and engaging writing into an instrument of love. Her passion for her subject is surpassed only by her desire to see humanity restored. She has become the conduit of a series of remarkable and colorful stories that demonstrate the full range of human possibility from devastation to hope. Her accounts provide a window into experiences and lives that might have otherwise been forgotten or misunderstood. In doing so, she offers readers an opportunity to realign their relationship to the events and individuals of one of Tulsa's most disturbing and formative events, and in turn invites all who are willing to proceed down a path of reconciliation.

Mrs. Gates may have started out intending to record the lives of the remaining survivors, but she ended up becoming a significant part of many of their lives. Her book not only brings its readers into contact with these real people and their memories, but it has the capacity to convey these life stories in a way that can have a profound effect on one's own.

Marlin Lavanhar
Senior Minister
All Souls Unitarian Church
Tulsa, Oklahoma

Acknowledgments

People

Rep. Don Ross
Senator Maxine Horner
Councilor Joe Williams
Councilor Roscoe Turner
Dr. Scott Ellsworth
Harry K. Dowdy
Dr. John Hope Franklin
Dr. Danney Goble
Hannibal B. Johnson, Attorney at Law
Robert Littlejohn
Curtis Lawson
Rose Wright
Kavin Ross
Sammy Weygand
Keith Jimerson, Librarian, Rudisill North Regional Library
Kim Johnson, Director, African American Resource
Center, Rudisill North Regional Library
Dr. Bob Blackburn
Rodger Harris
Millard House, Metropolitan Tulsa Urban League
Iman Arthur Farakhan
Ruford Henderson, Jack Henderson, Melvin Easiley,
Tulsa Chapter, NAACP
The American Red Cross
The United Nations of Eastern Oklahoma
Tulsa Metropolitan Ministry
The University of Tulsa
Ed Eakin and Virginia Messer, Eakin Press, Austin, Texas

Places/Organizations, Etc.

North Tulsa Historical Society
Greenwood Cultural Center
Greenwood Chamber of Commerce
Tulsa Chamber of Commerce
North Tulsa Heritage Foundation
Tulsa Historical Society
Oklahoma Historical Society
Oklahoma Commission to Study the
Tulsa Race Riot of 1921
Oklahoma State University–Tulsa
Tulsa City County Library
Rudisill North Regional Library
Tulsa Branch, NAACP
Metropolitan Tulsa Urban League
The University of Tulsa
The YWCA of Tulsa
The YMCA of Tulsa
The Salvation Army of Tulsa
The University of Tulsa Council

Special acknowledgments to my wonderful and patient husband, Norman, for his unconditional support of me and the various compelling causes that often take me away from home and hearth, and to my five grown children, Norman Gates, Jr., Kevin Jerome Gates, Derek Wayne Gates, Dianne Gates-Anderson, and Donna Gates Kelley, who love me (and some of my causes) passionately, who have mixed feelings about some of my causes, and who just tolerate others because they are "my things," who dutifully look at all the scrapbooks, photos, videos, and other memorabilia connected to my causes and world travel, and, most of all, who gave me seven of the most beautiful, intelligent, charming grandchildren in the world; to my daughter-in-law Scharyl Swinton Gates, who, in addition to being a loving new daughter, is one of the brightest young women that I have ever known. Her degrees from Oklahoma State

University and the University of Tulsa explain her expertise in sociology and psychology, but she has an equally sharp mind for business and has been an equal partner with my son, Derek, and is equally responsible for the success of his engineering firm in Tulsa. But what I am most grateful to Scharyl for is her keen insight into the Tulsa community. She cuts to the chase, analyzes things instantly, and protects me because she thinks I am too tenderhearted and vulnerable. She is my shield. She "sees the ball coming," while I don't know the ball is coming until it hits me! Thanks, Scharyl, for helping me through all this "race riot experience," and for knowing when I needed a dinner at Red Lobster to get the creative juices flowing! Scharyl's sister, Sonya D. Swinton, is a carbon copy of Scharyl. Thanks, Sonya, for taking me under your wing when I did riot research in Washington, D.C. She took vacation time from her capital-area job and helped me navigate the D.C./Maryland subway system and find all the capital-area buildings where I did research. My other children's spouses, Stephanie Gates, Norman, Jr.'s wife, Harry Kelley III, Donna's husband, and Tikisa Anderson, Dianne's husband, live out of town, but they support my causes, too; thanks to my sister-in-law Bertha Jean Owens Gates, who clips from the *Muskogee Daily Phoenix* newspaper in Muskogee, Oklahoma, all the articles that relate to any of my causes and sends them to me, and who calls me every time she sees a television program that relates to one of my causes.

Thanks to the following non-family members who were so helpful to me during this writing endeavor, such as Rose Wright, Tulsa Public Schools counselor, former social studies teacher, and longtime friend, who helped me with research for this book, and to James Kavin Ross, of Oklahoma State University, Tulsa, one of the best videographers I have ever known. Kavin's warm personality, together with his technical expertise, were invaluable to me during the videotaping of approximately forty-five black Tulsa survivors of the Tulsa Race Riot of 1921, twenty white eyewitnesses of the riot, as well as the videotaping of numerous local, state, national, and international print and electronic media personnel who came to Tulsa to do stories about the riot. To Fai Walker, director of the Greenwood Cultural Center, located in the heart of the old Black Wall Street area of North Tulsa, who came to us from New York City and fell in love with Tulsa. She is doing a wonderful job of preserving, promoting, and perpetuating the legacy of Tulsa's black community. To Jewel Hines, who lived in Africa for years and who so willingly shared her African experience with me. Thanks to Jewel, I knew what to look for in Africa and how to get the most out of my African experience. To Dr. Vivian Clark-Adams, division chair, Liberal Arts, Tulsa Community College, my soul sister in terms of philosophy of life and passionate commitment to causes. And many thanks to Marge Morgan, a reporter for twenty-some years at the *Tulsa Tribune*, who attended a forum on the Tulsa Race Riot of 1921 at her church, All Souls Unitarian, late in 2001. She said that her heart was touched and she began to think about what she could do to help in the healing of the hurts that had been caused by the riot.

The minister of her church, Reverend Marlin Lavanhar, wrote a moving column in the *Tulsa World* newspaper early in 2002 appealing for Tulsans to volunteer in some way to help promote racial healing in Tulsa, and to specifically help riot survivors. He listed many kinds of in-kind services that could be provided by the entire Tulsa community. Marge knew then just what she wanted to do. She called me and volunteered to use her journalistic skills to help me with this book. I knew just what I needed at that moment from Marge—help with the bibliography. Marge went to work immediately, helping me with typing. Thanks, Marge, for organizing all the resources used in the writing of this book. Marge wasn't turned off by the suitcase of hardback books that I left at the Greenwood Cultural Center for her to pick up, or the large laundry basket of pamphlets, booklets, magazines, and other sources that I left there. She did an excellent job.

Also, thanks to Col. Harry K. Dowdy of Bowie, Maryland, who late in 2001 sent me a videotape that perked up my spirit, which had begun to lag due to the slowness, and/or inaction, of federal, state, and local entities to provide justice and closure to the race riot that destroyed the Greenwood District in Tulsa. That tape, *Ida B. Wells* was just what I needed. I have always been an admirer of Ms. Wells (later Barnett). Harry's videotape has become my beacon light. I have shared it with some of my fellow commissioners. We are determined that like the indomitable Ida B. Wells Barnett, we will not falter; we will not stop until justice is done for the victims of that awful riot of 1921 and for the Greenwood District in general. Ida B. Wells Barnett had a bounty offered to stop her movement. Despite death threats and being run out of her hometown of Memphis, she never wavered. If she could perservere, so can we!

And finally, thanks to Ed Eakin, owner of Eakin Press, Austin, Texas, who was one of the most loving, spiritually-minded, unbiased individuals that I have ever known. Ironically, my paternal grandparents, Joseph and Rhoda Wesley Petit, were sharecroppers in the same Brazos River Bottom lands near Marlin, Texas, as the white, sharecropping Eakin family. Perhaps it is this background that made Ed Eakin so just and fair. Observing the black experience firsthand in his childhood (the same time period as my childhood), he knew of the struggles, tenacity, and perseverance of black families like mine. Ed loved history, especially southwestern history. Unlike some major mainstream publishers in the east, he did not view black literary efforts as a "soft" market with limited potential readership. He valued black writings and considered them just as vital as writings by other racial, ethnic, religious, social, political, or economic groups. His main criterion in selecting manuscripts for publication is quality—good research, scholarship, and writing. It should be no surprise that Eakin Press was greatly respected and revered by black authors. Thank you, Ed, for valuing and affirming all of God's children!

Prologue

In order to understand one's own history and culture, an individual must have a basic understanding of the significance of history and culture to all mankind. An understanding of man's curiosity, of his deep-seated need to share his own culture and history with others, and the ability to adapt to and accommodate other cultures (and to learn vital lessons from all these experiences) will help one to better understand all cultures, all history. I hope that this book will add to the reader's storehouse of knowledge and promote a better understanding of history, in general, and of the Tulsa Race Riot, specifically. What an exciting time in history the world's populations are experiencing today! Recent exciting archeological finds are leading to critical reevaluations of the history of mankind. Revision of history is the natural outcome of new discoveries, new historical approaches, and the natural upward progression of human thought. New levels of uplifted human thought are leading to a new age of apology, reconciliation, and healing of centuries-old racial, religious, political, economic, and social injustices in the world.

On the other hand, recent terrorist attacks on the World Trade Center in New York City, on the Pentagon in Washington, D.C., and on a U.S. airplane over Pennsylvania show new levels of hate, envy, and criminal behavior in the world. One can see that there is still much to do in uplifting the thought of mankind so that there can be peace, harmony, prosperity, justice, and equality for all mankind all over the globe!

My background as a beginning college student, military dependent wife, perpetual college student, and long-time history teacher prepared me well for teaching, researching, and writing history. (My English minor preparations also helped tremendously.) For five decades, I have done extensive research on riots, revolutions, reform movements, massacres, and wars at local, state, national, and international levels. My search for historical truth spread from the Tuskegee Institute campus in Alabama in the 1950s, to Europe three times, the Middle East once, the Caribbean twice, and to my first trip to the Motherland, Africa, in March of 2001.

I learned much history when I lived in the north of England, near Liverpool and Manchester. Liverpool has extensive records on the European slave trade, since the city was a major port on the Triangular Slave Trade route during the slave-trade era. I learned even more history the three years that I lived in London. My Holocaust study experience in Poland and Israel in 1991 added to my storehouse of knowledge, and I learn more history about the Americas every time I visit the Caribbean. But it was my research in our nation's capital in 1999, on behalf of the Oklahoma Commission to study the Tulsa Race Riot of 1921, that was the "pinnacle experience" of all my research! I examined historical records at the National Archives, the Library of Congress, the Smithsonian Institution, Howard University, historic libraries, and other museums. While the electronic age has made available vast resources via the internet to help scholars, historians, authors, and others, nothing takes the place of physically handling the fragile documents, books, and memorabilia that bind our nation together in unity.

So, it is hoped that after reading this book, every reader will be better prepared to contribute to peace, harmony, and justice in his or her own community, state, nation, and the world. If for some reason I had not had the opportunity to share all the ideas I have expounded upon in this book but was limited to only two sentences of advice, they would be: Get to the root of problems that seem to divide mankind today. Learn how thoughts and actions of the past impact the present, and how they will eventually influence the future.

When I first began to write this book, I was overwhelmed by the enormity of the task before me. I had tons of books, newspapers, magazines, pamphlets and booklets, documents, charts, graphs, notes on interviews, photographs, audiotapes, videotapes, and other memorabilia that I planned to use. When my computer room and library became filled, the overflow materials were spread out in two unused bedrooms in my house. I bought storage bins, made folders, and put everything in perfect order. But when I sat down at my computer to write, I was still overwhelmed. I finally came to grips with the situation by convincing myself that I didn't have to tell everything there was that related to the Tulsa Race Riot of 1921! I felt safe in doing this, as print and electronic media had converged on Tulsa beginning in the early 1990s, when books and films begin to trickle out of the city, and reaching a peak in the 2000s, when the Riot Commission report was released. So much was available about that riot that I thought only a person living in outer space would not know about it.

Still, when I began to "edit down" this book, I had trouble. The old "compassionate teacher syndrome" kicked in. Teachers are notorious for freely giving too much information to too many people in too many places in the world! You don't have to be of any particular age, race, religion, or class to receive this information, and you definitely don't have to ask for it. You just have to be perceived by the teacher as being in need of it. Sociologists, psychologists, criminologists, and other specialists have written that because of this "compassionate syndrome," teachers fall into the category of sometimes easy victims— easy prey for clever, conniving students, con artists, and, sometimes, fast-talking, hard-core criminals. On the other hand, my grandma had a saying that "God always looks after babies and fools." So things have balanced out for me. People who know me take my zealous sharing of information in stride and do not think negatively of me because of my constant snapping of photographs, asking for interviews, clipping of articles, making tons of scrapbooks, and freely giving advice. They know that is just me being me! People who don't know me, and other "compassionate syndrome" people, sometimes mistake our motives and actions, and label us as egotistical, as softies (or suckers and patsies), or as bossy busybodies. It used to bother me if my motives and acts were mistaken, but now I just take it all in stride. I thank God that my friends know me, know that I have no hidden agenda and that I am not money-driven.

If I sometimes seem to cross into overzealousness, they forgive me, for they know the real me.

Two things helped my "inner author self" win the battle over my "compassionate teacher self"—the flood of printed materials, and the flood of electronic media that spread news about the Tulsa riot all over the world. So I was able to let go of writing a massive, detailed book about the riot and focus on the survivors, their descendants, and other eyewitnesses of the riot. Still, I pondered over how to set the stage for the eyewitnesses' accounts of their experience. I decided not to recreate the wheel, for much has already been written about race, justice delayed, justice denied, revolutions, riots, and reforms in history. I decided that I would write short chapters of introduction, chock full of details, before the chapters containing eyewitness accounts of the riot. And that is what I did. Here is a brief description of what will be found in each chapter in the book.

At the beginning of each chapter, I have included information about the resources that have been most helpful to me in writing that particular chapter—books, pamphlets, magazines, newspapers, electronic media, photographs, oral history interviews, etc. I have striven to fully credit every resource properly. Direct quotes are within quotation marks and references to authors freely given within the text in each chapter to provide clarity. A more detailed description of resources can be found in the bibliography at the end of the book. Any errors regarding proper crediting of creators of the resources used to write this book, are unintentional and will be corrected in future editions of the book providing written complaints regarding improper credit are sent to the publisher.

Chapter 1 covers the complex topic of history in general—the who, what, where, when, why, and how of the human experience. I researched and explored the following aspects of history:

I   Who writes history?
II   What is history?
III   Where did history begin?
IV   When did history begin?
V   Why is history so important?
VI   How has history evolved, and how has it had so much influence on mankind?

In this chapter, there will be an examination of history, with an update on "Old History" and "New History" and the interrelationship between the two. Certain key vocabulary terms turn up in this chapter, and they will recur in each subsequent chapter. Some of the terms were

    treachery, fear, anguish, terror, tumult, danger
    hope, faith, persistence, prayer, deliverance
    bestiality, brutality, scorn, hatred, indifference,
    greed, graft, corruption, enemies, conquerors,
       mobsters,
    care, concern, compassion, tenderness, gentleness,
    dignity, patriots, advocates, defenders, survival
    injustice, inequality, bias, prejudice, discrimination,
    racism, ambiguity, paradox, cover-up, denial
    justice, freedom, equality, love, spirituality,
       democracy
    examination, investigation, acknowledgment,
       documentation, reconciliation, restoration,
       reparation, justice, freedom, equality,
    spirituality, love, democracy

This chapter will help the reader understand how the factors covered in this chapter—the early settlement of the Americas by Africans, the era of exploration by European colonizers, and their subsequent domination of the Americas, and the movement into North America—impacted the lives of the peoples who settled in the Louisiana Territory district that later became Oklahoma.

Chapter 2 covers the Tulsa Race Riot of 1921:
I   The historical effects of the Settlement of the Americas
II Early Oklahoma History
III Early Tulsa History
IV Six Case Studies Regarding Settlement in Oklahoma
V   Revolutions, Riots, Reforms in History
VI Riots in the U.S. in the 1900s
VII The Tulsa Race Riot of 1921

Chapter 3 covers the seventy-five-year conspiracy to cover up the Tulsa Race Riot of 1921. Information will be provided to show how city, county, and state officials deliberately destroyed documents, newspaper articles, military records, and other vital materials pertaining to the riot. It will also show how the riot was purged from memory—from black memory and white memory—for many different reasons and how the miseducation of students in Oklahoma, until breakthroughs in the late 1980s and the early 1990s, created a distorted history of the black experience in Oklahoma.

Chapters 4–8 are so important that I issued a warning to the reader about them.

WARNING TO THE READER:

Stop! Look! Listen! Whatever you do, don't skip chapters 4–8! Read every word in them. These poignant, personal, penetrating accounts of the Tulsa Race Riot of 1921 will not be found, in this magnitude, in any other book or anywhere else. They are from the people—black, white, and other racial, ethnic, religious, and cultural groups—who observed this riot with their own eyes and who shared it with their heirs, and with anyone else who would listen.

You can find other print and electronic sources that deal with this topic, but no other source will have this vast eyewitness account of an event that has been so scrutinized, by a state commission, no less! You should find these chapters extremely interesting to read. Today's readers are fascinated with lists, with capsuled accounts of history, etc. Look at how Tom Brokaw's best-selling book about the experiences of America's military personnel has captivated readers. This is the era of ordinary heroes and of focus on unrecompensed victims of past injustices. Print and electronic focus on South Africa's Apartheid history, and present reconciliation movements involving Jewish Holocaust victims' past history and present reconciliation and reparations movements are abundant now. The Tulsa race riot has garnered the attention of the world and led to a deluge of national print and electronic media upon the city since the creation, in 1997, of the Oklahoma Commission to Study the Tulsa Race Riot of 1921. Add to that the terrorist attacks in New York and in Washington, D.C., on September 11, 2001, which have opened up new dialogue about long-past conflicts and perceived, and acknowledged, injustices in the Middle East. I hope that this book will add insight into the nature of man's conflicts and will offer effective guidelines for the solving of old conflicts and for the prevention of new inequities and injustices.

Chapter 4 includes eyewitness accounts of the riot by most of the 137 known living black survivors as of October 1, 2001.

Chapter 5 includes the oral-history accounts of the riot by widows/spouses of deceased black race riot survivors

Chapter 6 includes the oral history accounts of the

riot by the thrity-two riot survivors who died after the riot commission was created in 1997.

Chapter 7 includes oral-history accounts of descendants of deceased black riot survivors.

Chapter 8 is about the claims of white victims of the Tulsa Race Riot of 1921. It is the shortest chapter in the book because white riot claims were handled quickly, some of them immediately after the riot, and most all other claims by 1936 when a white judge, seeking to clear the docket of riot claims, granted most white claims and summarily dismissed most black claims. Only a handful of black riot victims had their claims even admitted in court. Even fewer received remuneration for their losses. Eighty years later, they are still trying to get remuneration.

Chapter 9 includes oral history testimony of white accounts of the Tulsa Race Riot of 1921.

Chapter 10 covers the Oklahoma Commission to Study the Tulsa Race Riot of 1921, 1997–2001.

Chapter 11 includes re-examination of the Tulsa Race Riot of 1921 and a look at lessons that can be learned from the riot.

The epilogue represents the full-circle journey of the author, from Oklahoma sharecropper's daughter to black American citizen setting foot on African soil for the first time. This chapter is a record of my experiences in Africa—meeting the people of my ancestors, visiting various sites, and examining historical events of Africa—and of the profound affect that this pilgrimage to the Motherland had on me. Many questions were answered, much anxiety was relieved, and I was able to purge past fears and anger from my consciousness. I am a better person today because of my "Africa experience"!

CHAPTER 1

Guts, Glory, and Greed: the Settlement of the Americas
The Collective Black Experience

To understand the Tulsa Race Riot of 1921, one can't begin with the events of May 31 and June 1, 1921. One must begin centuries earlier with the settling of the Americas and thoroughly examine the complex patterns of good and of evil that set the stage for the political, economic, and social conditions that led to brutality, racism, revolutions, and riots in the Americas. A thorough exploration of the past is necessary in order to grasp the ambiguities of the history of the Americas and how those ambiguities came to one day affect Tulsa, Oklahoma.

Let us look at the basics of history—the who, what, where, when, why, and how of the recording of history in nations. Here are some basic questions that must be examined and answered if one is to know history and to benefit from its lessons.

WHO?

First, we must know who wrote history in the past and who writes history today. Basically, little has changed regarding the writing of history. In the past, it was the conquerors who wrote history, those leaders in control of the nations of the then-known world. They controlled their nations and greatly influenced political, economic, and social phenomena in their countries. The history being written then mainly chronicled the lives of the rich and powerful. Today, history is still being written mainly by the privileged, but there is more focus on the history of all individuals. Today one can read about women, minorities, environmental issues, and various other topics that cover a multitude of previously unthought-of topics.

WHAT?

History is the written record of human events. The invention of writing is one of the most important events ever to occur in the history of mankind. From it, mankind gained access to a greater knowledge of the world. Along with oral traditions, and artifacts, including human remains, mankind now had a better way of recording and sharing its history.

WHERE?

Since history is the record of human events, it is found, and made, all over the globe, from land masses and vast bodies of water on the earth, to outer space.

WHEN?

Many scholars, from many places in the world, have written about writing and the effects of written history upon mankind. One of my favorite sources on information about the significance of history and about the world's prominent historians of the past is *The Westminister Historical Atlas to the Bible,* edited by George Ernest Wright and Floyd Vivian Filson, the Westminster Press, Philadelphia, Pennsylvania, 1946. From that fine old masterpiece I learned who the first great historians were, who replaced them, and why, and what glorious legacies and lessons they left for all mankind.

WHY?

History is so important because it shows us how peoples and nations, from the beginning of mankind to the present, utilize their natural resources, determine their customs, culture, values, institutions, and organizations, develop ways of helping their people internalize those values, and pass those values on to future generations.

HOW?

There are so many powerful lessons to be learned from the study of history. Mankind can use the lessons of history to avoid patterns of thought and behavior that do not promote peace, harmony, and prosperity in the world. People can use and enhance patterns of thought and behavior that do promote peace.

In addition to the above short overview about the significance of history for all mankind, let us look briefly at some of the historical records of the past to see why certain topics were chosen for examination and recording, why certain topics were avoided, and what is happening in the world of history today.

In the past, the history that was recorded was "self-preservation" history, which means history that protected, and promoted, the status quo—the continuation of the political, economic, and social condition in nations at that time. Topics that would promote the collective good were chosen. Controversial topics that could lead to division in nations were avoided.

Today, historical topics are more inclusive. Topics previously avoided because they were thought to be divisive are now openly examined, discussed, and recorded both in print and via electronic media—topics such as race, religion, sex, and politics.

New finds constantly bring about changes to the historical record. In the past, events were sometimes ignored or even worse, covered up. Today, they are instant evening-television news, and formerly accepted "old truths" are purged from the records and "new truths" are inserted. That does not mean that the historical record is perfect today. There can still be hidden agendas, coverups, and conflicts regarding "new history." New discoveries in archaeology and history tend to cause excitement all over the world; they also bring controversy as experts struggle over what is valid from the past, what is not, and how to redefine history.

The historian is always about the business of
1. Locating primary sources.
2. Locating secondary sources.
3. Making assumptions and inferences based on those findings.
4. Writing compelling narratives about their findings.

Let us look further at the history of the Americas so we can see how attitudes, behaviors, and events of the past would eventually affect black people in Tulsa, Oklahoma, in 1921 and would result in the worst race riot in U.S. history. An understanding of this early history of the Americas, and of the people who settled there, is absolutely necessary if individuals and nations are to truly connect those long-ago events to the present and learn valuable lessons from the past that can help mankind have a better future.

In preparing for this chapter, I dug out books, class notes, and papers from my undergraduate study days at Tuskegee Institute in Alabama in the 1950s and from whatever university offered classes at the bases where my military husband was stationed. Between 1954 and 1968, I studied at Texas Southern University in Houston, Texas, the University of Maryland's overseas branch at Burtonwood Royal Air Force Base in Warrington, England, and the University of North Dakota. I also got out my graduate study materials from the University of Tulsa and from further study programs in which I participated after I received my graduate degree.

Books that were helpful were classic books about African history, about the settlement in the Americas by people from Africa, about various expansion movements and expeditions, and about the Atlantic slave trade such as "The History and Description of Africa, Leo Africanus, New York, (n.d.); "They Came Before the Mayflower," Lerone Bennett, Johnson Publishing Company, Chicago, 1959; "Central Africa and the Atlantic Slave Trade," Roland Oliver, Oxford University Press, England, 1968; "Topics in West African History," A. A. Boahen, Cambridge University Press, New York, 1969; "A Glorious Africa," E. Chu and E.A. Skinner, Doubleday-Zenith, Garden City, New York, 1965; "Through African Eyes: Cultures in Change," Leon Clark, Praeger Press, New York, 1969; "The African Slave Trade," Basil Davidson, Atlantic-Little Brown, Boston, 1961; "Great Rulers of the African Past," L. Dobler and W.A. Brown, Doubleday-Zenith, Garden City, New York, 1965; "A History of West Africa," J.D. Fage, Cambridge University Press, New York, 1969; "Peoples of Africa," James L. Gibbs, Holt, Rinehart, and Winston, New York, 1965; "A History of the African People," Robert July, Praeger Press, New York, 1986; "Tropical Africa: Land and Livelihood, Vol. I and Vol. II, George H.T. Kimble, Twentieth Century Fund, New York, 1960; "The Afro-Asian World," Edward Kolevzon, Allyn & Bacon, Inc., Boston, 1972; "The Peoples and Policies of South Africa," Leo Marquand, Oxford University Press, New York, 1969; "The Middle Age of African History," Roland Oliver, Oxford University Press, London, 1967; "An American Dilemma," Gunnar Myrdal, New York, 1962; "The Dawn of African History, Oxford University Press, Simon and Phoebe Ottenburg, New York, 1968;

"Africa: Tradition and Change," E. Rich and I. Wallerstein, Random House, New York, 1973; "West Africa and the Atlantic Slave Trade," W. Rodney, Northwestern University, Chicago, 1967; "The Peculiar Institution," Dr. Kenneth Stampp, Random House, New York, 1956; "The Black Man in the United States," Edgar Toppin, Allyn & Bacon, 1973; "The Lonely African," Colin Turnbull, Anchor Press, New York, 1963; "Pictorial History of the Black American," Baldwin H. Ward, 1973; "A Reader's Guide to African Literature," Hans Zell and Helene Silver, African Publishing Corporation, Holmes and Meier, New York, 1983; "They Came Before Columbus," Dr. Ivan van Sertima, 1976 (also other writings by Dr. van Sertima— "Egypt Revisited," 1990; "African Presence in Early America, 1987; "Early America Revisited," 1998); "Race Matters," Dr. Cornel West, Beacon Press, Boston, 1993 (a native Tulsan);

Helpful with the Reconstruction period of history, and the subsequent westward-migrations era with its history of conflicts and difficulties between migrating pioneers in search of Promised Lands, were the following books:

"Westward Expansion: A History of the American Frontier," Ray Allen Billington, Macmillan, New York, 1974; The South During Reconstruction, 1865-1877," E. Merton Coulter, Louisiana State University Press, Baton Rouge, 1947; "The Freedmen's Bureau, Dr. W.E.B. DuBois, Atlantic Monthly, LXXXVII, 1901. ("The Souls of Black Folk," also by DuBois, Amereon, Ltd., New York, 1977 reprint of 1907 ed., is a must-read book for all who want to learn how it feels to be conflicted by racism); "Reconstruction: Political and Economic, William Archibald Dunning, Essay Index Reprint Service, 1977 reprint of 1907 ed; "Documentary History of Reconstruction," Walter Lynwood Fleming, BCLI-U.S. History Service, 1993 reprint of 1907 ed; "Reconstruction After the Civil War," Dr. John Hope Franklin, University of Chicago Press, 1961; "The Buffalo Soldiers," William Leckie, University of Oklahoma Press, Norman, 1975; "The Conquest: The Story of a Negro Pioneer," Oscar Micheaux, University of Nebraska Press, Lincoln, 1994 reprint from 1913 ed; "Reunion Without Compromise: Reunion Without Compromise, 1865-1868," Michael Perman, Cambridge University Press, Boston, 1973; "New Viewpoints of Southern Reconstruction," American Historical Review, XLV, ; "Historians of the Reconstruction," A.A. Taylor, Journal of Negro History, XXIII, 1938; "The Negro in the Civil War," Benjamin

Quarles," University of North Carolina Press, 1961; "Origins of the New South, C. Vann Woodward, Louisiana State University Press, Baton Rouge, 1951;

Copies of old newspapers were helpful. Modern newspapers were also helpful to the commission. 2001 and 2002 have been banner years for the print media and its dissemination of information to the world should bear fruit as mankind becomes more educated about the inhumanity of man and seeks to solve the dilemma of racism, revolts, massacres, genocide, and wars forever. The following "Smoking Gun" headlines of the past three years garnered world attention and validated long-held theories by some of the world's experts that Africans were the first settlers in the Americas:

"Ancient Skull, an Americas Mystery," Rio de Janeiro, Brazil, REUTERS NEWS, September 27, 1999

"Archaeological Site in Peru Is Called Oldest City in Americas," NEW YORK TIMES, April 27, 2001

"Site Sheds Light on Ancient Urban Life," THE CHRISTIAN SCIENCE MONITOR, April 27, 2001

"The World of Science Becomes a Global Village," NEW YORK TIMES, May 1, 2001

"Human-Like Remains May be of Earliest Ancestors," Mark Evans, ASSOCIATED PRESS, July 12, 2001

"Peru May be a First in Urban Living," Paul Recer, ASSOCIATED PRESS, April 27, 2001

"Dealing with the Legacy of Slavery," FOR A CHANGE, August/September 2001

"The Art Behind Modern Behavior," THE CHRISTIAN SCIENCE MONITOR, March 21, 2002

"Learning: Lesson No. 1: Shed Your Indian Identify," THE CHRISTIAN SCIENCE MONITOR, April 2, 2002

Another most helpful resource for me was an unpublished manuscript written by Robert Littlejohn. That manuscript, and the personal help of Robert Littlejohn when I visited historical sites and research centers, was invaluable to me while I was writing this book. Littlejohn, an officer in the North Tulsa Historical Society, is one of the best researchers that I have ever known, barring none! He is a retired research scientist from Amoco Productions (now British Petroleum) in Tulsa. He has a degree in geology from the University of Tulsa and worked for years all over the U.S. and overseas at various oil sites. He did graduate study in paleontology and is one of a handful of black paleontologists. He is one of the most meticulous of researchers. He taught me to always carry plenty of change to print copies of research immediately. He learned the hard way, years ago, how the "hidden agenda" network works in a society that is not yet totally equal and just. In his early research experience days, he often went back to research and copy from documents he had previously examined only to find them missing. Officials would insist that they never had such documents, until Bob Littlejohn would pull out printed copies from his previous research. Some officials stubbornly "held their own" and kept the removed documents hidden. Others, quietly and secretively, circumvented the system, often at great risk, to get materials into the hands of those who were writing true history. Most of the writings about race-related history in the nation, and especially in Oklahoma, were "hidden agenda, "white-slanted" history. Black researchers jokingly refer to it as "three dot" history because when any references would have clearly defined the subject as black, those references were left out and the three dots (ellipsis) substituted. One can only speculate at what this country could have been if that editing of history had not occurred. Perhaps much of the racial turmoil that has plagued us for so long could have been avoided if the true story of all the people had been told.

To help people do better research and better writing, Robert Littlejohn has given lectures and workshops locally, statewide, nationally, and overseas. He teaches how to go to the original sources for historical information and how to fill in the gaps left by "three dot" historians. He specializes in mound cultures and carefully shows the audience how artifacts—human and material—show an African presence in the Americas that predates all other human explorations. His annual guided bus tours during Juneteenth to all-black towns are sellout events. Robert Littlejohn and Curtis Lawson, another North Tulsa Historical Society officer, a former state legislator and freelance writer, are writing a book about Africans settling the Americas. They are both descendants of these early African explorers who first settled in Central America, then migrated to Mexico, and then to North America, where their final settlement was in Oklahoma! (These people of African descent were never slaves like the majority of present day-African-Americans were.)

Documents that were helpful in preparing this chapter were :
Dawes Hearings Documents.
Curtis Hearings Documents.
Many other documents from the National Archives,

Library of Congress, Smithsonian Institution, and Howard University in Washington, D.C., which will be discussed in further detail in following chapters.

Electronic media productions are also very helpful in helping individuals understand history. One of the best documentary films that I have ever seen is the Robert J. Emery documentary film *The Genocide Factor: The Human Tragedy,* which aired six times on television in April 2002, and reached nearly 80% of the U.S. viewing audience. It would not surprise me if that film was nominated for an Oscar in 2003! The film begins with this quote:

In an attempt to present a complete examination of man's inhumanity to man, *The Genocide Factor* contains documented atrocities not officially classified as genocide, as originally defined by Raphael Lemkin or by the United Nations Convention on the Prevention of the Crime of Genocide. Along with the historical facts and documentation, this program presents the individual opinions of survivors, witnesses, scholars, experts, and government officials.

Among the government officials featured in the film are President George W. Bush and numerous other world leaders. Also in the film are major spokespersons for the United Nations, Genocide Watch, Amnesty International, and other organizations dedicated to the protection of human rights for all mankind. Scholars and experts on human rights, riots, and massacres from all over the world were interviewed, and their comments are vital and valuable. (The Oklahomans appearing in the film were Wilma Mankiller, former principal chief of the Cherokees, Tulsa Race Riot 1921 survivors Eldoris McCondichie, Juanita Burnett Arnold, and Otis Granville Clark, and me, Eddie Faye Gates, commissioner on the Oklahoma Commission to Study the Tulsa Race Riot of 1921).

Each of the hourlong segments of this thorough, impeccably documented film, which took three years to make, began with a quote from the Bible: "Take heed ... lest you forget the things which your eyes have seen, and ... teach them to your children and your children's children" (Deut. 4:9).

The series then proceeds to cover the history of genocide that has occurred in the world from Biblical days to the present. Sprinkled throughout the series are wonderful quotes on the subject of genocide by people caught up in it—the victims, perpetrators, observant world leaders who tried to help victims, indifferent leaders who denied that genocide was going on or ignored it, and others. Actor Jon Voight introduces each of the four segments. Then the topic of each segment appears, a map shows location of the genocide being covered in this portion of the film, and graphic photographs appear, showing the ugly legacy of genocide in the world. A warning appears at the beginning of each segment about the graphic nature of the photographs.

The entire history of the ugly legacy of genocide is covered in this film, beginning with Cain's slaying of his brother Abel and ending with a thorough examination and anatomy of the Israel/Palestine conflict that is causing such worldwide ramifications today.

The documentary aims to make children, and everyone else, aware of the common threads in genocide:

(1) A culture in crisis, something that has occurred in the culture—political, economic, social—that has demoralized the people, that has made them vulnerable, and has set them on a path leading to genocide.

(2) A lack of democracy. In totalitarian nations, there is no room for flexibility, for the discussion and contesting of ideas. People are forced to follow party lines and to move in a monolithic, single-culture mode. But genocide can and does occur in democratic nations, too. The Tulsa Race Riot of 1921 is a classic example. Even in nations with strong spiritual ideals and values, and strong democratic principles, people can delude themselves about one group in their culture, excluding it from the protections granted to other citizens in the nation. People in such a group often become victims of genocide.

(3) A history of violence in the nation.

Here is a brief overview about the settlement of the Americas and how that history played a role in the Tulsa Race Riot of 1921. For a long time, archeologists, historians, authors, and others have said that the artifacts found in ancient mounds across the Americas—from Central and South America to the furthermost parts of North America—were African. For just as long, that knowledge was kept under cover, as it collided with the collective world thought about race, culture, history, etc. Most universities, along with private and public presses, wouldn't touch such a controversial topic with a ten-foot pole. Still, some authors persisted; some authors published. Authors such as Robert Ryal Miller, John R. Swanton, David Hurst Thomas, Cecelia Klein, Ivan van Sertima, and Lerone Bennett eloquently and empirically defended their theories and provided documentation showing that Africans were the first settlers in the Americas. They showed the common threads that tied all the mound cultures to the African continent—human skeletons, language, religious icons, and the physical mounds themselves. All pointed to Africa!

Writers about the African settlement of the Americas provided detailed geographical information—maps, graphs, charts, and ocean travel history.—to show that Africans were already in the Americas when the European exploration age began. These experts on early African migration to the Americas provided documentation showing levels of migration out of Africa to the Americas: (1) early voluntary migration out of Africa in pre-historic times; (2) involuntary migration out of Africa when Africans who were fishing, or otherwise on the ocean, got caught in turbulent weather conditions and were forced into an Atlantic Ocean path that brought them to the Americas; (3) voluntary migration to the Americas by some Africans in the period before the European age of exploration, and, finally, the Atlantic Slave Trade and the mass movement of African slaves to the Americas. Experts on the settlement of the Americas continue to provide documentation and information about Africans being the settlers of America. That is why those "Smoking Gun" headlines listed on page 26 are so important today. Some other good sources on this subject of early settlement in the Americas are

David Hurst Thomas, "Skull Wars: Kennewick Man, Archaeology, and the Battle for Native American Identity," Basic Books, 1996

William Loren Katz, "Black Indians," Peabody Museum, Harvard University, Boston,

Massachusetts, American Legacy, Spring, 1997.

Curtis Lawson and Robert Littlejohn, Lecture, North Tulsa Historical Society Lecture Series Pamphlet, "The Settlement of the Americas: Go to the Original Documents," Tulsa, 1998

"Ancient Africans in Oklahoma: History's Missing Chapter," April 18, 1997

Essay, "Who Will Tell the People?" Russell Banks, Princeton University, Harper's Magazine, June, 2000

Whatever the reasons, Africans *did* end up in the Americas. They were in Central and South America before the European explorers arrived, they came into contact with those explorers and with the permanent European settlers who followed, and some Africans migrated into North America, both voluntarily and involuntarily. Some of them, and their descendants, ended up in North America in the territory that would become Oklahoma. The history of the settlement of the Americas, with its mixed legacy of good and evil, would follow them into their new land and would still have a profound effect on them. Some of the psychological, sociological, political, and economic baggage from the European colonization era would be brought into North America—imperialism and the subjugation of native populations, racism, which allowed justification for such subjugation, and preservation of the status quo (domination of the known world by the Caucasian race)—would be planted in the new land, would take root there, would grow and flourish, and would eventually have an impact on Tulsa, Oklahoma, where the worst race riot in American history occurred.

CHAPTER 2
The Tulsa Race Riot of 1921

Without a doubt, this was the most difficult chapter in the book to write. After three and a half years of research by the Oklahoma Commission to Study the Tulsa Race Riot of 1921, there was much new information about the riot to add to already existing riot information. That was the dilemma that authors faced—just what to choose to write about from that mountain of riot information that is now available.

Books that were helpful to me in writing this chapter were classic books such as "The Anatomy of Revolution," Dr. Crane Brinton . . . ; "The Etiquette of Race Relations in the South: A Study in Social Control," Bertram W. Doyle, Chicago, 1937; Dr. John Hope Franklin, "From Slavery to Freedom: A History of American Negroes," Alfred A. Knopf, New York, 1956 (and also four other books written by Dr. Franklin); "Color Complex: The Politics of Skin Color Among African-Americans," Dr. Ronald Hall, Kathy Russell, and Midge Wilson, Anchor Books, Doubleday, New York, 1992; "Thaddeus Stevens: Scourge of the South," Ralph Korngold, Greenwood Press, Westport, Connecticut, 1959 (and also "A Being Darkly Wise and and Rudely Great,"—about Thaddeus Steven's black housekeeper by Korngold, also published by the Greenwood Press, 1955; "The Negro in the American Revolution," Benjamin Quarles, University of North Carolina Press, 1953; "The Difference of Race Between the Northern and Southern People," Southern Literary Messenger, Vol. XXX, June 1860; "Democracy in America," Alexis de Tocqueville, Alfred A. Knopf, New York, 1945.

Other books not listed in chapter 1 were also helpful in writing this chapter. Some of the books were broad, general specific books about the generic black experience in America. Others were about the entire state of Oklahoma, while some were specifically about Tulsa. A few, like Arthur Farakhan's book about gangs, are not riot-related but show how residual effects of previous history affect current history. The race of authors is listed here for clearly historical, sociological, psychological, and cultural reasons. See chapter 10 in which I describe in more detail my great respect for those of other races, religions, and cultures who take up the gauntlet and fight battles for justice and equality for all mankind. We, of the oppressed groups, HAVE to fight for "the cause" each day of our lives. We live it (the fight/the cause) from the cradle to the grave. Those of "non-oppressed groups" don't. Therefore when they "take up the cause" and fight, there is great respect for them from oppressed groups.

White authors who wrote such books were: Maurice Willows, Nina Dunn, Sammy Weygand, Scott Ellsworth, and Rudy Halliburton.

Black authors who wrote about the black experience in America in general, and/or about the Tulsa riot, specifically were: Dorothy DeWitty, Arthur Farakhan, Hannibal Johnson, Mary Elizabeth Jones Parrish, and Clifton Taulbert.

Some of the new books, fiction and nonfiction, which were written by authors who had done research in Tulsa and around the nation, during the work of the riot commission were helpful also. Some of the authors attended commission meetings on a regular basis. Among these authors who wrote books about the riot that I have read were Jewel Parker Rhodes, Rilla Askew, Tim Madigan, Al Brophy, and James Hirsch. All of the chroniclers were probably sincere in their efforts to write good books that would stand the test of time and historiography. But even with the sincerest of motives and efforts on the part of honest researchers, cultural factors can enter the picture; the same events, data, and research could be interpreted differently when viewed through the lenses of one's own culture. Writing about the Tulsa riot was no exception.

Old newspapers from the Tuskegee University archives in Alabama were extremely helpful in showing how factors such as race, ethnicity, social status, and class impacted the media coverage of the riot. Modern newspapers written by the media that converged upon Tulsa from all over the world during the duration of the riot commission study were helpful, too.

Old magazines covering race, lynching, and violence were fascinating to read and provided valuable firsthand accounts of domestic and world thought on race. Especially helpful were the *Crusader* magazines of the African Blood Brotherhood Organization, 1920–1922, which had its headquarters in New York City, National Urban League documents, 1920, National Negro Business League documents, all from the National Archives in Washington, D.C., and *Time* Magazine, ... 1938

Maps, charts, graphs, documents, articles, papers, books, unpublished manuscripts, oral interviews, etc., were generously shared with me (and with other commissioners) by Jim and Ethel Blair, Robert Norris, and William O'Brien. The books and articles that Robert Norris shared with me helped me better understand the sociological, psychological, political and cultural conditions that drive mob behavior. I also learned that conspiracies and coverups, and the exoneration of mob participants from penalties, is standard behavior after riots. Among the most helpful of maps, graphs, and charts were the larger-than-life ones that Dr. Scott Ellsworth used at one of the commission meetings.

New magazines written by media that came to Tulsa to cover the race riot showed how far people had come (or had not come) in terms of views on the subject of race, conflict, and violence.

Old, jerky, spotted media finds from the past were powerful in showing the visual history of race, riots, and revolts in the past. New electronic media productions that came out from the "Big Guns" such as the History Channel, Media Entertainment, Tulsa's own Barrister Studio, *60 Minutes II*, BBC, London, and many, many others provided new information and promoted respect and credibility for the commission.

One of the most useful resources for writing this chapter was the documentary film, *Ku Klux Klan: A Secret History*, produced by the History Channel. This thoroughly researched and finely produced film was invaluable in showing the motives, methods, and tenacity of white racist

people who kept recreating the organization, regardless of whatever new name the haters used. Evidence clearly showed that it was the same KKK that Nathan Bedford Forrest had founded—just new names and new garb. Now, on with the story of the Tulsa Race Riot of 1921.

NEW NEWSPAPERS: The Media (See chapter 10)

OTHER HELPFUL DOCUMENTS

NATIONAL ARCHIVES
- Presidential Papers
- National Media regarding race, riots, lynchings
- U.S. Constitution—history of, laws, cases, etc.
- Department of the Interior, "Hearings Before the Secretary of the Interior on the Leasing of Oil and Natural-Gas Wells in Indian Territory and Territory of Oklahoma, May 8, 24, 25, and 29, and June 7 and 19, 1906
- Curtis Acts Primary Documents
- Dawes Commission Primary Documents

LIBRARY OF CONGRESS
- U.S. House of Representatives Journals, 1921, The 67th Congress
- U.S. Senate Journals, 1921, The 67th Congress
- Congressional Records, 1921, The 67th Congress
- Congressional Serial Set (Committee Reports), 1921, 1922, The 67th Congress
- U.S. Justice Department article, "Blacks Not Blamed for Fomenting Tulsa Race Riot," 1921
- NAACP papers
- Urban League papers, magazines, correspondence
- National Business League papers, magazines, correspondence
- African Blood Brotherhood papers, magazines, correspondence

HOWARD UNIVERSITY, WASHINGTON, D.C.
- General History, The Black Experience, information from the Ida Jones Manuscript Division, the Moorland-Spigarn Research Center
- Black History Week, Black History Month Celebration History from the Carter G. Woodson Gallery
- Primary Documents, the African Blood Brotherhood

SMITHSONIAN INSTITUTION, CAPITAL AREA PUBLIC LIBRARY
- Miscellaneous materials regarding the Black Experience in the Americas and the Tulsa Race Riot of 1921

SCHOMBERG BLACK HISTORY COLLECTION, NEW YORK, NY
• Primary documents: Black writers' correspondence during the 1920s regarding the Tulsa Race Riot of 1921

PRIMARY SOURCES REGARDING RIOTS IN THE U.S.
• "A Documented History of the Incident Which Occurred at Rosewood, Florida, in January 1923, Submitted to the Florida Board of Regents," 22 December 1993, Investigators, The Florida State University
• "We Have Taken a City," Wilmington, NC, Racial Massacre and Coup of 1898, Dr. H. Leon Prather, Sr., Fairleigh Dickinson University, London, Toronto Press

STATE ARCHIVES
• *Redfearn v. American Century Insurance Company*, Oklahoma Supreme Court, Case No. 15851, June 1925
• Oklahoma Historical Society, Oklahoma City, Oklahoma—source of much primary and secondary materials regarding the Tulsa Race Riot of 1921 (especially helpful were numerous "Chronicles of Oklahoma" articles)

LOCAL ARCHIVES
• Tulsa Historical Society, numerous primary and secondary materials regarding the Tulsa Race Riot of 1921; numerous photographs documenting Tulsa's history, University of Tulsa: The Special Collections Department, McFarlin Library—Ku Klux Klan Rolls, Tulsa County, 1928-1932
• Tulsa Chamber of Commerce Minutes, January 1920–December 1922
• Tulsa County Minutes of Meetings

OTHER SOURCES
• Primary documents/sources located for the Riot Commission by Ethel and Jim Blair—maps, charts, graphs, photographs, military reports, etc., regarding the Tulsa riot; original Mary Elizabeth Jones Parrish photographs, writings, and books that were part of the estate of Parrish's late nephew by marriage, Clarence Love
• Primary documents/sources located for Riot Commission by Robert Norris—primary and secondary sources about the role of the military in the Tulsa Race Riot of 1921, and prominent books and articles about mob behavior, such as:
1. Transcript of T. J. Essley interview, recorded summer, 1987. Essley, now deceased, was a First Sergeant,

Company B, Third Oklahoma Infantry Regiment, Oklahoma National Guard (later Company L, 180th U.S. Infantry Regiment, 45th Infantry Division
2. Report of Major C.W. Daley to Lt. Col. L.J.F. Rooney regarding "Information on activities during Negro Uprising May 31, 1921"
3. *Social Psychology: An Outline and Source Book*, Edward Alsworth Ross, Macmillan Company, 1919. See chapter 3, The Crowd
4. "Prevention and Control of Mobs and Riots," Federal Bureau of Investigation, United States Department of Justice, John Edgar Hoover, director
5. "A Study in Social Violence: Urban Race Riots in the United States," Allen D. Grimshaw, University of Pennsylvania, 1959
6. *Urban Racial Violence in the Twentieth Century*, Dr. Joseph Boskin, University of Southern California, Glencoe Press, a Division of the Macmillan Company, Beverly Hills
7. "Race Riot at East St. Louis (Illinois), July 2, 1917," Elliott Rudwick, University of Illinois Press, Urbana
8. "Civil Disturbance Riot Control Manual," New Jersey State Police Training Regulation 70-1, from U.S. Justice Law Enforcement Assistance, New York, New York
9. "Lynchings and What They Mean, General Findings of the Southern Commission on the Study of Lynching," Atlanta, Georgia
10. "A Sociological Study of a Texas Lynching," *Studies in Sociology*, Vol. 1, Durward Pruden, 1936
11. "An Historical Survey of Lynchings in Oklahoma and Texas," Oklahoma University, 1942
12. "The Sociology of Race Riots," Bernard F. Robinson, Department of Sociology, Morehouse College, Atlanta, Georgia
13. *Without Sanctuary: Lynching Photography in America*, James Allen, Twin Palms Publishers, 2000
14. "An Oklahoma Lynching" (Chickasha), Robert Bagnall
• Primary documents/sources located for Riot Commission by William M. O'Brien—primary and secondary sources about the role of the Ku Klux Klan and mobs in the Tulsa Race Riot of 1921. Included was O'Brien's own draft of his manuscript for a book about the Tulsa riot entitled "Who Speaks for Us? The Responsible Citizens of Tulsa in 1921"
• Ruth Sigler Avery, unpublished manuscript, "Fear, the Fifth Horseman," 1997
• T. Lindsay Baker and Julie P. Baker, *The WPA*

Oklahoma Slave Narratives, University of Oklahoma Press, Norman, 1996

• Angie Debo, *And Still the Waters Run,* Princeton University Press, 1940; Debo, *The Road to Disappearance,* 1941; Debo, *From Creek Town to Oil Capital,* 1943

• Dorothy DeWitty, "Tulsa, Tale of Two Cities," Langston University , Langston, OK, 1998

• Nina Dunn, "Tulsa's Magic Roots"

• Dr. Scott Ellsworth, *Death in a Promised Land,* Louisiana University Press, Baton Rouge, 1982

• Eddie Faye Gates, *They Came Searching: How Blacks Sought the Promised Land in Tulsa,"* Eakin Press, 1997

• Loren Gill, unpublished M.A. thesis, "The Tulsa Race Riot," the University of Tulsa, 1943

• Dr. Rudy Halliburton, *Red Over Black, Black Slavery Among the Cherokee Indians,* Greenwood Press, Westport, Connecticut, 1977

• Hannibal Johnson, *Black Wall Street: From Riot to Renaissance in Tulsa's Historic Greenwood District,* Eakin Press, Austin, 1998

• Mary Elizabeth Jones Parrish, *The Event of the Tulsa Disaster: The Race Riot of 1921,* privately printed; reprint, Out on a Limb Press, Tulsa, 1998

• Don Ross, *Impact* Magazine, June 1971

• Sammy Weygand, "Color Blind," Color Blind Productions, 1994

• Dr. D. Grant Williams, "Economic Dualism, Institutional Failure, and Racial Violence in a Resource Boom Town: A Reexamination of the Tulsa Riot of 1921," an unpublished article presented to the riot commission

• Maurice Willows, The American Red Cross Report, "The Tulsa Race Riot of 1921," December 1921

INTERVIEWS

• Dr. Scott Ellsworth and Dick Warner— Interviews of hundreds of white Tulsa riot eyewitnesses and information presented to the riot commission

• Eddie Faye Gates—see chapters 4, 5 of this book

• Ed Wheeler—numerous interviews of black and white eyewitnesses to the Tulsa riot. See *Impact* Magazine, June, 1971

OTHER

• Jim and Ethel Blair Papers, maps, graphs, chart, Old Newspapers

• Norris Papers

• O'Brien Papers

Given the political, economic, and social inequality between the races in the early twentieth century, it should be no surprise that race riots occurred all over the United States. Though these bloody confrontations were called "race riots," they were, in reality, most often "race massacres," or "race wars." Tulsa's racial confrontation of May 31, 1921, and June 1, 1921, which will be referred to as "The Tulsa Race Riot of 1921" hereafter because that was the term used in the official state-created commission to study this riot, a riot that has gone down in history as the worst race riot ever in our nation. But it wasn't the first race riot, or massacre, in the U.S. In fact, there had been so many bloody racial wars the summer of 1919 that the period was referred to as "The Red Summer" by poet James Weldon Johnson, who was secretary of the national NAACP in New York City. After the Tulsa riot, he would take a delegation of concerned black citizens to Washington, D.C., to lobby, unsuccessfully, for an anti-lynching bill. At first the Congress did not want to meet with Johnson and his "Nigger delegation," as was reported in newspapers. But due to heavy publicity from the African Blood Brotherhood's Crusader Magazines about racism, lynchings, and riots in the nation, and reporting in other newspapers and magazines sympathetic to blacks during this era of rampant lynchings, Congress relented and received the delegation, even cleaning up its language and "welcoming" Johnson and his "Colored delegation," as reported in local and national newspapers. But Congress failed to change the word "Nigger" to "Colored" in the Congressional Records for that day. In the official Congressional Record book that I personally pulled from shelves at the National Archives in Washington, D.C., during my research on behalf of the Oklahoma Commission studying the riot, I saw Johnson and his delegation referred to as the "Nigger delegation"!

The first major racial confrontation during this era occurred in Wilmington, North Carolina, in November of 1898. Other riots followed, such as in Atlanta, Georgia, 1906, Springfield, Illinois, 1907, Elaine, Arkansas, 1919, and Chicago, Illinois, 1919. Given the frequency of riots, it can be seen why black Tulsans were so fearful of them. What they so greatly feared became a reality in 1921, even though they fought desperately and bravely to prevent it.

To understand the Tulsa Race Riot of 1921, one must understand Oklahoma's turbulent, Wild West history, and even its history before that, all the way back to the first settlement in the land before the European settlers explored and settled in the Americas (which has been covered in the previous chapter). One must then look at all the settlers who came to Oklahoma Territory in the 19th century and, later to Oklahoma, the new state, in the early 20th century. Then it can be seen how the goals and ambitions, ideals, and philosophy of all these settler groups often came into conflict and how this set the stage for the worst race riot in American history.

Remember those "riot issues" listed in the prologue of the book? Now is the time to explore them again to see how some of those issues, especially the issue of race, impacted the young U.S. democracy, and still impacts the United States until this day. Alexis de Tocqueville, the French statesman who came to observe the U.S. prison system in the early 1800s, but who wrote about more than just prisons, wrote about many of his observations about the fledgling Republic, and its peoples. He said many wonderful things about them. But he also had one clear warning. He said that while the American people were deeply religious peoples who had a great love of law, they had one flaw that might undermine the greatest democracy that the world had ever known. That flaw was the nation's inability to deal with the issue of race. Alexis de Tocqueville was right. Americans still grapple with that issue of race. While the nation has made tremendous progress in its attempts to "level the playing field" so that all Americans can participate, on an equal basis, in the American Dream, it has not been able to purge, once and for all, the deep roots of racism from American society.

In later years, other Europeans saw this same flaw that de Tocqueville had noted earlier, historians, scholars, and authors such as Thorstein Veblen, Gunnar Myrdal, and others who wrote about it in the 1940s. In the 1960s during the civil rights revolution in the U.S., everybody from everywhere wrote about race and its ugly legacy. Among the most notable authors, writing about America's past and its racial turmoil, authors who have been an inspiration to other authors, scholars, historians, and researchers were Dr. Kenneth Stampp, Dr. John Hope Franklin, and Dr. Crane Brinton.

According to Dr. Crane Brinton, considered the foremost expert on riots and revolution in the world during his tenure as history professor at Harvard University, all the revolutions, reactions, riots, and reformation movements in history have had their roots in a common cause—upheaval due to deep-seated, long-range, long-simmering political, economic, and social imbalances (injustices) in society. Those conditions were certainly present in Tulsa, Oklahoma on May 31, 1921.

Dr. Kenneth Stampp, University of Wisconsin-trained history professor at the University of California, Berkeley, 1946-1965, visiting professor at Harvard University in 1955, and visiting professor of history at Oxford University in England 1961-1962, wrote the definitive book on race, delusion, and flaws in American society during the slave era in his classic "The Peculiar Institution." Dr. Stampp showed how the "peculiar institution" of slavery clearly conflicted with the high spiritual ideals and democratic principles upon which the American nation had been founded. He then shows how the American people dealt with this conflict. The nation gave in to a kind of self-delusion in which pseudo psychological and sociological "theories" were developed to explain away the inconsistences between professed ideals and the pragmatic application of those ideals in the nation. The myth of an "inferior African species" of man was created.

Dr. John Hope Franklin, considered one of the foremost historians in the nation, wrote the definitive book about slavery in the United States, the Civil War, Reconstruction, the Post- Reconstruction Era, and the effects of those events upon the American people forever. His book, "From Slavery to Freedom," has been elevated to near-Bible status in undergraduate and graduate studies programs all over the world! Dr. Franklin did his undergraduate study at Fisk University in Tennessee, and received a Master's degree and a Doctor of Philosophy degree from Harvard University. He taught at Fisk University, St. Augustine's College, Howard University, Brooklyn College, Cambridge University, the University of Chicago (1964-1982) and Duke University.

Ironically, today, in a new millennium, America is still grappling with the issue of race. Even on its Ivy League college campuses, the issue of race continues to divide. A good example is what is going on at Harvard University now. Dr. Cornel West, Dr. Henry Louis Gates, II, and others are involved in a controversy over respect, credibility, and the future of Black Studies programs at American institutions of higher learning.

This is a good place in this book to share briefly with the reader five short vignettes about some black settlers who came to Oklahoma looking for "the Promised Land." The most common factor that black settlers cited for their sojourn to Oklahoma was racism. Collectively, they shared a common experience—the search for a "Promised Land" free of bias and injustice. But, their stories are very different. Some of them were "Native Negroes"—those who had never been slaves.

Council Oak Tree, Tulsa, Oklahoma.

They were descendants of African explorers who had come to the Americas BEFORE European explorers.

Their African ancestors voluntarily came to the Americas from Africa, settled in Central America and later migrated to Mexico. From there, they came into the Louisiana Territory region of North America. And still later, they voluntarily migrated to the land that later became the state of Oklahoma. (At least two members of the North Tulsa Historical Society, Curtis Lawson and Robert Littlejohn, are descendants of such ancestors). Some blacks in the Americas were descendants of African slaves, and had no "mixed blood" in them, while others were Mulattoes, descendants of African slaves who had offspring by European slave masters and/or other whites who came into contact with slaves like some of the Wilson family, and the Petit and Minter families profiled in this chapter. Most settled in the United States, but some disgruntled black families fled to Canada and never returned to the U.S. Their black offspring reside in Canada today. One black family, the family of Jack Kelley, fled from Oklahoma to Canada, but did not stay long for they found that Canada was not a Promised Land either. There they found discrimination, prejudice, racism, and sometimes, violence just as they had experienced in Oklahoma. So the family returned to Oklahoma after just two years in Canada, all except the dear grandmother who died in Canada and is buried there. Listen to their spell-binding stories below!

I: THE WILSON FAMILY SAGA: "Get Out of Town Or You're Next—Horse Genitalia and Intimidation in Louisiana"

In the early 1900s, among the most prosperous families in the Opelousas, Louisiana area were members of the Wilson family, black families. Three grown brothers, Austin Wilson, Buddy Wilson, and Theodore Wilson, made the decision to migrate to Oklahoma. The catalyst that caused these brothers to leave their comfortable and affluent lives in Louisiana was a horse genitalia incident that happened like this. Theodore Wilson was a veterinarian and he and his teenaged sons loved horses. They trained some of their prized horses, and the boys rode in local rodeos. There was much resentment in the white community toward this prominent black family with the fancy rodeo horses. The Ku Klux Klan was active in the community, and often its members "did dastardly deeds" in the dark of night to show their displeasure. One morning when Dr. Theodore Wilson stepped out onto his front porch, he nearly

Early Tulsa.

Tulsa Indian Territory, December 1905.

Early Tulsa, before statehood.

Early Tulsa

Early Tulsa, Union Depot Railroad Station.

The Wilson family that migrated to Oklahoma from Louisiana; L-R. Florence, Theodore Wilson, Sr., (father); El Sandof Wilson (seated child); Theodore Wilson, Jr. (standing); Lincoln Wilson (baby); Lucille Wilson (mother, seated); Alice Wilson; Mary Wilson (back, standing) Mae Wilson (front, standing).

To the left:
Alice Wilson Prudhomme and Alexander Prudhomme, c. 1915.

stepped into a strange, unfamiliar bloody mass. It was the genitalia from one of his prized rodeo horses! A note warned that the same plight might befall his boys.

The Wilson brothers hurriedly took care of—as best they could on such short notice—the details of severing their Louisiana ties and moving to Oklahoma for a better way of life. Then the brothers and their families boarded a train bound for Oklahoma. Theodore Wilson's daughter, Alice, was a curious little girl and did not follow directions given to the frightened, departing black passengers. Train personnel had closed all curtains on the windows in the segregated black section of the train and warned that passengers keep the curtains closed and that they refrained from looking out the windows, for Klansmen were noted for boarding trains, removing black passengers and beating or even killing them. But nosy little Alice didn't listen. She gingerly lifted a curtain and looked out. What she saw remains a nightmare memory for her to this day. She saw the station platform filled with hooded Klansmen, sunlight glinting off their guns. But God was with the departing black passengers that day. No Klansmen entered the train, and the Wilson families made it safely to Oklahoma.

The Wilson brothers and their families settled in the Okmulgee, Preston, and Beggs area, forty-some miles south of Tulsa. Because they were not dirt-poor sharecroppers, like most of the blacks in the area, they prospered. Eventually, Theodore Wilson accumulated 300 acres of land in the area oil-rich land. Today, that land is still in the hands of Theodore's offspring.

Interview with Jean Prudhomme Kirkpatrick, Tulsa, Oklahoma, daughter of Alice Wilson Prudhomme and Alexander Prudhomme, granddaughter of Theodore Wilson, Tulsa, January 11, 2002.

II: JESSIE FLURRY AND FANNIE JACKSON FLURRY: A Cherokee Woman and Her Negro Husband's Search for the Promised Land in Arkansas and in Oklahoma

The numerous descendants of Jessie and Fannie Jackson Flurry live all over the United States. But they meet almost every year for a family reunion in Oktaha, Oklahoma, a tradition begun years ago by Irene Winn Oakley, granddaughter of Jessie and Fannie. They never tired of sitting around the farm home of Irene and Harold Oakley, both now deceased, and talking about their family history. Their children continue to carry on the annual family-reunion tradition, still held in Oktaha. They still eat tons of "the greatest home cooking in the world," and they still talk about how Jessie and Fannie came to Ft. Smith, Arkansas, just across the river from Moffett, Oklahoma.

From information gained from talking to the elders at these reunions, most any Flurry offspring can recite, verbatim, the fascinating story of the Flurrys, even the most minute details about Jessie and Fannie. Jessie Flurry was born a slave on May 2, 1837, on a plantation in Virginia. Fannie Jackson Flurry, a six-foot tall, full-blood Cherokee woman with waist-length hair (and who wore a size-twelve shoe), was born January 3, 1855, in Alabama. It is not known exactly how the two met or when they went to Arkansas, but according to the Sequoyah County, Oklahoma, 1910 census record they were living in the county at least by that date.

Jessie and Fannie Flurry had six children:

Louvenia Flurry Bivens Howard
Mary Elizabeth Flurry Smith
Edward Flurry (twin of Mary Elizabeth)
Adelaide Flurry Winn
William Flurry
Virginia Flurry

Adelaide Flurry married Samuel Winn and had nine children, six boys and three girls. Two of those children, eighty-five-year-old Oda Winn Jackson and eighty-three-year-old Odessa (Mickey) Winn carry on the oral tradition, in the manner of African griots, of preserving and perpetuating the family history. They were the source of much of the information used in this vignette.

Odessa (Mickey) Winn, a former navy man in World War II, has a mischievous nature, but when he is telling the family history, he is dead serious. He spoke of the burdens and wounds his parents, and their parents, carried with them to the grave—burdens that had their roots in the evil system of human slavery. It wasn't easy for young Odessa to learn this information, for in those days he said parents did not talk much to their children about the past, or about the present, for that matter, except to give chore assignments or to discipline the children. He said he learned about the past by hiding under the porch of their home in the Moffett, Oklahoma, area and eavesdropping as his father engaged in lively conversation with his two best friends. It was under that porch that he learned about Jessie and Fannie's early life, their marriage, and about the children. He also learned how his father, Samuel Winn, had met and courted his mother, the beautiful Adelaide, who inherited the best features of her Indian mother and her African father. And it was under that porch that he learned why his father so admired Masons, and how enamored his father was with Marcus Garvey, the founder of the Back to Africa Movement in the early 1900s. He said his father's dream, never realized, was to go to Africa.

Odessa Winn, the mischievous little eavesdropper, learned that his father, Samuel Winn, lived in the Ft. Smith, Arkansas area (exact year unknown) with his first wife (Amelia Wright?) and their children (number and ages unknown). Sam Winn got into some kind of trouble in Arkansas, the exact nature unknown, but it could have been for his avowed affection for Garvey. Anyway, he feared for his life and fled to Oklahoma. He was aided by a kindhearted white man, a Mason, who drove him to safety in a wagon. Sam had a blanket wrapped around his shoulders, a woman's bonnet on his head, and a Winchester rifle, covered by the blanket, across his knees as he sat next to his Good Samaritan benefactor. No one stopped them, and that night the man dropped Sam off across the bridge in Moffett, Oklahoma, where Sam hid in the nearby woods for days and slipped out at night to go to the bridge to wait for his wife and children, who were supposed to come to the bridge to meet him and to cross over into Oklahoma to begin a new life. They never came. The heartbroken Sam thus started his new life in Oklahoma alone. He became a schoolteacher and an ordained minister. It was in his classroom that he met the beautiful Adelaide Flurry. He courted her, married her, and together they raised their nine children.

Odessa (Mickey) Winn, with a twinkle in his eyes, said that he sure is glad that his father never caught him hiding under that porch all those years ago, for "if my dad had caught me under that porch, I wouldn't be here today to give you this interview!"

Interview with Odessa (Mickey) Winn, Muskogee, Oklahoma, January 26, 2002.

Eighty-five-year-old Oda Winn Jackson, daughter of Sam and Adelaide Flurry Winn, is in excellent health and walks five miles daily. Her doctor tells her, "Whatever you are doing, keep doing it!" Oda, listening in on her brother's interview, didn't have much to add to her brother's story. She did mention that one of her favorite childhood memories was when her aunt Mary Elizabeth Flurry Smith would come to visit. She said that her mother, Adelaide Flurry Winn, would have the "best old time" with her sister. "They would be in the kitchen making dumplings, pound cakes, and . . . The

smells were just delicious. They would be just chattering away and us kids couldn't wait to taste all that good food." Mary Elizabeth Flurry and Edward Flurry were twins, and they were kind of a novelty in the community when they were growing up.

Mary Elizabeth Flurry married Elia Smith (who was originally born a Thornton, but his name was changed to Smith when he was sold to a plantation owner named Smith). Elia Smith, twenty-five years older than Mary Elizabeth, was twelve years old when slavery ended. Mary Elizabeth Flurry Smith and Elia Smith had seven children:

1. Arizona Smith
2. Frances Smith Britt
3. Icsia Smith Gates
4. Younger Smith
5. Adam Smith
6. Nehemiah Smith
7. Elijah Smith.

Oda Winn Jackson showed me the "museum" that has been made in the bedroom of her mother's home in Muskogee, Oklahoma, which is next door to the modern brick home that Oda, now widowed, had built after she moved from Minneapolis, Minnesota, where she had lived and worked for years. Among the items in that precious little "museum" are a painted metal tray that Jessie Flurry ate from when he was a slave child, photographs of Jessie and Fannie Flurry, in their finest garments, taken in the 1800s, and numerous other photographs of the 1800s and early 1900s, so numerous that all walls of the room are filled, and items of clothing such as shoes, hats, and purses that belonged to the beautiful Adelaide.

Oda Winn Jackson said that her mother preached to her children each day that there were only two things that they really owned—their time and their health. She said that they must always take care of their health and that they must always use their time wisely. Adelaide Flurry Winn would be proud of her children. They did exactly what she told them to do!

Interview with Oda Winn Jackson, Muskogee, Oklahoma, January 31, 2002

III: JACK KELLEY: "To Canada and Back: All Except Grandma"

On February 15, 2000, I got a call from Jack Kelley in Fresno, California. He had just read a story in a newspaper about the Tulsa Race Riot of 1921 and he wanted to share some of his family's history with me. He said that he barely missed being born in the Tulsa area, but his parents moved to Edmonton, Alberta, Canada, in 1919 and he was born there in 1920. His sister had been born in 1918 near Henryetta, Oklahoma, an infamous white town that had "sundown" laws, meaning that black people had better not be caught in Henryetta after sundown. His parents moved from Henryetta to Jenks, Oklahoma, which is about ten or fifteen miles from Tulsa. The Kelley family had friends who lived in the Greenwood District and they heard all about the racial tensions in Tulsa. So the Kelley family felt that Tulsa and Jenks were not much better than Henryetta and decided to go to Canada. Here is what Jack Kelley says about his folks' move to Canada:

"Blacks were being warned to get out of Tulsa or else. Notes were left on doors, etc., and whites were in an angry mood. They had run out of space to build and expand their businesses and railroads. They needed and wanted lands that blacks owned, and when the blacks wouldn't sell, they began intimidating the black people. My folks just got fed up and fled to Canada. But many blacks stayed on and fought a good battle. They got caught up in the Tulsa Race Riot of 1921!

"In Canada, my folks met other blacks who had moved there to avoid the racial unrest in the U.S. My poor grandmother died in Canada and is buried there. She died directly from stress that had begun in Tulsa with all that racial hatred inflicted upon black people there at that time. She didn't die in Tulsa in the riot, but though she died in Canada, she died from the effects of the racial hatred that caused that riot!

"But Canada did not prove to be a promised land for my family. There was racial unrest there, too, so they moved back to the U.S.—to Fresno, California. My grandfather worked in the Stanford University region in Palo Alto, California, which is most noted for its famous Stanford University. But then it was also known for its rich farmlands too. My grandfather got a job working on the farm of Herbert Hoover, who later became president of the United States. My dad liked working for Mr. Hoover. He said Mr. Hoover hired mostly black and Mexican workers to work on his farm in this richest farm valley in California! He knew the difficulties that minorities were having in the U.S. at this time. Minorities were grateful to Mr. Hoover for the kindness he showed them and for the good wages he paid them. But Mr. Hoover was blessed, too. Those grateful blacks and Mexicans became outstanding laborers for him!"

Jack Kelley still keeps in touch with the Tulsa that he loves, via the *Oklahoma Eagle* weekly black newspaper, and through telephone conversations with me. I learned that the colorful Mr. Kelley attended Fresno State College, where he played football, and that after college he tried out for the national New York Yankees football team and played professional football in the Canadian League, where he was a running back.

Interviews with JACK KELLEY, Fresno, California, February 15, 2000; January 31, 2002.

IV: JOSEPH PETIT:
"Thirteen Wagons: From Texas to Oklahoma— Escape from the Texas Ku Klux Klan"

One day in 1904, thirteen buckboard wagons filled with thirteen black families and all their worldly possessions left Lott, Texas, a little all-black farming community near Marlin, Texas (Waco was the nearest big city), bound for the promised land in Oklahoma. These families were hardy people, many of them having been slaves on nearby plantations in the Brazos River bottomlands. All of them were trying to escape intolerable conditions of racism and injustice in the post-Reconstruction South. The final straw that precipitated this move was the Klan beating of the son of one of the Oklahoma-bound settlers. The young man's back was so bloody and lacerated by the strands of barbed wire used by some of the assaulters that it was a miracle that he lived. The men in Lott, heads of their households, protectors of their wives and children, knew that they could not tolerate another incident like this. They knew that if they stayed, they would have to kill their tormentors, and that would mean certain death for them and their families.

The journey was difficult. They endured the wagon trek, traveling over rough roads by day and sleeping in and under their wagons by night. Some just draped quilts over sapling trees along their route and made their own "village inns." Late in the evenings when it was getting too dark to travel, the little group settled down where they would spend the night. But first, the women had to cook the evening meal. Each family had brought along a supply of dried staples—flour, meal, hominy, other vegetables, and fruits. For meat, the women cooked what the men had killed that day, whatever wild animals had come across the path of the travelers—squirrel, rabbit, raccoons, ducks, geese, prairie chickens, pheasants, etc.

For a special treat, the women sometimes made peach cobblers, apple cobblers, or other fruit cobblers from wild fruit trees that they happened upon.

Of course, history shows that Oklahoma was not really the promised land that settlers had imagined. But it was indeed better for these black pioneers than their Texas homeland had been. Joseph Petit, his wife, Rhoda Wesley Petit, and their nine children (several more were born in Indian Territory) prospered in Oklahoma. They settled in the Okmulgee, Preston, and Beggs area. During the 1920s, some of the offspring moved to Tulsa. Today descendants of this pioneer family live all over the U.S. Most are college graduates and live useful, productive lives. They are grateful that their ancestor, Joseph Petit, made that wagon trip to Oklahoma many years ago.

Interview with ADA PETIT CULLOM, Okmulgee, Oklahoma, January 12, 2002

V: JAMES MATTHEW MINTER:
"I Can't Live in Texas One More Day— A Response to a Texas Lynching"

One day in 1918, James Matthew Minter, a young black man who lived with his wife, Retter Hardeman Minter, and six children (three more were born in Oklahoma) in Como, Texas, a little farming village near Sulphur Springs, Texas, made up his mind to take his family from the only home that they had ever known. The black people in Como were descendants of slaves who had lived and worked on nearby plantations during the slavery era. These people had never had lives of ease, but conditions for them worsened after the end of Reconstruction in 1877.

The catalyst for the return of oppressive "Southern Home Rule" in the South was a deal that the U.S. government made in 1877 with the former Confederate states that had returned to the Union. The Republicans needed the vote of the southern states to settle the contested presidential election of 1876, in which the Democratic candidate, Samuel J. Tilden, won the popular vote over the Republican candidate, Rutherford B. Hayes. But four states, Louisiana, South Carolina, Florida, and Oregon, sent in two sets of electoral votes, one from the Democrats and one from the Republicans. So there was controversy over who won the electoral votes. To settle the dilemma, Republicans promised that if the southern states would throw their support to Rutherford B. Hayes, Republicans would end Reconstruction in the South and the government would withdraw federal troops from the South. The southern states did as they were asked, and Hayes won by one electoral vote.

One of the first acts of Rutherford B. Hayes, as the new U.S. president, was to end Reconstruction in the South and to withdraw federal troops as promised. It was the beginning of the end for many blacks in Texas. All hope for peace and prosperity in their native state was gone. A reign of terror began for black people in the Sulphur Springs area, as well as in other parts of Texas. They felt that they were living in virtual slavery.

The breaking point came for James Matthew Minter the day in 1918 that he witnessed the lynching of his best friend in the woods near Como. The two young men, both married with many young children, were on horseback and happened upon a group of mobsters, some of them known Ku Klux Klansmen.

James Minter's best friend was spotted as he emerged from a thicket. (James hid in the thicket praying that his horse would not make a sound and betray him to the mobsters.) These young black men had done nothing wrong, but they just happened to be in the wrong place at the wrong time. During the lynching, James Minter heard the mobsters cursing and beating his friend before they hanged him. He heard them shouting that they were sick and tired of the way that their "good, peaceful slaves" had turned into "uppity niggers" during Reconstruction, and now that Reconstruction had ended, they were going to teach niggers a lesson!

When the mobsters had vented their fury upon James Matthew Minter's best friend and had left his body swinging from a tree limb, Minter left the thicket and went home to his loving wife and children. He told them to gather their things for they were leaving Texas that very day. They left with their meager belongings for the Sulphur Springs train station and set out for Oklahoma. They settled in the Wewoka area first and later in Okmulgee. James even took his family to Tulsa, where there was more prosperity, but he moved from Tulsa just before the riot of 1921. Racial tensions there at that time reminded him too much of Sulphur Springs, Texas.

James Minter's brothers, Orion and Clifton, also moved to Oklahoma, but most of the Minter family, as well as all of the Hardeman family, remained in Texas. James Minter never saw some of them after that day in 1918, for when that train crossed over the bridge and entered Oklahoma, he vowed that he would never set foot in Texas again. And he never did! Not even family reunions, nor funerals, could bring James Minter to Texas again. Retter Hardeman Minter visited her Texas relatives often, but not her husband. He kept his vow, and he hated Texas until his dying day in 1966.

The descendants of James Matthew Minter and Retter Hardeman Minter live all over the U.S. They, too, are grateful for their ancestors' decision to "get out of Texas" that day in 1918. They thank God for his protection of the Oklahoma-bound migrants on that train trip, and for all the blessings and benefits that have followed this family ever since.

Interview with Bertha Mae Minter Littlejohn, Tulsa, Oklahoma, February 2, 2002

Now that I have summarized how the issue of race contributed to the climate of thought that allowed revolts, revolutions, riots, and massacres to flourish in history, I will now continue with a brief chronological account of the Tulsa Race Riot of 1921. In this book, in later chapters, riot survivors, themselves, will be the main storytellers of the Tulsa riot. But here is a brief examination of The Scholars' Report and of the Final Report of the Riot Commission. Chapter 10 focuses completely on the Commission Report.

In addition to racial conflicts that contributed to the Tulsa Race Riot of 1921, there were other nonracial factors that were equally responsible, such as land needs, inflammatory media, and religious and cultural conflicts. Here is a look at Tulsa in 1921.

Perhaps the two recent resources that were most helpful to riot commissioners and others seeking information about the riot were the Scholars' Report, compiled and edited by Dr. John Hope Franklin and Dr. Scott Ellsworth for the Oklahoma Commission to Study the Tulsa Race Riot of 1921, and the Final Report of the Oklahoma Commission to Study the Tulsa Race Riot of 1921, itself.

Given the credentials of the two outstanding scholars Franklin and Ellsworth, it should be no surprise that their report was so helpful, and given the fact that riot commissioners examined over 20,000 documents during their three and a half years of research, and that they took their task seriously, it should also be no surprise that their document was so helpful and that even national and world organizations have cited its significance.

The Scholars' Report began with a brief historical introduction of the state of Oklahoma in 1997 as it prepared for a centennial celebration to be held in 1998. "It isn't difficult to look upon the history of our state with anything short of awe and wonder. In ninety-three short years, whole towns and cities have sprouted upon the prairies, great cultural and educational institutions have risen among the blackjacks, and the state's agricultural and industrial output has far surpassed even

the wildest dreams of the Boomers. In less than a century, Oklahoma has transformed itself from a rawboned territory more at home in the nineteenth century into . . . a shining example of both the promise and the reality of the American dream. In looking back upon our past, we have much to take pride in."

Though Franklin and Ellsworth stressed pride in Oklahoma, they did not ignore the heartache in our state's history. They began the report with this quote: "As any honest history textbook will tell you, the first century of Oklahoma statehood has also featured dust storms and a Great Depression, political scandals and Jim Crow legislation, tumbling oil prices and truckloads of Okies streaming west. But through it all, there are two twentieth-century tragedies which, sadly enough, stand head and shoulders above the others, the Tulsa Race Riot of 1921 and the attack on the Alfred P. Murrah Federal Building in downtown Oklahoma City by American terrorist Timothy McVeigh on April 19, 1995."

Though centuries of colonialism and conflicts between imperial powers and indigenous peoples, had set the stage for riots and massacres all over the world at

Ellis Walker Woods, Principal,
Booker T. Washington High School, Tulsa during the riot.

Black Tulsa Policemen, 1921

Juanita Lewis Hopkins, daughter of one of Tulsa's first black policemen, C.J. Alexander, Sr.

Family of Judge Amos T. Hall—seated Jean Williams McGill, her mother Lucille Hall Williams, sister of Judge Hall; standing L-R Dorothy L. Gordon, Edith G. Johnson, Carolyn Williams Tolliver

Atty. Edwin L. Goodwin, Publisher, The Oklahoma Eagle Newspaper, Tulsa, OK, (in operation 1921- present; Paper was founded by Goodwin's father James O. Goodwin who came to Oklahoma from Mississippi before the Tulsa riot

The famous Latimer family of Tulsa. The family included prominent Tuskegee, Alabama-trained builders and women who were college graduates and noted educators and business women at the time of the riot.

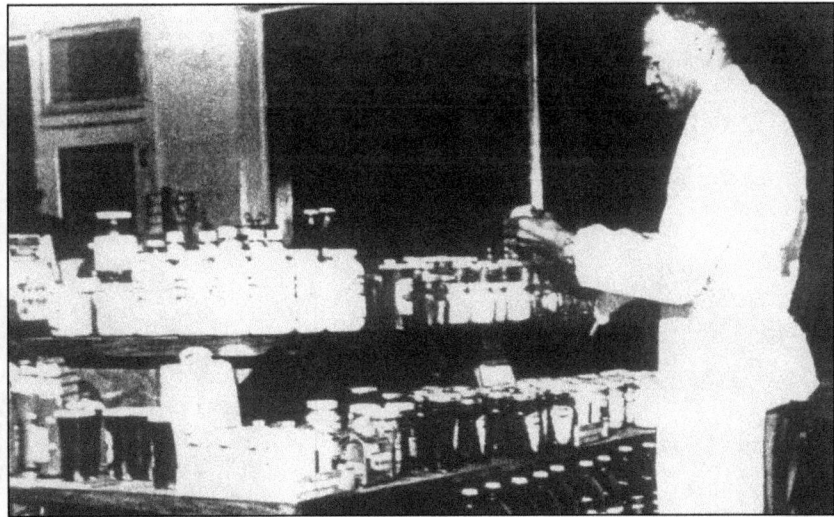

On the left: James Nails, one of the Nails brothers who had businesses on Greenwood Ave. at the time of the riot. Right: Wilson Hendrix Jarrett, whose store in the Greenwood District was legendary.

The prominent Alfred Stanley Dennie family of Tulsa. Paternal grandparents Howard and Ida Rodgers were riot survivors.

Simon Berry, Sr. and James Lee Northington were two of early Tulsa's most colorful pioneers. Licensed pilots, they provided air transportation for Tulsa's elite oil men, businessmen, and for the Sunday-after-church people who wanted a ride in an airplane!

various times in history, it was a seemingly insignificant confrontation between a young white woman, Sarah Page, and a young black man, Dick Rowland, on an elevator that was the catalyst that sparked the Tulsa Race Riot of 1921. Of course, there were deeper, longstanding problems in Tulsa.

Sarah Page, a seventeen-year-old white elevator operator, lived in a rented room on North Boston Avenue and was reported to have been attending business school in Tulsa. She was a native of Missouri. Dick Rowland was a black shoeshine "boy" who went that day, May 30, 1921, to use the only elevator in the downtown area that blacks were allowed to use, the elevator in the Drexel Building at 319 South Main Street. It was rumored, even in segregated Tulsa then, that Page and Rowland knew each other and that they may even have been lovers. Some of the survivors that I interviewed said that it was common knowledge in the black community, and among some in the white community, that the two were lovers. Some of these eyewitnesses actually lived in the same boarding house as the supposed lovers. One elderly black riot survivor who testified so was a former babysitter for Rowland. Whatever the two's relationship, the elevator incident changed Tulsa's history forever.

Given the terrible status of race relations in the U.S. at that time, it is no wonder that Dick Rowland went into hiding after the incident. Even looking at a white woman the "wrong way" could result in the lynching of a black man. According to Hannibal Johnson, in his excellent book *Black Wall Street: From Riot to Renaissance in Tulsa's Historic Greenwood District*, there were sixty-one recorded lynchings of black people in 1919. In 1920, sixty-one were reported, and in 1921, fifty-seven more were recorded. Black people all over the nation feared lynchings and sought ways to protect themselves from the carnage. Strong black Tulsa leaders, such as J. B. Stradford, A. J. Smitherman, and Dr. Robert T. Bridgewater, had so far been successful in keeping Tulsa's black men from the noose. They had even gone to other towns and stopped lynchings.

When a racist newspaper, the *Tulsa Tribune*, printed an inflammatory account of the elevator incident, already-tense emotions were further inflamed and the worst race riot in history erupted.

The media has always played a vital role in society. In the American democracy, it has been so strong and influential that it was sometimes referred to as the fourth branch of government. Those who control the media, from positions of status and power, often protect and promote the status quo. Those outside the loop of status and power in their nations often establish their own news sources. That has been the case in the United States, which has a legacy of a powerful black media. Born out of desperation due to the exclusion of their history in the mainstream media, black newspapers told the complete stories of black people, cradle-to-the-grave stories, not just violence and criminal-oriented stories, or biased and slanted stories whose ulterior motives were to keep the black race "in its place."

Spreading of the word (regarding revolts, riots, reformation movements, etc.) is absolutely essential in garnering support for such movements, in working out the details of the movements, and in the actual carrying out of the plans of such movements. In the past, messages and information to would-be supporters have been carried out via lanterns, shouting riders on horseback, and secret displays in varied and sundry places; nothing is more successful in getting the word out than the printed word. At the time of the Tulsa riot, its two black newspapers, the flagship *Tulsa Star* of Andrew Jackson Smitherman, and the *Tulsa Sun*, fulfilled their vital roles of keeping Tulsa's black population well informed about conditions in Tulsa and in the rest of the nation and the world. In fact, in the tense days just before the riot, Tulsa's black leaders met in the *Tulsa Star* office. It was from there that the black leaders, armed and determined to stop the lynching of Dick Rowland, went down to the courthouse on the night of May 31, 1921.

Since the early 1900s vigilante groups grew bolder and bolder. Some of them were card-carrying Ku Klux Klansmen; others were renamed groups, such as United Confederates Veterans and the Knights of Liberty.

The Klan, and offshoot organizations with a similar philosophy, tarred, feathered, beat, and intimidated people who were of the wrong religion, who stirred up labor discontent, or who weren't treating their families right. A few years before the Tulsa Race Riot of 1921, a group of Industrial Workers of the World (Wobblies) had been tarred, feathered, roughed up, and run out of Tulsa. And many an errant husband was tarred, feathered, and/or beaten during this era. But the severest punishment by Klan and Klan-like organizations was meted out to black men who had been accused of defiling white women.

In 1921, blacks in Tulsa were especially edgy because Tulsa, and surrounding areas, had been excessively harsh in dealing with white men in previous years. One incident, the lynching of a young white man named Roy Belton in 1920 for the murder of a white taxi driver, was really unsettling to the black community. A lynch mob had taken Belton from the county courthouse. It appears that County Sheriff Jim Woolley did little to stop them. Tulsa police officers, under the command of Police Chief John Gustafson, did not arrive in force until after Belton had been kidnapped. By the time the Tulsa police officers caught up with the kidnap victim and the mobsters, it was too late. The lynching was in process and was soon completed.

So after the racist *Tulsa Tribune* articles appeared the evening of May 30, 1921, and after the police had hunted down, caught, and arrested Dick Rowland the next day, A. J. Smitherman, in his *Tulsa Star* office, set his anti-black lynching agenda in place. Determined and armed black men set out to prevent the lynching of a black man (as they had done during the previous five months in places like Muskogee, Dewey, and even in Tulsa). But the Belton lynching had clearly shaken the men. They thought that if white Tulsans would do that to one of their own, what wouldn't they do to a black man? Still, they were determined to maintain the status quo—that is, that no black man had ever been lynched in Tulsa.

Dick Rowland was being held in the same jail where Roy Belton had been held. But the new sheriff of Tulsa County, Willard M. McCullough, was not like Woolley. He armed an adequate number of men, positioned some of them on the courthouse roof, secured the jail, disabled the building, and let it be known that there would be no lynching on his call. And there wasn't! But the nervous black men of Tulsa didn't know then what the outcome would be. Sheriff McCullough had tried unsuccessfully to disperse the white mob in front of the courthouse. He didn't want black "defenders" of Dick Rowland in the area, either. Neither did some black leaders, such as prominent businessman O. W. Gurley and well-respected deputy sheriff Barney Cleaver, who kept in contact with Sheriff McCullough regarding conditions at the courthouse. They argued for a more cautious approach. But despite assurances by McCullough that things were under control, Smitherman and his group had to see for themselves that Dick Rowland was safe. So at about 9:00 P.M. approximately twenty-five black men drove down to the courthouse. They offered to help the sheriff defend the courthouse; the sheriff declined their offer, assured them of Rowland's safety, and asked them to return to Greenwood. They did.

The white mob in the courthouse area became incensed over the actions of the black men, many of them former World War I soldiers. Some went home for weapons; others headed for the National Guard Armory at Sixth and Norfolk Streets, where they intended to break in and steal weapons. But a heroic officer, Major James A. Bell, quietly took the initiative and called guardsmen to duty (who were scheduled to depart for summer camp the next day). Major Bell, and the armed men awaiting summer camp, successfully held off the mob.

By 9:30 P.M. the white mob outside the courthouse had reached nearly two thousand persons, including men, women, children, and would-be lynchers. Good White Samaritans, like Reverend Charles W. Kerr of the First Presbyterian Church and a local judge, tried to talk the mobsters into leaving. The woeful inaction of the police chief was later fully documented and resulted in his dismissal from office after the riot.

The small, armed group of blacks in the *Tulsa Star* newspaper office, awaiting information about the situation at the courthouse, got another telephone call. Upon learning that the size of the mob had greatly increased, the men got in cars and again drove down to the courthouse. The situation was quite ugly then. Among the armed black men were the Mann brothers, prominent business owners in the Greenwood district. A white mobster challenged one of the Manns, asking the question, "Nigger, what are you doing with that gun?" The tall Mann brother replied, "I'm going to use it if I have to." The mobster said, "To hell you will" and then attempted to take the gun from the ex-soldier. A shot went off. The white man fell dead. The first casualty of the worst race riot in U.S. history sent the mob into a frenzy. The armed black men who had gone to the courthouse to offer their services to officials fought bravely, but they were greatly outnumbered. They were driven back into Greenwood. They left many in their entourage dead on the streets. (They also left whites dead on the streets of downtown Tulsa). The survivors of the mob attack made it back to their beloved Greenwood, took defensive positions to protect their neighborhood, and fought a good fight. But they were outnumbered, and when inept officials lost control of the city (many joining in with the mobsters, looters, and killers), and especially when airplanes were brought in and dropped incendiary devices down upon the Greenwood community, sending flashing white lights and flames into the community, the fate of the black community was sealed. Greenwood was at the mercy of white mobsters and some white officials and leaders who joined in with them.

When the carnage ended, the worst race riot in U.S. history had occurred. During the course of eighteen terrible hours, more than one thousand homes, twenty-three churches, and virtually all of the prominent black businesses on Greenwood were destroyed. Some forty square blocks were in ashes. In chapter 4, the people who lived through the riot will speak of their losses—human, material, spiritual, and emotional. An area that had been so prominent, so beautiful, so successful that Booker T. Washington had referred to it as a virtual "Negro Wall Street" when he visited the city while on his way to speak in Boley, an all-black town to the south of Tulsa, did not exist anymore.

The human losses were even more detrimental, for there is no adequate compensation for the loss of lives. Even though the riot commission researched diligently, we will probably never know the exact number of people who died in the Tulsa riot. We do know that the "official" estimate of nine whites and twenty-six blacks is a farce. There were more deaths in a week in Tulsa during normal times. This low estimate was the first step in the long-lasting conspiracy and coverup of the riot. Using resources such as the Maurice Willows' Red Cross Report, the Tulsa Police Department Yellow Tablet list of black riot victims that General Ed Wheeler observed, and the few existing funeral home and city cemetery records, we commissioners were comfortable with saying there were probably at least three hundred deaths (two hundred blacks and one hundred whites).

In conclusion, how did such a tragedy as this occur? After this riot decimated the black community in Tulsa, many individuals, organizations, and nations asked that question. There was not one clear-cut answer, not one specific cause, because many factors had contributed to the riot—racism, conflicts between settlers in a new Promised Land, greed, corruption, jealousy, envy, hatred, vice, and criminality, an inept government in the city at the time that failed to take early, appropriate action, an inflammatory media, Klan and Klan-like organizations that

Tulsa riot scene.

Tulsa riot scene, photo courtesy of Sand Springs Leader newspaper

Greenwood riot destruction, photo by Merton Houston.

*Above: Tulsa riot scene, recently discovered photo donated by Pat Lucy, Tulsa.
Photos taken by her late father Richard C. Alden during the Tulsa riot. Left:
Tulsa riot scene. Photo donated by Pat Lucy, Tulsa*

Tulsa riot scenes, photos donated by Pat Lucy.

Tulsa riot scene, photo donated by Pat Lucy.

Tulsa riot scene. Frisco Railroad and First St., photo courtesy of Sand Springs Leader newspaper.

fanned mob hysteria, and other reasons. But there certainly have been attempts to explain the riot and its causes. Immediately after the riot, the media descended upon Tulsa. Newspapers, black and white, large or small, sent their reporters to Tulsa to cover the riot. The riot commission spent much time examining those newspapers, many of which are stored in the archives at Tuskegee University in Alabama.

It is sad that the riot has come to be such a defining factor in Tulsa's history, for there was much good in the city also. This ambiguity, this conflict between the good, the bad, and the ugly in Tulsa is difficult to explain. But it existed, and so much has been said about the awfulness of the riot that the good has been neglected. There were many good and decent people in Tulsa at the time of the riot. They were church-going, law-abiding people, for the most part. There were many beautiful churches in Tulsa, so many on South Boulder Avenue in the downtown area that the street was called "Cathedral Row." There were beautiful homes in Tulsa, many of them show-off, do-you-one-better mansions of new oil barons and other wealthy entrepreneurs, many of them belonging to blacks like J. B. Stradford, A. J. Smitherman, O. J. Gurley, and many others that will be described in other chapters of this book. Tulsans, black and white, stressed education and had well-loved, well-cared-for schools with students performing at high levels of scholarship. There were exquisite, ornate buildings for business and for entertainment in the growing, sophisticated young city.

But there was also a "bad side" to Tulsa: vice, criminality, lawlessness, greed, corruption, and hatred. It was this side that gained control, and reigned, during those awful eighteen hours of the riot.

The "ugly side" of Tulsa extended to the riot's aftermath: the lack of proper attention for the blacks wounded in the riot, in contradistinction to the wonderful medical attention given to white wounded, the lack of dignity and respect (and funerals) for the black dead after the riot, also in contradistinction to the tender care given to white riot dead. This is covered in thorough detail by Dr. Clyde Snow in the Final Report of the Oklahoma Commission to Study the Tulsa Race Riot of 1921. Dr. Snow is one of the foremost forensic scientists in the world today. (See chapter 10.)

And so this concludes the chapter on the awful Tulsa Race Riot of 1921. Just as quickly as the riot captured national and world attention, interest in the riot waned. After a period of cleanup (forced, unpaid cleanup mainly done by black Tulsa refugees), the riot was purged from the minds and records of most Tulsans; it was forgotten by the national and world media.

A period of silence, referred to as a conspiracy by some, set in. It would be seventy-five years before the silence ended!

The Oklahoma Commission to Study the Tulsa Race Riot of 1921 was established to create a historical account of the riot. After the examination of over 20,000 documents, three and a half years of research and writing, and numerous public meetings, interviews, and speeches, the final report of the commission was completed, and it was presented to Governor Frank Keating and Mayor Susan Savage at the State Capitol in Oklahoma City on February 28, 2001. While it is not a perfect document, I am proud of the commission and the work that we did. We did the best that we could humanly do with the resources available, the normal limitations of historical research, and the normal cultural differences in people and in the world views that they brought to the dialogue table. A full account of the establishment of the commission and of its work and findings is in chapter 10.

CHAPTER 3

Aftermath: The Seventy-Five-Year Conspiracy and Coverup

Missing military records. Missing fire marshal records. Missing insurance claims. Missing funeral home records. Missing cemetery records. Missing bodies. Is this just coincidental? Not likely, according to the Oklahoma Commission to Study the Tulsa Race Riot of 1921. After three and a half years of intensive research, the commission found what had been hinted at for four decades. There had been a pattern of deliberate distortion of facts regarding the riot and even the destruction of vital documents and a subsequent coverup of the riot that had ramifications at state, local, national, and even international levels.

It has been said that history is the lie agreed upon. Well, nowhere has that statement been proven more than in Oklahoma after the powers that be agreed upon a lie about that riot which went unchallenged for seventy-five years. It was not until June 1, 1996, at the first annual Commemoration of the Tulsa Race Riot of 1921 ceremony at Mt. Zion Baptist Church in North Tulsa, right at the site of some of the most infamous battles of the riot, that the lie began to unravel. The work of the Oklahoma Commission to Study the Tulsa Race Riot of 1921 has helped tremendously to fill in the gaps in history relating to this worst race riot in the United States (and perhaps ever in the world). We commissioners examined primary and secondary sources and interviewed numerous people about the riot, and benefitted from the extensive print and media electronic coverage of the event. We searched high and low for riot information, from local areas to overseas. Still, there are holes in the history of the riot. I think Dr. Danney Goble sums up this subject best. One day at a commission meeting, he honestly said that we would probably never find all the answers we were looking for. He said that some things probably happened, but that we probably could not find proof that they happened; he said that some things probably did not happen, but we couldn't prove that either. So we concentrated on finding everything that we could. We found many things that we did not know existed. We felt that the hand of God was upon our mission, for how else could we account for the goodness of people toward us as we went about out task; how else could we explain things that fell into our hands? Some things were meant to validate a point and ended up validating a point we had not expected to validate! We entered our mission with love and affection in our hearts, and that love was reflected in love. Thanks to a good and loving God for that!

Many resources that were helpful to me in writing chapters 1 and 2 were also helpful in writing this chapter. Among the many other resources found and used in this chapter were:

• Dawes and Curtis Act Information, National Archives, Library of Congress
• National Guard Report, Company B
• Al Brophy Report
• Robert Norris' unpublished manuscript
• Bill O'Brien's unpublished manuscript
• Sections of the Scholars Report to the Commission
• Salvation Army Report
• Tulsa Chamber of Commerce Minutes, 1919–1922
• Tulsa County Commissioners' Minutes
• City of Tulsa Minutes
• Tulsa County Ku Klux Klan Rolls, McFarlin Library Special Collections, University of Tulsa
• Redfearn Case, Oklahoma Supreme Court
• Samuel Mackey Case vs. City of Tulsa
• William Walker Case vs. City of Tulsa
• Barney Weaver Case vs. City of Tulsa

- Other Cases vs. City of Tulsa (See Atty. Jim Lloyd's files)
- Old newspapers from the Tuskegee University
- Tuskegee, Alabama, archives that covered the riot and the period immediately following the riot
- Old magazines with riot articles
- Old films that had riot footage
- Contemporary newspapers and magazines (Note: After Dr. Vivian Clark-Adams and I participated in Tulsa Race Riot 1921 panel discussions, we received information from border states and other states about their own history of violence, lynchings, massacres, race wars, and riots. Newspapers in Monett, Springfield, and St. Louis, Missouri, and Duluth, Minnesota, sent clippings to me). Also, most all newspapers and magazines that came to Tulsa to do stories about the riot sent complimentary copies of their stories.
- Contemporary, complimentary copies of electronic media stories (radio, television, made- for-motion pictures media, and stage media productions, etc.).

Interview with Scott Zarrow, April 11, 2002

Just as modern archeological discoveries have led to a revision in history regarding the settlement of the Americas, and Africans are being acknowledged as the original settlers of the Americas by today's experts, perhaps one day old sources and documentation might be found which will validate completely that a conspiracy did indeed occur in Tulsa in 1921. On the other hand, it is probable that such corroborating documents may have been burned in the riot, and it is known that some documents and evidence were deliberately destroyed by perpetrators of the riot or by those who felt the need to cover it up. So we may never know the whole story. But many people feel that we already have enough proof of a conspiracy. Despite our best efforts to show a conspiracy and coverup in Tulsa in 1921, there were people who disagreed. Our critics said we made too many leaps of faith in drawing our conclusions regarding conspiracy. It is true that we had to dig deeply to get conspiracy data and to establish credibility for a conspiracy theory. We couldn't rely on surface, simplistic approaches. We had to get beneath the surface. When we couldn't find specific corroborating evidence, we did what historians do in such instances, and what lawyers do in cases where there is only circumstantial evidence. We used what we had. We made general observations of the sources; we also looked for patterns in history, for perspective. We had to look at the events in terms of the time period and through lenses that reflected thinking of the past and not modern-day thinking. We had to look at a lot of givens in human nature. We had to use the vast body of research and knowledge of the past to help us answer questions about that long-ago event, to answer questions about conditions in North Tulsa today, and to help Tulsa prepare for a better future for all its citizens by rectifying and repairing damage done to the community by the riot of 1921. I firmly believe that the evidence that we did uncover, and the patterns of thoughts, behaviors, and actions that we did examine, justifies our assumptions and inferences. I believe that the preponderance of the evidence we found validates our conclusions regarding conspiracy. I am satisfied with what we did!

My major regret regarding the commission report is that we did not pursue national culpability. There was a reason for that. Our legal advisor, attorney and law professor Al Brophy, advised us to concentrate on our strongest evidence, and that was evidence in the local and state realms. I still wish that there had been more a national focus. Even if we could not make a strong legal case that would stand up in court, we could have made a strong moral case about the federal government's distortion of our high spiritual principles and our revered, professed strong democratic principles. If the federal government had enforced the civil rights enacted during the ten years immediately following the Civil War (the Civil Rights Acts of 1868, 1870, 1871, and 1875), perhaps our history would have been different. Maybe we would not have had the 100 years of benign neglect of America's black citizens which ended only after the civil rights revolution of the 1960s. Maybe white Americans would not have become so entrenched in "white privilege" thinking that was so hard to break; some vestiges of that type of thinking still remain. But following the Ten Commandments, the Golden Rule, and the Beatitudes was not the norm in the nation for dealing with people of African descent at that time. And experts on genocide point out that even spiritually based nations and strongly democratic nations have had their share of unholy actions against peoples who had been excluded from their countries' legal protection. Mankind has always found causes, and ways, to justify such actions. For example, in our beautiful U.S. Constitution, the founders of the nation refer to any person of African descent as not a whole, God-created person but as three-fifths of a person! After the Civil War ended, the U.S. legislature enacted the Thirteenth, Fourteenth, and Fifteenth Amendments to the Constitution, which prohibited slavery, provided citizenship for people of African descent, and gave voting rights to this formerly disenfranchised group.

Once again, if the federal government had strongly enforced those laws, our history might have been different. But with the return of Southern Home Rule, laws circumventing those Constitutional amendments—Black Codes, etc.—were enacted in Southern and border states. Federal courts, including the U.S. Supreme Court in the infamous Dred Scott decision, upheld such laws. That is what makes culpability for race riots and massacres at the federal level so difficult to prove. But some of us on the commission felt that we should at least cite the examples of neglect of the federal government toward its black citizens. That is why some of us worked so hard to prepare that Preliminary Report of the Riot Commission, which was presented at the Oklahoma Capital February 4, 2001. In that report, we based our citing of federal government culpability on the following:

1. During the time period preceding, during, and immediately following the Tulsa Race Riot of 1921, there existed a climate in the American culture that perpetuated the status quo in the nation—that is, a privileged position for white citizens and a subservient, second-class position for black citizens.

2. There was a collective lack of concern in the nation for black people, black causes, black issues (there were some exceptions, of course).

3. This collective attitude of indifference was reflected in the American culture by a continuance of the status quo—namely of political, economic, and social inequities, and injustices against black citizens.

4. There was little focus on race relations, positive pro-active efforts to end lynching, racism, and injustices in the nation which were the norm in the American culture at that time.

5. Presidents at this time—Grover Cleveland, Woodrow Wilson, and Warren G. Harding—paid little more than lip service to using their executive status to provide moral leadership to end injustices in America, or to appeal to the legislative and judicial branches of government for action on these issues. (Woodrow Wilson has a record of opposing some proactive efforts to end discrimination when he was president of Princeton University.) Even after the Tulsa Race Riot of 1921, President Harding was not a strong advocate for redressing racial grievances.

6. The legislative branch of the federal government took little notice of the injustices in American society that black citizens endured on a daily basis. The incon-

sistencies that existed in the American nation—namely that there was a wide gap between the nation's professed high spiritual ideal of the brotherhood of man—did not seem to bother this group.

7. Even after documentation of over 3,000 lynchings in America (mostly of black men), the Congress could not muster enough support to pass the Dyer Anti-Lynching Bill (and this was after the Tulsa Race Riot of 1921!).

8. The federal courts, including the U.S. Supreme Court, tended to side with business and corporate plaintiffs, and decisions usually did not benefit or promote black causes, rights, or issues.

9. The federal government did little at this time to protect the Thirteenth, Fourteenth, and Fifteenth Amendment rights of black citizens, which were consistently being violated all over the nation.

10. There appear to be specific violations of these rights in Tulsa during and after the riot. For example,:

a. Blacks alone were forced to clean up, without compensation, after the riot or face arrest. This is a clear violation of the Thirteenth Amendment, which prohibits slavery, involuntary servitude.

b. There was an order by the City of Tulsa, prior to the Tulsa Race Riot of 1921, for merchants to sell munitions to whites only. They were specifically ordered not to sell munitions to blacks. This violates the Second Amendment, the right of all citizens to bear arms, the right to protect self and property.

c. The incarceration of only black males during the riot seems also to violate the Fourteenth Amendment and, perhaps, the Second and Fourteenth Amendments.

(Author's Note: A *Tulsa Tribune* article, "Sub Station of Post Office is Razed by Fire, One Violation of Federal Law Uncovered by Secret Service Agent," June 4, 1921, showed that the federal government could count at least one incident during the riot a definite a violation of federal law.)

The actions that the commission cited that seemed to point toward conspiracy and to county/state culpability were as follows:

1. Actions of the National Guard, which is under the control of the state—specifically the Guard's failure to protect black lives and property; the participation of some members of the Guard in the shootings and pillaging in the Greenwood district during the riot; and the Guard's incarceration of blacks only during the riot;

2. The state pays salaries of county officials, and thus wrongful actions that occurred in Tulsa County

during and after the riot during the cleanup process come under state domain.

3. The actions of County Sheriff McCullough seem suspect. In the book *Angels of Mercy*, author Maurice Willows questions why McCullough never revealed to the public that Dick Rowland had been secreted from the jail and driven to Kansas City, Missouri, during the early hours of the morning when the white mobs grew larger, eventually reaching 10,000 people. Wouldn't such information have resulted in the dissipation of the mob and of the black defenders of Rowland? Was the ultimate plan to have an excuse to go in and destroy the Greenwood community and have the land, which blacks would not sell, available to the white community at last? Some researchers have drawn those conclusions and cite the actions of the Tulsa Real Estate Commission after the riot, and the blacklisting of burned-out Greenwood blacks who sought loans and materials to rebuild after the riot, as supporting evidence.

There was an abundance of evidence that seemed to support city culpability in the Tulsa Race Riot of 1921. Among the evidence the commission cited in its Preliminary Report of February 4, 2001, were:

1. Early warnings to blacks in Tulsa, and surrounding areas such as Okmulgee, to vacate their properties and get out of town by June 1, 1921, or "suffer the consequences." Blacks testified that warning notes had been posted on the doors of blacks.

2. The "whistle" theory, expounded by both blacks and whites immediately after the riot, seemed to gain credibility after one of Dr. Scott Ellsworth's presentation to the riot commission at one of the commission meetings. While the media, commissioners, riot survivors, descendants of riot victims, and other interested observers sat spellbound, Ellsworth displayed huge maps, charts, diagrams, and photographs to set the stage for his depiction of the unfoldment of the race riot that thirty-first day of May in 1921.

According to Dr. Ellsworth, at 5:00 A.M. a whistle blew and whites responded from all quadrants of the city. The systematic takeover of the Greenwood district resulted. Was there some sort of plan to invade the Greenwood district? Probably. But hard evidence to prove this will probably never be found. We did find evidence of mobsters (some of them card-carrying Ku Klux Klan members) and Boy Scouts acting as sentinels into the Greenwood district. We also found evidence that the Bell Telephone System cut off phone service to the Greenwood district just before the riot, and the Ku Klux Klan rosters at the University of Tulsa's McFarlin

Library does include names of some telephone company workers. Many Boy Scout leaders (mostly high school teachers and principals) are also on the Klan rosters at the University of Tulsa. Even the superintendent of Tulsa public schools is on one of the rosters. So the conspiracy theory does not sound like a great leap of faith to many people. It sounds like a reasonable possibility given the thoughts and behaviors of white Tulsans at that time. Some of the riot survivors featured in chapter 4 spoke of the whistle incident and cited other examples of a coordinated attack.

3. The chief of police of Tulsa, John Gustafson, deputized whites who had gathered at the courthouse to lynch Dick Rowland. Gustafson deputized only whites though he mistakenly deputized a light-skinned black man, Walter White of the National Association of Colored People (NAACP), whose headquarters were in New York City. White was in Tulsa at the behest of black Tulsans who had sought national help, since they could not rely on their own local government leaders. A number of Tulsa policemen, as well as a number of Tulsa government officials, are listed on Tulsa City/County Klan rosters in the McFarlin Library Collections at the University of Tulsa.

4. Minutes of the City Commission of Tulsa from June 1921 to June 1922 show a systematic denial of black property loss claims for riot damages and losses, and a quick, orderly payment of white insurance claims for damages and losses.

5. The minutes of the City Commission of Tulsa from June 1921 to June 1922, also indicate the extent of the damages caused by the riot; city expenditures for riot control, damage, and cleanup totaled $40,000, which was a very large sum at that time.

6. Certain city officials and local aviators (mostly wealthy oil barons) flew over Tulsa's Greenwood district during the riot. Some incendiary devices were dropped over the area, which increased the destruction of the black community.

7. Firefighters did not properly and adequately protect the Greenwood district during the riot. According to reports by scholar Scott Ellsworth, a consultant to the riot commission, focus was on protecting white property and white lives. In the Redfearn case, heard before the Oklahoma Supreme Court, black and white eyewitnesses of the riot testified that some fire stations tried to respond to the riot but were kept from doing their duty by the "special" deputies (most of whom were the very mobsters who had gathered at the courthouse to lynch Dick Rowland the night of May 31, 1921);

The moment that law is destroyed, liberty is lost; and men, left free to enter upon the domains of each other, destroy each other's rights, and invade the field of each other's liberty.—Timothy Titcomb.

IT MUST NOT BE AGAIN

SUCH a district as the old "Niggertown" must never be allowed in Tulsa again. It was a cesspool of iniquity and corruption. It was the cesspool which had been pointed out specifically to the Tulsa police and to Police Commissioner Adkison, and they could see nothing in it. Yet anybody could go down there and buy all the booze they wanted. Anybody could go into the most unspeakable dance halls and base joints of prostitution. All this had been called to the attention of our police department and all the police department could do under the Mayor of this city was to whitewash itself. The Mayor of Tulsa is a perfectly nice, honest man, we do not doubt, but he is guileless. He could have found out himself any time in one night what just one preacher found out.

In this old "Niggertown" were a lot of bad niggers and a bad nigger is about the lowest thing that walks on two feet. Give a bad nigger his booze and his dope and a gun and he thinks he can shoot up the world. And all these four things were to be found in "Niggertown"—booze, dope, bad niggers and guns.

The Tulsa Tribune makes no apology to the Police Commissioner or to the Mayor of this city for having plead with them to clean up the cesspools in this city.

Commissioner Adkison has said that he knew of the growing agitation down in "Niggertown" some time ago and that he and the Chief of Police went down and told the negroes that if anything started they would be responsible.

That is first class conversation but rather weak action.

Well, the bad niggers started it. The public would now like to know: why wasn't it prevented? Why were these niggers not made to feel the force of the law and made to respect the law? Why were not the violators of the law in "Niggertown" arrested? Why were they allowed to go on in many ways defying the law? Why? Mr. Adkison, why?

The columns of The Tribune are open to Mr. Adkison for any explanation he may wish to make.

These bad niggers must now be held, and, what is more, the dope selling and booze selling and gun collecting must STOP. The police commissioner, who has not the ability or the willingness to find what a preacher can find and who WON'T stop it when told of it, but merely whitewashes himself and talks of "knocking chairwarmers" had better be asked to resign by an outraged city.

⚏ ⚏ ⚏ ⚏ ⚏ ⚏ ⚏

FOR TULSA

Don't let your eye escape the coupon on the first page. Put your pencil to it. The honor of Tulsa is at stake. The commercial stability of Tulsa stands in jeopardy. For reasons of justice, for simple, plain, good business reasons, Tulsa must do the right thing and do it NOW. Are you a Tulsan? Give. And give NOW.

children, one a baby a month old, Mrs. M. R. Travis of 1792 South Boulder, who is in charge of this case, is anxious to hear from anyone who knows of the whereabouts of Mrs. Love and the children. Her telephone number is Osage 2447.

JURY SUMMONS BEING ISSUED FOR RIOT QUIZ

BIDDISON ASKS THAT FREELING BE SENT HERE AT ONCE

OKLAHOMA CITY — Attorney General S. P. Freeling intends to go tomorrow to Tulsa where he will conduct an investigation into the race riot, as ordered yesterday by Governor Robertson, he said today. Evidence secured in the investigation will be presented to the grand jury, which meets June 8.

It was said at the governor's office today that am essage had been received from Judge Biddison of Tulsa asking that the attorney general be in Tulsa Monday. Mr. Freeling had planned previously, however, to go tomorrow and to start work on the date asked by Judge Biddison.

Jury summons were being issued today for service on the grand jury for investigating and fixing the responsibility of the race riots in district court, while a call was under way to Governor Robertson from Judge W. Valjean Biddison asking that Attorney General Prince Freeling be sent here Monday to prepare his case for the quiz on Wednesday. Freeling has already been ordered here by the governor.

Judge Biddison said today that jury summons were already under way and that he was in active direction of the empaneling of a grand jury ordered by Governor Robertson. The date set for the first sessions of the jury is June 8. The investigation by the state authorities will be carried on separately from that ordered by the department of justice at Washington.

no more right to invade it than a professional burglar. If the search warrant is not available, then it is the duty of the police to exercise common sense in their selection of houses that might justify a search.

The suggestion of the Real Estate Exchange that the negro district be moved out farther, the present burned-over area to be given over to industry and switch tracks is a sensible one. If Tulsa business is to expand, the ground occupied by the section now in ashes is by all odds one of the most necessary to such expansion.

The honor of a large number of Tulsans is being put to the test by the gun store men. They want their property returned.

Sat. June 4, 1921 editorial, Tulsa Tribune newspaper (blame-placing for Tulsa riot).

WWI black soldiers (attitude of black soldiers blamed for riot turmoil).

WWI military vehicle.

Arch of Triumph postcard sent from Paris to a Tulsa mother from her soldier son who was in WWI.

other firemen, totally insensitive to the black community, never left their stations; some who left their stations, but were prevented from going into the district, testified that they returned to their stations and slept through the riot.

8. The motives and methods of the Tulsa Real Estate Exchange seem suspect. The members of this organization, the politically, economically, and socially elite in Tulsa, had long sought the Greenwood district for white expansion. Merritt J. Glass, president of the exchange at the time of the riot, was reported in the June 7, 1921, *Tulsa Tribune* as stating that "real estate men will at once secure industrial purchases for property in the devastated area and also will get options on land farther to the north where the Negroes may build their homes and locate a new Negro district." A group of real estate persons issued an order to blacks whose homes had been destroyed in the riot that they must sell their land to whites for the purpose of industrial development. To further ensure that blacks would sell this Greenwood district land to whites, the City of Tulsa passed an ordinance regarding rebuilding the riot-destroyed area—an ordinance so stringent that blacks could not possibly meet the requirements. Attorney B.C. Franklin, father of noted historian Dr. John Hope Franklin, challenged the law all the way to the Oklahoma Supreme Court, where it was declared unconstitutional.

Immediately after the riot, Tulsa was faced with the tremendous task of cleaning up, burying the dead, and providing makeshift shelter for 9,000 black refugees. Some survivors tearfully speak of those tents they lived in during the unusually rainy and cold winter of 1921; some had relatives who contracted pneumonia and died. In chapter 4, the reader will see examples of black deaths after the riot that were directly related to the riot. The city also had to assess blame and mete out punishment for the riot, a task that seemed to be a priority for the white community. The media ranted and raved about the riot and about the "bad niggers" who started it. The *Tulsa Tribune*'s June 4, 1921, newspaper was the most strident of the press articles. Its "Old Nigger Town" editorial is the epitome of bigotry in the media.

On the first Sunday after the Tulsa riot, pulpits in Tulsa rocked to the rafters as white ministers pounded their podiums and denounced the "black criminal ruffians" for perpetrating the riot.

Even the courts placed blame for the riot on Tulsa's black population. But even though Tulsa had its collective villain for the riot, the people salivated for a specific victim, or better still multiple victims to crucify. Among the most hated black men in Tulsa before the riot were wealthy and powerful black businessmen. The two black scapegoats chosen by white Tulsans were J. B. Stradford and A. J. Smitherman. They were both run out of Tulsa, and neither ever returned to Tulsa or to their pre-riot status of authority and wealth.

General Charles Barrett, commander of National Guard troops during the riot, ordered Stradford arrested after the riot, but Stradford escaped via train to Independence, Kansas, where a brother of his lived. The next day he was arrested by Kansas officials, and he immediately called his son, Cornelius Stradford, who was an attorney. Cornelius got his father out of jail on bond, but J. B. Stradford, was not supposed to leave Independence. Fearing that he would not get justice in either Kansas or Oklahoma, J. B. made a decision that would have a profound effect on his life. The law-abiding, upright black man of wealth and status "went on the lam," to the big city of Chicago, where his son lived. He lived there until he died in 1935. Though Oklahoma failed in its extradition attempts, the state did indirectly sentence that noble man. He was given a life sentence of indignity and injustice!

J. B. Stradford never set foot in Tulsa after June of 1921; neither had any of his offspring, until October 18, 1996. In a moving ceremony at the Greenwood Cultural Center in Tulsa on that date, J. B. Stradford was exonerated. Before twenty-one of his descendants, who came from all over the U.S. and even from Europe, J. B. Stradford finally got delayed justice. Governor Frank Keating issued an executive pardon to Stradford and sixty-two other blacks listed in the indictment in the case of the *State of Oklahoma v. Will Robinson, et al,* June 15, 1921. Tulsa District Attorney William

Photograph from Lt. Col. (ret.) Major Clark who was a major source of information about the military for researchers until his death several years ago. Photo was taken in 1946 when he was in Leghorn, Italy where he had fought during WWII.

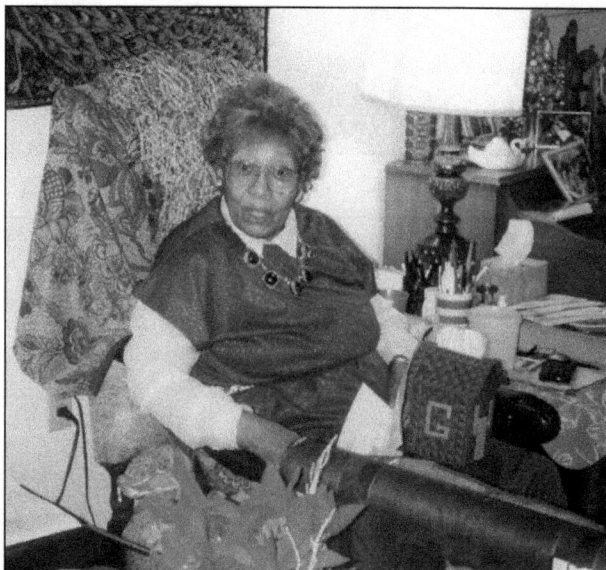

Alice Andrews who lived through the Tulsa riot shares personal information that she knew about the Dick Rowland/Sarah Page relationship.

B.C. Franklin, attorney, works, in a tent on Greenwood, on the case involving the Real Estate Board of Tulsa's Ordinance re: the rebuilding of the Greenwood District after the destruction caused by the Tulsa riot.

Dr. Lloyd H. Williams, Sr. in his drugstore on Greenwood Avenue after Greenwood was rebuilt after the Tulsa riot.

LaFortune (recently elected mayor of Tulsa) and Judge Jesse Harris officially dropped all charges on behalf of the City of Tulsa. After seventy-five years, J. B. Stradford finally had his day in court.

Stradford's great great-granddaughter, Ann-Marie Usher of Chicago, was interviewed several times by me on behalf of the riot commission, and she generously sent some primary documents of her famous ancestor to the commission, which were made a part of the official record. A daughter of Stradford's, Jewel Lafontant-Mankarious, a former U.S. Ambassador who was in Tulsa for the ceremony, has since died.

In interviews with Carol Smitherman Martin and her two grown children, Dr. Carol Dozier-Walton and Dr. Richard Dozier, I heard a story almost identical to Stradford's. Andrew Jackson (A. J.) Smitherman fled from Tulsa after the riot and settled his family in Buffalo, New York. He was never able to re-create the extremely successful life (and business) that he had in Tulsa. Mrs. Martin said that he donated his papers to the library in Buffalo. A poignant poem that he wrote about the Tulsa Race Riot of 1921 was given to all of the riot commissioners at a meeting in Oklahoma City.

After the Stradford and Smitherman sagas played out, after whites had been recompensed for their riot losses and a white judge had dismissed all remaining black claims against the City of Tulsa, it was if a giant eraser wiped the blackboard of the race riot clean. It would never make it into the history books; it would not be talked about by black or white Tulsans; it would vanish. It would be seventy-five years before this conspiracy of silence would be broken.

The process by which the conspiracy was broken was:

1. Opening up dialogue about the Tulsa Race Riot of 1921

2. Mass focus on healing and reconciliation

3. Healing/reconciling commemoration programs

4. Collective community effort in Tulsa by all races, religions, and political, economic, social and cultural groups to form a spiritually based, just, and equal society

5. Annual Tulsa Race Riot of 1921 Commemorations begun

6. The exoneration ceremony for J. B. Stradford.

Don Ross must be given credit for being the person most responsible for opening up dialogue about the Tulsa riot. He began what became for him a holy mission, the process of getting to the roots of this riot, when he was a fifteen-year-old student at Booker T. Washington High School in Tulsa. He never wavered in his love for the Tulsa community and his desire to learn the truth about the riot, which he wanted to share with all Tulsans. As a student, he went to talk to survivors of the riot and recorded their stories in his journal and in his mind forever. See chapter 10 for more details about how his dream that this story should be known by everyone became reality in the form of his House Bill 1035 resolution (co-authored with Senator Maxine Horner), which created the Oklahoma Commission to Study the Tulsa Race Riot of 1921. Without Ross's dogged persistence for four decades, the world wouldn't have learned the story of the Tulsa Race Riot of 1921.

Ed Wheeler's research of the Tulsa Race Riot of 1921 was poignant, potent, and powerful, too powerful to be handled by Tulsa in 1971 when Wheeler wrote an article about the riot. Wheeler, is best known as the military expert who was a captain in the Oklahoma National Guard and who rose to the rank of brigadier general in the U.S. Army. He was also an historian who did extensive research on subjects that interested him, and he was very articulate in sharing his ideas and research with others. He was such a good communicator that he was hired by Tulsa's KVOO radio show in the 1960s to broadcast short historical dramas. The dramas were so popular that they began to be aired on television also.

Larry Silvey, young white editor of the Tulsa Chamber of Commerce's magazine, *Tulsa*, asked Wheeler to write an article about the riot for publication in the magazine. Wheeler was happy to oblige the Chamber. He did extensive research in archives in the city and in the state, and was dismayed to find that many vital records and documents about the riot were gone. He also went into the black community in Tulsa and interviewed numerous survivors of the riot in their homes; he visited their churches and attended their social and cultural organization meetings, as well. Being a good historian, he also interviewed white eyewitnesses of the riot.

But when Ed Wheeler presented his report to the Chamber, the all-white Chamber board got cold feet. Wheeler's research on the riot had been a hot topic in Tulsa, and he and his family had even received death threats. So it should not have been a surprise to Wheeler when Clyde Cole, head of the Chamber, relayed the news to him that the article which the Chamber had requested would not be printed, after all. But Wheeler was not a man to give up easily. He then went to the *Tulsa World* newspaper and gave the article to an editor whom he personally knew. The editor concurred that it was an excellent story, but then he gave Wheeler the bad news that given the times and the controversy over "opening up the riot story again," the *Tulsa World* wouldn't touch that story with an eleven-foot pole. So, Wheeler went to the black community. He took his story to Don Ross, the young black editor of North Tulsa's *Impact Magazine*. Ross was skeptical that white Tulsans would ignore a black magazine. So he went to the *Tulsa Tribune* newspapers to see if two white reporters there would write the story. They did, but Don Ross didn't like their story. He thought it too liberal. He liked Ed Wheeler's balanced account of the riot. So he published it verbatim in *Impact Magazine* in June of 1971. The rest of the story is history. Dialogue about the Tulsa Race Riot of 1921 was reestablished at last.

The beginning of annual commemoration programs to reflect upon the history of Tulsa's black community, to respect and honor those who survived the Tulsa Race Riot of 1921, and to share dialogue on how to promote racial healing and harmony in the community must also be credited to Don Ross.

The first commemoration ceremony, on June 1, 1996, set the pattern for other annual commemorations. There were dignitaries and powerful speakers, Gospel singers who "lifted the rafters," children participants singing their songs and reading their poetry who lifted the spirit of the audience and, of course, the riot survivors and their descendants. Over 1200 people filled Mt. Zion Baptist Church in the Greenwood District to capacity. The entire spectrum of humanity was represented—black, white, red, yellow, the young, the old, the rich, the poor, local people and out-of-towners. What a beautiful audience! My heart overflowed when a young white man hugged me and introduced me to his wife and two young daughters. It was Tulsa attorney Scott Zarrow, his wife Hilary, and daughters Alison and Rachel. I first met Scott Zarrow when he was a teenaged student in my U.S. history class at Thomas Alva Edison High School in Tulsa. He loved history. I soon learned why. Scott's grandfather, Sam Zarrow, was a Tulsa businessman in the 1920s and had a reputation as one of the finest and fairest merchants in town. At a time when it was not the norm, not politically or socially correct, he befriended black people. Many elderly blacks in the Tulsa community today still speak of the kindness of Sam Zarrow. He was honored posthumously with a North Tulsa Heritage Foundation Image Builders Award in 2001.

In an interview with Scott Zarrow on April 11, 2002, I asked Scott for some more details that he had heard from his dad, Jack Zarrow, and from his uncle, Henry Zarrow, who was six years old when the riot broke out. Here is what he told me:

> My grandfather always talked about the terrible race riot in Tulsa in 1921. He said that on the day of the riot, when the black people were running for their lives, some of them ducked into his store, located at Sixth and Rockford, and hid behind (or in) food storage barrels, under counters, or anywhere else they found where they could be hidden from the view of the murderous mob. Grandma Rose said that she hid some small black children under her skirt!

> My grandparents' store was destroyed in the riot, and they built another store after the riot at 352 North Greenwood Avenue. There is a photograph of my grandparents and my uncle Henry in that store on display at the Greenwood Cultural Center. My dad, Jack Zarrow, was not born until after the riot.

The national media covered that commemoration and set the pattern for the subsequent siege of Tulsa by media from all over the nation and the world.

And so, this dark period in Tulsa's history has been scrutinized under the microscope of the Oklahoma Commission to Study the Tulsa Race Riot of 1921, by worldwide media, and subsequently by people who have digested this media with a passion that surprised everyone. The Tulsa riot has gone from being one of the most covered-up events in history to being a household word all over the world. Much healing has already gone on. Tulsans have overcome the denial stage; some are even into the acceptance-of-responsibility stage, while other individuals and organizations have proceeded with passion to the action stage, in the form of pressing for reparations to survivors from culpable entities, raising and distributing voluntary donations (moral-based gifts), establishing scholarship funds, and making in-kind donations of goods and services to survivors. The Tulsa Reparations Coalition was founded by the Tulsa Unitarian Church, the Church of the Restoration, and has spearheaded the reparations drive in Tulsa. The Unitarian Universalists Association of Cleveland, Ohio, raised the initial $20,000 gift donation for Tulsa riot survivors. Another $8,000 was raised by All Souls Unitarian Church, Church of the Restoration, College Hills Presbyterian Church, and Metropolitan Community United Church, all of Tulsa. Mike Wilkerson of Barrister Studios donated $10,000 to a scholarship fund at Tulsa Community College, and

Tulsa Senior Services (with the Greenwood Cultural Center) established a program to aid survivors. The Metropolitan Tulsa Chamber of Commerce has committed to raise funds from the business community to give each riot survivor $5,000. The hearts of Tulsans have been touched by the survivors. (See chapter 10 for information regarding city, county, and state culpability and reparations.) I am so proud that some Tulsans have taken the first steps toward reconciliation and healing:

1. End of the denial syndrome:

2. Acceptance of the collective deed (not personal responsibility . . .) (Inheritance of collective good; collective debt concept)

3. Proactive actions to right the wrong

We have to wait a while longer to see what the final solution to the Tulsa Race Riot of 1921 will be. But we can rejoice that the process of healing has begun. Naturally, it is hoped that a just settlement will be offered to the victims of the riot and to their descendants for the great losses that they suffered—human, property, emotional losses. James Baldwin, the prominent, late black author, had a favorite saying about dealing with past injustices. He said that, "You can't fix what you don't recognize." Thank God, Tulsa has finally recognized that an injustice was done in the past, an injustice to black people caused by the Tulsa Race Riot of 1921. Now we are in the process of fixing it.

CHAPTER 4

Eyewitness Accounts of the Tulsa Race Riot of 1921 by Known Living Black Survivors

I have always loved babies, children, the elderly, and animals—those that seemed vulnerable and in need of the help of the tender-hearted. And tender-hearted I am! When I studied in my major field (history) and in my minor field (English), I learned that the critical researcher, writer, or journalist is supposed to remain unemotional and detached from the subjects being studied. I just can't do that. I could no more have remained detached from these precious survivors (and their fascinating offspring and heirs) than I could have stopped the sun from rising. My professors always forgave me this "flaw," if it is a flaw, because my research never suffered. In fact, some people believe that this tender concern for subject populations enriched me as a human being and helped me to do the things that I do best, such as record oral history. I was so touched by what my fellow University of North Dakota alumni Tim Madigan, an award-winning journalist at the *Fort Worth Star-Telegram*, said about me in his new book, *The Burning: Massacre, Destruction and the Tulsa Race Riot of 1921*. He spoke of my tender concern for the riot survivors. Even author James Hirsch, who was sometimes strident in his descriptions of Oklahomans in his book about the Tulsa riot, *Riot and Remembrance: The Tulsa Race War and Its Legacy*, acknowledged my unabashed compassion for riot survivors.

A recent article that appeared in book section of the *Tulsa World* about the "tender-hearted" historian Will Durant and his success despite that "flaw" made me feel better about my tender-heartedness. So whenever I worry about my tenderheartedness getting in the way of historiography, I just think about Will Durant and how he laughed all the way to the bank after the sales of his numerous books, and I also think about the Bible verses Ephesians 4:31, 32, and Galatians 5:14,

about tenderheartedness. And I rejoice that I am tenderhearted!

The eyewitness accounts of the living Black survivors of the Tulsa Race Riot of 1921 are extremely significant, for they are a primary source of vital riot information given by one of the most important groups in Tulsa at that time, the besieged black population of Tulsa who suffered the most during that awful holocaust May 31–June 1, 1921. Some of the accounts are compelling examples of the terror of traumatized children during the riot. Some are accounts of the black warriors of the riot, ranging from eleven-, twelve- and thirteen-year-old-boys who formed a "munition brigade" to hack open boxes of ammunition and to pass boxes of bullets, to Greenwood's black men who were trying desperately, against all odds, to keep mob elements and militia from destroying their beloved Greenwood. One of the bravest of this group was Horace "Pegleg" Taylor, whose daughter Lena Eloise Taylor Butler of Seattle, Washington, told the author of Taylor's last earthly efforts on June 1, 1921. Other accounts give poignant inner-circle views of what Tulsa was like in the 1920s—two cities divided by race. Some of the testimonies of the riot are long, detailed, thorough. Others are terse but telling. A few survivors gave no testimony at all, for they are no longer capable of sharing their thoughts, due to the effects of aging or illness.

Oral history has "come to a new place" in the world today, to a new respectability. It is especially popular in American history. Note the focus on slave narratives, on holocaust survivors' testimonies, and on war experiences, such as Tom Brokaw's *The Greatest Generation*. On an ABC evening news program August 6, 2001, the credibility of oral history was discussed. The expert interviewed stated that traumatic memories, such as those cited by riot survivors and other witnesses of mass trauma, tend to be surprisingly accurate when cross-referenced with other accounts (written, visual, etc.) of the same events. These types of emotional memories are often engraved with clarity and permanence in the minds of the eyewitnesses, though they might not remember whether they have eaten a meal that day or where they parked their cars! Dr. Ed Linenthal, a University of Wisconsin, Oshkosh expert on mass tragedies and memories, was brought to one of our Riot Commission meetings and provided valuable insight and guidance to the Commission.

The survivors whom the Oklahoma Riot Commission interviewed ranged in age from 80 to 108. Their physical and mental status ran the gamut from physically and mentally robust, like ninety-eight-year-old Otis Clark, who is extremely healthy and agile, and who still drives himself from Tulsa to California and Seattle, Washington, once a year, to those whose physical capacities confine them to walkers and wheelchairs. Some have had their mental capacities dimmed by age, while some suffer from the dreaded Alzheimer's disease. Still others told me that they are just "keeping up and keeping on" despite daily visits from "Arthur" (arthritis) and "Al" (Alzheimer's)!

Some of the survivors live in Veterans Homes, where they relive the stories of the Tulsa Race Riot of 1921 and World War II. Some live in care centers that cater to the elderly, and others live in residential housing devoted to senior citizens. Surprisingly, a number of them live in private homes, with spouses or grown children. A goodly number live alone and take good care of themselves.

TULSA'S EARLIEST PIONEERS

(Uppercase names indicate individuals who were interviewed for this book.)

Male Business Entrepreneurs: Property and Losses

A. J. Smitherman, J. B. Stradford, John Williams, Samuel D. Hooker, Samuel McGowan, O. W. Gurley, J. H. Goodwin, William Walker, Wilson Hendrix Jarrett, Osborne Monroe, Arthur Chester Curvay, the Nails brothers (James and Henry), the Rodgers/Dennie families, the Sipuel family, the Cannon family, the Small family (which owned the famous Hotel Small on Greenwood and Archer), the Grayson family (who had moved from Grayson, Oklahoma, a town named for the family, and built a restaurant on Deep Greenwood), Hosea Vaden

Female Business Entrepreneurs: Property and Losses

Loula Williams, Carrie B. McDonald, Mabel B. Little, Annie McNeal, Mrs. Partee

The Medical Profession

Dr. A. C. Jackson, Dr. Sylvester Kimbrough, Dr. Sneed, Dr. Keys (many survivors mentioned these two doctors, but none could remember their first names), Dr. Robert T. Bridgewater

Faith Communities

Most survivor testimonies include some reference to faith, religion, and, often, specific reference to the survivor's own church. Black churches most often mentioned were First Baptist Church, Mt. Zion Baptist Church, Vernon AME Church, Paradise Baptist Church (where black males of all ages, from boys of eleven to men in their eighties, hacked open boxes of ammunition, armed themselves, and went forth to protect their beloved Greenwood district), and St. Monica's Catholic Church. But sometimes, little churches would be mentioned, such as "the little church that wouldn't burn" during the riot despite repeated dousing of a church wall with gasoline. Church members consider it a miracle of God.

Some references are also made of white churches in Tulsa at the time of the riot, and to present activities of churches and faith organizations, such as the Unitarians and First Presbyterian Church of Tulsa, and the Tulsa Metropolitan Ministry, which have taken an active role in remembering the history of the Tulsa race riot and given strong support to reparations for survivors.

Education

E. W. Woods and Henry Clay Whitlow Jr. were the educators most mentioned, idolized, and honored by riot survivors and the Black Tulsa community in general. They were both principals at the renowned Booker T. Washington (BTW) High, which was known for its molding of future black leaders. The account of survivor ERNESTINE GIBBS, who herself became a BTW teacher, is exceptionally effective in conveying the significance of the school.

Legal Profession

Amos T. Hall, B. C. Franklin, Primus Wade, P. A. Chappelle, H. A. Guess are the attorneys of the riot era in history whose names turn up frequently in testimonies and in key historical documents relating to the riot, such as court cases, including the famous case *Redfearn v.*, which went to the Oklahoma Supreme Court.

Government/Politics

Due to rigid segregation in Oklahoma at the time of the riot, access to political, economic, and social positions were limited for black people. Nevertheless, some of them earned "political plum" positions in government and politics, given to them by the grateful white establishment for keeping the black community "in line" and for doing the bidding of the white establishment. The main political patronage in Tulsa at the time was the appointment, by white officials, of black policemen (who were restricted to the black community and allowed to take limited action). Black law officials (at city and county levels) were extremely respected in the black community. Some of them were riot survivors, such as C. J. ALEXANDER, one of Tulsa's first black policeman, and JOHN SMITHERMAN. For a detailed look at Tulsa's black police force in the 1920s, see *They Came Searching: How Blacks Sought the Promised Land in Tulsa*, Eddie Faye Gates, Eakin Press, Austin, Texas, 1997. C. J. Alexander's three sons share vital information regarding their father and those early Tulsa policemen. For information on John Smitherman, see testimony of his daughter, survivor JEWEL SMITHERMAN ROGERS, Perris, California, in which she tells of how even she failed in trying to get her father to talk about his encounter with the Ku Klux Klan in the 1920s. Read about the incident in which Klansmen cut off part of Smitherman's ear and tried to make him eat it.

The Military

Riot survivors served their country well during World War II and the Korean War. See the testimonies of JAMES D. BELL, JOE BURNS, SAMUEL CASSIUS, Hackensack, New Jersey, ALMADGE J. NEWKIRK, Barstow, California, and BERTRAM WILLIAMS, Seattle, Washington, to find out who was the Buffalo Soldier, who lives in a retirement home and whose good friend is a former Tuskegee airman, where they fought, and what medals they won.

Social and Cultural Institutions, Museums, Etc.

Survivor JULIA BONTON JONES had a famous relative, Arna Bontemps, a black Harlem Renaissance literary figure, who has a museum in his honor in Louisiana.

The Riot: Shot and Killed

One of the most famous of the Tulsa riot victims who was shot and killed was DR. A. C. JACKSON, a surgeon who trained at the Mayo Clinic in Minnesota and who was called by his professors "one of the finest surgeons in the world." Some of the riot survivors mentioned with pride that they had been delivered by Dr. Jackson. Read how his death affected his niece, Tulsa riot survivor WILHELMINA GUESS HOWELL. Mrs. Howell also talks about her grandfather, H. A. GUESS, the famous Tulsa attorney who represented riot survivors in lawsuits after the riot.

Riot survivor CECIL WHITE, Berkeley, California, talks about the death of his mother's brother, George Jeffries. Read how the death of an unidentified old man, who was shot from a low-flying airplane, affected riot survivor J.B. BATES.

ELWOOD LETT became a media favorite because he was one of the few riot survivors who witnessed the shooting of a relative. Over and over, he told the story of how his grandfather was shot and killed as he tried to take his family, including Elwood Lett's mother and little sister, to safety. A mobster walked right up to the horse-driven wagon and asked Mr. Lett, "Nigger, where do you think you're going?"

Mr. Lett replied, "I'm taking my family to safety in Nowata, where I have relatives."

"Like hell you are," snarled the mobster as he raised his gun and shot the old man three times in the head. Six-year-old Elwood Lett should not have seen this violent death. He and his sister had been hidden under a blanket in the back of the wagon and were sternly warned to stay completely covered. But little Elwood was always an active little boy, and he just couldn't resist looking out to see what all the commotion was about. He regretted that decision all of his life, for he could never forget the sight of that raised gun and the sound of those three bullets that penetrated his beloved grandfather's head. Read the rest of the story in chapter 6, which covers the testimony of survivors who died after 1997.

The Riot: Shot and Wounded

"The bullet hit his belt buckle, then ricocheted and slit open his stomach. His intestines were hanging out." Read how survivor ROSELLA CARTER, Kansas City, Missouri, witnessed this shooting of her husband. Learn how he suffered from that wound until it killed him.

Survivor WILMA MITCHELL JOHNSON, Belen, New Mexico, said that her father, William Willis Mitchell, was shot three times by rioters and left for dead. He miraculously survived.

Read about other eyewitness accounts of shootings. See testimonies of JUANITA DELORES McGOWAN BURNETT and ELDORIS McCONDICHIE.

The Riot: Missing, Presumed Dead

Tom Bryant, stepfather of riot survivor OTIS GRANVILLE CLARK, was last seen running from his home on Archer Street as white mobsters were pursuing fleeing blacks. He was never seen or heard from again. Read how that event still affects Mr. Clark, as does the disappearance of two dear neighbors, the Greens, who were also never seen or heard from again. Survivor SIMON R. RICHARDSON also still mourns the loss (and presumed deaths) of his dear neighbors, the Butlers. They were last seen leaving the Greenwood area in a wagon pulled by a team of mules during the height of the riot.

The Riot: the Beaten, Bruised, Burned, 'Buked, Scorned, and Bused

Survivors KINNEY BOOKER and Sister, DOROTHY BOOKER BOULDING, St. Louis, Missouri, hid with their mother in the attic of their home, where their father, downstairs, tried to talk mobsters out of setting the house on fire. He failed. The children feared they would burn to death.

Survivor JAMES L. STEWARD had a similar experience. When mobsters set the Steward home on fire, all the doors welded shut. His distraught father, unsuccessful in opening any door, had the presence of mind to break out a window and push four-year-old James and his mother out of it. He then jumped, just before the mobsters entered the house. Read the rest of the story. You must see the meticulous account of the riot that Mrs. Steward later wrote.

Survivor BESSIE MAE AUSTIN VESTER still talks about how her sister, Lucille, was burned in the riot.

The Riot: Other Harrowing Experiences

ELDORIS ECTOR McCONDICHIE broke away from her father during their flight from mobsters and ran and hid in a chicken coop. She had to be forcibly removed by her father. BEULAH LOREE KEENAN SMITH remembers fleeing blacks having to duck down and hide in Sour Dock weed patches to dodge bullets. She also remembers her fleeing group spending the night in a hog pen. (The media, with reverence, tenderness, and respect, referred to her as "the hog-pen lady" and couldn't get enough of her "hog pen story.") Everywhere the group asked to spend the night of May 31, 1921, they were turned away by frightened people. A kind white man, who was afraid to let the group stay in his house, told them they could hide in the hog pen. Read the rest of the story to find out how their hog "neighbors" behaved that night. Survivor ANNIE BIRDIE CARTER BEAIRD never forgot what it felt like to be running from a mob and to have no place to hide except down in the bowels of the earth in an abandoned strip mine pit. The adults were grateful to stumble across that pit as they fled from fast-advancing mobsters. But the children, who had been dropped down into that pit, hated it, especially when the mobsters had fled the area and the fleeing riot survivors knew it was safe to get out and to go farther north to safety with relatives. Perhaps that memory was one of her last earthly thoughts before she died on August 28, 2001.

Survivor ERNESTINE GIBBS and her mother feared that the young son (and brother) in the family was killed in the riot when he got separated from them during their frenzied flight down Greenwood just barely ahead of raging mobsters. But after the riot, they found him in Sand Springs, Oklahoma, where he had fled. He had swum down the Arkansas River to safety from the mobsters who controlled the streets of Tulsa that day. Other frightened blacks jumped into that river. Most made it to safety; a few are believed to be still resting in the sands beneath that river today.

The Riot: Traumatized Children and "Punitive" Losses

Much has been written about the great loss of property when the Negro Wall Street was destroyed in the Tulsa Race Riot of 1921, but "punitive" losses are just as significant. Child survivors of the riot, now at least eighty years old, touched my heartstrings as they told about their losses. Here are just a few:

ART BUCKNER, San Francisco, California. Read the whole story of how eleven-year-old Art lost his size-twelve shoes during the riot. Not realizing the seriousness of the riot, young Art poked around right in the middle of the commotion so he could get a better view. Not until a horse right in front of him was shot dead and the blood spurted onto Art, did he realize the significance of what was going on! Then he joined fleeing blacks who were running down the Santa Fe Railroad track trying to get to safety farther north in the addition across from Pine Street. Read the rest of his story to find out how he was suckered out of his shoes by a bare-footed black man. Read about Art's bloodied feet.

Here is another shoe story. Survivor JOYCE WALKER HILL, Kansas City, Missouri, and the rest of the WILLIAM WALKER family also fled down the Santa Fe Railroad tracks, as did the Buckner family. But Joyce lost only one of her shoes. Read the rest of the story to find out how that one shoe provided protection not only for Joyce, but also for her sister. Soft-hearted Joyce lent the shoe occasionally to her sister, to give her brief respites from the merciless gravel of the railroad tracks. Thus the sisters had one less bleeding foot!

There were other shoe stories. New shoes were extremely significant to female child survivors, especially those who had received them as birthday presents right around the time of the riot. One survivor, in a nursing home, daily asks a nurse which pair of new sandals she should wear—the brown ones or the black ones. The nurses don't have the heart to tell that dear, sweet little woman of the time lapse and of the situation regarding those new birthday sandals. (They burned up in the 1921 Tulsa riot!)

Child survivor DOROTHY WILSON STRICK-LAND, Chicago, Illinois, still feels shame when she thinks about the panties she lost during the riot and the trouble she had concealing her nakedness. Read how this child was snatched so quickly from her bed the morning of June 1, 1921, that she had time to grab only a red winter coat (on top of a pile of winter clothes that her mother was to put away June 1, 1921) to go over the panties that she had worn to bed the warm night of May 31, 1921. The red, buttonless coat gaped open frequently. But that was not so bad as long as the child had on her panties. Read of how the child lost those panties during a "bathroom break" behind a tree in the Mohawk Park hiding place. Wouldn't you know that that would be the exact time that the group would be found!

LOUIE BARTON, Los Angeles, California, has a similar distressed-child story regarding clothes. Mrs. Barton says that early in the morning on June 1, 1921, she was to help her mother with some chores, so she put on her most ragged dress and an old bonnet. She still regrets that for the next three days, during the flight from mobsters, and, later, during their stay in a holding center, that all the people she came into contact with saw her in that ugly dress and old bonnet, and that those were her only worldly possessions, since everything the family owned had been burned up during the riot. Read her story.

Some child survivors describe a single lost treasure or a group of lost treasures. VERA INGRAM still longs for her big brown Teddy bear named, appropriately, Ole Teddy. She says she never went anywhere without Ole Teddy, that is until June 1, 1921. Her mother, aware of the perils of remaining in the Greenwood district, which was becoming a war zone, dragged the screaming child from their house before she could get her beloved bear. Read the rest of the story and see how much Mrs. Ingram still misses Ole Teddy.

Child survivor HAZEL HACKETT, Tuscaloosa, Alabama, longs for her most cherished possessions—a brown-skinned doll with curly black hair, and a little white china plate with red flowers that she won at Mt. Zion Baptist Church for being the first child in her Sunday school class to learn to recite the New Testament books of the Bible.

BEULAH LOREE KEENAN SMITH does not long for dolls, toys, or clothes, but for her precious school books that she left behind, and the papers and drawings of hers that were displayed on the Honors Board at Dunbar Elementary School on May 31, 1921. The child, who dreamed of becoming a teacher someday, usually didn't leave her beloved books at school, but since she had no homework and the next day would be the last day of school, she had made an exception. She still regrets that, and she also regrets that she never had the opportunity to become a teacher. After the riot, she had to drop out of school and work to help with family expenses. Read the rest of her story for further details about the riot, including the hog pen experience.

MADELEINE DUNN HAYNES doesn't remember material losses; she remembers the loss of her peace of mind, the loss of her sense of safety. During the riot, Madeleine's sister, whom she referred to as "Hard-headed Margaret," disobeyed their mother and went outside, "peering and poking around to see what she could see" and got caught up in the crush of fleeing blacks and was lost from the family for days. That caused anguish among the Dunn family, especially to sensitive, quiet, obedient Madeleine, who clung to her mother for safety.

RUTH DEAN NASH was so traumatized by the sight of gun-toting guards in the Greenwood district that she jumped from the car that was carrying her family to safety in Muskogee, Oklahoma, and fled into the street. She got lost in the crowd of fleeing blacks and was missing from her family for two days. Read the rest of the story to find out what happened to this child during those two days, and what happened afterward.

One of the most heart-wrenching child survivor stories is that of LEROY LEON HATCHER. Only eight days of his life were riot-free. Born May 23, 1921, he was carried in his terrified mother's arms as she fled, barefoot and in her nightgown, from mobsters who threw "Molotov cocktails" (or some kind of incendiary devices that exploded and burned, leaving in their wake a bright trail of light, according to Mr. Hatcher). Whatever those devices were, one of them set the Hatcher house on fire. Read the rest of the story to find out how the terrified family got out of the house after all doors were welded shut, where they fled to, and what happened to Augustus Hatcher. Read of little Leroy Hatcher's constant pestering of his mother with his daily "Mama, where is my daddy" questions; read of the grown-up Hatcher's search for *any* of his father's relatives; read of how he found them and what role "gray cat eyes" played in the search. If this testimony doesn't make you cry, then you have no working tear ducts!

The Riot: Pregnant Women—Untimely Births, Premature Births, Miscarriages, Deaths of Newborns, Deaths of Mothers

From pre-history to the present, all societies and cultures recognize the significance of procreation, a process that ensures the very continuation of human society. Thus certain rituals, customs, and procedures have been developed for dealing with the birth process. One of the basics is tender concern and care for the pregnant woman, especially during the delivery of her child. Wars, riots, and revolutions are so tragic, for all the civilizing aspects of the birth process are abandoned then and women give birth under the most horrible circumstances and conditions. Nowhere has this been more evident or tragic than during the Tulsa Race Riot of 1921! For heart-wrenching examples, see the following survivor testimonies about: JAMES D. BELL'S mother's riot-stressed forced ten-mile walk and the birth of her child;

MILDRED LUCAS CLARK'S pregnant mother's ordeal; MILDRED JOHNSON HALL'S mother's riot-related death and the dying woman's request of her mother; EDWARD EARVEN JONES'S mother's flight from mobsters with him (a baby) in arms, and a toddler by the hand; PHINES BELL'S mother's ordeal.

The Riot: Temporary Shelters— Making Silk Purses out of Sows' Ears

Read where survivors lived when their homes were destroyed in the Tulsa Race Riot of 1921—places like hog pens (BEULAH LOREE KEENAN SMITH); chicken coops (ELDORIS MAE ECTOR McCONDICHIE); abandoned strip pit mines (ANNIE BIRDIE CARTER BEAIRD); garages (WILLIAM A. SCOTT).

Compelling Testimonies: Political, Sociological, Psychological, and Economic History of the United States

Some of the best testimonies in this category are those of: BEATRICE CAMPBELL-WEBSTER, Los Angeles, California (a masterpiece!); VENEICE DUNN SIMS (read about her missed Booker T. Washington high school prom, which was scheduled for June 1, 1921. See how she felt at being named "Honorary Queen" of the Booker T. Washington High School prom in 2000; Survivor JAMES L. STEWARD'S mother left a hand-written description, on lined tablet paper, that is priceless. What thought, care, and concern went into her document. It means as much to me as the documents I personally handled during my riot research at the National Archives, Library of Congress, the Smithsonian Institution, and Howard University in Washington, D.C., or the Schomberg Center in New York City;

MARY TACOMA MAUPIN, Louisville, Kentucky, gave a testimony that is deeply analytical, with vivid descriptions of her life as the adopted daughter of her biological uncle, Dr. Robert T. Bridgewater, one of Tulsa's prominent black leaders. She covers all aspects of life in Tulsa's two cultures—black and white. But what I liked equally as well was her story-telling style. Not only is her testimony educational, it reflects her wit, humor, tenacity, intellect. and, most of all, her deep, lifelong agony over the riot. Her descriptions of her feelings of despair at her first sight of her former elegant home, with its beautiful furnishings, classy wardrobe of each family member, fine musical instruments, and other "fineries" of a typical upper-class Tulsa family viciously destroyed by mobsters should move even the most stone-hearted individuals. Just out of pure envy and hatred, mobsters had ripped down and burned laced curtains from Belgium, and they took the time to break up and pile in the center of the dining room elegant, hand-painted china from Europe. Mrs. Maupin's descriptions equaled those of writers of antique and collector magazines;

DR. HOBART JARRETT'S testimony is also deeply analytical, as well as fun to read. He covers Tulsa's history from his boyhood days of clerking in his dad's grocery store to the family's rebuilding of their lives after the riot. You will clap your hands when you read of their success—especially when you learn that their only assets after the destruction of Greenwood was $13 (left in Hobart's Little Boy Blue bank, which was sitting on the fireplace mantle);

Survivor JAMES DURANT, Detroit, Michigan, gave testimony that was very helpful to the Riot Commission. We were looking especially for survivor testimony that would corroborate conspiracy theories and/or assaults on Greenwood from the air. He knew key people and gave vital information regarding real estate and police activities during and after the riot.

The Lilly sisters, MURIEL LILLY CABELL, HATTIE LILLY DUNN, and JIMMIE LILLY FRANKLIN lived through that terrible 1921 riot together; now they live together in a shared house in Los Angeles, California. (Other siblings who live together now, or who lived together once, are the Hooker sisters, and formerly one brother, White Plains, New York, and the McNeal sisters, formerly three of them, oldest sister THERESSA McNEAL GILLIAM and twins ARNETTA McNEAL ANDERSON, who passed away in 1999, and JEANNETTE, formerly JOHNETTA McNEAL BRADSHAW, Chicago, Illinois.) The neatly printed-in-ink testimonies of the three Lilly sisters make delightful reading. They are carefully written, detailed accounts of Tulsa's history before, during, and after the riot, and their descriptions of property losses were among the most detailed sent to the commission. JIMMIE LILLY FRANKLIN'S vivid description of her lifelong battle with post-riot nightmares will make even the pacifist want to sue local, state, and national entities for punitive damages for her sufferings.

DR. OLIVIA J. HOOKER's specificity and meticulous details, and old photographs, calendars, and other memorabilia that she sent, were invaluable to the Riot Commission.

EUNICE CLOMAN JACKSON added information about the care (or lack of care) of black dead during and after the riot that no one else in the world could have provided. Her husband, whom she married after the riot, was Samuel M. Jackson, noted funeral home owner in Tulsa. The commission had access to City of Tulsa death statistics, funeral home statistics, etc., which showed that the city paid Samuel Jackson to embalm black bodies. Only EUNICE CLOMAN JACKSON knew the minute details! Read about them for yourself.

Survivor WESS YOUNG shared much information with the Riot Commission about Tulsa in the 1920s, especially about the economy and culture of oil-rich Tulsa at that time. Wess Young knows a lot about oil barons. His father worked for one who lived in the Brady Heights district in North Tulsa in an elaborate mansion. Today, Wess Young lives in the Brady Heights district in North Tulsa (now on the National Historic Register) in a lovely manor house built by an oil baron. He can often be seen working in his beloved flower beds in the yard of his Denver Boulevard historic home. How about that for poetic justice?

COLORFUL, "UNIQUE" RIOT EXPERIENCES, RIOT TESTIMONIES, ETC.:

Feisty Females:

Two of my favorites were NELL HAMILTON HAMPTON and MARIE WHITEHORN

1. NELL HAMILTON HAMPTON makes no bones about it. She has always liked to party. Even when she and her good buddy, the late riot survivor ELWOOD LETT, a Hollywood professional dancer in his younger days, were in their eighties, they went out dancing (and she admits they had a drink or two). Read the testimony of this delightful woman and see how she is coping now that her "partying days" are over.

2. MARIE WHITEHORN'S testimony touched me deeply because she had had such a rough childhood (worse than that of even her fellow riot survivors). I interviewed this still-vibrant woman by telephone when I visited the San Francisco Bay area. I had already read a charming story about Mrs. WHITEHORN in her hometown newspaper, The Sacramento (California) Bee.

Read her testimony for yourself and see the tragic things she had to endure as a child and, later, as a young teenager in Tulsa, Oklahoma. When she was two years old, little Marie's mother died and the toddler was sent to the orphanage for black children in Taft, Oklahoma.

An aunt rescued her and raised her like a sister to her own children. Read how as a feisty teenager working for a "ritzy" woman who didn't like her, she was framed and sent to jail! Continue on into her account to find out who the people were who mentored the plucky teenager and got her onto the "right track" in life.

Colorful Males:

All of the survivors that I interviewed were wonderful, but some of them stand out because of their wit, humor, seriousness, or special experiences that set them apart from other survivors. Here are a few of the exceptional ones; there are many others, but these are the accounts that I was compelled to share with you readers:

JAMES "BOTTLEHEAD" HILL, Los Angeles, California. My twenty two years experience as a classroom teacher came in handy when I interviewed numerous riot survivors. Teachers develop sensory skills that rival, if not surpass, those of FBI, CIA, and other such agents charged with keeping order and peace in nations. We seem to have eyes in the back of our heads and acute hearing (the better to see and hear what's going on in the back of the classroom) and an ability to learn names, faces, and voices of hundreds of students yearly (and thousands of students in a life-time career). After one or two conversations with a person, I have the uncanny knack of recognizing the voice of that person. That doesn't mean that teachers are always one step ahead of students. Teachers also have the reputation of being so tender, caring, and trusting that they can easily be duped. We have often been tricked by our students. One of the most embarrassing examples is of teachers responding to messages left by the public. I have often returned telephone calls to Mr. Lyon or Mr. Tiger (there are numerous Creek Indian Tiger families in Oklahoma), only to find that the "public" person who left the message was a mischievous student, and that the telephone number was for the Tulsa Zoo!

Survivors get the greatest kick when I respond to their calls by instantly greeting them by name. JAMES "BOTTLEHEAD" HILL told me that since he was a young boy, he has been known as "BOTTLEHEAD" by his childhood friends and classmates, and later by his closest friends. He said I could call him that, too, since he considered me a dear friend. So it never stops amazing BOTTLEHEAD that I recognize his voice instantly and greet him with a "Hi, BOTTLEHEAD, how are you" each time he calls. Read his fascinating story and find out how he earned his nickname, and how he and

some of his little playmates stole rides on the downtown jitney (public transportation vehicle) and got caught in the middle of a riot June 1, 1921.

BINKLEY WRIGHT, Los Angeles, California. Read the spell-binding testimony of BINKLEY WRIGHT (as I did before the riot Commission's public meetings). His description of the actions of his childhood Warrior Brigade as they helped Tulsa's armed black men try to save their beloved Greenwood district will keep you riveted to your seat. His future wife, CLOTIE LEWIS, was performing in an elementary school play in the near downtown area when the riot broke out. That's why BINKLEY WRIGHT and his buddies stole the jitney rides downtown. See her account also.

ALLEN WHITE, Dayton, Ohio, first cousin of survivor ELDORIS MAE ECTOR McCONDICHIE has become a dear friend of mine. He telephones frequently and he gave me the scare of my life on September 11, 2001. On that day, which goes down in infamy, he left home for a scheduled flight via TWA, from Dayton (which is near the area where terrorists brought down a plane in a Pennsylvania field), with a stop in St. Louis, and a final destination of Tulsa where I was to pick him up at the airport. He was in the air bound for St. Louis when terrorists struck the twin towers in New York City, the Pentagon in Washington, D.C., and the Pennsylvania field. For two days, no one knew where Mr. White was. Read his oral history account and find out where he was, who was frantic while he was missing, why he was missing, and how he was reunited with his loving wife.

LENA ELOISE TAYLOR BUTLER, Seattle, Washington, who passed on before the riot Commission report was completed, gave me a wonderful interview early in our riot research period. Read her poignant testimony to find out how her famous father, HORACE "PEGLEG" TAYLOR got his nickname—the result of a most brutal experience! Her father is the "Greenwood Warrior" most often referred to by survivors and historians because of his brave, but futile, attempt to stop the destruction of his beloved Greenwood district.

ALMADGE J. NEWKIRK, Barstow, California— see Military.

Entertainment:

HOSEA VADEN. Read survivor DeLOIS VADEN RAMSEY'S account to see what notable people visited her father's famous pool hall in Tulsa.

HAROLD "CORNBREAD" SINGER—Read

SINGER'S testimony, and letter, to get first-hand information from a long-time Jazz expatriate in Paris, France.

Survivor References to "Good White Samaritans:"

Besides being heart-warming, heart-wrenching stories, these "Good White Samaritans" stories are significant because they show how people of different races and cultures can come to the aid of their fellow man who may be so different from them. It also shows how people of the same race and same culture can behave so differently. For instance, while many whites were warm and loving toward the besieged black Tulsa population during the riot, even risking their lives to help them, other whites were extremely brutal, and often deadly, in their relations to the blacks. Research and documentation seem to corroborate some survivors' accounts that there was a white conspiracy in the fomenting of the Tulsa riot. The testimonies of some of the black riot victims certainly do seem to show that some whites had prior knowledge of the riot and made specific arrangements to protect their black employees. The acts of good white Samaritans range from making prior arrangements for their black employees (including having a supply of necessities—food, clothing, personal care items, blankets, beds, cots, etc.—already on hand and ready for their employees in the homes or offices of the caring employees BEFORE the riot broke out) to hiding blacks under hay in wagons, holding off white mobsters hell-bent on taking trusted employees away from their white employers' homes, to even risking bullets and death, themselves, by going into the Greenwood district at the height of battle to bring their respected black employees to safety. See the testimonies of:

JAMES D. BELL, Tulsa, Oklahoma and Massachusetts

JUANITA DELORES McGOWAN ARNOLD, Tulsa, Oklahoma

SIMEON L. NEAL, Chicago, Illinois

VENEICE DUNN SIMS, Tulsa, Oklahoma

GENEVIEVE TILLMAN JACKSON, Tulsa, Oklahoma

KINNEY I. BOOKER, Tulsa, Oklahoma

MILDRED MITCHELL CHRISTOPHER, Jacksonville, Florida

EFFIE LEE SPEARS TODD, Oklahoma City, Oklahoma

LUCILLE B. BUCHANAN FIGURES, Tulsa, Oklahoma

HAZEL HACKETT, Tuscaloosa, Alabama

ISHMAEL MORAN, Santa Barbara, California

QUEEN ESTHER LOVE WALKER, Muskogee, Oklahoma

Unluckiest Riot Survivors:

TISHIE WRIGHT who chose May 31, 1921 to visit her cousin PEARL OLIVER in Tulsa and got caught smack-dab-in-the-middle of the worst race riot in U.S. History!

All SURVIVORS with birthdays on May 31 and June 1.

Miscellaneous Tidbits:

MABEL B. LITTLE'S FUNERAL—Dr. Calvin McCutchen loved his long-time church member MABEL B. LITTLE (the feeling was mutual) and knew well the legend of her "being difficult to get along with." They got along fine, with both the minister and the parishioner often giving each other a little leeway. Read MRS. LITTLE'S testimony and find out how she planned her own funeral four times. You'll hear some of the excerpts from Dr. McCutchen's warm, loving, and elegant eulogy of the great lady. You'll also read about how she kept demanding back those funeral plans three times within the last twenty years. The fourth set of funeral plans were followed to the tee by Dr. McCutchen. Even in death, the great lady still wielded power. No one dared to cross her. Not even then!

JOHN MELVIN ALEXANDER'S FATHER'S OBEDIENCE TO GOD—When the race riot on Greenwood accelerated and black people began to lock up their homes and flee, JOHN MELVIN ALEXANDER'S father, WALTER ALEXANDER, was going to lock his doors and flee too, but he didn't. He said he just couldn't though that was his first inclination. He said a strong thought came to him, almost audibly, "Leave the door unlocked!" Recognizing in his heart that this thought was from God, he left his door unlocked and his house was the only one on the block in his neighborhood which was not burned down. Read the rest of the story and see how that house became a "safe house" for riot refugees when they were allowed to leave detention centers.

MARY ELLEN STREET WALTON'S MOTHER'S EMPLOYER—MARY ELLEN STREET WALTON'S parents, Prince and Alva Street, lived at 413 E. Latimer Street at the time of the riot. Long after the riot, in the late 1940s or during the 1950s, Mrs. Street was the laundress for a white family in Tulsa. She talked to her children about the three rambunctious sons in the family—twins about six or seven and a younger boy. She was very fond of those boys and the feeling was mutual. One of the rambunctious boys was Frank Keating, former governor of Oklahoma! Read the rest of the story for further details, including a warm letter to me from Governor Keating in which he spoke of the family's love and respect for Mrs. Alva Street.

Survivor Media Personalities:
the Darlings of the Media:

GEORGE D. MONROE, OTIS G. CLARK, KINNEY I. BOOKER, GENEVIEVE TILLMAN JACKSON, ELDORIS MAE ECTOR McCONDICHIE, VENEICE DUNN SIMS, BEULAH LOREE KEENAN SMITH

Most Supportive Survivors:

Attendance at Commission meetings, other meetings, commemoration programs, interviews with media, telephone calls, thank you notes and letters, and various acts of random kindness
ANNIE BIRDIE CARTER BEAIRD—oxygen tank
GENEVIEVE TILLMAN JACKSON—walker or wheelchair
MILDRED LUCAS CLARK, Parkin, Arkansas (June 3, 2001 Commemoration Ceremony—See photo)
KINNEY I. BOOKER—walker, diabetic snacks, liquids
THEODORE PORTERFIELD—emaciated little body, piercing brown eyes at at most every riot meeting until his death!
THERESSA McNEAL GILLIAM, Chicago, Illinois
LEON GRAYS, SR., Wasco, California
HAROLD "CORNBREAD" SINGER, Paris, France
MARY TACOMA MAUPIN, Louisville, Kentucky

Most Distressful Incident(s) to Eddie Faye Gates During the Three Year Commission Study

ALLEN WHITE, Dayton, Ohio—MISSING SEPTEMBER 11, 2001 on flight from Dayton to Tulsa! See p. 105 for the complete testimony of MR. WHITE containing all the details of that harrowing experience.
THELMA FORD MITCHELL'S TELEPHONE CALL TO COMMISSIONER EDDIE FAYE GATES, Sunday September 30, 2001. The deadline for submitting the formal, completed list of riot survivors, spouses/heirs, survivors who died between 1997 and October 1, 2001, and descendants of riot survivors to the Oklahoma Historical Society in Oklahoma City was October 1, 2001. To be on the safe side, I Fed-Exed the lists to Oklahoma City on Friday evening, September 28, 2001 to make sure they reached there BEFORE October 1st. The Oklahoma Historical Society had someone in the building at all times on Saturday September 30th to receive the materials. And then came Mrs. MITCHELL'S call which threw me into a tizzy. How could I follow the letter of the law and still have Mrs. MITCHELL'S name on the official list? Thank goodness things worked out. Dr. Bob Blackburn, Director of the Oklahoma Historical Society, had me fax Mrs. MITCHELL'S name and information to him and she was officially added to the list. I was so distraught over the thought of the sweet little woman being left off the list, that I blurted out to her, "Where have you been during all this media blitz about the Tulsa Race Riot of 1921? On Mars?" The sweet little lady had been right here in Tulsa, Oklahoma and had not heard a thing about the riot!

INCORRECT DEATH NOTICE of ELDORIS MAE ECTOR McCONDICHIE in a local newspaper, November 22, 2001. Mrs. McCONDICHIE, with her shy, sweet, enduring nature, had been one of the most endearing of the riot survivors. She had a reputation in the community for making gift packets of elegantly wrapped, delicious assortments of home-made cookies for her family and best friends. Yes, I made Mrs. McCONDICHIE'S "best friends" list. That sweet little woman makes the best cookies in the world! I was a little suspicious of the "In Memory" tribute to Mrs. McCONDICHIE in the paper that week, for I had heard the same tribute read at the dear little lady's 90th birthday party. I went by the newspaper but it was just before the Thanksgiving holiday and all key personnel had left. The skeletal crew that was closing up the building knew nothing about the article. So I picked up the phone and rang Mrs. McCONDICHIE'S telephone number. My heart burst with gratitude as, once again, I heard that gentle, lilting voice!

The 169 living black survivors that I interviewed between 1997 and 2001 were the most interesting population pool that I ever had the privilege of working with. They ranged in age from 80 to 108. Unfortunately, most the centenarians have passed on, including 104-

year-old Tulsan Lillie Skelton Rice and 104-year-old Mabel B. Little.

Some of the survivors were fragile, mentally and physically. Others were agile, even robust, like spry 98-year-old evangelist Otis G. Clark, who drives himself to California and to Washington state each summer. I recently helped him in his attempt to get a U.S. passport so he could go to England for an evangelist meeting. It is not easy getting a passport for a 98-year-old who never had a birth certificate! The normal procedure, which I used when getting my passport to go to England, didn't work. There were no neighbors, teachers, or others alive who could testify to their personal knowledge regarding the birth. I got another bright idea to help Mr. Clark get his passport. I thought that if he had met Oklahoma legislative requirements to be qualified as a bona fide riot survivor he could surely use that information to meet the passport requirement standards. So I called local officials on Mr. Clark's behalf. But I was wrong. That information did *not* satisfy the passport-issuing officials. The matter was finally settled when Mr. Clark found old Booker T. Washington High School (BTW) records that confirmed his attendance at BTW during certain years.

The survivors live all over the United States, and one lives in Paris, France. Oklahoma has the largest group of survivors, followed by California and Illinois. The political, economic, and social status of survivors varies. Some lead well-to-do, vibrant, active lives in

their communities despite advancing age. Others are not well off and lead subsistence lives. One was evicted from her Tulsa home during the Christmas holidays, 2001.

Thanks to widespread media coverage of them for the past three and a half years, the survivors have earned a place in the hearts of people all over the world. They are warm, wonderful people who have shared their history with us.

Below, in their own words, are the fascinating, compelling, passionate, and powerful accounts, in alphabetical order, of the Tulsa Race Riot of 1921 by all of the known black survivors living today who were interviewed by me, 1997–2001.

JOHN MELVIN ALEXANDER, Tulsa, Oklahoma, b. December 22, 1919

My parents, Walter S. Alexander and Ida Jones Alexander, moved to Tulsa from Guthrie, Oklahoma. They lived at 1621 North Norfolk, and I was born there. During the Tulsa Race Riot of 1921, all houses around our house burned to the ground, but our house was not touched. Instead of locking the doors to his house before he and his family fled the oncoming white mob, Dad left his house unlocked. He said the Lord told him to leave the house unlocked. Dad had no guns in the house, so when the mobsters and the militia went into the house, they just left it like it was. Dad and his family fled the mobs by going up to Pine Street. But we

5th from left—John Melvin Alexander.

were interrupted by the National Guards, who picked up the men and took them to the ball park on Eleventh Street, where Home Depot is located today. The women and children were taken to Brady Theater or to churches. After a day or two, the men were released to their white employers and the men found their wives and children in whatever shelter they were, and those that were lucky and had homes to return to, like my father, returned home. Dad was so kindhearted that he was always referred to as "the kind-hearted Brother Alexander." Well, my kind-hearted father let people who had lost their homes come to our house, and he let them bring the things they had taken with them as they fled. He let as many as could fit in come to our house.

Dad didn't talk much about the riot for many years, but in later years he did begin to talk about it. He spoke of how God had guided him to leave his house open that day and how his obedience to God had saved his house. He also talked a lot about a certain photograph of the riot. What photo?

I often think about that riot, and when I'm asked whether I favor reparations, I say yes, I certainly do! If Japanese Americans got reparations for their suffering during World War II, we black Tulsa Race Riot survivors deserve it for our suffering in 1921. We went on and fought for this country, the USA, in World War II. I was a steward on war ships. First, I was stationed for twenty-two months in Norman, Oklahoma. I fought, in Hawaii, Guam, Philippine Islands, Iwo Jima, and Okinawa in the eastern hemisphere. Then I was assigned to the USS *Anzio,* CVE# 57 and went to Europe. I went to Korea near the ending of the war in that country in the east. Another riot survivor from Tulsa, Samuel McGowan, was at a naval air station with me. Yes, I did my duty for this country. I suffered during that Tulsa riot and I suffered during those war years. I feel that I deserve reparations!

JUANITA DELORES BURNETT ARNOLD,
Tulsa, Oklahoma, b. July 27, 1909

At the time of the riot, my parents, Eugene Lawrence Burnett and Mary Jane McGowan Burnett, lived at 1000 North Lansing, just south of the railroad tracks. They owned the house. My grandfather and grandmother lived farther north on Madison where they owned their house and an adjoining grocery store. My grandfather had moved to Tulsa first. He and my grandmother had lived in a little all-black town called Redbird, where he had been a schoolteacher and she

Juanita McGowan Burnett Arnold

had been a schoolteacher and postmistress, the first black postmistress in the U.S. In Tulsa, my grandfather bought two lots. He built a large house on one lot, and a grocery store on the other lot.

Dad got tired of teaching, so he got a job in Tulsa working at the Oil Supply Company in the Drew Building on Boston Avenue between Third and Fourth Streets. His boss was Frick Reed (or Reid). My mother sewed for wealthy white Tulsa "oil women" at an exclusive shop on Fifth Street between Main and Boston. The shop was next door to Vandevers Department Store. My mother was an expert seamstress. Those wealthy white women loved wearing fashions that she created.

Trouble had been brewing in Tulsa before the riot broke out the night of May 31, 1921. We children noticed grownups, frowns on their faces, talking in whispers about bad race relations in the city and about rumors of a showdown coming. In fact, the day before the riot there was an incident right in front of our house. A group of angry white men were roaming up and down our street.

They were so full of anger, jealousy, and rage. They were using the "N" word in every sentence they spoke. It was "Nigger this," and "Nigger that!" They were especially jealous of men like my father and grandfather, who had nice homes and businesses. My dad got his gun and went out into the yard and ordered the men off his property. He told them to respect his wife and children. All the men left, except one man who was obviously intoxicated. Dad drew his gun on him and told him to leave. The angry, defiant man finally did reluctantly leave.

The next day, when the riot was on, and after we had fled to safety farther north, a person who was in the area described an armed, angry white mobster who stood in front of our house and snarled, "Where is that uppity Nigger who was so bold yesterday?" If my father had still been in our house, he would surely have been killed by that hate-filled man.

Now let me tell you how we escaped the mobsters and how my grandfather's store was saved from destruction during the riot. We stayed at our house as long as we could, but when it became obvious that white mobs were in control of the Greenwood District and surrounding black areas, my father told the family that we had to leave. So we joined the fleeing black refugees. But my dad stopped to help tend to a black man who had been shot. He sent us on ahead. He told us to stay with the crowd and go on to safety and that he would join us later. We didn't want to leave my dad, but we did what he told us to do. We kept up with the running crowd until my mother befriended an elderly woman who couldn't keep up. That was just like my mother. She was an angel who couldn't stand to see anyone suffer. I think her kindheartedness had something to do with her being the oldest of the ten McGowan children. She knew nothing but loving and caring for the young, as well as for the elderly. Well, when that old lady fell behind and couldn't keep pace with those frightened-out-of-their-minds fleeing blacks, Mother decided she couldn't leave that old lady alone. She told my brother and me to go on ahead with the people, that she and the old lady would join us later. But we wouldn't go. We were crying and pitching such a fit. We just wouldn't go! But you know God blesses his angels. He sent my dad's boss, who worked at the oil supply company, to find us. And he did find us in the midst of that fleeing mass of black refugees. When he saw my mother, he yelled for her and us children to get into the car and he would take us to safety. But Mother told him we couldn't get in, for we couldn't leave this poor, helpless old lady to the mobs. The exasperated Mr. Reed (or Reid) threw up

his hands and said, "All right, she can get in, too." And she did. Some kind of way we all squeezed into that car!

My grandfather's store was saved because of the kindness of some white salesmen (called "drummers" in those days) who came to his store every three weeks. They came to deliver orders, to take orders, to share the latest trade news, local and/or out-of-town news, or just to plain sit and chat (gossip) for a while. It so happened that on the heaviest day of rioting, June 1, 1921, the three drummers came to Grandpa's store. They saw the mobs when they first arrrived, and saw the damage they had done on Greenwood and surrounding areas, and the damage that they were continuing to do. So those drummers stayed all day guarding Grandpa's store. They just wouldn't leave. When mobsters came up to the store to burn it, the drummers would shout a loud "NO!" They told the mobsters, "The man who owns this store is a good man. He worked hard for his property. He has done you and no one else any harm. You WILL NOT destroy the efforts of this man's hard work." And they DID NOT! God bless those men. They were angels sent by God to protect us. I believe there is a heaven, and in heaven I know at least five angels there now because they earned their places because of their angelic acts during that awful Tulsa riot: my beloved, kind-hearted mother, Dad's boss Mr. Frick Reed (or Reid), and those three drummers!

AGNES BAGLEY, Kansas City, Missouri, b.

Agnes Bagley was unable to be interviewed. Her devoted niece, Erlene Crosslin of Kansas City, Missouri, contacted the Riot Commission and provided information about the Bagley family. She said that her grandmother, Mattie Bagley, lived on Latimer Street at the time of the riot with her children Fannie Mae (mother of Mrs. Crosslin) and Agnes. Mrs. Mattie Bagley and Fannie Mae Bagley are deceased. Mrs. Crosslin had no riot information to share other than the address of the Bagley family during the riot. Except for her aunt, Mrs. Agnes Bagley, she knows no one else to talk to about the Bagley family experiences during the riot. The Commission is grateful to Mrs. Crosslin for her contact, for she helped the Commission to create a more accurate list of riot survivors.

J. B. BATES, Tulsa, Oklahoma, b. June 13, 1916

At the time of the Tulsa riot my grandparents, Green and Mary Bates, my father A. B. Bates, my mother, Minnie Kirkendoll Bates, and my uncles, Percy and Howard Bates, all lived on Bullette Street (the name of the street was later changed). I was only five years old, but there was so much turmoil that day that some of the events are still vivid in my mind. Of course, I was too young to know the significance of a riot, but I do remember that my mother was so frightened that I knew something was terribly wrong. Also, we had a double tragedy that day. My grandfather was deathly ill. In fact, some men came to the house and took Dad and my uncles away to be at my grandfather's side. When my grandfather died, a white undertaker came and took the body away. Then the militia took Dad and my uncles to detention. While they were busy taking the young men in the family away, my mother slipped away with my sister Roxanna and me and ran to hide in a chicken house. With us was an old man using a walking stick. While we were running, an airplane flew over real low and someone in the plane shot and killed that old man! But Mother kept running with us children and got us to safety in that chicken house. When things quieted down, we slipped out of the chicken house and went somewhere else. I don't know where.

Four years after the riot, Mother and Dad separated. My sister went to live with Mother in the country, and I lived with Dad out on Bird Creek. My mother talked often about the riot, but my dad NEVER talked about it!

ESSIE LEE JOHNSON BECK, Tulsa, Oklahoma, b. April 29, 1915

My Johnson relatives had acquired 700 acres of land in Arkansas after the end of the Civil War, but there was such hatred and envy of black landowners by southern whites that my family lost all that land. Due to a deliberate racial injustice to take the land, my rela-

Essie Beck

tives secretly fled Arkansas. They did this to spare the life of one of Mother's brothers. That is how my mother arrived in Tulsa just before the Tulsa Race Riot of 1921.

THELMA DUNN BEDELL, Springfield, Missouri, b. May 18, 1918

See biography of Mrs. Bedell's sister, VENEICE DUNN SIMS, for information on the Dunn family at the time of the Tulsa riot.

Thelma Dunn Bedell

JAMES D. BELL, Tulsa, Oklahoma, b. June 12, 1921

At the time of the Tulsa Race Riot of 1921, my father, J. D. (Dick) Bell, and my mother, Ida Mae Bell, lived at 418 North Cincinnati Avenue in Tulsa. My mother was eight months pregnant with me. Dad and Mother had moved to Tulsa from St. Louis, Missouri, to get in on the oil boom in 1918. Dad was a chauffeur for rich Tulsa oilmen and businessmen, including Tate Brady, Judge Shea, and the owner of Crosby Farms. But of all the people Dad chauffeured, his favorite was a wealthy white oilman named Dale Bowmaster. The Bowmasters lived in a big mansion at 1434 South Cincinnati. They had a nanny, a governess, a laundress, a Japanese cook, a black maid, and as I said before, they

James D. Bell

had Dad as chauffeur. Mother baby-sat the Bowmaster sons, Dale and Najor. Mother said when I was born, ten days after the Tulsa riot began, the boys called me "our little brother."

When the riot started, Mother and Dad fled along the Santa Fe Railroad tracks with other fleeing black refugees all the way to Mohawk Indian Nation Park. When they returned ten days later, they found that Little Africa had been totally burned down. Mother went into premature labor and I was born. We all had to live in a tent, since our house had been burned. Dad later rebuilt.

After the riot, Dad returned to his chauffeuring. But he had always had a fascination for police work. Appointments of blacks to jobs as policemen in those days were always "political plum" appointments. In 1925, two Tulsa commissioners, Thomas I. Monroe and A. P. Bowles, Democrats, recommended that Dad be appointed to the police force. Dad was elated and loved being a policeman. The next election resulted in a Republican victory and, of course, Dad lost his job. Then at the next election a Democrat won, and Dad was back on the force.

Though Dad loved the police force, he still loved cars and he still chauffeured sometimes for Mr. Bowmaster. I remember that as a teenager, I was fascinated with Mr. Bowmaster's fine automobiles. I have a photograph of me, when I was about thirteen, with my father in Mr. Bowmaster's fold-back Dodge convertible. I felt like a millionaire that day in that car! In between his time on the Tulsa police force in the 1920s and 1930s, Dad moved to Albuqueque, New Mexico, and to Vancouver, Washington, where he also served on the police force in those cities.

But Dad returned to Tulsa in the 1940s and once again worked for Mr. Bowmaster.

In 1944 or 1945, Dad did his last job for Mr. Bowmaster. A despondent Bowmaster called Dad and said he was going to commit suicide. He said he just couldn't take it any longer. He had gone broke and had lost the big mansion on Fourteenth and Cincinnati. He had moved his family to a small house on South Boston Avenue near his daughter. He told Dad to come and clean up the mess. By the time Dad got to the Bowmaster house, sure enough Mr. Bowmaster had shot himself in the head. Dad cleaned up the mess.

The widow, Mrs. Bowmaster, always stayed in touch with our family. The grownup Bowmaster sons always loved my parents. They used to come and visit them frequently. They'd take Mom to lunch, and they even gave her a mink coat. They treated us like family.

PHINES BELL, Tulsa, Oklahoma, b. August 16, 1918

I was born in Okemah, Okfuscee County, Oklahoma, but my parents, Lonnie and Rosella Bell, moved to Tulsa, Oklahoma. At the time of the riot, they lived at 500 Jasper Street in a rented house. They lost all their belongings in the riot. After the riot, my mother gave birth to a premature baby which died.

FRANCES BLACKWELL, Tulsa, Oklahoma, b. February 12, 1913

I was eight years old during the Tulsa riot, and I lived at 630 E. Booker (now Latimer Place). My mother and her husband lived with Mrs. Parker. All members of the family fled the mobs that were rampaging the Greenwood District. We walked ten or twelve miles out past Sperry, where we hid until it was safe to return to Little Africa. That was a mighty lot of walking for a little girl!

JUANITA SCOTT BLAKELY, Chicago, Illinois, b. August 5, 1914

At the time of the Tulsa riot, my parents, Arthur and Marie Gilkey Williams, were separated. My father was in Chicago, and my mother lived in Tulsa in a four-bedroom home on North Frankfort Place which she owned. Mother had been born in Greenwood, Mississippi, and Dad in Pittsburg, Texas. They met and married in Tulsa. But, as I said before, by 1921 they had separated and Dad had moved to Chicago.

I remember that during the riot, when the mobs were taking over the Greenwood District, militia officials herded us black people like cattle. Before they put us on trucks and took us to detention centers, we looked back at our houses and saw mobsters setting them on fire. It was so sad. We could see trucks pulling up to the houses and people taking things out of our houses before they set them on fire. You see, those awful mobsters/looters knew exactly which homes had the best items to loot. For many of those mobsters dealt with the black community in a variety of ways. Some were vendors who delivered goods into the community; others were insurance agents who collected policy money from black folk weekly. My mother told me that some people paid a small amount weekly (as little as 25 cents a week) to insure their belongings. But some of the wealthiest black people in the United States lived in the Greenwood District, and those agents knew where the good stuff was! The insurance agent had a little book in which he recorded his transactions. My mother always told me that greed and conspiracy caused the Tulsa Race Riot of 1921. She said white people coveted the Greenwood area and they were determined to get it one way or another. Now they have it. I recently visited Tulsa, and I did not recognize my old Greenwood hometown area. The Oklahoma State University–Tulsa campus sits right on the spot where many homes of my family and neighbors' families were located. George Monroe was one of my childhood friends who lived in the OSU-Tulsa area. I couldn't recognize where his house used to be. I couldn't even recognize where my house used to be. It is so sad. They took away our Greenwood!

JUANITA SMITH BOOKER, Tulsa, Oklahoma, b. January 15, 1914

Everything about that riot was terrible. I remember that we were all riding on a flatbed truck, trying to escape the approaching mobs. The truck was going so fast. The driver made a sharp turn on a corner and hit the curb. A lady fell off the truck and was killed!

With all this talk about the Tulsa riot, I have been thinking about my childhood days before the riot. I remember a little playmate named Juanita Scott. [See JUANITA SCOTT BLAKELY, who now lives in Chicago.] At the time of the riot, we lived near the Samuel Jackson funeral home, which was located on Archer Street. The Scott family was nearby. Oh, those innocent days before the riot! Nothing was ever the same again.

KINNEY I. BOOKER, Tulsa, Oklahoma, b. March 21, 1913

At the time of the Tulsa Race Riot of 1921, my parents, and the five of us children, lived at 320 North Hartford. We had a lovely home, owned by my parents, filled with beautiful furniture including a piano. That beautiful home with the elegant furnishings, and all our clothes and personal belongings, was burned up during the riot.

My dad, Hood Booker, was born in Greenfield, Texas, but came to Oklahoma to get in on the oil boom business. Actually, very few blacks became oil barons. Most did the next-best thing. They worked for white oil barons. That is what my dad did. He got a job working as chauffeur for a prominent white Tulsa oilman named Wilcox who had an office building downtown on Sixth Street. Mr. Wilcox had a yacht and spent summers with his family in Michigan. He would take Dad with him to Michigan, for Dad had one of the sharpest minds, when it came to mechanical or engineering-oriented things, of any man I know. Mr. Wilcox felt that way about Dad, too. Once, while Mr. Wilcox was sailing his yacht on Lake Michigan, the yacht developed mechanical problems. When his fancy engi-

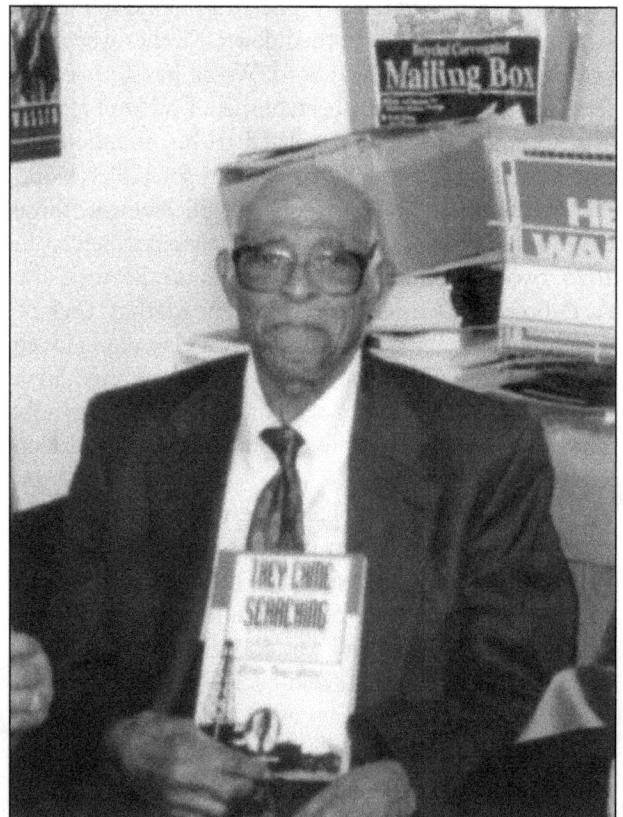

Kinney I. Booker

neering expert couldn't fix it, Mr. Wilcox turned to Dad and said "Hood, do something with it." Dad fixed the ailing yacht! I have had to fight bitter feelings about the way blacks were treated then. They did not have opportunities to develop their talents to their fullest extent. My dad was a mechanical genius. He could have been another Thomas Edison if he had had a chance. America did not nurture its black citizens then. But that's another story. Now back to the day of the riot.

Early on the morning of June 1, 1921, my parents were awakened by the sounds of shooting, the smell of fire, and the noise of fleeing blacks running past the house. My dad had awakened us children and sent us to the attic with our mother. We could hear what was going on below in the house. We heard Dad pleading with mobsters who had broken into our house.

We could hear him begging, 'Please don't set my house on fire. Please don't burn my house." But, of course, that is exactly what they did. We could smell the smoke. Dad pretended to leave the house, and when the mobsters left after they had sprayed our house with gasoline or kerosene and set it on fire, Dad returned and rushed to the attic and rescued us. We joined the fleeing black refugees who were trying to get out of Tulsa to the safety of the countryside. What a pitiful bunch we were. In our nightclothes . . . barefoot . . . electric lines falling down around us . . . smouldering relics of once-beautiful homes . . . the sight and smell of death and destruction all around us. There we were, men, women, children running like frightened animals fleeing a forest fire. We saw things that day that no human eye should ever see. My little sister's comment sears my soul to this day. She asked me, "Kinney, is the world on fire?" I replied, "I don't think so, but we're in a lot of trouble!" And, oh Lord, we black people of Tulsa were certainly in a lot of trouble that day. My family and the people who were fleeing with us were captured by the Guards and taken to a detention center, Convention Hall (now the Brady Theater).

After the riot, Dad rebuilt us a nice house, but to us, it was never as fine as that first house, and we sure did miss the elegant furnishings we had in that first house, especially that piano.

DOROTHY BOOKER BOULDING,
St. Louis, Missouri, b December 2, 1915

See the above Kinney I. Booker biography for details of the Booker family. Dorothy, now a senior citizen, will forever be immortalized as the frightened little girl who asked her brother if the world was on fire. She is an icon of the traumatized child of the Tulsa Race Riot of 1921. That question of hers—whether the whole world was on fire—touched hearts of riot researchers, the media, and anyone else who did not have a heart of stone.

AUTHOR'S NOTE:

When the Oklahoma Commission to Study the Tulsa Race Riot of 1921 was created in 1997, Arnetta McNeal Anderson, her twin Jeanette (formerly Johnetta) McNeal Bradshaw, and Theressa Cornella McNeal Gilliam, daughters of prominent Tulsa business woman Annie McNeal, lived together in a house in Chicago, Illinois. Mrs. Arnetta McNeal Anderson has since passed on.

JEANETTE (formerly JOHNETTA) McNEAL BRADSHAW, Chicago, Illinois, b. June 28, 1918

At the time of the Tulsa riot, my sisters, Annetta McNeal Anderson, Theressa Cornella McNeal Gilliam, and I lived with our mother, Annie McNeal, a Tulsa businesswoman, at 911 Fairview Street (later Haskell Street, and now John Hope Franklin Blvd). We had a lovely home, and next door was a hotel. Mother was a dressmaker to rich white women, and wealthy black women, as well. She had a large inventory of fabric and completed fancy dresses which were lost in the riot. Everything we owned was lost in that riot.

Jeanette Bradshaw

MATTIE BRIDGES, Muskogee, Oklahoma, b. September 16, 1905, died Jan. . . . 2002

Mrs. Bridges lives in a Muskogee, Oklahoma care center and was unable to share riot information with the Commission. Her grandnephew and guardian, Ambrose Bolling, lives in Weirton, Virginia.

TERESA EARLEE DYSART BRIDGES, Corpus Christi, Texas, b. December 11, 1917

At the time of the Tulsa riot, my father, Willie Dysart, and my mother, Annie Marie Morton Dysart, and us three children—I was the oldest, born in 1917, Irene, born in 1918, and Orlee, born in 1920—lived at 514 North Hartford in a rented home on railroad property. A baby boy was born in 1922. Dad worked for the Atchison, Topeka, Santa Fe Railroad. We had some nice furnishings, including two pianos and an organ. My mother said she had nice, handmade Indian jewelry and Dad had a Rooflee Model car.

JOHNNIE L. GRAYSON BROWN, Tulsa, Oklahoma, b. July 5, 1914

Before the Tulsa riot, my parents, John L. and Cenia Simmons Grayson, lived in Cushing, Oklahoma, a famous oil town. My father died before I was born, and my mother couldn't keep me. At the time of the riot, I was living at 31 North Kenosha with my aunt, Corine Edwards, in a little shotgun house facing the railroad tracks. She rented the home from the parents of Tulsa's first black policewoman, Mrs. Horne.

I just can't remember much about the riot . . .

LEE ELLA STROZIER BROWN, Lancaster, California, b. January 29, 1919

My grandmother, Laura Bell, and my mother, Johnnie Glover, lived on North Kenosha at the time of the riot. Grandmother lived in a house in the rear; Aunt Rosie Anderson owned the house in the front where my mother and I lived. The houses and all our possessions were burned up in the riot. I am blessed with a gift of memory. But sometimes I wonder if that memory is a gift or a curse when I think about all the things I was told about that riot. Mother described what it was like for black Tulsans to be running for their lives from those white mobs determined to kill them and to destroy Greenwood. She said they fled north in a wagon drawn

Johnnie Grayson Brown

by two horses. After the riot, she said, we lived in a tent for a long while. She described how inconvenient it was living in a tent and having to cook outside. She said that riot was an awful thing, and that the memories of it just stuck in the mind like glue. She said there was no way for survivors to forget that painful event.

CLARENCE BRUNER, Muskogee, Oklahoma, b. July 28, 1904

Mr. Bruner lives in a Muskogee, Oklahoma, nursing home and was not able to give an interview. His cousin, Bertha Jean Owens Gates, remembers that when he was younger, he talked about living in Tulsa and surviving that race riot in 1921. At the time, he worked at Mills Hotel as a bellhop.

ART BUCKNER, San Francisco, California, b. August 28, 1909, d. August 2001

At the time of the riot, my parents, Dr. George Arthur Buckner and Julia Buckner, stayed in an area called Lightning Creek.

On June 1, 1921, when the riot was getting worse, I was too young to know the significance of what I was witnessing. I was just a curious young boy. At first, I was just watching from the porch. I was looking at the shooting going on up on top of the Hill (Standpipe Hill). But I went into the yard to get a better look. A

Art Buckner, age 11.

I wore a size-thirteen shoe. A black man who was running barefoot down the track asked me, "Boy, what size shoes do you wear'" I replied that I didn't know. He told me to take them off and let him try them on. So, silly me, I took my shoes off, and the man put them on and tied them up and the next thing I knew he was running down the railroad track in my shoes! He yelled out, "They fit me just right, boy." That's the last I saw of that man or my shoes. I sure did miss those shoes. By the time I ran over the gravel on that track and got to safety five miles from where I started, my feet were bleeding.

Military troops stopped us and took us to a shelter where we stayed three days. My mother frantically searched three days for me. She was overjoyed when she found me. An aunt who lived in the San Francisco, California, area (Monroeville) came and got us. She was so mad when she saw what those whites did to us. She angrily said, "They ought to burn the whole damn state of Oklahoma down!"

LULA BELLE LACY BULLOCK, Kansas City, Missouri, b. April 22, 1920

[See interview with Artie Lacy Johnson, Kansas City, Missouri, sister of Mrs. Bullock's for details of the Lacy family's riot experiences.]

JOE R. BURNS, Tulsa, Oklahoma, b. February 5, 1915

My parents, N.T. and Doshia Burns, lived at 517 Latimer Court in a rented house at the time of the riot. For some reason, the mobs did not burn our house. Unlike other black Tulsans, we suffered no property losses. But we did suffer from the turmoil of fleeing mobsters who were bent on killing you! I was only six years old, but the events of that day are engraved indeliby in my mind.

My folks had come from Dumas, Arkansas, to Tulsa seeking a better life. Little did they know . . . I remember running with my parents, siblings, and other fleeing blacks. The first night, we made it to safety and slept in the grass, in a little ravine, on Apache Street, near where the Northside Post Office is located today. It was June, and Oklahoma is noted for its hot summers, but it was so cold that night. I remember that my mother tried to keep me warm under her own body. I will never forget how cold and scared I was that night.

My riot experience was my first encounter with a "war" experience. During World War II, I fought in my

bullet nearly hit me—it just whizzed right over my head and hit a horse. When that horse dropped dead, I then knew this was serious business and that I had better take cover. So I ran and hid under the porch. But when I saw the smoke and fire, and the black people running away to safety, I came from under that porch and ran with them.

We ran down the Santa Fe railroad tracks. Some people hadn't had time to put on shoes, and the gravel was tearing up their feet. But I had my shoes on. I'd put them on early that day and was just nosing around outside when the riot broke out. I had big feet for my age.

Joe Burns

L-R. Sisters—Jimmie Lilly Franklin, Hattie Lilly Dunn, and Mignon Lilly Cabell

first real war experience. On April 2, 1944, my unit landed in Australia. Two days later, General Douglas McArthur came. Yes, I've done my duty. I have suffered. I have fought a good battle, both in Tulsa as a fleeing child survivor of the Tulsa riot, and in the eastern hemisphere, where we fought to protect freedom for peoples of the world. It is time for the world to acknowledge the suffering of Tulsa's riot victims and for those in the U.S., the state of Oklahoma, and the city and county of Tulsa, who were culpable for the riot, to acknowledge their wrongdoing and to rectify the damages done. It is long past time for healing and justice!

[NOTE: The Oklahoma law that created the Oklahoma Commission to Study the Tulsa Race Riot of 1921 required that one of the eleven commissioners be a Tulsa Race Riot survivor. Joe Burns was the survivor on the Commission.]

MURIEL MIGNON LILLY CABELL, Los Angeles, California, b. December 29, 1913

I was born in Jacksonville, Florida, but in 1921, the three Lilly girls, Hattie, Jimmie, and I, lived with our parents, Henry Walter and Florence Wells Lilly, in Tulsa in the Greenwood District that was looted and burned to the ground. I'm not sure whether we owned the house or rented. Our house was the third house burned during the riot. We lost everything, and we had some

nice things including a Kimball piano, photographic equipment, tools, furnishings, one Ford sedan car, one Ford coupe car, and miscellaneous things.

We were pitiful after that riot. All our possessions, hopes, and dreams were gone. But we were strong people, us Tulsa black people. We recovered, and we went on with our dreams. Some of my childhood friends were George Monroe, John Hope Franklin, Kinney Booker, Eldoris Ector McCondichie, and Joe Burns. We all went on and made something of our lives. My sisters and I graduated from Booker T. Washington High School and went off to college and became teachers. We're all retired and widowed now. We live together in Los Angeles, California, now. One thing we will always share is the memories of that awful race riot in 1921.

BEATRICE CAMPBELL-WEBSTER, Los Angeles, California, b. March 5, 1914

At the time of the riot, we lived at 906 North Greenwood across from Latimer's bakery. We had a beautiful home and lovely furnishings, including a piano and a Victrola with a little white dog on top of it (RCA Victor), leather couches and chairs, etc. I lost my most prized possessions—a little alphabet set, dolls, and a swingset in the back yard which I just loved. I was always out in that back yard swinging!

When the riot broke out, I was seven years old. We were awakened by a man running down the middle of the street yelling for everyone to get up and get dressed. He said that whites were on their way to kill all the Negroes. Living in our house was my mother, father, an invalid aunt, and a cousin my age that my mother had raised since her mother died when my cousin was three months old. My father was fortunate to have a friend that owned a truck. They loaded my aunt on a mattress and placed her in the truck; then the rest of us got in. We spent the rest of the day running from one place to another, as we heard that the mobsters were on the way and about to catch up with us. Eventually, we ended up in a little town called Alsuma, where later in the day the militia located us. Some blacks fled, some climbed trees and hid in ditches. But most were found. The militia took the men to the ball park, and women and children were taken to Convention Hall (now the Brady Theater).

An aunt who lived in the serving quarters of a white family in south Tulsa came looking for us. She took us home to her serving quarters, and we stayed with her until the family arranged for us to go stay with a relative in Denison, Texas.

My father returned to the home site and found all the surrounding homes had been burned to the ground. My uncle's street had been spared due to the fact that one of the rioters recognized him as the janitor who

Beatrice Cambell-Webster

worked at one of the white theaters which the rioter attended. He directed the men to spare this block.

All this suffering, all the looting, burning, killing happened because a white woman accused a Negro man of rape. That's what started the ball rolling. Some things we forget, or only have a vague memory of, but the deaths, the burnings, and the running for hours from mobsters is just as clear to me today as it was June 1, 1921. Some stories are being labeled as fabricated or impossible. This one is true. I lived through it!

JAMES DALE CARTER, Kansas City, Missouri, b. November 26, 1920

I was a seven-month-old baby during the riot, so naturally I don't remember anything about it personally. But my mother, ROSELLA GRAYSON CARTER, remembers it well and will share her information.

ROSELLA CARTER, Kansas City, Missouri, b. June 20, 1900

I may be 101 years old, but my memory is still good. I remember well the awful Tulsa Race Riot of 1921, which my husband, son, and I lived through. I remember how scared we were. We were just running, just desperately trying to get out of harm's way. Every which way we looked, there seemed to be harm! I had my seven-month-old son, James Dale, in my arms. My husband was running down the middle of the street when he got shot in the stomach. The bullet hit his belt buckle and ricocheted. It caused a split right in his stomach. When he was found, the people who found him thought he could not possibly survive that wound, as his intestines were actually hanging outside! But he did live, though he suffered from that wound the rest of his life. In fact, for the rest of his life he always had some sort of stomach complaint—locked bowels, severe pains, cramps, or something. He died in December of 1935. His death was directly connected to that bullet wound he got during the riot. That bullet cheated my son out of his father's lifelong love and guidance. There were many casualties from that riot. Some were worse than others. That bullet wound to the stomach of my husband was one of the worst!

SAMUEL CASSIUS, Hackensack, New Jersey, b. May 2, 1921

I was just one month old during the Tulsa riot, but I often heard my parents, Frank and Ellen Cassius, talk about the devastation that riot caused to the whole black community in Tulsa. My dad had always been sort of an activist. He formed the first black American Legion Post in Guthrie, Oklahoma. After the rioting, looting, and burning of black Tulsa during the riot, my family moved to North Peoria Avenue, where the neighbors included the prominent Tulsan Dr. George Lythcott and Tulsa dentist Dr. Everette Hairston who was my uncle. His wife, Anita Hairston, became the first black graduate of the University of Tulsa. I also knew Simon Berry Sr., whose jitney stopped right in front of our house on Peoria. The jitney driver was always getting out and making small talk with us. I found out it was because he had a crush on my beautiful cousin, Birdie Hairston, who gave herself the more glamorous name of "Dixie" when she sang with Count Basie's band.

Although I was just a baby during the riot, that riot did have an effect on me. It made me mad, and I vowed to fight racism and injustice anywhere I saw it. And I have done just that all of my life. I attended Langston University in Langston, Oklahoma, where I got good grades and had good attendance (except when the fish were biting). I was in the U.S. Navy during World War II and fought at Pearl Harbor, Coral Sea, and other places in the Eastern battle zone. I met my wife at Pearl Harbor. She was a messenger. She would walk from corridor to corridor with messages. It was unusual for a black woman to have such a job then. Ususually only "Aunt Jemima" and "Uncle Mose" type jobs were reserved for black personnel. After the war, my wife and I flew with a civilian airline. We were on the Denver-to-Boulder route. One of the pilots was former Tuskegee airman Richard Biffle.

I continued to fight racism and injustice when I moved to Los Angeles, California, fifty years ago. I once pushed over a Ku Klux Klan cross there and helped chase some Klansmen up Laurel Canyon. I worked with the group that helped California Attorney General Kenny get the Ku Klux Klan charter revoked in California.

I also worked with groups that publicized the injustice of the military regarding the awarding of citations for bravery during wartime to black military personnel. White personnel routinely received medals for their acts of bravery; blacks were routinely ignored when they performed similar, or even more outstanding, acts of heroism and bravery. It was not until the Bill Clinton administration took an interest in rectifying this blot on America that justice was finally done and black military

heroes received, at last, their recognition and awards. The governor of New Jersey presented the Medal of Honor to me on June 27, 2000. At last my country had recognized what I had done and had rewarded me for a job well done!

NAOMI HOOKER CHAMBERLAIN,
White Plains, New York, b. January 26, 1918

At the time of the riot, my parents, Samuel D. and Anita J. Hooker, lived in a house on Independence Street and owned a large store at 123 North Greenwood Avenue. The home was damaged, but not burned down. The business was a total loss. The estimate of our parents' loss is covered in more detail in my sister's Tulsa Race Riot, 1921, testimony. (See Dr. Olivia J. Hooker)

MILDRED MITCHELL CHRISTOPHER,
Jacksonville, Florida, b. October 19, 1913

At the time of the Tulsa riot, my parents, James and Jessie Cunliff Mitchell, lived on King Street between Elgin Street and Greenwood Avenue. My brother is Nathaniel C. Cannon, and my sister is Johnnie Cannon. Cannon's Drygoods Store was a popular store during the old Greenwood days.

I was seven years old during the riot. I remember being awakened by my parents and joining the crowd of black people running from approaching mobs. We were half-naked—in our night clothes, some of us without shoes. I remember when the Guard's truck came upon us. The sun had come up then, and I watched as the sun shined on the men's bayonets. Some of the women screamed; some of them prayed loudly to God to save us. The black men raised a white flag. The Red Cross came. We were taken to the Tulsa fairgrounds, where we were given food and milk. We were given baloney sandwiches, pork-and-bean sandwiches and a cup of milk each. That was my first experience with a pork-and-bean sandwich. I didn't take to it then, and I don't take to it now!

The husband in the white family that Mama worked for, Mr. Pate, came and got us. He carried us to the servants quarters. Then he went back to look for Papa. He brought Papa home to us about twelve or one o'clock.

We lost everything we owned in that riot. Papa went back and looked through the ashes where our house stood. He said he could find no evidence that we had ever had a happy, normal home life there. He said he couldn't even find evidence of our piano—there were no keys, no wires, no nothing! The mobsters must have taken our beautiful things. All that was left of black peoples' former happy lives was billowing smoke. We saw that smoke, smelled that smoke on our way back from to Tulsa, back to the fairgrounds. What a sad sight. What a pitiful end to our dreams.

MILDRED LUCAS CLARK, Parkin, Arkansas, b. October 15, 1921
(born premature due to riot trauma effects upon her mother, who died five months after the birth)

The Tulsa Race Riot, 1921, affected me before I was born; the trauma of that riot caused my mother to give birth to me prematurely in the Greenwood District, which was like a war zone. My family, and other riot victims, were like war refugees. That riot also deprived me of a mother, for my mother died nine months after the riot from riot-related stress and pregnancy complications. So no amount of reparation, restitution, reconciliation, medals, or memorials can restore to me what I lost. I have never known a mother's love!

At the time of the riot, my parents, Daniel and Lela Lucas, lived at 1012 North Elgin Street, at the foot of a hill, just off Latimer Street. On the night of May 31, 1921, my dad joined a group of black men and went down to the Tulsa jail to keep the young black shoeshine man, Dick Rowland, from being lynched. Dad said he saw dead black bodies piled like stacks of logs. He said he also saw black bodies being dumped into the Arkansas River. He said the river looked like "a river of blood." Later, while Dad and some of the black men were hiding out, the militia caught them. They were taken to the armory by the guards. My dad never got over the tragedy of that riot. He never forgot about my mother's suffering. He died in 1940.

OTIS G. CLARK, Tulsa, Oklahoma, b. February 13, 1903

At the time of the Tulsa riot in 1921, I lived with my grandmother, Ellen Clark, my stepfather, Tom Bryant, and my mother, Ellen Bryant, at 805 East Archer Street near the Midland Valley railroad tracks that went straight into and across Greenwood Avenue. This area was the heart of mob action in the early pre-dawn attack upon Greenwood. Some prominent white industrial buildings were on the south side of Greenwood, and prominent black businesses were on the north side of Greenwood, such as Jackson's Funeral Home which had just purchased a new, state-of-the-art ambulance. Archer was the dividing line between white and black

Mildred Lucas Clark

Otis G. Clark

Tulsa. The upper stories of some of those white industrial buildings were used by white snipers to kill blacks who were defending Greenwood. During the riot, I got caught right in the middle of a gun battle. Some white mobsters were holed up in the upper floor of the Ray Rhee Flour Mill on East Archer, and they were just gunning down black people, just picking them off like they were swatting flies. Well, I had a friend who worked for Jackson's Funeral Home, and he was trying to get to the place where the new ambulance was parked so he could drive it to safety. I went with him. He had the keys in his hand, ready for the takeoff. But one of the mobsters in the Rhee building zoomed in on him and shot him in the hand. The keys flew to the ground, and blood shot out of his hand and some of it sprayed onto me, as I was just behind my friend. We both immediately abandoned the plan to save the ambulance and ran to save our lives. We ran north on Greenwood. I was trying to make it to my cousin Bertha Black's cafe/choc joint just North of Pine Street. But when we got there, the mob had beat us to it.

It was burned down, and my cousin and her family had fled farther north.

Later, I fled farther north and caught up with my family. We hid in Nowata until the riot was over and it was safe to return to Tulsa. I never saw my stepfather again. He just vanished at age forty-five and was never seen or heard from again. An old couple, the Talbots, who lived near us on Archer were also never seen or heard from again. We believe they are among the nameless dead, buried who knows where! Oh, yes, we had a little pet bulldog named Bob that everybody just loved. Bob was so protective of our house. He was never seen again. I just know that Bob fought bravely to protect our house. I do believe he was a victim of that mob, too. When things cooled down in Tulsa and it was safe to return, I went to our home site. There was nothing there but ashes. I raked through the ashes trying to find something to cherish from the past. But I couldn't find nothing. Absolutely nothing. I believe Bob's remains were in those ashes.

[AUTHOR'S NOTE: Ninety-nine-year-old Otis G. Clark has been one of the most interviewed of the black riot survivors. He takes great pleasure in speaking to print and electronic media from all over the world. But his eyes fill with tears, and, momentarily, he cannot speak when he thinks of his stepfather, the Talbot neighbors, and Bob, the beloved little bulldog. Mr. Clark is one of the most avid survivor supporters of reparations.]

SANDY CLARK, Tulsa, Oklahoma, b. 1907

Mr. Clark was unavailable for an interview, but his nephew, Calvin Johnson of Tulsa, said that his uncle, when asked about the riot, would always sum it up with the following remark: "All I remember about that riot is that I was RUNNING LIKE HELL!"

BLANCHE CHATMON COLE, Bristow, Oklahoma, b. April 21, 1904

My folks had come to Tulsa from Clarksville, Oklahoma. They had heard that there was a lot of money to be made in Tulsa and that families could have a good life there. They lived in a rented house or a boarding house in the Greenwood District area.

On the day the riot broke out, we were just walking, and running, trying to get to safety. We saw men standing around, directing the fleeing blacks to safety. Somehow we got out of Tulsa! We went home to Clarksville. Child, I was a nervous wreck. It had been a rough journey, I tell you.

Later, when we came back to Tulsa, we found that we had lost everything. Everything we had had been stolen or burned. I wondered why we had come back. There was nothing to come back to. The rented house was badly burned and everything stolen or burned. Even my child toys and treasures had been taken. What the mobsters hadn't stolen, they scattered about, set on fire, or smashed and damaged. I just sat down and cried. I was a nervous wreck.

WORDIE (PEACHES) MILLER COOPER, Sand Springs, Oklahoma, b. February 4, 1911

Mrs. Cooper was unavailable for an interview.

CARRIE HUMPHREY CUDJOE, Tulsa, Oklahoma, b. April 6, 1913

My parents, David and Hattie Humphrey, moved from Ft. Gibson, Oklahoma, to Tulsa. At the time of the riot, they lived at 1211 North Lansing Avenue in a home which they owned. They attended the Holiness Church on the corner of Marshall and Lansing. The pastor was Reverend Nichols. There were six of us children then. We had a house, a horse, a cow, and some chickens. Our home was burned down during the riot and we lost everything that we had. That riot was an awful thing. It scarred us.

Carrie Humphrey Cudjoe, left.

CORINE LOVE CUMMINGS, Chicago, Illinois, b.

Mrs. Cummings was unavailable for an interview. Her contact is her sister Queen Esther Love Walker of Muskogeee and Mrs. Walker's daughter Brenda J. Lykins of Muskogee, Oklahoma.

LaVERNE COOKSEY DAVIS, Tulsa, Oklahoma, b. May 24, 1904

My family moved to Pawnee, Oklahoma, from Royce City, Texas, in 1916. They left Texas because conditions were just terrible there for black farmers then. In 1919, they moved to Tulsa, which was a booming oil town. We heard there were many good jobs in Tulsa for black folks. But I didn't find Tulsa to be much different from Texas. In Texas, my first job when I was eleven or twelve years old was washing dishes for a white lady in exchange for piano lessons. In Tulsa, the only job I could find was being a maid for a white doctor in south Tulsa.

When the riot began, late the night of May 31, 1921, I was in the servant's quarters at the doctor's house. I had gone to bed, and after midnight I got a call from the doctor, who was still downtown. He told me not to go into Little Africa. That is what white Tulsans called the black district of Tulsa then. I thought it was strange for him to tell me that at that early time of morning. I wouldn't have been going into north Tulsa at that time anyway. Well, later on the doctor called me again. This time he was more urgent in his warning. He

said, "Hell has broken loose in Little Africa. Don't go down there!"

I was safe in my maid's quarters, but many of my friends in the Greenwood area had their homes burned to the ground. Before their homes were burned, some of the people were taken out of their beds. They went to detention centers in their pajamas and housecoats because the police wouldn't give them time to dress. I was so disturbed. I didn't know where my family and friends were. Later, I found that most of them had been taken to the Convention Center. Five or six days after the riot, blacks could get passes from the militia to go into the Greenwood area to try and find relatives and friends. That riot was a tragic thing, and it has stayed on my mind all these years.

Although safe in my maid's quarters, I could see that red blaze in the sky over our beloved Greenwood. When I did get down to Greenwood after the riot, I was so hurt by what I saw. To wake up and see nothing but ashes and buildings burnt to the ground—I couldn't keep the tears from falling.

After the riot, work conditions were still bad for black Tulsans. The only jobs available to them were in the serv-

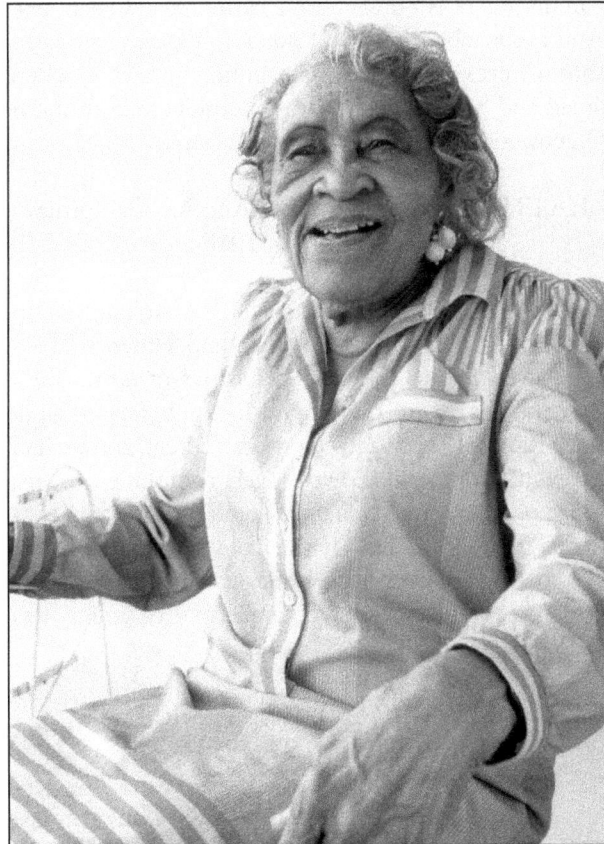

LaVerne Cooksey Davis

ices—in hotels, restaurants, lounges, etc., or as maids and housemen in the south and west Tulsa mansions of oil millionaires or other prominent white Tulsans. That is why I left Tulsa. I first went to Pittsburgh, Pennsylvania, where I worked seven years in the millinery business. Then I moved to Kansas City, Missouri, and improved myself by going to nursing school and becoming a Licensed Practical Nurse. I enjoyed my career in nursing, but I returned to Tulsa in the 1970s to be near my sister, Katherine Butler, who worked for the wealthy white Mayo family, which owned the famous Mayo Hotel and other choice Tulsa real estate. I worked thirteen years for the Red Cross in Tulsa and retired in 1984.

I have seen many changes in Tulsa since I first came here. Urban Renewal moved many of us elderly blacks out of our neighborhoods. The little house where I lived, which was packed with my memorabilia from all the places I have lived, no longer exists. That neighborhood has been leveled to make room for "modern improvements." I was moved to a Senior Citizens home where I stayed for a few years. Now I am living in a nursing home. My dear sister has passed on, and I don't have a single living relative left. Sometimes, I think of my parents and of our dreams for a better life in Oklahoma. And I remember that awful riot as if it were yesterday. I shut my eyes. I see that blaze lighting up the sky when greed and hatred caused white mobsters to burn down Greenwood. Then the tears come again . . .

HATTIE LILLY DUNN, Los Angeles, California, b. March 16, 1918

I was born in Charlotte, North Carolina, but in 1921, my parents, Henry Walter and Florence Wells Lilly, lived in the Greenwood District of north Tulsa that was burned to the ground in the infamous Tulsa Race Riot of 1921. We lived on Elgin Street, and we had a beautiful home filled with lovely furnishings, linens, tools, photographic equipment, clothing, and miscellaneous items. Papa Lilly had a Ford sedan, and Uncle Fred had a Ford coupe. We lost everything, including all of Uncle Fred's medical equipment. Everything was lost! (*See photo on page 60.*)

JAMES DURANT, Detroit, Michigan, b. January 27, 1915

At the time of the Tulsa riot in 1921, my parents, Arie B. and Glovenia Durant, lived at 201 North Detroit in the Greenwood District of north Tulsa. They

James Durant

were buying their home. Some of the finest black homes that were burned on the second day of the riot, June 1, 1921, were on Detroit Avenue. The site of these elegant homes, magnificently furnished, so infuriated white mobsters that they smashed fine dishes, hacked up valuable pianos, victrolas, musical instruments, tore down fancy lace curtains from Europe—those that were not loaded onto trucks and carried off to their homes—and set fire to everything. According to evidence, the Detroit area was burned by mobsters after National Guard troops arrived in Tulsa the morning of June 1. The loss of this Detroit area caused a lot of hard feelings and controversy in north Tulsa.

Although I was only six years old at the time, I remember that riot as if it were yesterday. When Dad heard that inflamed mobs were headed into the Greenwood District intent on burning down the property of the black people, and killing the people, he bravely tried to protect our family. He and my uncle barricaded the doors and windows of our house with mattresses from our beds and they told us to lie down on the floor. We could hear bullets hitting against the house. It was an awful experience that I will never forget. Our home and everything we owned was burned to the ground. Dad rebuilt us a home at 1144 North Elgin Street, but it wasn't as nice as that home we had on Detroit. That is why I believe I am owed reparations. My family lost a lot. Things might have been different for me had that riot not happened.

After the riot, there was a lot of talk about what caused it, who was involved, and was there a coverup. My father and my uncle knew Dick Rowland and his family well. They always said that the riot was a conspiracy thing. They said those were trumped-up charges against Dick Rowland. They said the elevator incident was a staged event, the creation of an excuse for the mobsters to go in and burn down Greenwood. The leaders of Tulsa wanted that area to expand into, and when blacks wouldn't sell it to them, they had to have an excuse to get the mobsters to go in and take it for them. That's what I heard. I remember hearing Dad and my uncle say that maybe it was an all-white conspiracy. But some blacks said that some fellow blacks were "bought off" and became involved in the conspiracy, too. Oh, yes, that riot was a terrible thing. I wish I could forget it, but I can't. It's just engraved in my mind. I can shut my eyes and feel the terror I felt as a six-year-old lying on the floor listening to bullets hitting our house.

AUTHOR'S NOTE: There were conflicting views about one black Tulsan in particular—Sheriff Barney Cleaver. On the one hand, many Tulsans praised him, saying he was a well-respected Tulsan who really cared about his north Tulsa community. He was known to be especially concerned with the black youth of Tulsa, often counseling them like a loving father and herding them off the streets. One survivor said the youth affectionately called him "Uncle Barney." On the other hand, there were some blacks who were suspicious of Barney Cleaver and wondered if he had been a political pawn of the white political and economic establishments. They noted that Cleaver was one of a handful of blacks who were paid for their riot losses. (See Tulsa City Minutes.) There is no hard evidence regarding any wrongdoing on the part of Cleaver, but he did come to possess a lot of north Tulsa real estate. Some survivors insist that is no accident, but was part of the "conspiracy." The enigma about Barney Cleaver is typical of the aftermath of the Tulsa riot.]

LUCILLE B. BUCHANAN FIGURES, Tulsa, Oklahoma, b. January 9, 1909

At the time of the riot, I lived with my mother, Mattie Vaden Buchanan, at 521 North Elgin Street in the house where I was born. We had a nice home which had two bedrooms, a living room, dining room, kitchen, and a porch. We had a piano, and I took piano lessons from a lady who lived on Frankfort Avenue. We did not own a car, but my mother did own the house. Mother did laundry in her house for wealthy white families.

I remember that the riot broke out the day after we had attended the funeral of a friend, Adonia Dupree, who lived in Haskell. We called her "Big Girl." The funeral was held at the Holiness Church on Independence Avenue, which was right around from Brickyard Hill. I remember when we returned from the funeral, I sat on my uncle's porch (H. O. Vaden, owner of Vaden's Pool Hall on Greenwood Avenue). I was sitting in the swing. While I swinging, I was listening to the men talk. I heard them talking about a riot which was supposed to break out soon. While they were talking, my mother came running up to the house. She had my cousin Delores Vaden (now Ramsey) and her little brother, Sam, with her. They had come running, around from the Cherry family's house, to warn my uncle that the riot was on. Sam was wearing knee pants, long white stockings, and shoes that were too big for him. Sam's father, my mother's brother, worked downtown at a bank. The whites always gave him cast-off shoes from their children. So whatever shoes they gave my uncle, that's the size shoes Sam wore!

We joined the scared black people who were running from the mobsters. We crossed the Midland Valley railroad tracks and made it to Samuel McGowan's mother Adelle's store. We were taken to some center, where we stayed until a white man that my mother did laundry for came and got us. His name was Mr. V. Fahnstock, and he was German. We were so glad to have someplace safe to stay after that awful riot.

ARCHIE JACKSON FRANKLIN, Los Angeles, California, b. November 11, 1915

I was only five years old when the Tulsa riot occurred, but I remember the awful feeling of not having a home to go to. For our house, which my parents owned, was burned down. We lost everything in that riot. There was so much grief in our family. Everywhere we looked in our Greenwood District, there was nothing but ashes, ashes, ashes! Our family had to live in one of those Red Cross tents for months. My sister Hazel Franklin Hackett is much more vocal than I am. She can tell you more about the riot than I can. But I *can* tell you the awful feelings of terror I felt, and how I hated living in that tent all those months!

JIMMIE LILLY FRANKLIN,
Los Angeles, California, b. June 12, 1915

My sisters, Muriel and Hattie, and I lived with our parents, Henry Walter and Florence Wells Lilly, in a beautiful home on North Elgin Street at the time of the Tulsa race riot. It was a large home with four bedrooms, one bath, living room, dining room, and an office which was used by Papa, who was a photographer. The house was furnished with beautiful things, including a living room which had a Kimball piano, two sofas, two upholstered chairs, a settee, and four bedrooms full of oak furniture, and a dining room which contained an oak dining room set. Papa had a photographic studio, a darkroom, and several large cameras. Papa also had numerous household, carpentry, and plumbing tools which the mobsters took. (Our uncle, Fred Wells, was a prominent Tulsa physician and surgeon, and he lost all his fine medical equipment when mobsters burned the hospital where he worked.)

My mother and us girls had beautiful jewelry and clothing, almost all of which was stolen. Mobsters took all our birthstone rings, but Mama was wearing her better jewelry and the mobsters didn't get that! They did take our watches, bracelets, and a strand of pearls. Two cars were lost—a Ford sedan and a Ford coupe.

The worst thing about the riot wasn't the loss of those beautiful material possessions, though, no matter how much we loved them. The worst thing lost was my peace of mind. For many years after the riot, I suffered horrific nightmares of the bloody killings, the strewn, mutilated injured, the dead bodies, and of the searing-hot blazing fires that burned our homes to the ground. In my troubled sleep, I had vivid memories of the unusual but defining sounds of airplanes flying low in the smoke-filled skies above, and of the loud blasts of the bombs [sic] that the planes dropped on burning structures as innocent black men were desperately trying to extinguish the devastating fires while striving to protect their families and their property.

As we sat huddled together in the middle of Elgin Street with other homeless women and children, I often dreamed of being so scared. The sheer terror of these frightening events were a constant reoccurrence in the nightmares that came so regularly.

At night I dreaded going to bed. I was desperately afraid to go to sleep because of the fears I harbored about the sinister, menacing, hooded invaders who looted our home of prized possessions and then with lighted torches set fire to our homes. The acrid smell of smoke constantly burned in my nostrils as I twisted, turned, talked, and cried aloud while I slept so restlessly and dreamed.

The recurring nightmare of seeing Papa Lilly and Grandpa Wells being hog-tied and taken away at gunpoint, to only God knows where, was always included in the invading nightmares. One of my parents shook me as they awakened me gently, softly assuring me that it was just another one of those bad dreams I was having, and reassuring me that I was indeed safe and secure.

For years, my parents kept a small light burning in our bedroom to help chase away the horrific events that invaded the recurrent dreams that for years disturbed and invaded my restless sleep. That was my legacy from the Tulsa Race Riot of 1921! (*See photo on page 60.*)

JOAN HILL GAMBREL, Bronx, New York

Mrs. Joan Hill Gambrel is in a nursing home in Bronx, New York, and is not capable of giving interviews now. A cousin of hers, two generations removed, attorney Eddie Renard Hadden, a graduate of Hofstra University in New York, New York, contacted the Riot Commission and shared information about the riot that Mrs. Gambrel had given years ago when she was mentally and physically fit. He thought this information from his distant cousin, whom he affectionately calls "Aunt," ought to be shared with others interested in riots and human injustices.

Joan Gambrell Hill

ERNESTINE GIBBS, Tulsa, Oklahoma, b. December 15, 1902

When the riot broke out in Tulsa, I was doing what I always did during the school year; I was studying. Oh, how I loved Booker T. Washington High School in north Tulsa! And I loved the principal, E. W. Woods, just as much or more. Mr. Woods was such a motivator. He inspired and motivated all—students, teachers, parents—to do our very best. And we did! Even though black

Ernestine Gibbs

schools in Oklahoma were segregated then, and not equal to white school in terms of facilities, books, and money spent on schools, we got the best education possible under those conditions, thanks to educators like Mr. Woods. I will never forget a message he gave to the student body in the 1920s. He said that we (black students) were as good as ninety-nine percent of all people, and better than the other one percent.

So the night of the riot, I was studying for my finals at school the next day. We lived on King Street in the middle of a train track area. A man ran up on our porch and knocked on the door. He said, "Put out that light! There is fighting and burning on Greenwood." So I put out the light and my parents and my brother went to bed. Soon a young man, a family friend, came from a hotel on Greenwood where he worked and knocked on our door. He was so scared he could not sit still nor lie down. He just paced up and down the floor, talking about the "mess" going on downtown and on Greenwood.

When daylight came, black people were moving down the train tracks like ants. We joined the fleeing people. My mother, a cousin who was staying with us, and I soon lost my brother and the friend who had come to warn us. My poor mother was beside herself with panic and grief when she couldn't find my brother. Everyone was just running hard as they could, trying to get to Golden Gate Park, located on the east side where Crawford Park is now, near Thirty-Sixth Street North. It was just weeds, grass, and trees then. But we made it safely to that place. We lay down on the ground and rested. I remember lying flat on my back, on the bare ground, looking up at the stars, and sleeping fitfully through the pre-dawn morning. We fled to this area because we had been warned to beware of highways and railroad tracks, because whites were shooting down blacks who were fleeing that way. Some of them were shot by whites firing from airplanes in the sky.

Around twelve noon, another group of fleeing blacks joined us. There was a house nearby where whites lived. One of the black men in our group went up to the house and told the owner about the black refugees. He told him how thirsty we were. The white man came back with the black man who had gone to the house to ask for water. He told all of us to come on up to his house. We did, and he gave us all the water we wanted.

After the sounds of shooting had stopped, and the flames seemed to be lessening, some of the black men decided to go back to the downtown area and the Greenwood area to help bury the dead. One young man gave his gun to Mama to keep for him. When the young man came back to where we were hiding, Mama gave him back his gun. We forgot to ask about the dead.

About 4:00 P.M., we were found by the guards and taken to the fairgrounds. We were given mattresses to sleep on and food and drinks. When a white man who knew my mother offered to take us home, we were allowed to leave the fairgrounds. Going back to Greenwood was like entering a war zone. Oh, what a pitiful sight! When we got to our house, we found nothing but ashes and metal. All around, the entire

Greenwood District, was nothing but ashes and metal. The only things that were not burned were iron and metal—stoves, bedsteads, etc.

All the trees were burned. Everything was gone! People were moaning and weeping when they looked at where their houses used to stand. Oh, Lord, it was an awful thing, that riot was. Oh, one good thing happened, though. My brother was found! Trains were running again. So my mother, my cousin, and I caught a train to Sapulpa to stay with relatives, since we no longer had a home in Tulsa. When we got there, there was my brother! During the heat of the riot, when he got lost from us, he and a friend ran west, and they jumped into the Arkansas River to dodge bullets aimed at them. They swam across the Arkansas River to safety. Then they walked to Sapulpa to our relatives' house. My mother was just overjoyed to find my brother alive. She just hugged him and kissed him, and cried. Oh, I will never forget that riot as long as I live. I can shut my eyes and still see the smoke, fire, and ashes that destroyed our beloved Greenwood. I'll never forget it. No, not ever!

HAROLD GIBBS, Tulsa, Oklahoma, b. January 16, 1920

I was just one year old during the riot, and I don't personally remember anything about the riot, but I do remember what my mother, Minnie Gibbs. told me about the riot. She said the morning of June 1, 1921, my dad, Lodious Gibbs, and his good friend and work partner, Ike Evans, had left early for work. Dad owned a wagon and a team of work horses, and he and Ike worked for the City of Tulsa. I don't know what exactly their line of work was. But Mother said they had helped with the building of Tulsa's Dunbar Elementary School.

My mother said that she had joined the crowd of running men, women, and children trying to escape the mobs who were approaching the Greenwood area. She had me in her arms and she was terrified. She said she and the group she was with ran all the way to Claremore, Oklahoma. Then a truck of soldiers came and took them to a detention center in Tulsa. I don't remember which center she said they were taken to.

After the riot, she was reunited with my father, who was in another detention center while she and I were in the one we were taken to from Claremore. Dad never heard a word from the city about where his wagon and his two work horses were. He never got a dime from the city from the loss of his "work capital"—that wagon and those two horses!

THERESSA CORNELLA McNEAL GILLIAM, Chicago, Illinois, b. October 11, 1911

Mrs. Theressa Cornella McNeal Gilliam is the oldest of the three daughters of prominent Tulsa businesswoman Annie McNeal, who owned a boarding house in the Greenwood District at the time of the riot. Mrs. Gilliam, exercising oldest-sibling authority, was clearly the "boss" in the household where the three sisters lived. Legally blind, she could not fill out the riot questionnaire, but she dutifully answered all questions verbally as I filled out her questionnaire. Arnetta McNeal Anderson had had a stroke when the riot study began but could communicate with her sisters by holding up one finger for "yes" answers and two fingers for "no" answers. Mrs. Anderson has since passed on. Mrs. Gilliam designated Jeanette (formerly Johnetta) McNeal Bradshaw spokesperson for the three sisters. Mrs. Bradshaw handled all written correspondence between the three sisters and sent photographs to the commission.

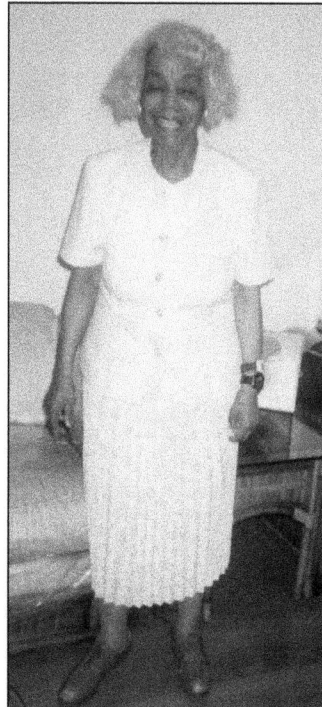

Theressa C. Gilliam

Mrs. Gilliam handles all verbal communication with the Riot Commission. She makes frequent calls for updates on the commission, or just to chat. There is a special bond between this author and those sweet sisters who lived through the Tulsa Race Riot of 1921.

ADELL HOPSKINS ARTEBERRY GRADY, Tulsa, Oklahoma, b. October 7, 1911

Mrs. Grady was unable to give an interview.

LEON GRAYS, SR., Wasco, California, b. August 5, 1915

My father, Ben Franklin Grays, was born in Nashville, Arkansas, in 1881. He moved to Oklahoma, looking for a better life than he and other black folks

Leon Grays, Sr.

had in Arkansas. At the time of the riot, he and my mother were living in a little house that they rented for $6 a month. Their furnishings were worth about $800, I guess. The furniture consisted of chairs, a couch, beds with mattresses filled with straw, rugs, work benches, and other ordinary stuff. My father also had a field wagon and some farm tools which were probably valued at $1,100. I was too small to remember any other details from then.

My father was one of the black detainees taken to a detention center. I heard him later talk about how miserable conditions were for black Tulsans during and after the riot.. He said they suffered terrible mistreatment from the hands of their own fellow Tulsans, white Tulsans.

I have lived to see eighty-six years, and I am glad to see something good come out of this terrible event. I am so grateful to Rep. Don Ross and Senator Maxine Horner for sponsoring the bill that created the Riot Commission. I am grateful to the commissioners, who have been working so hard to gather information about that terrible riot, especially Mrs. Eddie Faye Gates, who has been so faithfully contacting and interviewing us survivors. I remember all the sacrifices the Grays family had to make because of that riot. I remember all that we suffered. The most awful thing that riot did to us was what it did to our minds. It took away our safety, our security, our peace of mind. The suffering we endured was immeasurable. Eventually, it got so bad that Dad was forced to seek greener pastures elsewhere. We children moved with our mother to Muskogee in order to have a

more meaningful life. We just had to escape the racial tensions in Tulsa.

All my adult life, I have prayed that someday there would be a healing of all the hurts that riot caused, that something good would come from that terrible event.. Thank God, that time seems to have come. I do feel that now I could go on to glory knowing that the story of my father, Ben Franklin Grays, has finally been told. I find peace in knowing that his detention, under unjust conditions, is now known around the world. And I pray that nothing like that ever happens again. Once again, I thank the Riot Commission for all it has done to help heal the senseless tragedy that occurred during my boyhood days when my father, Ben Franklin Grays, was unjustly detained by the authorities of Tulsa, Oklahoma.

BERTHA HOPSKINS GUYTON,
Tulsa, Oklahoma
Mrs. Guyton was unable to give an interview.

HAZEL FRANKLIN HACKETT, Tuscaloosa,
Alabama, b. October 11, 1918

I was born in Meridian, Logan County, Oklahoma, but in 1921 my parents, Jackson Washington and Frances Franklin, had moved to Tulsa and lived at 604 E. Independence Place. Our home was burned to the ground in the riot and we lost everything—house, furni-

Hazel Franklin Hackett

ture, clothes—just everything in the world that we owned! I was nine and a half years old, and I was so traumatized by the riot that I lost most all of my prior memories. My mind just seems to have been wiped clean of memories, all memories except two. I remembered my two most treasured possessions—a little brown-skinned doll with curly black hair, and a plain little plate with flowers on it which I won at Mt. Zion Baptist Church for learning the books of the Bible. I can see those two things in my mind as plain as day. I wish I still had them.

My dad worked at National Supply Company on Archer Street. He left for work every morning at 5 a.m. and returned home at 8 or 8:30 A.M. for a quick breakfast. Then he returned to work. On June 1, 1921, Dad left for work at 5 a.m. as usual, but he returned home about 5:30 instead of at 8 or 9 as usual. My mother was so surprised. She asked Dad why he came back so quick. He replied, "Wife, get the children up quick. We have to get out of here!" He told my mother that he was almost to work when he met so many colored people—just a mass of people—coming down Greenwood, coming our way, going away from Greenwood. He said he asked them why were they leaving and where were they going. One of them said, "Jack, go home and get your family up, and get them out of here. The white folks are burning up this town and shooting all the colored folks!" So we joined the crowd.

We walked to Mohawk Park. But we left one old lady in our neighborhood, Mrs. Johnson. She wouldn't leave with us. She said she was too old and too sick to run. So she stayed in her house. After the riot was over and everyone had settled down again, I heard Mrs. Johnson tell what happened to her in the riot. She said when mobsters broke into her house she told them, "I'm an old woman and I'm sick. I didn't feel like running with the other colored folks. So you'll just have to shoot me." She said the mobsters just looked at her, and then they turned and left her house.

The militia found us at Mohawk Park and took us to the fairgrounds, where we stayed three days. The Red Cross fed us. White employers came to the fairgrounds, called out the names of their employees, and took them away. My dad's National Supply boss came and claimed my dad. My mother's sister, Muzzy Hood of 527 Latimer Place, did not get burned out, so we went and stayed with her for two weeks. But Dad was anxious to be on his own. Some white people from National Supply built us a small house on the lot where our burned-down house had been. Dad later added onto the house, and the addition he built faced Greenwood Avenue.

The riot caused my mother so much stress. I know that her high blood pressure problems started right after the riot. We didn't have any relatives killed in the riot, but I knew Dr. A. C. Jackson, the prominent Mayo Clinic-trained surgeon who was shot to death by a mobster after he had surrendered and had his hands held high in the air. We colored folks were so saddened by the burning down of the newly refurbished Mt. Zion Baptist Church during the riot.

AUTHOR'S NOTE: When the present minister of Mt. Zion Baptist Church, Dr. G. Calvin McCutchen, first came to Tulsa to be the minister of the church in 1940, he stayed in the home of Mrs. Frances Franklin until his home was ready. Jackson W. Franklin was dead then.

MILDRED JOHNSON HALL, El Sobrante, California, b. October 17, 1919

During the riot, my parents, George and Katie Lee Staples Johnson, were living in a little shotgun house, which they were buying, in the Greenwood area. My folks fled the riot along with the other fleeing colored folks, my poor mother carrying me, eighteen months old, in her arms. My mother never recovered from the trauma of that riot. She was sickly ever after, and she died when I was two. Homeless black people were put in tents which were put up in the burned-out area by the Red Cross. The living conditions in those tents were terrible during the fall of 1921 and the winter of 1922. It was just too much for my mother. First, she first caught pneumonia. Then she got tuberculosis. My grandmother told me that my mother was so sick and so sad after that riot. She was so upset about their losing everything. And she hated living in that tent. She just lost the will to live. On her death bed, she pleaded with her mother to always keep me, to raise me. My grandmother made a promise to my dying mother that she would always keep me, even if we had only bread and water to live on! My grandmother kept that promise. She kept it even after Dr. Motley, the prominent Tulsa black doctor who had delivered me, wanted to adopt me when he heard my mother had died. But my grandmother held firm. She wouldn't let that rich doctor adopt me. She stood by me. But my daddy didn't. He deserted me.

Grandmother kept her word. She lovingly raised me and insisted that I get a good education. I graduated from Booker T. Washington High School in Tulsa in 1938. I moved to California in 1962.

Oh, by the way, I did find my father. I was determined to lay my eyes on the man who fathered me and left me. I located him through a Methodist bishop (Green) who had married Dad's sister. When I met my father, he was married to a white woman in St. Louis. He heard from the bishop that I was looking for him. He came to Tulsa to see me. My grandmother had prayed that she would live until my father and I were reunited so she could verify to me that he was my father. She did live to witness the reunion. One month later she died. She died a happy woman because I now had the father I had never known, and she had kept her promise to my mother. I felt a sense of peace. I felt that those two women who had loved me so could now rest in peace. I also felt a sense of sadness, and a sense of bitterness about that riot. That riot cheated me out of knowing what it was like to have a mother. That riot caused the death of my mother. I will never get over that loss!

NELL HAMILTON HAMPTON,
Tulsa, Oklahoma, b. March 4, 1911

My parents, Milton Hamilton, Sr., and Alice Moore Wiley Hamilton, lived at 1420 North Kenosha. But just before the riot, they had separated, so only my mother and I were living at the house when the riot broke out. I remember that things began to get uneasy in the Greenwood area the evening of May 31, 1921. We saw people with bundles of belongings just walking north, and we saw wagons, loaded with people and belongings, lumbering along the streets, also going north. Around midnight, conditions were getting worse. We could hear voices and noises of people running down the road near the Midland Valley Railroad tracks; many were headed to the section line near Pine, or to the Peoria area, or to parks or other hiding places. My mother decided we had better join the fleeing crowd, and so we did. We went down the Midland Valley Railroad tracks, and when we got to Pine, my mother remembered she had left the deeds to our property in our house. She felt she just had to have those deeds or she would never get her property back later when all this trouble was over. So she told me to go on with the group, that she would find us. But she didn't find us; she didn't rejoin our group. We had gotten separated. I had no choice but to stay with the group. We hid in the residence of John Huddleston. He hid everybody who could fit into his house! He told us we could not have any lights on in the house and that we had to keep absolutely quiet. I was so frightened. I was just terrified out of my mind by all the commotion

going on—bullets, airplanes overhead, smoke, fires, noise, people running for their lives, and me separated from my mother. I had already been missing my father so much since he had left. Now the last straw was being separated from my mother! I was so stressed out that my nose began to bleed. Lord, I was a bloody, pitiful-looking, terrified child that day, June 1, 1921. Eventually, I was reunited with my mother. Black folks had lost just about everything in the Greenwood area. But we went on with our lives and did the best we could.

I've lived a long life and have some good memories, too, to go along with the bad memories of that awful riot. This riot study the last three years has caused us riot victims to get in contact with each other and with our old classmates and friends who moved away from Tulsa. One of my best buddies was Elwood Lett, a riot survivor who died a year ago. We sure used to have a lot of fun together. We'd go out on the town and other places and reminisce about the old days of Greenwood. We just had the best old time just carousing around! I used to also hit the casinos and go out of state to other places with my friends. Now my age is catching up with me. I don't go out carousing anymore, and I don't go to the casinos any more. I just sit at my window and look out at the traffic going by and hope someone will come and visit me. I sure do miss the good old days and my old buddies, and all that carousing we used to do!

LEROY LEON HATCHER, Tulsa, Oklahoma,
b. May 23, 1921

At the time of the riot, my parents, Augustus and Lois Muster Hatcher, were living in Tulsa. I don't know exactly where, but I believe it was in the Greenwood area, somewhere over near Brady Street. I don't know if they owned the house they were living in or if they were renting. They had come from Arkansas or Louisiana looking for a better way of life. Mother often talked about the riot. My dad never did talk much about it. Mother said on the day of the riot, she ran with other blacks who were running trying to get out of Greenwood, desperately trying to dodge bullets and fire from the sky. She said she ran nine miles with me, a nine-day-old baby, in her arms.

The commotion at our house began early the morning of June 1 while my parents and I were still sound asleep. The mobsters kicked in our door, threw in a Molotov cocktail or something or other, which set things on fire in the house. She said the wall in the house just lit up! Dad got Mother and me up and pushed us outside through a window. He told her to run, to join the crowd that was wildly running down the street trying to outrun the mobsters. He said he would be coming right behind us, that he would find us. But he never did. I don't know if the mobsters grabbed him and killed him right there in the house or what. All I know is that he was missing. We hid all day and all night somewhere. I don't know exactly where. But we were found and taken to some detention place. I don't know exactly which one. My mother called the white man that my father worked for and he came and got us.

After the National Guards got control of Tulsa, Mother looked and looked for my father. But she never found him. His loss haunted her the rest of her life, and it ruined my life. As a little boy, I used to worry Mama to death. I was always asking her, "Mama, where is my daddy?" She would say, "Son, I don't know. But I believe he would come to us if he could." Somehow that just didn't comfort me at all. I just wanted my daddy! During my teenage years, I seriously searched for my father. But I didn't have any more luck in finding him than my mother did immediately after the riot. When I couldn't find him, I searched for some of his people. I felt driven to find my relatives on my father's side. But for years I couldn't find a single relative of his. Then, by luck, I found one! I was out in California and I got injured and was taken to the hospital. There was a nurse at the hospital who saw my name on a roster. The name rang a bell with her. That was her family name, too. She came to check on me. When she saw me, she looked into my eyes and I looked into her eyes, and we knew we were kin. We had the same gray "cat eyes" that were typical in our family. At last, I had found my father's people! I found that he had a lot of relatives in Alabama.

Those gray "cat eyes" caused me a lot of grief when I was young. Kids at the Catholic school I attended in Tulsa were always teasing me about my eyes. You know how cruel kids can be when someone looks different. But those eyes united me with my father's family, and for that I am grateful. But I always carry a sadness in my heart. I am now eighty years old, but I still feel like that little boy who used to ask his mother, "Where is my daddy?" If my dad was killed in that riot, I wish I knew where he was buried. That riot caused us black people so much grief. Nothing can ever repay me for the hurt that riot caused me. It caused me to grieve a lifetime for my lost father.

MADELEINE HAYNES, Los Angeles, California, b. June 7, 1912

At the time of the riot, I lived with my mother, Georgia Dunn, at 544 E. Pine Street near a railroad track. Mother worked for a Daddy Fletcher. On the evening of May 31, 1921, about dusk time, I was in church with some other children. The church was on the corner of Greenwood Avenue. But Mother came and got her children. She said there was going to be trouble in Tulsa that night. She said a black boy (Dick Rowland) was going to be lynched that night. She took us home and gave us strict orders to stay in the house. We were not to come out of that house for anything! Then all the adults went down to the courthouse to try to save that boy.

We were so scared. We'd peep out the windows. We finally went to sleep. The next thing we knew, Mother was waking us up. She said there was shooting downtown and it was coming our way! We could see flames shooting up over the Brickyard Hill area. We went to the kitchen and quickly packed some food to carry with us. We looked out windows and saw scared, running black people who were trying to get away from the shots and fires that were fast approaching our area. I heard screams of people, and I saw bloody people running. By nine or ten in the morning, the sky was dark with smoke over the Greenwood area. Greenwood was being burned down.

My sister Margaret was always hardheaded. She slipped out of the house so she could see more. But at the time, we didn't know she had slipped out. I hung by my mother's side. For some reason, my mother decided to stay in the house. She didn't take us kids to the street to join the scared, running people. Some people were just too scared to remain in their houses. The looters just scared some people to death—kicking in doors, setting houses on fire, crashing, trashing, and burning what they didn't take with them. But Mama decided to stay in our house. Mobsters did come. There were no men in our house, so the mobsters did no hitting or shooting. They did set fire to the house. Then they left. I was so scared. While the mobsters were there, that is when we discovered Margaret wasn't with us. Mama had been so calm all during this riot thing, even when the mobsters set the house on fire. When they left, she calmly put out the fire with dirt and buckets of water. But when she couldn't find Margaret, she fell apart. She was crying and running through the house but Margaret was nowhere to be found.

After the mobsters left, and while we were running through the house looking for Margaret the soldiers came. They kicked open our door and asked for our guns. We had no guns. They then marched us to the section line, Pine Street. I noticed that all the soldiers were white. I saw no black men in authority. Just white men. Women and children were taken to the Ball Park and men to the fairgrounds. They gave each of us a sandwich and milk at the Ball Park. Then my mother's white employer came and got us and took us to the servants' quarters, where we lived for two months.

Oh, yes, my hardheaded sister, Margaret, was found at the Ball Park. When she went out of the house so she could see more, she went to help neighbors put out their house fires and she was picked up by troops and taken to the Ball Park, too. My mother was so overjoyed to find Margaret that she didn't scold her for going out of the house without permission. She didn't have to worry about me leaving the house without permission. I clung to Mama like glue the day of that riot. I was so scared. I often think about what that riot did to me. It took away my feelings of safety and security. It just paralyzed me with fear and grief. But you know, there is something else I have never forgotten. I lost my two most cherished possessions that day—a little teddy bear that I just loved and a little rocking chair. No amount of reparations can restore what I lost that day!

JAMES FRISSELL "BOTTLEHEAD" HILL,
Los Angeles, California, b. October 25, 1919

My name is James "Bottlehead" Hill. I got the nickname "Bottlehead" when I was a boy. One day I went to the Dreamland Theater on Greenwood Avenue to see a movie and I got in an argument with another boy. That boy slipped up behind me and hit me in the head with a bottle. Lorenzo Kemp nicknamed me "Bottlehead," and to this day everyone who knows me calls me "Bottlehead."

At the time of the Tulsa riot, my parents, James Duffy and Sarah Stamps Hill, lived at 441 E. Latimer Street. They had come to Tulsa from Arkansas. My dad worked for the Frisco Railroad. He worked in the roundhouse on the steam engines. That was a good job for a black man in those days. My dad owned a rent house and a store, and he was buying the house the family was living in at the time of the riot.

When the riot started, Mother was home with me and I was just a baby. Dad had gone to the movies with a man called Mr. Goodkid. Since I was too young to re-

James "Bottlehead" Hill

member the riot personally, I can't tell you much about the riot itself. I do remember my mother talking about how they lost everything they owned and how they had to live in a tent after the riot. She hated living in that tent!

I remember growing up in the Greenwood District after the riot. I was a "wild child" in those days. I remember my days at Booker T. Washington Elementary. I used to cross Brickyard Hill on my way to my classes. We had good teachers in those days and they were real strict with us students. I remember Mrs. Neal tore me up every day. Mrs. Armstrong was a real mild-mannered teacher. She had the reputation of not whipping nobody. But she whipped me! 'Course, I deserved it.

Our parents were strong disciplinarians at home, and everybody in the community corrected us, disciplined us. Barney Cleaver, the police deputy, talked to us kids and disciplined us, too. I remember Barney Cleaver and his father, Mr. Cleaver, once whipped me for staying out late at night. But it didn't do no good. I'd still slip out with my boyhood friends Johnny Tate, I.V. Tate, and George Monroe and go to the Dixie Theater. Then we'd roam the streets late at night. We didn't do anything really bad. We just felt we had to slip out.

When I got grown, I worked a while at the Frisco Railroad like my dad did. My friend Izory Daniels, who I had known since Carver Junior High School, worked there, too.

During World War II, I volunteered to go into the U.S. Army. First I was sent to Ouahu in Hawaii, then to Canton Island, which is now called Bora Bora. I was in the Twenty-Fourth Infantry. The military was very segregated then.

I've had a good life. I have lived in California for years. I sometimes think of Tulsa, and I remember how sad my parents became whenever they talked about that Tulsa race riot. I am glad that I was too young to remember all the horrible details of the riot. I do remember how those who were old enough to remember said how terrible it was and how they could never forget it.

A good thing about all this research on the Tulsa Race Riot of 1921 for the past three and a half years is that riot survivors were able to meet people like Mrs. Gates, who have worked so hard to find us survivors and children of dead survivors. I can't express my gratitude enough to these wonderful people. Mrs. Gates and I talk frequently, and she keeps me updated about the whereabouts of survivors, many of whom were my childhood playmates. She tells me where they are and what they are doing. And, sadly, she tells me who has recently died and gives me details of their funerals.

Lately, I've been thinking a lot about my old buddy Cecil White, who lives in Berkeley, California. Before the riot of 1921 burned us out, we lived on the same street in the Greenwood District—Latimer Street. Cecil's house was three or four doors from mine. We used to walk home from Booker T. Washington Elementary School together. For some reason, Cecil would always jump on me and fight me when we would be coming home from school (probably to impress the other children). I'd come home crying. One day when I came in from school sniffling and crying, my grandmother, Chaney Stamps, told me, "Boy, if you let that boy beat you up again, you're going to get another beating when you get home. I'll whip you myself!" Well, the next day when school was out and we started home, before Cecil could jump on me, I jumped on *him* and beat him up good! After that, we became friends, and we're good friends to this day. I sure would like to see my old buddy Cecil White again.

JOYCE WALKER HILL, Kansas City, Kansas, b. December 18, 1908

My parents, William and Lillie Holderness Walker, owned a lovely eight-room house called "The White House" at the time of the riot. It was located at 322 North Frankfort Avenue. It was a two-story house.

Joyce Walker Hill

They also owned a cleaning and pressing shop on the corner of Archer Street and Greenwood Avenue. They also owned a restaurant which was not burned during the riot.

During the riot, I remember all us colored people running down the street, desperately trying to escape the white mobs that were right on our heels. I remember that our family fled with the Cloman family members (see Eunice Cloman Jackson vignette), and my dear childhood friend Edna Touchett was running beside me. We made it to safety to Mohawk Park. I remember that during all that riot confusion, I lost one of my shoes. And when we were running from the mobs, we ran down the Midland Railroad tracks as we were trying to get to the section line on Pine and then on to Mohawk Park. Well let me tell you, that gravel on the railroad tracks tore up the feet of us poor scared souls running away from those mobsters hell-bent on killing us! My one unshod foot bled. I was softhearted and felt sorry for my barefoot sister, who hadn't had time to put her shoes on before we fled. Well, I took off that one shoe and let her wear it awhile. It sure helped her out, but that act of kindness caused me to have both of my feet bloodied during that riot. But I didn't mind. My heart led me. I just had no choice. I had to share that one shoe with my sister!

ROBERT DANIEL HOLLOWAY, JR., Pasadena, California, b. December 11, 1918

My parents, Robert Daniel Holloway, Sr. and Roberta Smith Holloway (his first wife), lived at 1224 North Greenwood Avenue at the time of the riot. I remember my father saying that he and my mother lost everything they owned in the riot, but not as much as my grandmother Wilson lost. She owned a lot of rent houses which burned down.

OLIVIA J. HOOKER, White Plains, New York, b. February 12, 1915

My parents, Samuel D. and Anita J. Stigger Hooker, came to Tulsa from Holmes County, Mississippi. At the time of the riot they owned a home on Independence Street which was valued at $10,000 and a store at 123 North Greenwood Avenue which was one of the most prominent stores in the Greenwood District. The home was damaged but not destroyed in the riot. Furnishings valued at $3,000 were either stolen or deliberately smashed and destroyed. Jewelry valued at $1,000, furs valued at $1,000, and silver valued at $500 were also stolen. The estimated total loss of goods that were displayed at the store was $100,000. That makes a total loss of $104,000 to our parents during that riot. There is a record in the Tulsa Court on this, for my father sued the insurance company. A judge threw the case out in 1926 or 1927. Papa's chief witness had a "lapse of memory" on the stand. Papa never got over the chicanery of that witness!

My parents were distraught over the loss of the many beautiful things they had purchased with their hard-earned money. The mobs hacked up our furniture with axes and set fire to my grandmother's bed and sewing machine. After the riot, my mother saved all the artillery shells that mobsters had put in all our dresser drawers!

We did go on with our lives after the riot, but the memories of what happened to us then will never go away. The injustices we suffered the two days of the riot, and the injustices we suffered after the riot when insurance companies failed to pay riot victims for their losses, and when court officials summarily threw out all riot victims' cases between 1926 and 1936, are blots on Tulsa's image that have not been erased to this day.

I graduated from Booker T. Washington High School and went off to college. After I graduated from college I became a teacher. For years, I was at Fordham University in White Plains, New York.

AUTHOR'S NOTE: In a personal letter to the author after the completion of the Tulsa Race Riot Questionnaire, Olivia J. Hooker had this to say:

"I am so enjoying your book *They Came Searching: How Blacks Sought the Promised Land in Tulsa*. Some of the people featured in your book were dear childhood friends of mine, such as Robert Fairchild and his sister, Ruth, who was one of my close friends. We were all in the same class with John Hope Franklin and his sister, Anna Franklin. Helen Foushee and AlmaLene Williams were my other close friends, and also Jewel Smitherman. I was chief 'baby tender' for Jewel's younger sister, Verdell Johnson.

"Have you ever thought of writing a book about 'Great Teachers from Booker T. Washington High School in Tulsa, Oklahoma?' Even after all these years, I attribute much of my love of learning to 'Dad' Mitchell, Gertie Berry, Mr. Roberts, Horace Hughes, and, of course, to the music teacher Carrie Persons, as well as to Mr. J.T.A. West, who was my Papa's closest chum! I was delighted to read so much in your book about Maurice Willows and the noble actions of the Red Cross during the riot. I had never known about his pioneering spirit. Say hello to my dear friend Jeanne Goodwin and to Keith Jimerson, my good friend at Rudisill Library."

Dr. Olivia J. Hooker

SAMUEL HOOKER, JR., Evergreen Park, Illinois, b. January 6, 1918

Until 1999, Mr. Hooker lived in White Plains, New York, with his sister, Olivia. But he now lives in a transitional care center in Evergreen Park, Illinois (a Chicago suburb), and is unable to give interviews.

WILHELMINA GUESS HOWELL, Tulsa, Oklahoma, b. April 25, 1907

When I was a little girl, I used to visit my dad's law office on Greenwood Avenue (Attorney H. E. Guess) and my mother's brother's office, which was also on Greenwood. My uncle was the famous Mayo Clinic–trained surgeon Dr. A.C. Jackson. My family still has a document written by a doctor at the Mayo Clinic in Minnesota in which my uncle was referred to as one of the finest surgeons in the nation! But all that medical stuff didn't mean a thing to me. What was important to me was that this man was my favorite uncle and he had saved my life when I came down with a severe case of scarlet fever when I was eight years old. For a while my family feared that I would die. But my uncle doctored me and I lived. From then on, he was my hero! That is why I was just devastated when I heard that he had been killed in the Tulsa riot. He had already surrendered and had his hands held high in the air. But a young mobster shot him, and he agonized for hours with his mortal wound. He asked for medical help, but he didn't get any. He was thrown into a truck by guards with other captured Negroes and taken to the Convention Center. Before he could enter the center, he died just outside the center's door. The mindless acts of a bunch of hate-filled thugs led to the death of my beloved uncle. They took him away from me, and I will never forget that.

Wilhelmina Guess Howell

The fact that the riot which destroyed my father's office and which led to the death of my uncle occurred in Tulsa seemed very ironic. My relatives had come to Oklahoma to get away from racism, violence, and death in Tennessee. In fact, my grandfather Guess just barely made it out of Tennessee alive. The night before he left Memphis for Tulsa, which was being called a promised land for black people, the mob came for him. But he had gotten word that the mob would be coming, and he had fled to a kind white man's house, where he was hidden in a corn crib under mounds of corn which was in storage for animals' winter food. If it had not been for those kind, courageous neighbors, the mob would have lynched nine black men that night instead of the eight they lynched, and I would not be here today! Those men, and my grandfather, were considered "uppity niggers" because they strived to uplift themselves and to better the lives of their families.

My father had uplifted himself. He had gone to Howard University and had graduated with a degree in law. After the riot burned down his office, he rebuilt and continued to practice law until his death in 1931. My grandpa Guess was also proud of his other son, Dr. James Guess, who was medical doctor in Okmulgee, Oklahoma, for over fifty years. He was a graduate of the famous Black Meharry Medical College in Nashville, Tennessee. I will never forget my daddy, my uncle, A. C. Jackson, my other uncle, James Guess, my maternal relatives, the McMullens, who were equally strong pioneer people, and all the other black people who fled the Ku Klux Klan in the South, and poverty, and poor schools, and a bunch of other problems to come to Oklahoma in search of a promised land. I am sorry that so many of them got caught in that awful riot. But many of them, like my relatives, started over. My dad, H. A. Guess, rebuilt his office and practiced law until he died in 1931. Before he died, he was proud that he had represented black riot victims in their lawsuits against the City of Tulsa. Of course, with so much racism, they didn't win, but I am proud that Daddy put up a good fight for justice!

I tried to carry on the legacy of my families—the Guess and McMullen relatives. I believe the strong old pioneers would be proud of what I did. I tried to uphold the family tradition of educational excellence and service to mankind. As an elementary school teacher in Tulsa for forty years, I tried to give young black students a sense of pride in their ancestry and history. I tried to motivate them to develop their talents, to excel, and to contribute their talents and services to the community. Most of them did. I believe my grandfather would have been proud of me. I sure am glad that he got out of Tennessee that night before the mob got him!

AUTHOR'S NOTE: Mrs. Howell's famous grandfather, Attorney H.A. Guess, was the chief lawyer in lawsuits filed by two black riot survivors, William Walker, in *Walker v. the City of Tulsa*, and Samuel Mackey, in *Mackey v. the City of Tulsa*.

CHARLES HUGHES, Detroit, Michigan

Mr. Hughes lives in a nursing home in Detroit, Michigan, and was unable to give interviews.

MYRTLE WELLS HURD, b. April 24, 1913

Mrs. Hurd was not available for an interview.

VERA INGRAM, Tulsa, Oklahoma, b. March 4, 1914

I was seven years old when the Tulsa Race Riot broke out. My father, Ike Wilson. was working when some men came into the Greenwood neighborhood and told the men to "Get your guns. Come on. We're going downtown to save that boy from being lynched!" They were talking about Dick Rowland, a young black man who had been accused of assaulting Sarah Page, a young white woman. Papa was a janitor at a barbershop on Greenwood, and he had to finish cleaning up the shop. Then he came home and got his gun and went to join the men. He told Mama he was "going to take care of some business." But Mama (Augusta Wilson) knew he was going to join those men who had gone downtown to save that boy from being lynched. She begged Papa not to go, but he said he just had to go. But first, he hitched up some horses to a wagon and had us all pile into the wagon, along with some neighbors, and he sent us out of the Greenwood District to seek safety farther north. We went as far as Lynn Lane, where we stayed all night, hiding in thickets and bushes and sleeping on the ground. I remember seeing bullets being shot from airplanes, seeing the bullets fall to the ground all around us. I saw one woman get shot by bullets that came from a plane.

When the riot was over and we returned home, it was such a sad homegoing. Greenwood was burned to the ground. Our house, which was at 1342 N. Lansing Avenue, was nothing but ashes. I had a big brown bear that I had named "Teddy." I thought a whole lot of Teddy. I slept with him every night. Ever since I had had a memory, I never remember going to bed without old Teddy. But in the rush of leaving our house when the

mobs were coming into Greenwood, I left old Teddy behind. I never saw him again. I sure did miss old Teddy. I still do!

EUNICE CLOMAN JACKSON, Tulsa, Oklahoma, b. August 27, 1903

My mother, Betty Pearce, had moved to Tulsa from Lake Village, Arkansas. At the time of the riot, we were living at 401 E. Marshall Street. Our home was not burned. After the riot, we learned why. There were some poor (economically) whites who lived near us colored folks in the Greenwood District, and they put out the fires that were set in our house. Every time a group of mobsters would set fire and leave, those neighbors went in with buckets of water and dirt and put out the fire. When another set of mobsters would come, set fire, and leave, those neighbors would go in again and put out that fire. They kept doing that all day until the riot was over. Thank God for those kindhearted white neighbors of ours!

Eunice Cloman Jackson

The riot that destroyed our Greenwood District was a terrible thing. It caused so many people so much grief. When the riot began late in the evening of May 31, we sitting out in our yard and people were just running, just running toward us and hollering. Mama yelled, "What is the matter? Where are you people going?" Someone replied, "There's a riot over on Brickyard Hill (in the Greenwood Avenue area). They're just shooting everybody they can!" More colored people came running by, so we joined the running crowd—men, women, and children—all just running like the devil himself was after them. We were stopped by the police at Pine Street and Greenwood Avenue, which was called the section line. Then we were taken to the Convention Center. While we were marching to the Convention Center, one of the policemen noticed a bag my mother was carrying. He said, "What you got in the bag, Auntie?" All the colored folks were just staring at the white policeman. They were scared out of their wits. Mama slowly opened the bag. The policeman looked in and slowly took out my brother's gun! We were all paralyzed with fear, but all the policeman said was, "You don't need this." He kept the gun and we continued on our journey to detention.

After order was restored in Tulsa, white bosses came to various centers where colored folks had been taken and took their employees home with them. My mother's white boss lady took us to her home and fed us and cared for us.

Samuel Malone Jackson, who owned Jackson's Funeral Home at 614 E. Archer, became my husband in 1923. During the riot, he roomed at a boarding house, Howell Rooms. He had a real nice funeral home with modern equipment and a brand-new ambulance. (See Otis Clark's vignette regarding the new ambulance.) Because all the colored funeral homes had been burned in the riot, the City of Tulsa was in a dilemma about what to do with black corpses. I have heard that most were disposed of quickly without any ceremony or anything. But almost all of the few blacks who were embalmed were embalmed by my future husband, Samuel M. Jackson. He told me about that experience.

My husband was paid $25 per body to help Mowbray Funeral Home embalm the few colored riot dead who were taken to funeral homes.

GENEVIEVE ELIZABETH TILLMAN JACKSON, Tulsa, Oklahoma, b. June 29, 1915

My parents, Charlie and Ellen Ersalene Richards Tillman, moved to Tulsa from Arkansas. At the time of the riot we lived on Frankfort Avenue on a hill by where Oklahoma State University-Tulsa is located today. It was called Brickyard Hill then. Our home was rented, and we lost everything in that riot. I was six years old at the time of the riot. Mrs. Whipple kept us Tillman children while our mother worked in the home of a wealthy white man who lived on a hill overlooking downtown Tulsa. The day of the riot, I was with my mother while she worked. Early that morning of June 1, 1921, I was out in the yard and I was just flitting around everywhere, looking at everything—just drinking in with my eyes everything that I saw. What I saw puzzled me. I saw smoke and flames in the sky over the Greenwood area, and I saw what I thought were little black birds dropping out of the sky. But those were no little birds; what was falling from the sky over the Negro district, as it was called in those days, were bullets, and devices to set fires, and debris of all kinds. I always was a curious child. I took notice of everything. Mother, sensing the danger of the situation, told me to go in the house, which I did. But soon as Mother turned her back, I went right back outside to look some more! My mother saw me running around outside and she came and got me again. She said "You sure are a nosy little thing. You just see too much!" I sure did notice everything then. I still do.

Seated: Genevieve Tillman Jackson, riot survivor. Standing L-R: Otis G. Clark, riot survivor, Eddie Faye Gates, Useni Perkins at premier of Perkins' play, "If We Must Die," Greenwood Cultural Center, Tulsa, April 27, 2001

Later on that day, I saw something else that fascinated me. I saw a truck load of dead bodies being carried somewhere. I was just spellbound looking at those bodies—bodies that looked like they had just haphazardly been thrown onto that truck, with arms and legs just dangling. I got closer so I could see better, and I noticed that the faces and arms were black but that when the arms dangled, a person could see white at the top of the arms. I asked about that. I learned that those were white men who had painted their faces and arms black so they could get into the Greenwood community under false pretenses. But when they started shooting down the black people, their game was up and they themselves got shot down.

After the riot we went back to our rented house and found that everything we owned had been lost, either stolen or burned—all our clothes, furnishings, and all other earthly possessions. We heard a lot of talk after the riot about a conspiracy, about how this had not been a spur-of-the-moment thing, but a well-planned conspiracy by the white leadership and the inflamed lower class white mobs to gain control of the Greenwood area. I do believe that this was a conspiracy. My mother said she remembered her white boss and his friends having quiet discussions in which they seemed to be talking about something very serious. It was her boss who insisted that she bring us children to his house in the days before the riot. He must have known that Greenwood was going to be invaded by whites. And he wanted us to be safe.

WILLIE BELL WHITE JACKSON,
Dayton, Ohio, b. June 4, 1910

Mrs. Jackson did not wish to be interviewed and requested no publicity regarding the Tulsa riot. Her wishes have been respected by the Riot Commission.

DR. HOBART JARRETT, New York, New York,
b. November 1, 1915

My parents, Wilson Hendrix and Jo Pearl Nicholson Jarrett, came to Tulsa from Gainesville, Texas. At the time of the riot, their home was located at 1213 North Greenwood Avenue (later changed to 1209), and their store was located on Easton Street. The store was burned down. The home was not burned, though it was thoroughly looted. We had a lovely home that was filled with beautiful furnishings. All that the mobsters left was a phonograph and my Little Boy Blue

Willie Bell Jackson and her brother Allen White,
Tulsa riot survivors.

bank, containing $13 in change, which always sat on top of the piano. That $13 was the family's only income after the riot!

Racial trouble began brewing in Tulsa the night of May 31, 1921, after the *Tulsa Tribune* newspaper carried inflammatory articles about the arrest of the black young man, Dick Rowland, who was accused of assaulting a white woman. From six p.m. on, things kept getting worse and worse. About six that evening, my parents were walking me to a church to recite a poem. From the other end of town—the Brady Street area—the wind was blowing trash toward the north. Trash kept blowing where we were walking, toward Pine Street. It sure seemed like a long walk to me, a six-year-old boy. We saw several men who were going north on Greenwood, going home from work downtown. They were walking so fast! Dad asked them where they were going in such a hurry. But they were in such a hurry, they didn't bother to stop and talk to him. Then Dad saw a man he knew, and he went right over to him and put his hands on the man's shoulders and stopped him. He asked his questions, and he got his answer! The man told him about the Rowland story. That worried Dad. He had seen men with guns and had wondered what was going on. Now he knew. So he turned around and took us home. I sure was disappointed. I had my heart set on reciting that poem!

We went on back home, past Brickyard Hill. My parents were puzzled. They didn't know what to do. On our way back home, we saw that mobs had already reached some of the homes and had burned some of them. We got to 1214 North Greenwood. Then we went on up to my step-grandfather and grandmother's house at 1201 on the corner of Marshall and Greenwood.

My step-grandfather sat on the front porch, holding his gun in his lap. Also at the house were other relatives who had gathered there—the Chester Wilson family, the Roy Wilson family, and the Charles Turner family. Chester Wilson was my grandmother's brother, and he was married to Dora Wilson, a milliner. Roy Wilson was my grandmother's other brother, and he was married to Bessie Mae Nicholson Wilson. Charles Turner was married to my grandmother's sister, Alice Nicholson Turner. Alice and her husband Charles were befriended by his white boss during the riot. What a house full of relatives were there! My great-grandmother was even there visiting. Her daughter from Ft. Worth, Texas, and her ten-year-old son were with her. The men got all the family members together and decided that it was too dangerous to stay. They had seen too many homes nearby that had been burned. They said we were going to run, to run to safety. My uncle, Eugene Wilson, knew where he could get a truck. He came back with a small Ford truck, and all the family members attempted to get into that little truck—five families in all: the Jarrett family, the Chester Wilson family, the Roy Wilson family, the Curry family, and those Wilson daughters. My step-grandfather wouldn't go with us; he remained on the front porch with the gun in his lap. Uncle Gene drove the truck north beyond Pine Street toward Dunbar Elementary School. Then he turned near the Midland Valley Railroad tracks into an area where there was an old rundown park. Nothing was really there but some little old food stands. Mother, Dad, and I found a hole (a little cave) and we hid there. We prayed together. I was so frightened! We wondered where the other family members were hiding. We were so worried about them. We heard a shot, which scared us out of our skin! Some of the men hiding in the area were determined to protect the women and children, so they went toward the shot. The men were armed. Dad had his pistol which he had carried home from work that evening. When the men left, the women and children began crying. Mother was crying, I was crying, and so was my little cousin, Dorothy Wilson, who was hiding in the cave with us. We were all just crying up a storm. Soon the men came back and said they saw no one shot. But they said they did see armed white men. We remained in the cave until morning. Then we continued north into the country. After two hours, we made it to a farmer's house. Dad knew the farmer, because the man bought groceries on credit from Dad's store. The man fed us, and then we continued on north. We stopped at a place near a burial ground and rested a while. Some people passed by and told us that the military had gained control of Tulsa and that we could go home now. This was now June 2, and we had been on the run three days.

When we returned to Tulsa, we were shocked at all the burned homes and businesses we saw, but we were elated that our house had not been burned, though it had been looted of everything except my Little Boy Blue bank and the phonograph. And would you believe it, when we got back, my step-grandfather was sitting on the porch with his gun in his lap! His house had not been burned, but across the street, the rent homes that belonged to his neighbor, Mr. Emerson, had been burned.

Though our house had not been burned, it had been desecrated. All of the good, quality things the looters took with them. What they didn't want they piled in the middle of the floor. Some showed evidence that mobsters had tried to set some pile on fire. Records were smashed, documents, valuable papers, and memorabilia, had been crumpled and torn, if time permitted. And there was evidence left that showed some mobsters urinated and defecated on some items in the house. Oh, yes, they desecrated our house!

Since our house was not suitable for living in at that time, we were taken to the fairgrounds with other homeless black refugees. We were taken in National Guards' trucks. A deputy at the fairgrounds ushered us into a long soup line. We were served pork and beans. People were so hungry they were glad to get anything to eat! I ate two big bowls of pork and beans. For many years, I couldn't stand the thought of pork and beans. They were too connected to my memories of that riot. Years later, I thought to myself, "I'm a grown man and I've got to get over my fear of pork and beans." So I ate a few pork and beans (but not many).

After the riot, my parents thought about moving to Kansas City, Missouri. But they decided to rebuild right in Tulsa. And so they did. Immediately after the riot, when all their inventory had been stolen, the only things they had to sell were Irish potatoes and sweet potatoes. But they soon reestablished their store, and it became a landmark in the Greenwood District until the era of supermarkets ended the mom-and-pop grocery business.

That riot will remain in my memory for the rest of my life, but I didn't let it destroy me. I went on and got my medical degree and was a doctor in New York City for many years. I am now retired and living out the rest of my life in New York City, where I share an apartment with my wife.

ARTIE LACY JOHNSON, Kansas City, Missouri, b. July 29, 1915

At the time of the riot, my parents lived on a street that was called Bullette at that time. Of their four children who lived through the riot, Ovied, Jr., Robert E., Lula Belle, and I, only Lula Belle and I survive. Our house was between the Daniels and the Spears families' homes.

That's about all I can tell you about the riot.

WILMA MITCHELL JOHNSON, Belen, New Mexico, b. August 14, 1919

Mrs. Johnson's nephew, Dale Mitchell of Detroit, Michigan, shared the following information about the Tulsa riot that his aunt had often shared with the family when she was in good health:

The parents of my aunt, Wilma Mitchell Johnson, were William Willis and Barbara Ann Taylor Mitchell, who lived at 1421 North Kenosha at the time of the riot. They owned a restaurant in the Greenwood area. During the riot, William Willis Mitchell was shot three times and left for dead, but he miraculously survived! The restaurant was burned down.

EDWARD EARVEN JONES, Red Bird, Oklahoma, b. March 24, 1920

My parents, James E. and Hattie Helen Sharp Jones, lived on East Davenport Avenue during the riot of 1921 in a house they rented from a cousin. They had come from Morrilton, Arkansas, looking for a better way of life in Tulsa. I was just a baby, and of course I don't remember the riot at all. But I heard from my mother what happened that day in June when they got caught up in the riot. My mother said she was visiting friends when a man came by and said a riot was on. Mother went to the house and got Dad, and they started walking down Easton between Greenwood Avenue and Hartford Street. Mother, who was pregnant with her second child, carried me in her arms sometimes; then Dad would take me to give her a rest. A man drove by us in his Model T Ford car. He picked us up and took us three blocks to get us out of the street. He took us to the place where the street dead-ended at the Sand Springs Street Car Line stop—on Pine Street.

About that time, Mother said some whites in a truck came by. They had their faces painted black. About that very moment, an airplane flew over low and dropped some kind of explosives which hit that truck

Edward Jones, age 22.

with the white men with painted faces in it, killing a lot of them. Those white men were camouflaged guerillas who had sneaked into Greenwood. On the east side of them was another group of whites who had gotten into Greenwood. Mother said one of the men opened a valve on a Midland Valley truck. The group of men who were with him kept urging him on. One kept yelling, "Open it up, open it up!" He got the valve open and set the oil that poured out on fire. We were hiding on the west side in a brushy area, and thank God they didn't see us. The colored men who were guarding and watching us told the hiding Greenwood people to lay low and keep quiet. Everyone did, even including the babies like me. This was in the area where Carver Middle School is located now. Two blocks from there, a man picked us up and took us to Louis Harris' home on North Lansing. We stayed there three to four hours. Then we turned right on East Apache Street by Dirty Butter Creek. We went to Dick Barton's home. He was a white pawnshop owner who was known to be friendly to blacks, who often pawned their good clothes and their guns at Barton's. Whenever they needed their things, they'd go and get what they needed out of pawn. When I grew up, I sometimes went to Barton's to do business. Mr. Barton's wife gave us sandwiches. According to my mother's story, we left the Dirty Butter Creek area and went to a bridge, which they crossed over to Fifty-sixth Street North. There they met up with hundred of scared colored folks. Some of them were half-clothed—women in nightgowns and house slippers if they were lucky, or just barefoot if they had not had time to find shoes; some of the men were in pajamas or long-legged underwear. We were on the north side of a creek near Crown Hill Cemetery. Then we went on to Catoosa and stayed at a gambling house. We met up with an uncle who took us to our relatives in Red Bird.

In Red Bird, we stayed with relatives in the little shanty-house where I had been born. It had only one room and one door (a front door), and it had a little porch on the front. My baby brother was born there a few months after the riot. When he was a crawling baby, he got a hold of some dried beans that had fallen on the floor and ate them. They gave him terrible gas and colic; they just locked up his stomach and his bowels. My dad sent for a doctor, but Red Bird was way out in the country from Muskogee, the nearest town. By the time the doctor got there, my little brother was dead. My parents sure suffered a lot of tragedy in their lives. The worst was that Tulsa race riot and the death of my little brother.

HAZEL DELORES SMITH JONES,
Tulsa, Oklahoma, b. January 19,1919

I am the eighth of thirteen children born to my parents, Willie and Maggie Smith, who lived at 1205 North Madison Avenue at the time of the Tulsa riot. All the seven older children are dead. They could have told more about the riot than I can tell. I was only two and remember only what I was told.

My mother said that on June 1, 1921, my father had gone to work and she was home with the children. She heard the big commotion outside and looked to see what was happening. She saw trucks with militiamen putting black people into the trucks. They were just trying to get all the black people into those trucks! She said she and her children were put into one of the trucks and taken to the fairgrounds, where they stayed two or three days. That is all I can remember that she told me about the riot.

JULIA BONTON JONES, Tulsa, Oklahoma,
b. June 7, 1915

At the time of the Tulsa riot, my parents, Arthur and Emma Bridgett Bonton, lived at 700 Williams Street (now Latimer Street) between the Midland Valley and the Santa Fe Railroad tracks. They owned their home, which burned down in the riot. They lost everything in the riot—furnishings, clothing, and everything else that they owned.

AUTHOR'S NOTE: Mrs. Julia Bonton Jones is a member of the famous Bonton (or Bontempts, as some of the family members spell the name) family, originally from Louisiana. The most famous member of the Bontempts family is Arna Bontempts, the noted Harlem Renaissance writer. A cultural museum in Alexandria, Louisiana, houses many of the Arna Bontempts memorabilia highlighting his literary accomplishments.

THELMA THURMAN KNIGHT,
Tulsa, Oklahoma, b. May 30, 1915

At the time of the Tulsa riot, my mother, Maggie Murray, lived at 619 East Cameron Street (right off Greenwood Avenue). She lived in a rooming house owned by Mama Lula Robertson. The rooming house was behind the Stradford Hotel. That riot was a terrible thing. My mother lost everything she owned. It might not have been a whole lot, but it was hers! I lost everything I owned, including my birthday presents, which I had just received the day before the riot broke out. I had gotten a new white china doll, some other toys, and some new clothes. It sure did hurt me that I never got to enjoy those birthday presents!

Thelma Thurman Knight

LEANNA JOHNSON LEWIS, Tulsa, Oklahoma, b. August 24, 1919

Mrs. Lewis was unable to give an interview.

KATIE MAE JOHNSON LIVINGSTON, Tulsa, Oklahoma, b. May 6, 1921

At the time of the Tulsa riot, my mother, Louvenia Payne, my older sister, and I lived with her parents, Frank and Katie Payne, who had moved to Tulsa from Clarksville, Oklahoma, trying to get in on the good life that was supposed to exist in oil-rich Tulsa. Mother said that riot was the worst experience she ever lived through. She said she was just scared to death. She was running in terror with my sister, who was born when Mother was just thirteen, at her side and with me, a three-week-old baby, in her arms. She said there was fire and shooting everywhere! People were just running wildly trying to get out of the inferno on Greenwood that day. Some kind of way my mother made it safely out of the inferno on Greenwood. She later went to Clarksville and stayed with relatives there.

ALICE HIGGS LOLLIS, Tulsa, Oklahoma, b. June 21, 1906

I just happened to be visiting in Tulsa and got caught right in the middle of the worst race riot in American history! I was staying with a friend of my mother's, a Mrs. Richardson, who lived somewhere in the Greenwood District. One of Mrs. Richardson's sons ran into her house and said, "Get your clothes on. LET'S GO. A riot has begun!" We quickly got half-heartedly dressed, got in his car, and fled to Sand Springs to Dad's sister's house (Aunt Ellen Bryant). We stayed there all night and all the next day. We came back to Tulsa when the guards had regained control of Tulsa. It was a sad sight—nothing but burned-out buildings everywhere, and smoke, smoke, and more smoke everywhere! When we got permission to leave Tulsa, we went home to Rentiesville.

ROANNA HENRY McCLURE, Tulsa, Oklahoma, b. Feb. 21, 1914

My father, William Henry, died before I was born. At the time of the riot, my mother, Lula Row Henry, and I were living with my grandmother, Katie Row, in a house on Pine Place, I believe. On the day of the riot, we left home in fear for our lives. We first sought shel-

Roanna Henry McClure

ter at Dr. Key's house. Dr. Key was a prominent colored physician who lived in a big two-story house on Virgin Street. Then we moved on again. I was a sickly child. I had rheumatism and couldn't walk very well. Grandma carried me in her arms, but she was walking too slow for me. I said, "Put me down. I'll walk myself!" I remember we all got picked up and taken downtown. Then, later, we were taken to a place on Fifteenth Street. The officials in charge put a bunch of mattresses on the floor for the ill colored children. That is where I lay.

ELDORIS MAE ECTOR McCONDICHIE, Tulsa, Oklahoma, b. September 8, 1911

At the time of the riot, my parents, Howard and Harriet Ector, lived at 1431 North Iroquois Street. Our home was not burned in the riot, but we were just scared to death during that riot. As a child, I suffered with fears and nightmares after the riot. Some of those fears, bad feelings, and sadness linger on to this day!

On the morning of June 1, 1921, I was sound asleep when my mother shook me hard and said, "Wake up!

Eldoris Mae Ector McCondichie

Wake up! The white folks are coming and they're killing all the colored folks." I was just petrified. In my nine-year-old mind, I pictured white folks lining up colored folks of all ages and just going down the line killing every colored person in Tulsa! I was so frightened that as we ran with the crowd of folks down the street, going north, parallel to the Midland Valley Railroad tracks, I broke away from the group and ran into the nearest dwelling I saw off the street. It was a chicken coop, and there were some colored people already in there hiding. But my father ran after me and he crawled to the furthest corner of the coop, where I was curled up, just frozen with fear. He dragged me out and we kept running.

I felt that the world was coming to an end. I was just scared to death. On top of everything else going on, airplanes flew low over us as we were running. They were low enough to shoot dead anyone on the ground underneath them. I heard the bullets dropping on the ground, and I saw colored folks dodging bullets, yelling and screaming, and running for their lives. But the

thing that frightened me the most—more than the white mobs right behind us, more than the airplanes, was the sight of the huge, billowing, mountain of black smoke over Greenwood. I later learned that smoke was from the burning homes, schools, churches, and businesses in the beloved Greenwood area. I thought that smoke and fire would catch up with us and that we would all be burned to death.

When we got to the Pine Street area, my father stayed behind to help the wounded and to take care of the dead. Mother, my brother, and I continued on with the crowd, which was going on farther north. A kind white man let us stay at his house. He said, "Y'all come on in. As many as can fit in this house, come on in." The kindness of that man was so comforting to us who were fleeing for our lives. I'll never forget that kindness. We kept on running north, and in Pawhuska we stayed in the home of a black family.

After the National Guard gained control in Tulsa on June 3, people were allowed to come back to the Greenwood area. We returned to our home in the Addition, which had not burned. But we went on up to Greenwood to see the damage that had been done. I walked with my father, who held my hand, from Greenwood to Archer and then on over to Detroit Avenue. It looked like a war zone. Our beautiful Greenwood District, with the famous Black Wall Street business district, existed no more. It had been burnt off the earth!

On Detroit Avenue, I saw something that just became engraved in my mind. It became a symbol of the riot, an icon you might call it. You see, Detroit Avenue is where the wealthiest black people in Tulsa lived—people like Dr. A. C. Jackson, Dr. Bridgewater, and other prominent black doctors, lawyers, teachers, and professionals. Well there was one house that just mesmerized me. That is, the *remains* of that house mesmerized me. For the house had been burned to ashes, along with all its contents that would burn. But along one wall, the fireplace still stood and a section of the wall that had two little windows in it. Well a part of a curtain had remained untouched and was gently blowing in the wind. I was just puzzled by this sight. I wondered how, with everything around it burning, how could that little piece of curtain have survived. I still see that image in my mind to this day.

Another thing that escaped burning during the riot was our church, the little white frame church on a hill on Independence Avenue. Not that mobsters didn't try to burn it. They did. We saw evidence of how the walls of the church had been splashed with some kind of flammable liquid, repeatedly. There was evidence that there had been some combustion, but that the flames would always go out. There was no serious damage to the church, just a black smear on the wall. Our minister, Rev. Burgess, would never let us paint over that smear. He wanted it left for all to see. He said it was a legacy—a gift from God—to us. He said it was proof that God saved our church from the devil. People still talk to this day about the miracle of God that occurred the day of the riot.

Although the church didn't burn, it was left in shambles. It seems that mobsters just went into a frenzy destroying and vandalizing the inside of the church (perhaps because they were angry because it wouldn't burn). Our minister was so distressed about the riot. He died soon after. I remember that when I went to pay my last respects to our beloved minister, I had to step over riot debris which church members had not had time to clean up. Everyone said that terrible riot killed our minister as surely as if he had been shot or burned. His heart was so saddened by what he saw. He just couldn't live with it. There were so many casualties of that riot. I was a casualty myself. For most of my life, I've had nightmares and fears going back to that riot. And I kept things from my children. I would not tell them anything about Tulsa's past history. I didn't want to saddle them with my fears, and I didn't want them to be bitter toward white people. So I just held a lot of things inside myself. It is only after all this focus on the riot the last three and a half years that I have opened up and talked about Tulsa's history—the good and the bad. And my fears have lessened. I am finally coming to terms regarding that riot. I am finally gaining some peace. But I still can't get the image out of my mind of that little piece of curtain gently blowing in the wind in that former elegant home of a prominent black Tulsan!

AUTHOR'S NOTE: Mrs. McCondichie, with her warm, gentle demeanor and excellent recall of events, has been a favorite with the print and electronic media that have covered the Tulsa race riot. She recently fretted because she could not remember the favorite Negro hymn of Allen Burgess, pastor of the little church that wouldn't burn during the riot, but she has found it! And here it is:

THE TRUMPET OF ZION

Blow ye the trumpet of Zion
Sound aloud the Holy Command,

The earth's habitation trembles
Who shall be able to stand.

What a weeping and a wailing
From among the sinful throng,
Men are dying, nations falling
For the day of the Lord is come.

ODESSA BELCHER MALONE, Los Angeles, California, b. September 6, 1912

Mrs. Malone has Alzheimer's disease and was not capable of being interviewed. Her daughter, Marie Taylor, with whom she lives, said that her mother told her children to *never* talk about the Tulsa race riot. She says that her mother never got over that riot, that she never forgot it. It seemed to haunt her all her life. She never got over her hatred toward whites for what they did to the black people in Tulsa. "It wasn't really hatred. It was disrespect for the whites of Tulsa for what they did during the riot," according to Mrs. Taylor. Now, only since she came down with this debilitating disease, does she have relief from those riot memories.

At the time of the riot, she lived with her parents, Robert and Annie Tennel Belcher, in the Greenwood area. Her parents had come to Tulsa from Boley, Oklahoma, the most prominent little all-black town in Oklahoma. Two years after the riot, the Belcher family moved to California.

Mrs. Malone had a sister, Wilma Belcher Kirkwood. Mrs. Kirkwood's daughter, Lorraine McFarland, lives in Los Angeles, California, and told this author the following blood-curdling story:

"My parents, like my Aunt Odessa, never talked much about that Tulsa riot with us children. But Mother did tell us one story that I will never forget. One event of the riot was so engraved in my mother's mind that one day the memory of it just spilled out and she told us of the awful incident she had witnessed during the riot. That incident haunted her every day of her life, until that day in 1995 when she died. On the day of June 1, 1921, when authorities had lost control of Tulsa's Greenwood area to murderous mobs, she and her brother were out walking in the fields near their home in the Addition, a housing area near Pine Street. They had walked into a wooded rural-type area just past the Pine and Greenwood area. They saw some white mobsters in the area. One man had a rope in one hand and a gun in the other. She and her brother, sensing imminent danger, held hands as they hid in some bushes, where they had a good view of what later happened. They saw the mobsters marching a black man and a heavily pregnant black woman to a tree. One of the men hanged the black man first. Then he hanged the black woman. While the woman was hanging from the tree, he cut the baby out of the woman's stomach. The baby was alive and was kicking and screaming. The man then stomped the baby to death!

"My mother said she just blotted everything about that riot out of her mind. She said she had to or she would have gone crazy. But she said the one thing she *couldn't* blot out of her mind was the memory of that lynching. That's why she told us children about it. She said she thought if she talked about it, maybe she could forget it. Maybe it would just fade from her memory. But it didn't. She said the memory of that hanging still haunted her. It was probably the last thing she thought of that day in 1995 when she died."

CAROL SMITHERMAN MARTIN,
Fayetteville, North Carolina, b. December 22, 1912

At the time of the Tulsa riot, my father, Andrew Jackson Smitherman, owned the famous black weekly newspaper in Tulsa, *The Tulsa Star*. Of course, his newspaper building was targeted by hate-filled mobsters, and they burned it to the ground the night of May 31, 1921. Dad was one of the most hated black men in Tulsa because he owned much property and he was so outspoken. He, and a handful of other prominent, outspoken black men like his brother, John Smitherman, J.B. Stradford, O.W. Gurley, and James H. Goodwin, were leaders in the north Tulsa area. Some of them, like my father, had been powerful enough to stop lynchings. They would surely have been killed if they had gotten into the hands of mobsters. During the riot my mother was so worried about the safety of my father, and also she feared for her own life and for us children. But we all survived.

After the riot, my family fled east and we settled in Buffalo, New York. Immediately after the riot, my father's brother, John K. Smitherman, had part of his ear bit off, which he was forced to chew, by white mobsters, purported Ku Klux Klansmen, because he wouldn't tell them where my father was. My father never had the success in New York that he had in Tulsa. When he died, he was buried in Buffalo. But his heart was always in Tulsa. We gave his papers and memorabilia to the Public Library of Buffalo, Erie County, New York.

MARY TACOMA MAUPIN, Louisville, Kentucky,
b. November 9, 1905

My mother died when I was two years old and I was adopted by my mother's brother, Dr. R. T. Bridgewater and his wife. I always called him "Uncle" and I called his wife "Auntie." I was brought straight home from the funeral to live with them. My three older brothers and a sister went to Missouri to live with our father.

My uncle had a good relationship with white people in Tulsa, where he had been Tulsa's first black physician in 1905. He was a graduate of Meharry Medical School in Nashville, Tennessee. Of course, he never got the full recognition he should have in the community, because he was black and there was so much race discrimination in Tulsa then. He ran the hospital where he worked, but white Tulsa wouldn't give him the dignity of being called the director of the hospital. They listed a white man, who never worked there, as director and listed my uncle as the white man's assistant. That's the way things were in Oklahoma then!

I had a good life growing up in the Bridgewater house. My uncle was a strict adoptive parent. He didn't believe in young people attending dances. So balls, proms, etc. were off-limits to me. My uncle's home was at 507 North Detroit Avenue. This was the area where blacks lived in the fanciest homes in Tulsa. My uncle entertained some famous guests, such as Chautauqua stars including lecturer Roscoe Conkling Simmons, artist Samuel Coleridge

Mary Tacoma Maupin

Taylor, artist Clarence Cameron White, dancer Katherine Dunham and her troupe, elocutionist Richard B. Harrison, blind pianist Briane Boone, Mary Church Terrell, and author W.E.B. DuBois, who stayed at the Gurley Hotel when he came to Tulsa early in 1921.

Now, about that awful riot. I was fifteen years old, so I have a good memory of that riot.

There had been rumblings and trouble in the Greenwood community beginning around dusk dark on May 31, 1921. The next morning, things were so bad that we joined the scared blacks who were running down Greenwood to get away from mobs that were pursuing them. Greenwood was under attack, just like in war time. While we were running, airplanes flew over us and began dropping some kind of devices. I don't know exactly what they were dropping, but whatever it was, the devices exploded and set everything they touched on fire. I remember hearing someone yell "Move on! They're bombing us from the air!" Just as I moved, a device dropped from the plane and fell to the ground just behind my heels, right where I had been standing a moment earlier! Dirt flew up where the device had hit the ground, and some of the dirt landed in my hair.

Our house, located in the prestigious Detroit area which had some of the finest black homes in Tulsa, was burned but not destroyed. This area of Tulsa was especially targeted and was the last part of the black district to be looted and burned. White mobsters were especially envious of blacks who resided in this area, like my adopted father, Dr. A. C. Jackson, and others. One mobster was heard to angrily say, "These Niggers have better things than we do!"

Our house was looted and heavily vandalized, but it did not burn, thanks to the intervention of a white judge who knew my father and had helped him with some deeds. The mobsters had begun the fire just before Judge Oliphant arrived at our house. First the mobsters had put into sacks all the good things they wanted to carry with them. Then they broke, defaced, and vandalized what they couldn't take with them. Some of the things were destroyed just out of pure meanness. Our beautiful hand-painted china dishes, gorgeous crystal glassware, vases, etc. were smashed to pieces and piled in the middle of the floor. Windows had been shot out. All my lovely jewelry was gone forever. Every single piece was stolen! My beautiful clothes, many of them lovingly made by my Auntie (adoptive mother) from the finest fabrics in America, were stolen. The everyday clothes which the mobsters didn't want were piled in a mound on the floor.

There were women and children among the looters, and they looked for our "pretty things," our souvenirs and mementoes that were irreplaceable. They stuffed our treasured things into shopping bags and took them, and our memories, away from us forever.

The men mobsters did the fire damage. When Judge Oliphant made it to our house, the mobsters had just poured some kind of flammable oil into my music cabinet and set it on fire. Judge Oliphant said he yelled at the mobsters, "Put that fire out! This is my house." Another group of mobsters had taken my uncle's safe out into the yard, where they had just torn the door off. They believed Judge Oliphant when he told them that this was his house. So they gave him the deeds and other valuable papers of my uncle. The mobsters weren't interested in the papers anyway. They were looking for money. Many black people didn't trust banks during that time and kept large sums of money in their homes in mattresses and other hiding places, or in safes like my uncle did if they could afford a safe.

After the riot was over, after the detention period in which blacks were held in detention camps in Tulsa was over, the National Guard troops allowed us to go back to our homes, or to the piles of ashes that were once homes for most of the black people of Greenwood. It was so sad looking at the destruction. My aunt and I wept when we saw what the mobsters had done to our beautiful things. What they didn't take with them, they had viciously and deliberately destroyed. Some of the looted goods did trickle back to rightful owners. Some recovered articles were taken to fire stations or churches in the Greenwood area, where riot victims could reclaim them after giving appropriate proof of ownership. But most all the looted property was never returned. But I did get a favorite blouse of mine returned, thanks to the persistence of my aunt. Just before the riot, I had made a beautiful blouse. My aunt saw a white woman wearing that unique blouse after the riot. Well, Auntie followed that woman all the way to the woman's house. That woman had no chance of escaping my auntie that day! At the house, Auntie began to hassle that woman. She made her case that that was *my* blouse. She hassled that woman so that the woman took off the blouse and gave it to Auntie. So I did get one treasured thing back after that riot, the blouse that I had made. I was so proud of that blouse. It's curious how a little thing like getting a blouse back made me feel a little bit better after that riot.

My uncle had a rough time after that riot, just as he had before the riot, due to racism and injustice in Tulsa at that time. Uncle was on a "hit list," together with

J. B. Stradford and A. J. Smitherman, before and after the riot. White Tulsans wanted the property of black Tulsans in the Greenwood District. They had tried to buy them out and when they refused to sell their property, they were threatened and intimidated. They especially hounded Mr. Stradford, Mr. Smitherman, and my uncle. They thought if those prominent black Tulsans caved in, then the rest of the blacks would follow suit. When that didn't work, they were besieged by mobsters who destroyed most of the property of Greenwood.

To make matters worse, after the riot the Tulsa Real Estate Board passed an ordinance which was designed to make it impossible for black Tulsans to rebuild the Greenwood district. The fire protection clause just made it impossible that the black district could be rebuilt. Greedy whites thought they had won. They thought they had finally succeeded in running blacks out of Greenwood so they could make an industrial center and a railroad center. Thank God that black attorney B. C. Franklin took up the fight for blacks of Greenwood. He won a lawsuit in which the Oklahoma Supreme Court overturned the Real Estate Commission law regarding the rebuilding of Greenwood. Blacks remained in control of their beloved Greenwood, though it looked like a war zone then.

Mr. Stradford and Mr. Smitherman fled Tulsa during or immediately after the riot, for they were in danger of losing their lives. They were blamed for inciting the riot. The *Tulsa Tribune* had the nerve to say that Uncle ought to be cited for starting the riot because he had brought W.E.B. DuBois to Tulsa to speak, and that blacks had been all riled up ever since!

Many black Tulsans never did recover from that riot. Many moved away, taking nothing with them but bitter memories. Others just rebuilt their lives the best they could. That is what I did. I went to Wilberforce College in Ohio, an African Methodist Episcopal College. I met my husband there. Later, my husband and I moved to California, where we stayed. Now I plan to live out the rest of my life here in Louisville, Kentucky. I still remember that riot as if it occurred yesterday. But I try to not dwell on it. I won't let that riot have the victory over our beloved Greenwood!

WILLIE MUSGROVE MEANS,
Louisville, Kentucky, b. August 24, 1916

In an earlier interview, in 2000 when Mrs. Means lived in Los Angeles, California, she confirmed that at the time of the riot she lived with her father, William

(Willie) Means and her mother in a home on Queen Street, perhaps 760 E. Queen Street. Her father owned the home.

She could not remember much else about the riot.

THELMA FORD MITCHELL, Tulsa, Oklahoma,
b. May 25, 1920

I was just a baby during the riot, and of course I don't remember anything about it except what my mother told me. My mother said that our home at the time was in the Y area on King Street. She said there was a King Street Park nearby. I remember playing in that park when I was a young girl and also playing in an area located between the Midland Valley Railroad track and the Santa Fe Railroad track.

But back to the riot. My mother said things got out of hand so quickly and got so furious and dangerous that she just panicked. In fact, she became so hysterical that she just started running down the street, trying to get away from the approaching mobs, bullets, yelling, and cursing, etc. She even forgot about me. I was left behind! But things worked out all right. Someone got me and carried me to safety, and we all got together again at some detention camp.

Years after the riot, my mother laughed about forgetting me in that riot. But it was no laughing matter during that riot. I wondered how a mother could be so frightened that she would run off and leave her own child. But I knew it could happen, because it did happen and I *was* the forgotten child. I am glad I was too young to feel the panic like my poor mother felt and that the other poor fleeing black people felt during that awful riot of 1921.

ISHMAEL S. MORAN, Alameda, California,
b. January 1, 1920

At the time of the Tulsa riot, my parents, Julius and Edna McLeod Moran, were living at 313 N. Elgin Street by the railroad track near Cameron Street. My dad worked for the National Bank of Tulsa in downtown Tulsa. Before the riot got out of hand, people from the bank came and got us. We lived there for a week. It seems like the people there were aware that the riot was going to happen, for the bank was all set up for us—cots, mattresses, bed coverings, food, etc.

My parents never talked much about the riot. Later, when I asked them about the cause of their silence, they said they didn't want to disturb us children. They didn't want us burdened with riot memories like they were. I have learned more about the riot since 1997, when the Oklahoma Commission began studying the riot, than I did in all my previous years.

I knew a lot of the old-timers who lived through that awful riot—Dr. Bridgewater, Mrs. Cynthia Petit Bankhead, whose husband was in real estate and owned a lot of property in the Detroit Avenue area, and attorney H. A. Guess, who had a law office on Greenwood (and who handled many of the post-riot lawsuits filed by black riot victims). I knew a lot of the riot victims who were my age—Kinney Booker, George Monroe, Dorothy Monroe, and a lot of others. Oh, and I remember the famous Mt. Zion Baptist Church!

RUTH DEAN NASH, Tulsa, Oklahoma, b. September 9, 1915

My parents, John and Lydia Stokes, moved to Tulsa from Moffett, Oklahoma, when I was five years old. At the time of the riot, I believe we lived in a house on Latimer Street. I don't remember if we owned the house or not. I was so traumatized by that riot, I don't remember much about anything, except for my terror. I'll never forget that.

When things began to really get ugly on June 1, 1921, an aunt of mine took us to Pine Street, where we were to meet up with a cousin who would drive us to Muskogee in his Ford car. Well, when we drove down Pine Street to Peoria Avenue, gun-bearing guards met us. I remember one came right up to the car and he had a long bayonet in his hand. I was so scared of that guard and that bayonet that I jumped out of the car and started running back toward Pine Street, where my aunt lived. My mother jumped out of the car and ran after me. Meanwhile, while all this commotion was going on, my cousin couldn't wait on Mother and me. He just slipped away and drove the rest of the family to Muskogee! I don't remember where we stayed in Tulsa during the riot. I believe we were taken to the YWCA in downtown Tulsa. All I know is that I kept my mother and me from getting to safety in Muskogee.

SIMEON L. NEAL, Chicago, Illinois, b. August 31, 1920

My parents talked very little about the Tulsa riot. I do remember that they told me the story of how we got out of Tulsa during all the shooting, looting, and burning of the Greenwood District. My dad had a white friend who came and got us and took us out of the area that was soon to be destroyed. The friend had a wagon, and he had us all lay down in the wagon and he covered us with hay and took us out of Greenwood! Thank God for that kind white Samaritan! While my father lost his tailor shop and three rent homes, all of which were burned to the ground, our lives were saved by that good white man.

ALMADGE NEWKIRK, Barstow, California, b. October 13, 1913

My father, Amos Newkirk, moved from Hennessey, Oklahoma, to Tulsa in 1914. At the time of the riot, he, my mother, and us four sons lived at 119 North Greenwood Avenue, which was our residential dwelling place as well as my parents' place of business. I don't know if Dad owned the building or rented. The business consisted of a bakery and confectionery shop, and a photography studio. We were across the street from the Dixie Theater, near Samuel Hooker's store. The J. E. Hardy family lived on one side of us, and the Gits family lived on the other side of us. Smith's Grocery Store was across the street from us.

On the day of the riot, June 1, 1921, my father left home early with some other men. My mother, a lady friend, and us children headed for Berry Park on the other end of town, where black people were seeking safety.

I was just a nosy eight-year-old boy at the time of the riot. I didn't understand the significance of what was going on. I remember that during the heat of the riot, my mother, my twin brother, and another woman

Almadge J. Newkirk

were running down Greenwood just barely ahead of the mobsters. We were trying to make it to Berry Park to safety. But right in the middle of the riot, my curiosity overtook me. I stopped to look all around to see where the commotion was coming from. But when bullets started falling near me, I was startled and I got the significance of the riot, and I lit out running to keep up with my mother!

After the riot was over, we were allowed to leave the detention areas where we had stayed. When we returned to our home and business, we were so saddened. Everything had been burned, and our pet watchdog had been killed. Shortly after the riot, our family broke up. My mother took sick and sent my twin brother and me off to the Deaf, Blind, and Orphans Institute in Taft, Oklahoma. Her condition worsened and she died. My twin brother and I remained at Taft until we graduated from high school. Our stepfather moved out of the state. The two older boys were old enough to remain behind in Tulsa and to be on their own. I am the only member of my family still living. I sit and think sometimes about that riot. I still remember how it felt to be running from a mob intent on killing you. I'll never forget how it felt to be dodging bullets!

AUTHOR'S NOTE: Mr. Almadge Newkirk lives in a Veterans Home in Barstow, California. He and I have had some wonderful conversations about life in general, about the Tulsa riot, specifically, and about Tuskegee University (my undergraduate alma mater).

One of Mr. Newkirk's retired military buddies at the Barstow, California, Veterans Home is RUSSELL DESVIGNES, a Tuskegee Airman. Mr. Desvignes and this author have had some wonderful conversations about their beloved Tuskegee Institute, about black military personnel in World War II, about racism, the Tulsa riot, and the status of black Americans today. He has sent me autographed photographs and articles about his life as a Tuskegee Airman.

MYRTLE NAPIER OLIVER, Tulsa, Oklahoma, b. 1911

At the time of the Tulsa riot, I was living with my grandparents, James and Fannie Napier, at 526 North Elgin Street. They rented the house from a Mrs. Porter. The reason I was living with my grandparents is because my twenty-six-year-old mother, Martha Colbert, had died two weeks before the riot.

My grandfather was a railroad worker, and my grandmother took in washing for wealthy white folks.

GERALDINE McCOY PAGE, Tulsa, Oklahoma, b. May 16, 1911

On the day the Tulsa riot broke out, I was with my mother in the Cincinnati Avenue home of her white employers. When we saw Greenwood after the riot was over, it looked like a war zone. Our beloved Negro Wall Street had been totally wiped out by the rampaging white mobsters, who had gone on a two-day massacre. It was such a sad situation.

HELEN WASHINGTON PARKER, Tulsa, Oklahoma, b. 1914

Mrs. Washington was unable to give an interview. See questionnaire of her brother, OSCAR DOUGLAS WASHINGTON, for information about the Washington family at the time of the Tulsa riot.

JUANITA MAXINE SCOTT PARRY, Tulsa, Oklahoma, b. June 21, 1919

My father, Julius Warren Wiggins, was born April 15, 1888, in Jacksonville, Florida. My mother, Daisy Scott, was born October 16, 1897, in Blevins, Arkansas. At the time of the Tulsa riot, they lived at 341 (or 404) North Elgin Street. Later, they lived at 707 North Greenwood Avenue. They owned a home and two rent houses. They had a grocery store in front of one of the houses.

My mother was a first cousin of I. H. Spears, who survived the Tulsa riot, also (with his wife, Rowena). Attorney Spears is noted for working in a "law office" (a tent on Greenwood Avenue) with attorneys Peter A. Chappelle and B. C. Franklin. They filed many claims on behalf of black riot victims.

After the riot, the Spears moved to Pasadena, California. The Wiggins family lived on Hartford Avenue in Tulsa after the riot.

IDA BURNS PATTERSON, St. Augustine, Florida, b. January 25, 1919

See questionnaire of JOE BURNS, brother of Mrs. Patterson, for details about the Burns family during the Tulsa riot.

FREDDIE PAYNE, Chicago, Illinois, b. November 8, 1914

See questionnaire of Mrs. Payne's brother, William Scott, for details of the Scott family during the race riot.

JUNE ALEXANDER POWDRILL, San Diego, California, b. March 24, 1917

See questionnaire of JOHN MELVIN ALEXANDER, brother of Mrs. Powdrill, for information on the Alexander family.

ALICE PRESLEY, Los Angeles, California, b. March 8, 1921

My parents, Thomas and Grace Harris Presley, were born in Mississippi but moved to Tulsa seeking a better way of life in the oil-boom town. They were members of the Greenwood community until that race riot destroyed it.

After the riot, my parents moved to Los Angeles, California.

FRANCES BANKS PRICE, Chicago, Illinois, b. October 5, 1913, d. December 2001

My parents, Henry and Irene Banks, came to Tulsa from Coffeyville, Kansas. At the time of the riot they lived at 405 E. Marshall Place in a rented house. The home was not burned. In the early hours of June 1, 1921, we could hear such noise—shouting, screaming, shooting—that we ran from our home. It was about daylight, and we ran down alleys and behind houses until we got to Pine Street. We stayed out of the street and off the railroad tracks, because that's where whites were doing most of the shootings. When we got to Pine Street, a cargo of Home Guards came by. We were marched to Convention Hall (or maybe it was McNulty Park), where we were given sandwiches and drinks. We were kept there through the night and all day the next day. Then we were released.

DeLOIS VADEN RAMSEY, Tulsa, Oklahoma, b. March 5, 1919

My father, Hosea Oscar Vaden, owned one of the most popular pool halls in Tulsa at the time of the Tulsa riot. Vaden's Pool Hall was located on Greenwood Avenue next to Art's Chili Parlor.

DeLois Vaden Ramsey

Across the street was another popular pool hall, Spann's Pool Hall. Younger people went to Spann's, and older people came to my dad's pool hall. Famous people were always coming to play pool at Vaden's Pool Hall. Boxer Joe Louis always came by Dad's pool hall to buy newspapers. Dad sold Black Despatch papers and also white Tulsa newspapers.

My parents also owned a home on Elgin Street which burned to the ground in the riot.

I was too young to personally remember details of the riot, but I heard my parents talk about the riot—how bad it was, how it destroyed so much property that blacks had worked so hard to acquire, and how it burned up the family's pet German shepherd dog.

After the riot, Dad rebuilt on North Peoria Avenue. I graduated from Booker T. Washington High School in 1936.

CORA HAWKINS RENFRO, Chicago, Illinois, b. April 28, 1920

Mrs. Cora Hawkins Renfro is in a Chicago nursing home. The author did interview her once, but she had little recall of what she had been told about the riot. The author did talk to some of the second-generation Hawkins family members, who shared information about the family's riot experiences. Mrs. Renfro has a living relative who is also a Tulsa riot survivor. See account of EFFIE LEE SPEARS TODD.

SIMON R. RICHARDSON, Tulsa, Oklahoma, b. February 12, 1914

At the time of the Tulsa riot, I lived with my grandparents, Eli and Angeline Campbell, who were also raising a cousin of mine, Angeline Williams, who is now deceased. My grandparents had come to Tulsa from Elmore City, Oklahoma, and they lived somewhere on Greenwood, where they owned a home. Their home was heavily looted, but it was not burned.

My uncle, Isom Newberry, lived on Lansing Avenue, and the mobsters burned his house down.

On June 1, 1921, when things got so bad, my grandparents sent me on with our neighbors, the Butlers. The Butlers hooked up two mules to a wagon, and we headed for Mohawk Park to get away from the fast-approaching mobsters. My grandmother and my cousin, who was like a sister to me, were picked up by the Guards and taken to the Red Cross. Men and boys were taken by the militia to the Convention Center. In all the commotion, my grandmother didn't know where I was. I was missing from her for two days, and she was so worried. She was just sick with grief. She thought I had been killed. In a few days after the riot, blacks were released from the detention center and most were reunited with their families. When Grandma saw me and we ran to each other, it was the happiest day ever for both of us! But some people were not reunited; some were never heard of again—like the Butlers, who took me to safety in their wagon pulled by the two mules. I tried to locate them after the riot and even years later, but they were never heard of again. It's like they vanished from the face of the earth. I wonder if they were among the dead that were just dumped somewhere during that awful riot. I wonder if they were buried in some secret place.

Another thing I always wondered about was the death count. I know there was lots of talk about the stacks of black bodies, but I heard about whites who had been killed by black men. My grandfather had a rifle, and he knew how to use it. A lot of black men at that time had excellent weapons and weren't afraid to use them for their protection. I often wondered if Grandpa had killed any white men during that riot.

JEWEL SMITHERMAN ROGERS, Perris, California, b. June 12, 1917

I am the only biological child of the late, famous black Tulsa police deputy John K. Smitherman. My mother, Abbie Billingsley, later married a man named Johnson and had a daughter with him. Dad had two stepsons, Clyde and Donald McGowan. Clyde, Donald, and I spent some memorable times together. Clyde is now deceased, but Donald still resides in Tulsa and continues to be an important figure in my life.

People are always asking me about the "ear incident" my father had with some Ku Klux Klansmen. I asked my father about the incident, but he would never talk to me about it. He just gently changed the subject. I knew he didn't want to talk about it, but I seemed to have such a need to know about it that I'd keep asking him about it. He refused to answer, in a gentle, but firmer, way. I now know that it was just too painful for him to talk about that ear incident; it was just too painful for him to relive it.

At the time of the riot, my parents lived on Elgin Street in a home which I believe they owned. The house was burned down during the riot.

Although my father wouldn't (couldn't) talk about the painful experiences he had with racism before and during the riot, my mother sure did talk. She was a hairdresser, and you know how women talk when they are in a beauty shop! I was raised in a beauty parlor, and I heard much about the awful Tulsa riot from women who were getting "prettied up." It was not a pretty sight that they talked about. No, it was not a pretty sight. That riot was an ugly blemish which has not yet been wiped away.

GERLINE HELEN WRIGHT SAYLES, Markham, Illinois, b. October 26, 1916

At the time of the Tulsa riot, my parents and my grandmother, Nancy Wright, lived at 435 E. Booker Street (later called Latimer Place). My parents owned the home, which was valued at $10,000. The furnishings were valued at $2,000. My grandmother was a beautiful woman. She was part Comanche Indian and had hair that hung down to her waist. I look just like Grandma, and my hair is nearly as long as hers.

Grandma didn't come directly to Oklahoma. She had first lived in Canada. Then she and her family went to Mexico. Finally, they settled in Tulsa. When Grandma Nancy first got to Tulsa, she came down with a bad case of Mexican smallpox. It spread to some of her neighbors. One of them was Jackson Franklin. I remember that that smallpox left some of our neighbors, and Grandma, with some pox scars. (See account of ARCHIE JACKSON FRANKLIN.)

We had lovely neighbors. One of them was Dr. A.C.

Jackson. I was especially fond of Dr. Jackson because I had been told by my family that he was the doctor who delivered me. It sure did hurt me to learn that he had been shot dead by a young mobster after he had done everything that young thug had told him to do! He had surrendered and had his hands held high in the air. Yet he was gunned down like a wild beast. My father was right by Dr. Jackson when he was shot dead. I thank God he wasn't killed, too. Dad was with Dr. Jackson when he, Dr. Jackson, went to check on his house. He witnessed Dr. Jackson's shooting. He said the poor doctor died an agonizing death. The militia ignored his pleas for medical aid. They just let him suffer. He just bled to death. Dad said it was a slow, agonizing death. That riot was just awful. It caused terrible suffering to Tulsa's black people.

JULIUS WARREN SCOTT, b. September 23, 1921, in a tent in riot-devastated Greenwood area

Of course, I don't remember anything about the Tulsa riot, but I remember my mother telling me about it. Mother remembers running down the street, six months pregnant with me, dodging bullets that were dropping all around her. She said that it was a miracle that she escaped alive and that I was later allowed to come into this world. She always thanked God for our safety. My sister, JUANITA MAXINE SCOTT PERRY, also a Tulsa riot survivor, knows more about our family history and the riot than I do.

ORA LEE SCOTT, Los Angeles, California, b. August 4, 1912

My parents, Thomas and Grace Harris Presley, lived in Tulsa at the time of the race riot.

After the riot, they moved to Los Angeles, California. They seldom talked about the riot, so I don't know any of the details of that riot. But I do know that we were in it and that it caused many black Tulsans to lose everything they owned. And many of them left Oklahoma, never to return again. We were among that group that left. My sister and I live together in Los Angeles. We understand that the largest number of Tulsa riot survivors live in California. The second largest number, of course, live in Oklahoma.

WILLIAM A. SCOTT, Chicago, Illinois, b. March 15, 1913

At the time of the Tulsa riot, my father Arthur and

my stepmother lived at 620 North Elgin Avenue in a home that they owned. Everything burned to the ground. My grandmother, Willie Yancey, had a little shotgun house that was left untouched. But only the garage remained on our property. We all lived in that garage—my dad, stepmother, grandmother who came to be with us, and my sister, Freddie Scott (now Payne). We all stayed in that small garage until Dad could rebuild us a home.

TULETA S. DUNCAN SHAWNEE, Los Angeles, California, b. September 7, 1903

At the time of the Tulsa riot, I lived with my parents, James L. and Carrie Duncan, at 1062 North Lansing Street. They owned their home, but I don't know what the value of it was. During the riot, we fled to fields to escape the pursuing mobs, where we hid for three days. I was the only girl among bunches of male Duncans.

After the riot, when National Guard troops had regained control of the city, we returned home. The Greenwood area was like a war zone. But our home on Lansing was far enough from the Greenwood area that it escaped the mobsters' torches. It was not burned. My folks chose not to remain in Tulsa after the riot. First we moved to Detroit, Michigan. Later we moved to Los Angeles, California, where I live to this day.

Tuleta Duncan Shawnee

VENEICE DUNN SIMS, Tulsa, Oklahoma, b. January 21, 1905

My father, Arthur Fritz Dunn, was born in Florence, Alabama, and my mother, Lillian Anderson Dunn, was born in Topeka, Kansas. At the time of the Tulsa riot, they lived at 1027 North Kenosha Street. Our front yard looked up to Standpipe Hill. On June 1, 1921, there had been rumblings the day before and throughout the night that there was going to be trouble in Little Africa. That's what white people called the black part of town. But we hadn't paid much attention to the rumors. In fact, my siblings and I were out in our front yard. We were just looking around to see if we could find what all the commotion was about. All at once, bullets began dropping into our yard. I was just terrified. When bullets are falling all around a person, you just don't know what to do. I didn't know whether to drop down on the ground, or whether I should run. For a while I just stood rooted to the ground. I was just paralyzed. My father had heard bullets hitting the roof

L-R Veneice Dunn Sims, riot survivor, Michael Rosenbaum, Senior Producer, "60 Minutes II," Eddie Faye Gates, riot commissioner.

and the sides of our house, so he ran to find us children. He called us into the house. Then he decided we had better run to safety. The mobsters were getting too close. We could see cars full of white men going down Greenwood Avenue, guns blazing and bullets flying at running black people.

My father's boss, a Tulsa businessman named Sandy McMullen, saved our lives. My dad had the reputation of being one of the best mechanics in Tulsa, black or white. Before he went to work for Mr. McMullen, he worked as a mechanic/driver for Simon Berry's Jitney Service/Bus Company. Papa could fix any car or bus! And he was an excellent bus driver, too.

Anyway, as we were running from the mobsters and just scared out of our wits, who did we see driving down the road? It was none other than Mr. McMullen. He had come to rescue us. I have never been so glad to see anyone as I was to see Mr. McMullen the day of that riot. He took us to his home and kept us until it was safe for us to return to the Greenwood area.

The McMullens had a lovely home. I remember he had a front porch that had glass windows all around it. From that porch, we saw the burning down of Greenwood. It was a pitiful sight.

After the riot, we returned to the Greenwood area and found it just devastated. There were smouldering ruins everywhere. Because they had to flee so suddenly for their lives, black Tulsans lost everything. They didn't have time to get their valuables out of their homes. But the loss of house and furnishings was not my greatest sadness. My greatest sadness was that us Booker T. Washington students missed our Junior/Senior Prom dance, which had been scheduled for the night of June 1. I had been so excited about that prom. The day of May 31, I had been to the hairdresser to get my hair done, and I had laid out my prom clothes. Blue is my favorite color, and there on the bed was the centerpiece of my prom wear—a peacock blue prom dress. Along beside the dress were matching blue shoes, and a pearl necklace that I had borrowed from Mrs. Broaddus, the seamstress who had made my prom dress. Oh, yes, I had a boyfriend that I was looking forward to dancing with at the prom. Of course, he couldn't pick me up at home. Papa didn't allow us girls to date. But I was going to meet up with him at the prom, and I was set to dance with him until midnight, when the prom was to end. But that riot occurred and we never got to have our prom. I never saw my boyfriend again. I heard that he and his family fled to Detroit during the days immediately after the riot. That's what happened. Some blacks walked to safe places in Oklahoma, up to sixty miles by foot. Others hopped freight trains and went north, east, or west. Others were never heard of again and are presumed to have died in the riot and to have been hastily buried who knows where. I've heard they were buried in mine pits, or dumped in the Arkansas River, or incinerated at the park in Sand Springs. I don't know where the bodies were buried. But I do know that we never saw some of our friends and neighbors again. Neither did they communicate with anyone again. I believe in my heart that they were killed in the riot.

A lot of people who did research on this riot—writers, historians, newspaper reporters, and filmmakers were always asking us survivors if we knew Dick Rowland and Sarah Page, the young couple whose actions set off the riot. Well, I did know Dick Rowland and Sarah Page. I knew Dick Rowland's family well. Dick lived with his adoptive parents. His mother was Damie Rowland. They lived at the corner of Independence and Kenosha in one of Simon Berry's rent houses. Although there was strict segregation in Oklahoma at that time and interracial mixing of the races was strictly forbidden, some interracial relationships certainly did go on, especially between people who came into contact with each other on a daily basis. That happened in Tulsa, especially at the hotels and boarding houses, restaurants, entertainment houses, sporting houses, and such places. That's what happened to Dick Rowland and Sarah Page. Sarah Page often visited the Rowland house, which was a combination home and boarding house. I lived near the Rowlands, as I said before, and I saw this with my own eyes, as did many other neighbors. It was common knowledge in the black community that they were lovers. And some whites who came into contact with Rowland and Page on a daily basis had to know it, too. After the riot, we heard that Rowland and Page met up and lived together as man and wife in Kansas City, Missouri.

When things settled down and the military had gained control a day after he riot, blacks who were not taken to detention centers but who stayed with Good Samaritan whites, or with black people who lived outside the riot zone, could return to the Greenwood District. We did that. Oh, Lord, it looked like a war zone. I was just devastated. I wanted to do something to help. There was no school. There had been no prom. I was just ambling about aimlessly. So me and some of my classmates decided what we could do to help black Tulsans. We went over to Booker Washington High School, which had not burned even though it was in the heart of Deep Greenwood. The school had been made an emergency center for people who had been wounded in the riot. The Red Cross had sent supplies, but we were always running out of supplies. I remember that us girls tore up our underslips to make bandages for the wounded. Oh, the wounded people just made me weep. People had bullet wounds everywhere—in their legs, arms, chests. Black men had been especially targeted, and many had been shot right up close by mobsters. But there were some wounded women and children, too. You know a bullet is no respecter of any person! The wounded were in a certain area of the school, and the dead were taken to another room at the school. Many of the wounded men were so badly shot or burned that they soon died. Someone was always going out the door of the wounded room to take a person who had just died to the death room. The dead bodies were buried quickly, without proper counting, or without funerals. You know black people are very religious. We couldn't have survived in this country with all the racism we endured without our faith in God. It sure did hurt black people that their dead were not counted properly, were not treated properly in real hospital facilities (but by laypeople like me and those Booker Washington girl volunteers who had no medical training whatsoever), and, most of all, that they had no funerals.

There was a lot of anger in me at that time, during the riot, right after the riot, and a long time after the riot. A lot of black people felt that way. Some just left Oklahoma and never returned. Others did return and rebuilt their lives here. My family never left. When I am asked what I think about Tulsa today, I tell people that things are better now. The racial segregation by law is gone, but there are still differences between the races. North Tulsa, where most blacks live, is still unequal. It is underdeveloped. It is nothing compared to the great Black Wall Street we had before the riot of 1921

HAROLD (HAL) "CORNBREAD" SINGER,
Nantere, France, b. October 8, 1919

Mr. Singer, during the great popularity of the jazz era, left Tulsa to play the new music in Paris, France. He never returned. He lives in the Paris suburb of Nantere, and he sent the following letter to the author, who was chair of the Survivors Committee of the Riot Commission.

Hal "Cornbread" Singer, Paris, France

"Dear Mrs. Gates:

"I am glad that, at last, the world knows what happened in Tulsa in 1921, and I want to thank you and all the people working with you for taking their time paying this service. Since I was just one year old during the riot, I have no direct memories, and my parents gave me a few details but it has been so long ago that I have forgotten most of them. The last time I was in Tulsa, in 1998, George Monroe took me to what used to be Frankfort Place (now Oklahoma State University-Tulsa) and told me that this was the site of my parents' first home.

"My thanks again and best wishes to you.

"H. Singer"

AUTHOR'S NOTE: Included in the letter from Mr. Singer was the Riot Questionnaire, which included the following information about the Singer family in 1921. Mr. Singer stated that his estimates were based upon what his parents had told him about the riot:

"At the time of the riot, my parents lived on Frankfort Avenue. I can't remember the exact street number, but the house was in the exact location where the university is located today, at 720 North Greenwood Avenue. It was a two-bedroom house with a living room, kitchen, and bath. It was right in the center of black Tulsa and had a small garden.

"It had the normal furnishings for a comfortable black family in Tulsa at that time. The family had plenty of clothes—summer clothes, winter clothes, and Sunday clothes. I estimate the family's loss in 1921 at about $2,200."

BEULAH LOREE KEENAN SMITH, Tulsa, Oklahoma, b. May 20, 1908

My parents, W. M. and Roberta Keenan, lived at 1411 North Lansing at the time of the riot. Their first home in Tulsa had been at the corner of Reading and Norfolk. Before that, they had been guests in the home of Rev. Curtis and his family when they first came to Tulsa from Lovell, Oklahoma. My dad was the first black child born in Lovell. He was part Indian. My mother was, too. They were light-skinned blacks with high cheekbones. I look just like them. Their home was not burned in the riot. The mobs stopped at Marshall Street, which was the street just before our street. Papa was a common laborer who worked at Mann's Grocery Store, which was located at the corner of Lansing and Oklahoma. It was east of the Midland Valley Railroad tracks and west of Greenwood Avenue. The area was called the Lansing Addition.

My first knowledge of the riot was at four a.m. June 1, 1921. I always had to get up at four o'clock to fix Papa's breakfast before he went to work at the meat counter at Mann's store. When I went into the kitchen, I looked out the window and I saw fire. Mann's store was on fire! Mobsters had knocked a hole in the side of the store and had set it on fire.

That was the saddest day of my life. And when I got up that morning, I was so happy. It was the last day of school, and there was a tradition in our school that the day before the last day of school, we would put up our finest exhibits. Then that last day of school, we would have a glorious day. We'd be proudly showing off our exhibits, gathering up our books and things to take home for the summer, and having tearful goodbyes with our best friends. I treasured my books, so that I usually took them home every night. But the day before the last day of school, I had been so focused on putting up my finest exhibits that I had left my books and personal things at school. I never saw them again. They burned up in the carnage that began that night, May 31 and raged all day the next day.

I just loved school. In fact, I had made up my mind to become a schoolteacher when I grew up. But that riot put an end to that. We lost everything we had, and I had to drop out of school to work and help with family support. Not only did I not become a schoolteacher, I was not able to even finish high school. What a loss that was to Tulsa and to society. I had such a calling for the teaching profession, and I had such love for learning and for teaching. I know in my heart I would have been a good teacher.

Back to that riot. When I got up at four a.m. to cook my papa's breakfast and noticed that fire, I ran to wake everybody up. Papa had been warned by neighbors about 11:30 p.m. the night before about trouble between the races. But he didn't believe it. So we went on to bed as usual. But now he saw for himself that Greenwood was on fire. He walked up to Norfolk Street to his friend Eli's home, to see what he knew about what was going on. Eli knew Dick Rowland, and he explained to my father what the trouble was all about. So Papa came on back to our house and loaded my mother and us five children into a wagon and headed north to Peoria Avenue. We met up with other colored people who were fleeing. Then we went east and made it to Turley. We first stopped at the Green family's home, but they were too afraid of the white mobs and wouldn't let us stay at the house, but told us to go on up further where there was a hog pen where we could stay. But before we got to the hog pen, mobsters nearly caught up with us! Child, we had to duck down and hide in the tall sourdock weeds when the mobsters got too near us. One of the colored men would raise up his head to see if it was safe for us to move on; then he would give us the signal to move on if it were safe. And we would run on, desperately trying to get away from the fast-approaching mobsters. Once they got so close. We were shot at three times. My papa owned two guns, and he had his best gun with him—a long army gun. I believe he said it was a "45-70" gun. I remember that it had long bullets.

We successfully dodged bullets from those mobsters all day long, and we made it to the hog pen. We spent the night in that hog pen. Now, it might sound disgusting to be sharing quarters with hogs, but to us it was heaven. We were safe, and that hog pen was smooth and dry. And the hogs were quiet. Now, hogs are usually nosy creatures. They usually poke around at strange things, strange people. And they're usually very noisy—sniffing, poking, and grunting when they are disturbed. But this day, they didn't make a sound. I call it a miracle. Just as God shut the mouths of lions to protect his children in biblical days, he shut the mouths of those hogs and saved our lives during that Tulsa riot!. I remember that I slept by leaning my back against the wall of the hog pen. It wasn't a comfortable position, but I remember being grateful that at least I was safe from the mobsters. But the next morning, my back and neck sure did hurt.

Mr. Green sent for the women and children and hid us in his granary and fed us. About nine a.m. some white folks came looking for people. We were scared, but they convinced Mr. Green that they were friendly. They were the militia that had come to take colored people to safe centers. They informed him that the riot was over and that the National Guard had gained control. So we came out of hiding. When we got back to Tulsa, we found that our home had not burned down but everything in it was lost—either stolen, mutilated, or burned. Mother was most upset over the loss of her bolts of cloth. She was quite a seamstress. She had a big bolt of blue plaid material, a bolt of yellow material, and a little bit of bleached muslin. That's what she was most upset about, the loss of that material. I was most disturbed when I learned that our fine exhibits, our books, and personal keepsakes had burned up at Dunbar Elementary School.

Of course, there were much more serious losses during that riot than bolts of cloth and school books. Many people lost their lives, and others disappeared without a trace. A neighbor boy who was my classmate, Teddy, who was kin to the Morris family, just disappeared. He was never seen or heard from after the riot. An older couple, the Tolberts, were never heard of again after the riot. Oh, Lord, that riot caused so much grief and suffering!

GOLDEN WILLIAMS SMITH, Tulsa, Oklahoma, b. May 20, 1916

At the time of the Tulsa riot, my mother, Willie Williams Pannell Dawson, lived with her second husband in a one-story house on Greenwood Avenue. Mother worked for a white lady, Mrs. Van Horn. During the riot, my mother, stepfather, and I fled the riot area with a lot of other colored people. I don't remember much about the riot. I do know that our home was burned down and that we were taken by authorities to the fairgrounds.

JAMES L. STEWARD, Tulsa, Oklahoma, b. July 12, 1917

At the time of the Tulsa riot, my parents, Finclair and Lillian Clark Steward, lived at 444 E. Marshall Place in a home that they owned. Of course, I was just four years old and don't remember much about the riot. But my parents told me about our terrible experience during that riot. The mobsters set our house on fire. Dad said he tried every door to get us out, but at every door there was a fire! So he knocked out a windowpane

James Steward, right, as a child a few years after the riot.

James Steward as an adult.

and put my mother through it. Then he put me through the window into my mother's arms. We joined the crowd of running, scared black people. They told me how they saw airplanes flying low overhead and dropping some kind of devices that set everything they touched on fire!

Thank God, we all survived the riot. My mother always like to keep notes about things, about people, and events.

AUTHOR'S NOTE: Among the most meticulous and detailed descriptions of Tulsa conditions at the time of the race riot of 1921 that this author examined are Maurice Willows' notes (Willows was Red Cross director in Tulsa), and the handwritten account, on a lined tablet, written by riot survivor James Steward's mother, Lillian Clark Steward.

DOROTHY WILSON STRICKLAND,
Chicago, Illinois, b. November 6, 1912

My parents, Chester and Dora Jordan Wilson, moved from Gainesville, Texas, to Tulsa. At the time of the riot, they lived at 419 E. Latimer Court. My father also built a store on Elgin Street. The store burned down in the riot.

We were asleep when the riot broke out the night of May 31, 1921. Dad's store must have been one of the first buildings set afire by the mobs. I remember that officials came and got Daddy and took him down to where the store was. When he came back, I asked Mama, "What did they do to Daddy?" When he had left he was standing tall and upright. When he came back he was stooped over and pitiful-looking.

I guess authorities thought they had control of the Greenwood District the night of May 31, so when Daddy came back from his burned-out store, we all went to bed. But authorities did not have control of Greenwood at that time. Fighting, looting, burning, and commotions went on all night. Finally, Daddy decided we had better get out of the area. So we hurriedly got dressed and got into Daddy's grocery truck and fled to the Mohawk Park area, where some other black people were hiding in the bushes, undergrowths, and ditches around the park. We had left in such a hurry, I hadn't had time to dress properly, which happened to a lot of other fleeing blacks, who were also improperly dressed. It had been warm inside our house, so I was sleeping only in my panties. But as we were getting ready to get in Daddy's truck to run for our lives, Mother rushed me. She said, "It might be cool tonight. Get a coat." So I grabbed my little red winter coat. That's all I had to wear during the rest of our time as riot refugees—my panties and that little red winter coat. I don't remember why, but the little coat often gaped open and showed all of my body except for the little panties. I guess the coat didn't have any buttons on it. And would you believe it, I lost those little panties! It happened like this. While we slept on the ground at Mohawk Park, mothers tried to keep their young children warm with their own bodies. Well, during the night, I had to relieve myself. A kind woman knew Mother was trying to keep her youngest child warm, so she told Mother not to move and that she would take me to a bush behind where we were sleeping. And she did. But she told me to take my panties off and she would hold them for me. She didn't want me to soil them. So I did. And wouldn't you know it, that is the exact time that the mobsters found our Mohawk Park hiding place! That good, kind lady pulled me up so fast and got me back to the fleeing group that my panties were left behind. I tried so hard to keep that little red coat together to hide my nakedness. But sometimes, it just gaped open and I was exposed. I was so embarrassed, so ashamed. To this day when I think about that riot, I can shut my eyes and still feel that shame and embarrassment washing over me!

When the Guards did finally find us, we were taken to a shelter where a kind white lady gave me a cup of hot milk. I can still hear her sweet voice as she handed me the milk. She said, "Here, baby, drink this." I replied "No, thanks, I don't like hot milk." So that sweet lady went and got me an apple. I still don't like hot milk, but looking back, maybe right in the middle of a riot, I shouldn't have been so particular!

Sarah Tatum, left.

SARAH TATUM, Hartford, Connecticut, b. April 27, 1910

Mrs. Tatum was unable to give an interview. However, her son, Willie Mann, an attorney in Hartford, Connecticut, sent a copy of an audiotape to the commission that his mother made when she was in good health.

LOIS WHITE TAYLOR, San Jose, California, b. September 27, 1919

My older sister, WILLIE BELL JACKSON, and my older brother, ALLEN MATTHEW WHITE, can tell more about the Tulsa riot than I can, but I swear that as young as I was, I can remember one detail about that riot. And that is I can remember us running to get away from the danger (I later learned all the terrible details of the shootings, burning, looting, etc.), and I remember seeing a train on fire on the Midland Valley Railroad track. I remember pointing to the train and asking Mama, "Why is the choo-choo train burning?"

Though I can't remember anything but that detail about the riot, I remember my growing-up days in Tulsa well. I call them my "barefoot days!" We weren't dirt-poor, but we didn't have too much, either. My father worked at the Rainbow Bakery, and the bakery always gave their workers plenty of day-old unsliced bread to bring home. My mother always had a saying that "Wherever there's butter, there's bread!" Well, we had plenty of bread. Mama used to go out in the country to Bixby and pick up nuts to supplement our food supply.

I remember the happy times I had in school—Dunbar Elementary, Carver Junior High School, and Booker T. Washington. We had wonderful teachers and highly motivated students. I loved school and I studied hard. I got double promoted and ended up in the same grade as my older brother, Allen. I sure was proud of that!

Another thing I remember about Tulsa (and Oklahoma in general) is the many Burma Shave signs that advertised Burma shaving cream. One just stuck in my mind all these years:

A peach is pretty with its fuzz
But a man is no peach and never wuz
USE BURMA SHAVE

Isn't it funny what a person will remember about childhood? Those are two things that bring back memories of my childhood in Tulsa—the burning train on the railroad track during the Tulsa riot of 1921 and that Burma Shave ad.

WILLIE MAE SHELBURN THOMPSON,
Tulsa, Oklahoma, b. December 4, 1912

At the time of the riot, Willie Mae Shelburn lived with her stepfather, Dr. Sneed, and her mother, Harriet Jones Shelburn Sneed, on Lansing Avenue near First Baptist Church. They lived in a large brick house, and they lost everything in the riot. Mrs. Thompson could not remember her stepfather's first name. She was very young then, and immediately after the riot, she went to live with her father in Austin, Texas.

AUTHOR'S NOTE: Some of the survivors of the Tulsa riot, who were young children at the time of the riot, mentioned that they had been delivered by Dr. Sneed. So did some of the descendants of riot survivors.

EFFIE LEE SPEARS TODD, Oklahoma City,
Oklahoma, b. November 5, 1908

AUTHOR'S NOTE: Mrs. Todd lives in a senior-citizens center in Oklahoma City, but she told the author that she still has her good mind and good memory. She was right! Here is what she said about the Tulsa riot.

At the time of the riot, I lived with my parents, William Henry and Johnnie Spears. Our house was four or five blocks from Greenwood Avenue, near the railroad tracks. My folks had come to Tulsa from Macon, Georgia. I was a student at Dunbar Elementary School

Effie Lee Spears Todd

which burned up in the riot. Almost all of the Greenwood district burned up in that riot!

On the day of the riot, June 1, 1921, my father had gotten up early. He woke my mother and then he got my brother and me up. We could hear shooting, and we could see smoke and fire everywhere. Everyone in the neighborhood was running. Papa said we had to leave. So we started running, too. My older sister, Lula, was not with us. She worked in a private home in south Tulsa for a white family. Some whites stopped and picked us up. My father and my brother were taken to McNulty Ball Park. I was taken to the house where my sister worked.

When the troops gained control of the city, we were allowed to come back into the black neighborhood. It was in ruins, just like a war zone would have looked. I stayed out south with my sister until my father found another place which he rented. We suffered so much during that riot, and after it, too. A lot of people were killed, and a lot of property destroyed, just burned up by angry, hateful mobs. I feel that survivors of that riot and their descendants deserve reparations.

MELVIN C. TODD, Oklahoma City, Oklahoma,
b. April 12, 1910

Mr. Melvin C. Todd lives in a nursing home and was not able to give an interview. His son, Dr. Melvin Todd, also of Oklahoma City, said that the family home was located on Elgin Street and that it was destroyed in the riot.

KATHRYN MAE TAYLOR TOLIN,
Fullerton, California, b. August 27, 1910

Mrs. Tolin lives in Fullerton, California but was not able to recall much information about the Tulsa riot.

JOHN ANDERSON TOOLE, Chicago, Illinois,
b. February 13, 1915

Mr. Toole is a grandson of the famous Tulsa riot survivor J. B. Stradford. He lives with his niece, Ann-Marie Usher, who is writing a book about the Stradford family, in which she will use many primary documents, including early writings of J. B. Stradford, himself.

BESSIE MAE AUSTIN VESTER,
Perry, Oklahoma, b. September 28, 1919

Mrs. Vester's memory is not good now. She said that all she could remember about the Tulsa riot was that her parents, Simon and Snora Lee Austin, lived on Greenwood Avenue and that her sister, Lucille, was badly burned in the riot.

QUEEN ESTHER LOVE WALKER,
Muskogee, Oklahoma, b. May 4, 1921

Mrs. Walker lives in a nursing home in Muskogee, Oklahoma and was unable to give an interview. Her loving daughter, Brenda Lykins of Muskogee, Oklahoma, supplied the Commission with what limited information she had. She regrets that her grandmother, who used to talk incessantly about the riot, has passed on and that her mother and her aunt, CORINE LOVE CUMMINGS of Chicago, living survivors, are no longer able to share their memories of the riot. Brenda implores people to record their elders stories—in writing and by videotapes so they will not have the void in their family history that exists in the Love family today.

SAMUEL ELIJAH WALKER, Kansas City,
Missouri, b. prematurely in a tent in burned out North Tulsa on September 28, 1921 (his pregnant mother fled from mobsters on June 1st and suffered complications in her pregnancy thereafter)

I have been told that I qualify as a Tulsa riot survivor because I was born prematurely as a direct result of that riot which so traumatized my mother as she ran through the streets, fearful of losing her life (and mine).

Samuel Walker

And my first home was one of those Red Cross tents put up for black riot victims. Our father, Samuel, and his brother, William, lived next door to each other on Frankfort, Avenue. Both owned property in Tulsa. Our big two-story home, which we owned, burned down. So did Uncle William's big two story house which he owned. Uncle William also owned lots of other property in Tulsa including a cleaning shop and some other businesses. After the riot, he and Samuel Mackey were among the first black riot victims to file lawsuits against the City of Tulsa. Of course, the cases were thrown out of court by prejudicial judges. We fled to Mohawk Park to escape the rabid rioters. My sister, Joyce Walker Hill, lost one of her shoes while we were running. See Questionnaire of JOYCE WALKER HILL. Another sister survived the riot, as did a brother, TROY SIDNEY WALKER.

My Dad and his family were early founding members of Vernon AME Church on Greenwood Avenue which was not burned, though the domes on the top suffered some damage.

AUTHOR'S NOTE: Evidence gathered by the Commission that studied the Tulsa riot, and testimony from black riot victims whose claims for damages suffered in the riot were denied, seems to corroborate what Mr. Walker, and other blacks who were denied reimbursements and or compensation, said about biased judges. The Walker lawsuit and the Mackey lawsuit were part of the 20,000 documents that riot commissioners examined during the three and a half year study of the riot. An interesting aside is that among the lawyers for the Walker and Mackey cases was black riot survivor H.A. Guess, and among the lawyers for the City of Tulsa's defense was a white lawyer, Harry Halley, whose name is on the Ku Klux Klan Rolls of the 1920's-1930's at the McFarlin Library at The University of Tulsa. Black survivors said that with lawyers and judges like Halley, Wash Hudson, Jonathan P. Boyd, all card-carrying Ku Klux Klansmen, and many others like them, it was no surprise that they were not compensated for their property losses after the riot as whites were routinely compensated. The minutes of the City of Tulsa, the Tulsa County Commissioners Office, and the Tulsa Chamber of Commerce support this claim. Those minutes show that whites had their claims promptly and routinely admitted at monthly meetings starting in July of 1921. Most claims by whites were almost always promptly and routinely settled. Most black claims were marked "Not Admitted" in the minute records and the few black claims that were marked "Admitted" were usually marked "Claim Denied" in subsequent meeting records. Given the racial attitudes of the time, black Tulsans were not surprised when a white judge summarily, and routinely, dismissed all the claims by black riot victims that, in his opinion, had "clogged up the court system for too long." The Oklahoma Commission to Study the Tulsa Race Riot of 1921 felt that justice had been delayed too long. Its five recommendations, in both its preliminary report of February, 2000, and its final report on February 28, 2001 were attempts to rectify this situation. Situations such as this (the blatant denial of legitimate black riot damage claims in 1921) were one of the reasons that some riot commissioners fought so hard for reparations to be included in the Commission's recommendation, and the reason there is a strong reparations movement in Tulsa today spearheaded by the Tulsa Reparations Coalition.

TROY SIDNEY WALKER, Seattle, Washington, b. August 26, 1918

See Questionnaires of JOYCE WALKER HILL and SAMUEL WALKER, siblings of Troy Sidney Walker for details about the Walker family during the riot.

MARY ELLEN STREET WALTON, Tulsa, Oklahoma, b. June 26, 1921 three weeks after the riot; in the turmoil after the riot, the family could not get a midwife or doctor to assist in the birth, so the baby was delivered with only the help of distraught, untrained relatives

Troy Sidney Walker

Mary Ellen Street Walton

I came into this world as a result of the stress caused by the Tulsa riot of 1921. My parents, Prince and Alva Ford Street lived in the 400 block of Latimer Street, 413, I believe, in a home that they owned. They had come from Louisiana.

My parents had to flee for their lives as the mobsters converged upon their street. Their home was burned to the ground. They also lost a barn.

Our mother worked as a laundress for the Keating family in the 1940s or the 1950s. The Keatings had three boys—twins Frank and Daniel, and a third son who was younger than the twins whose name I cannot remember. Frank Keating is now governor of the state of Oklahoma!

OSCAR WASHINGTON, St. Louis, Missouri, b. February 18, 1912

My parents, Douglas and Ernestine Washington, lived in the 900 block of Queen Street, at 921 I believe, during the riot. My grandparents Henry and Hannah Hale lived on the family farm at Fifteenth Street and North Peoria.

I was nine years old when the riot began and my sister, HELEN WASHINGTON PARKER, was seven. We were out playing in the yard that day of June 1. We looked up in the sky and saw airplanes flying low. Later that evening, things had gotten so bad that black people were just running everywhere trying to get out of the commotion. There were shootings, burnings, looting, airplanes dropping something from the air, (we thought they were bombs) that set everything on fire, etc. in the Greenwood District and surrounding areas. There was just pure chaos and terror everywhere!

The black deputy policeman Barney Cleaver rode his horse through the community warning people to get out quick, to seek safety to the north. So we joined the running, scared-to-death crowds. We took just the first handful of belongings we could grab and ran down the Santa Fe Railroad track. I remember that the item my father picked up was his gun. Instead of running north as did most of the black crowd, we went east to Vinita where we had relatives. We walked every step of the way to Vinita. It sure was a long walk, especially for children.

When peace was restored in Tulsa, we returned home and found out that we were one of the lucky black families in Tulsa. We found that our home had not been touched!

AUTHOR'S NOTE: Most black Tulsa riot refugees fled to nearby settlements and towns such as

Sand Springs, Sapulpa, Alsuma, and Turley. But other fled much further, some of them walking the entire distance. Some went to the north to places such as Nowata. Still others went east to places like Vinita, walking by foot the entire way—fifty miles or more!

MARY LEON BROWN WATSON, Tulsa, Oklahoma, b. October 9, 1909

At the time of the Tulsa riot, my parents, John and Eva L. Brown, lived in the Webb Hotel which was located on the corner of Greenwood Avenue and Archer Street. My mother's sister, Jeanetta Webb, owned the hotel. I was eleven years old. I remember that we lost everything that we owned in that riot—all our clothes, furnishings, treasured things, etc. We fled to my grandparents' farm. My grandparents were Graysons who were Creek Indians who had been in Oklahoma a long time. They had nine children and each child had an allotment of land out in an area called Mingo.

Back to the worst day of the riot, June 1, 1921. We got early notice that trouble was brewing in Tulsa and that there was going to be violence. My uncle, Bailey Webb, was a Tulsa policeman so he had access to prior knowledge about bad race conditions in Tulsa and his warning to us allowed us to get out of Tulsa early. So we didn't stay until the situation got so bad like many of our black neighbors and friends did. We left early and so we didn't have to dodge bullets, fire, and airplanes like so many people did.

ALLEN MATTHEW WHITE, Dayton, Ohio, b. February 4, 1917

On the morning of the worst day of the Tulsa riot, June 1, 1921, my parents, Elias and Clara B. White, joined the crowd of black people trying to get out of the Greenwood District to safety from approaching mobsters. We lived at 1431 North Lansing Street, two blocks from the old Dunbar Elementary School which was near Mann Brothers Grocery Store. We left early enough that Simon Berry's Jitney bus service was still running, so our family hopped on a bus. I was just four years old and I vaguely remember being scared and crying. My mother and my older sister often talked about the riot. That's what I'm telling you now, things I was told about the riot. My mother and sister said that airplanes were flying over the area dropping something that set fires on whatever they hit. Back to the jitney bus. Mostly women and children were picked up by the

Allen Matthew White

jitneys. And oh, what a sight it was on the buses. Women and children were looking out windows at their men folks, and others, who were trying to outrun the mobsters. Babies were screaming. My mother said there was a white man on the bus and he took pity on the fleeing black mothers and their screaming babies. He said "Y'all come with me," and he took them all home with him and hid them from the mobsters.

CECIL WHITE, Berkeley, California,
b. April 5, 1919

My parents, Floyd and Ellen Jeffries White, lived at 427 E. Latimer Street, just off Greenwood, at the time of the Tulsa riot. I was just two years old and don't personally remember details of the riot but I remember what my mother told me about the riot. Her brother, George Jeffries, got shot to death in the riot. My mother never got over the grief of her brother getting killed so brutally in that riot. She grieved about it until her dying day! I know that riot survivors lost a lot of property as a result of the Tulsa riot, and that is a terrible injustice to lose

everything you had sweated and worked to accumulate. But nothing compares to the loss of life. That was the most tragic aspect of the Tulsa riot. And I know about that kind of loss first-hand. I know what it did to my mother's family. Nothing can every make up for that.

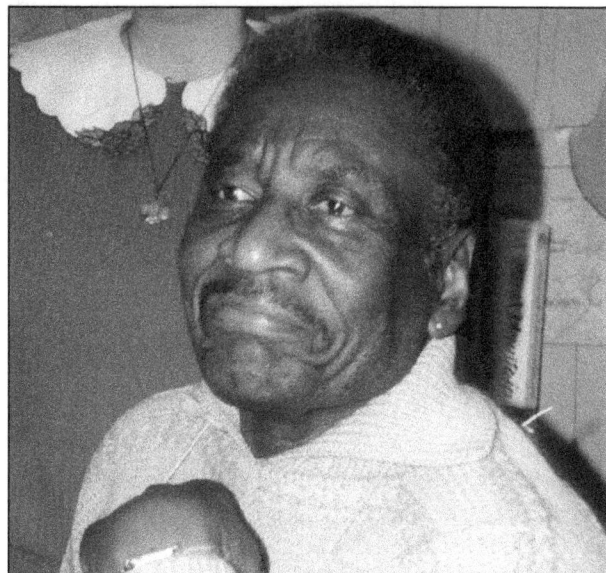

Cecil White

MARIE WHITEHORN, Sacramento, California,
b. April 24, 1910

At the time of the Tulsa riot, I was an orphan and lived with my aunt, Tully Smith who was my guardian, on Greenwood Avenue in a home which she owned. The home was not burned in the riot, but Oh, Lord I sure was traumatized by that riot! I'll never forget that

Marie Whitehorn

day as long as I live. Black people were just running everywhere trying to get away from the mobs and away from bullets and fire that were dropping down out of the sky. The whites who were chasing us were so cruel. We could hear them swearing and cursing us. Every other word they said was "Nigger." It was "Nigger this," and "Nigger that . . ." They treated us like animals. Honey, I was just scared to death!

I have had such a rough life. My mother died when I was very young and I was sent to the Deaf, Blind, and Orphans Institution in Taft, Oklahoma. I had an aunt, Goodson, who lived in Taft. The people at the Institution asked her to take me in. They said children were better off if they were raised by family members. She said the Institution was for children who had no family whatsoever. So my aunt took me in and she raised me with her many children. She was so good to me. She died eight years ago in Kansas.

When I was seventeen, I went to work for a well-off black lady in Tulsa. For some reason that lady didn't like me. We were always getting into it. I *was* a feisty teenager. I had always had to look after myself since I didn't have parents (though my aunt and her children were always good to me). Deputy Police Chief John Smitherman talked to me about the many arguments and fights I got into. He said to me, "Honey, you need to control yourself. Get that anger under control. You'll only hurt yourself. You'll make things worse." But I was young and headstrong then. I didn't listen. Oh, about that black well-off woman I worked for who didn't like me. Honey, she played a number on me. She stashed a lot of her fancy clothes somewhere and called the police and said I had stolen them. Do you know the police arrested me! I was in jail for thirty minutes before my aunt got me out. Oh, what a trauma that was! I never wanted to see the inside of a jail cell again. And I never did.

Oh, yes, I had a rough time during my childhood, but without a doubt the loss of my mother when I was young and suffering through the Tulsa riot of 1921 were the worst things that ever happened to me.

MILDRED EVITT WILBURN, Tulsa, Oklahoma, b. January 17, 1921

Mrs. Wilburn was not available for an interview.

BERTRAM C. WILLIAMS, Seattle, Washington, b. September 22, 1920

At the time of the Tulsa riot, my parents, Johnell and Lucille Hall Williams, lived at 543 E. Latimer Court

Bertram C. Williams during WWII.

Bertram C. Williams at retirement celebration in Seattle, Washington, 1985

in a house owned by my uncle, noted Tulsa attorney Amos T. Hall. I was told that during the riot, my mother, brother, female relatives, and I fled the commotion on Greenwood with other black people to a vicinity near Mohawk Park where we were picked up by troops and taken to a camp.

After the riot, black people who remained in Tulsa tried to resume their lives midst such awful ruins and memories. I attended Dunbar Elementary School, Carver Junior High School and Booker T. Washington High School. I graduated from Booker Washington in 1938. I served five years in the U.S. Army during World War II. I was with the 92nd Infantry (Buffalo Division) in Italy. I was awarded the combat infantryman's badge, three battle stars and campaign ribbons.

I have been married to my wife, Ernestine R. Rutledge Williams for fifty-four years. She is a retired registered nurse. I am a retired Boeing Company manager. We had three children, two girls and one boy. Our youngest girl is deceased.

Today, I am the oldest living member of the Hall/Williams clan. I am proud of my pioneer Tulsa relatives. My grandfather, Cecil Hall, was an architect, builder, and Mason. He and his sons built some of the old black churches in Tulsa before and after the riot. And, of course, almost anybody who has heard of Tulsa, has heard of my uncle, Amos T. Hall. I am the only riot survivor of the clan still alive.

LOUIE BARTON WILLIAMS, Chicago, Illinois, b. September 21, 1912

At the time of the Tulsa riot, I lived with my grandmother, Mary Calvert, on Greenwood Avenue. My grandmother was a cook for a wealthy white man, Jack Strinson, and his family. She stayed in the servants quarters behind the "Big House." During the week, she boarded me out with a lady in north Tulsa. During the weekends, she would come and get me and I'd stay with her in the servants quarters.

I remember that riot well. On May 31, 1921, I went to a movie show with some other children. A fight broke out between some blacks and some whites so we left. When we got home, we began to hear shooting. The fighting and shooting kept getting worse and worse. And it kept getting nearer! But we stayed in our homes. Early on the morning of June 1, I got up and put on my raggediest dress, wouldn't you know it! Well we were ordered to leave our homes and I had no time to change. Child, I was so embarrassed. Here I was run-

ning from mobsters, right in front of crowds of people, and I was in that ugly, raggedy dress! Course, that dress should have been the least of my worries, but you know how children are. Anyway, we were running like cornered animals. We were dodging bullets. We were just following the crowd trying to get away from those cruel, hate-filled mobsters. And wouldn't you know it, another tragedy befell me. I got lost from Grandma! I was just wild with fear and panic. But when I couldn't find Grandma, my instinct just told me to keep following the crowd, to get away from those guns, bullets, airplanes, and fire. By the end of the day, we were away from the danger. We were way away from Greenwood. The militia found us and took us to some kind of shelter where we were given bologna sandwiches and milk. It was like a madhouse—children screaming, women giving birth. It was three days before Grandma found me. If I live to be 100, I'll never forget that riot!

I had no relatives killed in that riot, but a part of my soul was killed. I felt so scared, so alone, not a possession left in the world except that ugly, raggedy dress I had on and a bonnet on my head. I'll never forget being ordered out of our house by the white mobsters. I can still hear one shouting, "Get out! "We're going to set this house on fire." I can still see one of the mobsters

Louie Barton Williams

pouring gasoline over our house as I scrambled out of the house in that awful dress and the little bonnet which was gathered at the brim and had two little string ties that hung down at my neck . . .

WILLIAM HAROLD WOOD, Portland, Oregon, b. May 18, 1921

William Harold Wood was one of the most difficult-to-find survivors. But when we did finally connect, it was well worth the wait! I first heard of Mr. Wood when his nephew Gary Slaughter, a Tulsa policeman, told me about his favorite uncle. Uncle Harold, as his devoted family members call him, did not fit the pattern of other survivors and elderly descendants I had interviewed during my four years research.

After having interviewed over 200 known living black survivors of the riot, over 300 descendants of deceased black riot victims, and hundreds of white witnesses with riot information, I had interviewing and filling out questionnaires down to a science. I had learned that the elderly didn't like early-morning interviews; they said they needed time to get rid of that unwelcome guest from the night before, "Arthur"—meaning arthritis. They didn't like to be interrupted by calls or visits during lunchtime. Some took afternoon naps and certainly didn't want to be awakened from naps. Many went to bed early, such as the now oldest known living black survivor, 103-year-old Rosetta Carter of Kansas City, Missouri. So I learned how to time my interviews. But Mr. Wood was never home when I called! His patient little wife took messages from me and left me his cell phone number. How many eighty- or ninety-something people do you know who need cell phones to track them down? William Harold Wood worked daily in Portland, Oregon, with his nephew Ken Berry.

After numerous attempts to interview Mr. Wood, I finally thought I was all set, but his nephew Ken picked up the phone and told me that he was sorry but I had missed his Uncle Harold once again, for he was half way up a ladder on his way to repair a roof.

But Harold Wood's story was worth the wait. His parents, George Wood and Florence Cherry Wood, owned their own home in the Greenwood District. They also owned a restaurant. During the riot, the Woods and their children joined the crowd of terrified blacks running for their lives down Greenwood.

They were captured by militia and put in a detention camp. When his dad was let out, he moved the family to Coffeyville, Kansas. He just couldn't bear to

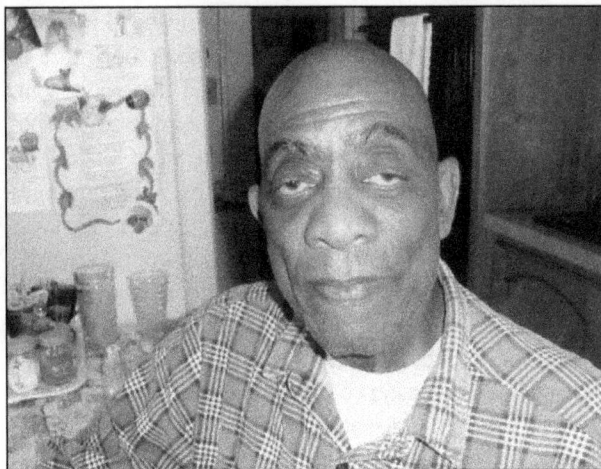

William Harold Wood

remain in Tulsa after that riot. Though the Wood family could not remain in Tulsa, they still have relatives and roots here. They come annually to visit graves and to pay respect to their beloved elders.

BINKLEY WRIGHT, Los Angeles, California, b. November 23, 1909, d. January, 2002

At the time of the Tulsa riot, my parents, Claude and Laura Hamlin Wright, lived at 435 E. Booker Street, which became known as Latimer Street after the riot. Years before the riot, it was known as Henry Street.

About that riot, I was part of it. Yes, siree, I was part

Binkley Wright

of that riot! I didn't actually do no killing, but I was part of the "pass-the-ammunition" team that took part in the fighting June 1, 1921. It happened this way. Wait, I'm getting ahead of myself. Let me go back to the beginning, to the night of May 31. There were lots of celebrations going on that night. Whites were having a school play at the Convention Center (now Brady Theater). Black Tulsans were having their play at the Dixie Theater. My future wife, Clotie Lewis, was ten years old and she was in the play being performed by seniors of Booker Washington High School. She was playing the little sister of one of the seniors, I believe.

My young buddies and I stole a ride on a jitney to downtown Tulsa so we could see that play. We had a lot of experience in jumping onto jitneys going from our home in north Tulsa to downtown Tulsa! One of my buddies was Toussaint Smitherman, the youngest Smitherman boy, who lived on North Detroit where the most prominent Tulsa blacks lived in some of the fanciest houses in Tulsa. His older brothers were Andrew Jackson (A. J.) Smitherman who owned the *Tulsa Star* newspaper and John Smitherman who was a deputy sheriff. John was the one who was kidnapped by the Klan who cut off part of his ear and tried to force him to eat it! The Klan was very active in those days. They were always burning crosses. Even in front of the number 2 Fire Station, the Klan burned crosses! I was always playing with Toussaint and his "poor white trash" neighbors and Mexican neighbors who lived on the east side of Detroit. I remember we were always playing cowboys and Indians. One day while we were playing and horsing around, Toussaint shot and killed a boy over there. But he got out of that trouble because of his influential relatives.

Back to the jitneys. This is how we boys would steal rides. The jitneys would come into north Tulsa and pick up people all along Greenwood, Pine, and the Addition outside of those two areas, and take them downtown. Each jitney had a spare tire on the side of the vehicle. If a boy jumped upon the slow-moving jitney, he could grab the spare tire and hang on for a free ride. The driver couldn't see the kid hanging onto the spare tire. His vision of that area was blocked. There was no glass window on the jitney except for the windshield. So us boys would jump on a jitney, hang onto the spare tire, and steal a ride to town. We'd cling to that tire and we'd jump off when the jitney crossed Cameron Street and Greenwood Avenue. Then we'd slip into the Dixie Theater. That's exactly what me and my buddies did the night of May 31, 1921.

But after the play had been on in the Dixie Theater for only about ten minutes, the bright lights of the theater came on. The manager asked us to leave. No explanation was given. Outside, we heard and saw all kind of confusion—people running, people upset, people talking about a "race riot" being on. We boys didn't know what a "race riot" was. But we sensed that it was something serious. So we each caught a jitney and rode back into north Tulsa on a spare tire. We jumped off the jitneys in the Addition, now the Greenwood and Latimer Place area of north Tulsa. When we got off the jitney, we were talking about that term, "race riot." One boy told me to ask my daddy what the term meant. So I did. Daddy said, "Boy, what you talking about?" We told him about the jitney drivers yelling out at people, warning them about a "race riot." We told him about black men like Mr. Wilson Jarrett and Mr. Chester Wilson yelling to black men to "Get your guns, get ready to defend yourselves and your families; a race riot has broken out!" Daddy put on his hat and said he was going to check things out for himself. He came back later and said "It looks bad!" He carried us out to Mr. Holderness' house. Two of the Holderness boys, Len and Clark, in their twenties, went to Mt. Zion Baptist Church to help a "protective brigade" fight off mobs entering Greenwood. They went high up into the church, into an attic room and they killed many white mobsters who entered the Greenwood area. The Holderness brothers survived, but many black men who were defending Greenwood from Mt. Zion Church were killed when heavily armed white mobs broke through, and when airplanes flew over, dropping bombs or something that exploded and burned everything they touched. Those brave men were no match for that kind of assault. Mobsters falsely accused Mt. Zion Church of being an arsenal for guns and ammunition.

After my dad got us safely to the Holderness house in the section line addition, where there were eight or nine other black families hiding, he went back downtown. Dad worked as a janitor in the Fourth National Bank Building at Fourth Street and Boulder Avenue. Mr. Holderness, the father of Len and Clark, worked there, too, and also a man named West. Before Dad left, he gave Mother his gun and told her to use it if she had to.

Meanwhile, downtown, Dick Rowland was in the city jail on Boulder Avenue just behind the bank building. My daddy knew Dick Rowland who was a porter in a bank building at Second Street and Boulder Avenue. Dad said Dick was going with (courting) Sarah Page, the young white elevator operator in the Drexel

Building. Dad said he met her when he stocked the concession where she worked.

Now back to the riot, back to the fighting, and how I got involved in it. When the white mobs came across the Frisco Railroad tracks, blacks put up a brave fight to keep them out of north Tulsa. But they were outnumbered, so the whites forced their way into Greenwood, shooting, wounding, and killing blacks, and burning down everything in their path. They even burned Mt. Zion Church where those brave men fought so hard to keep the mobs out. They burned it down to its concrete foundation!

Jitneys had driven ammunition into the north Tulsa Greenwood area from downtown where it had been stored and it was then placed behind Paradise Baptist Church. Horace "Peg-Leg" Taylor said "They're getting too many. They're killing too many of our people. I'm going on the hill and take 'em." He was talking about the hill between Haskell and Jasper Streets—Brickyard Hill. Later, he and the blacks who were defending north Tulsa moved on to Standpipe Hill to try to defend the people of north Tulsa who were under attack.

Peg-Leg and the other black defenders of north Tulsa met and "conferenced" behind the steps of Paradise Baptist Church. Then they made a human chain and went up the hill to defend blacks from the white mobs. They told three of us young black boys, Douglas Jackson, Virgil Whiteside, and me, that we could help to defend our people. They told us that the Mayor of Tulsa had opened the Armory and given two machine guns to whites and that whites were using those machine guns to mow down our people. They told us we could be part of history, that we could help defend north Tulsa. And so we did! Our job was to stay behind the steps of Paradise Church and load and reload guns for the human chain of black defenders. And so we did. But the shotguns and rifles of those brave black men could not compete with those machine guns. But those men sure did do their best to save north Tulsa, and me and my buddies did our part to help them! We used hatchets to cut open those boxes of ammunition that the jitneys had brought in earlier, and we kept those guns loaded and reloaded, and we kept that assembly line going, we kept passing those loaded guns to the human chain. But it was all in vain. Those brave black men who were outnumbered were picked off like flies by the white mobs and by guardmen in uniform who were firing those machine guns. Still, our black people put up a brave fight, and my buddies and I were proud to be a part of that movement that tried to defend north Tulsa May 31 and June 1, 1921!

CLOTIE LEWIS WRIGHT,
Los Angeles, California, b. February 21, 1911

Mrs. Wright is not in good health and was not available for an interview. For information regarding her activities during the Tulsa riot, see questionnaire of her husband, BINKLEY WRIGHT.

Clotie Lewis Wright

WESS YOUNG, Tulsa, Oklahoma,
b. February 20, 1917

Note: At the time of the Tulsa riot, Wess Young lived with his parents, Josh and Janie Ford Young, in the 300 Block of North Hartford Avenue, across from the Midland Valley Railroad track going north out of Tulsa. He describes the riot as follows:

On the day of the riot, black men, women and children who were running from white mobsters were picked up by guardsmen. The women and children in our group were taken to Booker T. Washington High School on the corner of Elgin Street and Frankfort Avenue. The men were marched to the fairgrounds in the area of Fifteenth Street and Harvard Avenue. The captured blacks were given vaccines and food. They stayed from three or four days, or as long as two to three weeks, until some white person came and claimed them.

The troops put up tents for the homeless black people. The tents had tops of canvas and sides of lumber. It

Wess Young

was a terrible time for black people after that riot. But they were strong-willed people and they did rebuild Greenwood. All the wonderful buildings, commercial and residential, on Greenwood had been burned to the ground during the riot. It was an exception for a building to remain untouched, though several did. From 1922-1932, black people were busy securing loans, getting money, to rebuild. They had to go out of state for money and building supplies. White Tulsans didn't want black Tulsans to rebuild. They (whites) still wanted the Greenwood area so they could expand northward. But blacks were determined to rebuild. There was new prosperity in the Greenwood area. In fact, Tulsa had recovered so well that it hosted the National Negro Business League Convention in 1926! That League had been founded by Booker T. Washington in the early 1900s. There was such a determination in those black Tulsa businessmen in those days. They just could not be kept down.

AUTHOR'S NOTE: Wess Young is an example, himself, of the determined black business man of Tulsa. He worked hard from the age of nineteen and accumulated real estate in the Tulsa area. He now lives in a beautiful home on Denver Avenue in north Tulsa's Brady Heights Historical District, not far from the Tate Brady Mansion. Tate Brady was a wealthy Tulsa oil man and civic leader at the time of the Tulsa riot. He committed suicide after the riot when evidence was uncovered that cast suspicion upon him (regarding some of his civic and community actions before and during the riot, and regarding his membership in racist organizations).

Wess Young can often be seen in the yard outside his lovely home which was built before the Tulsa riot and which he keeps painstakingly restored and refurbished. Much of the yardwork he does himself.

AUTHOR'S NOTE: In addition to recording the testimonies of survivors onto Questionnaires, about one-third of the survivors were videotaped. James Kavin Ross of Kavision, Tulsa, Oklahoma, is an unsung hero of the Oklahoma Commission to Study the Tulsa Race Riot of 1921. With the blessing of his employer, Oklahoma State University-Tulsa, where he serves as Project Coordinator for Community Relations, he became the glue that held together the local, state, national, and international print and electronic media and the Survivors Committee of the Riot Commission during the numerous videotaping sessions of survivors. His professional training in broadcast journalism and media production, and his experience with Houston, Texas television stations, prepared him well for this task.

Known affectionately as Kavin—(pronounced Kevin; he long ago gave up trying to tell people how to pronounce Kavin as KAVIN. He now just answers to Kevin!—this multi-talented young man helped survivors get to various interview sites. He then helped them with their walkers and wheelchairs, and for diebetics, their snacks, got them settled in their chairs, and with his gentle, warm and caring personality, he put them at ease, and recorded their vital information for posterity.

Before the videotaping of riot survivors, the spotlight was on me as producers from the major television and radio studios from all over the U.S., and the world, converged on Tulsa seeking riot information. I was their contact with the survivors and my phone number became a well-known number to them for a while. Add to that journalists from major local, state, national and international newspapers and magazines and you will get the picture—a picture of frenzy, a feeding frenzy, to satisfy the world's sudden demand for Tulsa's riot information. During the post-production period, after interviews with riot survivors, the focus of national media shifted to Kavin where his media expertise was in demand.

After the interviews with survivors had been completed, the spotlight shifted to Kavin. It was his phone ringing off the hook then, instead of mine, as Michael Rosenbaum and Jill Landes of *60 Minutes II,* producers of *Dateline, Nightline, the Today Show,* Tony Brown's Journal, Tim Reid's Productions, Tavis Smiley, Tom Joyner, Mike Wilkerson of Barrister's Studios of Tulsa, and others prepared their productions for airing. These producers, and I, learned what a joy it is to work with this gentle, quiet, unassuming, talented young man. He is a tribute to his parents, Don Ross and Diane Ross. You two did a great job raising that son of yours (and your other five children)!

CHAPTER 5

Known Widows / Widowers / Heirs of Deceased Black Survivors

The widows of riot victims, strong, successful women in their own right, cherish the memories of their beloved spouses and often share with authors, researchers, the media, and others what their pioneer spouses told them about the Tulsa Race Riot of 1921. There was one widower, Theodore Dargan, when this riot study began but he has passed on. Below are listed the names of each riot survivor followed by the name of each spouse or heir.

PETER ADDISON CHAPPELLE—heir Elizabeth Cooley Chappelle, widow of Peter Addison Chappelle's son Dr. T. Oscar Chappelle

OPAL LONG DARGAN—heir Theodore Dargan, widower

ROBERT FAIRCHILD—heir Florence Fairchild, widow

JAMES H. GOODWIN—heir Jeanne Osby Goodwin, widow of James H. Goodwin's son Edwin L. Goodwin

LYNN HOLDERNESS—heir Jobie Elizabeth Holderness, widow

JAMES HAROLD LATIMER—heir Hazel Latimer, widow of Fred Latimer, Sr., son of James Harold Latimer

Elizabeth Cooley Chappelle

Jobie Elizabeth Holderness

RICHARD WESLEY LOUPE—heir Mary Loupe, widow

MARY PAYNE, heir Lorell Kirk, widow of Thomas Kirk, son of Mary Payne

LOYD REED ROLLERSON—heir Myrtle Fagan Rollerson, widow

THEODORE SMITHERMAN—heir Claudia Maude Smitherman, widow

MARVIN SPEARS—heir Betty Spears, widow

SYLVESTER STRIPLIN—heir Rose Striplin, widow

DELMAR TILLEY—heir Pansy Tilley, widow

Myrtle Rollerson

CHAPTER 6

Known Black Survivors of the Tulsa Race Riot of 1921 Who Were Alive at Time of the Creation of the Oklahoma Commission to Study the Tulsa Race Riot of 1921, but Who Have since Died (Estates Still in Probate)

One of the saddest things for a researcher doing interviews for a significant project is to have one of the participants/subjects die. This happened thirty times after the Oklahoma Commission to Study the Tulsa Race Riot of 1921 was created in 1997. I grieved thirty times. They came so close to justice, but they died without recompensation!

But in August 2001, when we lost five survivors during the month, I began to simply write by each deceased person's questionnaire testimony, "DECEASED," and I noted the date of death. Most who died since 1997 are listed below, but refer to the Living Black Survivors List for the names of those who died near the end of 2001 and whose testimonies could not be added here due to time constraints.

ARNETTA McNEAL ANDERSON, Chicago, Illinois, b. 1916, d. 1999

Mrs. Arnetta McNeal Anderson was one of three delightful sisters, all survivors of the Tulsa Race Riot of 1921, who lived together in a house in Chicago, Illinois, which they all loved and shared. (Other riot survivors who share a home are the Lilly sisters, Muriel Mignon Lilly Cabell, Hattie Lilly Dunn, and Jimmie Lilly Franklin, who live in Los Angeles, California).

The oldest sister, Theressa McNeal Gilliam, was the acknowledged "head of household," or "boss" of the precious little family. The twins, Arnetta McNeal Anderson and Jeanette (formerly Johnetta) McNeal Bradshaw, were faithful followers. Mrs. Gilliam, the wittiest of the sisters, joked that between the three of them they would comprise one healthy human. She had the sharpest hearing and was the ears for the family. Jeanette had the best eyesight and read for the family.

Mrs. Gilliam has lost so much of her sight that she is classified as legally blind. The three sisters adapted gracefully to their aging and utilized their remaining physical abilities as best they could and went on with their peaceful lives as they always had.

The three sisters were so appreciative of what the Oklahoma Commission to Study the Tulsa Race Riot of 1921 did for survivors and descendants of the riot. As Chair of the Survivors Committee of the Commission, I became their favorite Commission contact. They telephoned me frequently, sent thank-you notes, photographs, and news articles, called in to their favorite Chicago talk show hosts and chatted about the riot and the work of the Commission, and called me when they needed to hear a Commission update, or when they just needed to hear the voice of one who cared about them.

The death of Arnetta McNeal Anderson was a blow to the two remaining sisters. I comforted them as best I could, and they shared with me information about Arnetta's nine surviving children. I will never forget those three sweet sisters and their loving, peaceful little family in Chicago. They are typical of the strong, loving, religious people that were born and raised in the Greenwood area of Tulsa, Oklahoma, who could not be stomped down not even by the worst race riot in American history!

ANNIE BIRDIE CARTER BEAIRD, Tulsa, Oklahoma, b. June 13, 1913, d. August 28, 2001

During the last week of August of 2001, Tulsans reeled with sorrow, for we lost four survivors in Tulsa that week and learned of the death of a fifth one in California. One of the deaths that was mourned was that of Annie Birdie Carter Beaird. Just before the funeral, a member of the Beaird family called me and informed me

Annie Birdie Beaird

that Mrs. Beaird had not received the letter of commendation, the resolution of honor, and the survivors medal that other survivors had received in June. I immediately canceled all my engagements and pursued the task of locating those items before Mrs. Beaird's funeral. The Greenwood Cultural Center staff and Rep. Don Ross' staff at his Capitol office in Oklahoma City joined me in the search. Mrs. Beaird's packet was not at either location, so it had not been returned, but must have been lost in the mail or misplaced at the Beaird house during the days of her final illness. Frances Fleming, of the Greenwood Cultural Center, used her computer to create the missing documents, and she gave me another medal for Mrs. Beaird. When I delivered the items to the grieving family, they were elated that their beloved relative finally had the documents she had longed for and the medal to be buried with.

Before her death, Mrs. Beaird, with her portable oxygen tank in tow at all times, had been a faithful attendant at Riot Commission meetings in Tulsa, where she often gave interviews to visiting media persons from all over the world. She is sadly missed by all those who ever came in contact with her!

SAMUEL LANGFORD BELL, SR.,
Niland, California, d. 2001

In April of 1999, Samuel Langford Bell, Sr., sent me a long, handwritten letter in response to an article he had read in the *Los Angeles Times* about the Tulsa riot. I responded with a telephone call, and we had the best old time reminiscing about Tulsa. He shared information with me about his Tulsa days, his military experiences during World War II, and about his life in Los Angeles after the war to the present. As I was once a military-dependent spouse in the U.S. and in Europe, we had some things in common. Below are excerpts from Mr. Bell's letter:

Dear Mrs. Gates:

I am a Tulsa boy. Sorry Mrs. Gates, I don't write so good. I have had a stroke and heart attack. I'm trying to do my best. (Author's note: Mr. Bell's writing was fine, was perfectly legible. One thing that Tulsa teachers had stressed in the elementary years of the riot pioneers was good penmanship. All the riot survivors signed release papers on their questionnaires with perfect penmanship. Their teachers would be proud of them!)

My parents, Dick and Ida Mae Bell, and my Dad's parents, Ike and Mollie Bell, all lived on Elgin Street, near the old Booker T. Washington High School, at the time of the 1921 race riot. They are all on the 1918 Tulsa census rolls.

I fought in the Philippines on Luzon in 1944 and 1945. When I returned to Tulsa after the end of World War II, I attended high school in Sand Springs, Oklahoma and graduated in 1948.

I later moved to Los Angeles, California, and have been here ever since. I am a retired bus driver of R.T.D., Los Angeles, which is now known as M.T.A. I have a home here in Los Angeles and I also have a motor home. Sometimes, I go all over the U.S. in my motor home. I hope to hear from you sometime.

Yours truly,
Sam Langford Bell

AUTHOR'S NOTE: Mr. Bell's children, Sandra L. Bell Perkins, Samuel Bell, Jr., and Rena L. Bell, live in Tulsa.

LENA ELOISE TAYLOR BUTLER,
Seattle, Washington, d. 2000

One of the most interesting of the 167 survivors that I interviewed was Mrs. Lena Eloise Taylor Butler, for she was the daughter of one of the most respected and revered black Tulsa pioneers—the legendary Horace "Peg Leg" Taylor, who stretched his one-legged body prone on Standpipe Hill and shot invading white mobsters who were destroying his beloved Greenwood district.

Mrs. Butler, her children, and her grandchildren first heard about the Riot Commission on a CNN television broadcast on August 3, 1999. She described how she felt when she saw Charles Zewe of CNN and me walking around in the cemetery at Sixth Street and Peoria Avenue. When she saw me pointing at the only two riot-victim graves with headstones (those of Ed Lockard and Reuben Everett), she had the daughter whom she lived with contact me. She needed to talk about that riot. And oh, did she talk! She said that at the time of the riot she was nineteen years old and lived in a rented house on the corner of Easton Avenue and Exeter Street, which was just east of Booker T. Washington High School. Her father owned eight storfront properties in mid-Greenwood, which included business offices downstairs and twenty-one upstairs rooms. She said there were no riot deaths in her family but they suffered much property loss. She remembers how sad she was when she saw black men, with their arms raised high over their heads, being marched to the Convention Center. She described how mobs of whites—old men and women, young men and women, and children, jeered and threw things at the men.

Though I had asked many people how Horace "Peg Leg" Taylor had lost his leg, no one knew. I knew his daughter would know. She did. Here is what she told me. When he was nineteen years old, Horace Taylor was still living at home and did what most black children in rural Oklahoma did in those days. He worked on nearby white farms to help supplement the family's meager income. That fall he was picking cotton on a nearby farm. He had picked hard all day, had gotten paid, and was getting ready to go home. But the boss, the man who owned the farm, happened to come by at that time. He felt that it was too early for Horace to leave. He ordered Horace to pick some more cotton until it got too dark to pick. Horace had other plans and refused to remain. As he started to walk away, the man grabbed him, overpowered him, and began to beat him. Mrs. Butler was not sure, but she thinks some other white men must have aided the boss, because she remembers hearing what a strong and powerful young man her father was then. Anyway, she said that Horace Taylor was tied up and carried to a nearby railroad track, where his whole body was tied to the tracks. Mrs. Butler is not clear about why the train did not stop. All she knows is that it did not stop and that one of Horace Taylor's legs was severed. The impact of the train threw the young man away from the track and into some weeds, where he lay moaning and bleeding for a long time.

Two little white ladies heard the moaning. There are no details about who they were, whether they lived together, or whether one was visiting the other. What is known is that those two ladies saved the life of Horace Taylor. They followed the sound of that awful moaning until they came upon the suffering man. They dragged him to the farmhouse. Mrs. Taylor said their dad often talked about those "two little angels" that God sent to him that day. He said they cauterized the bleeding stump to destroy any dead tissue and to prevent infection. Then they took turns nursing him around the clock for two weeks. Though he was eternally grateful to those two little ladies, Horace longed to get back to his own home, which was just a little shanty in the Oklahoma backwoods. After two weeks, the "little angels" thought their patient was well enough to go home. So they took him home. His mother, who had spent every waking moment, in prayer—silent and verbal—was overjoyed to see her son, though she nearly fainted when she saw his leg. So I finally learned how "Peg Leg" Taylor lost his leg.

ROSA L. GREEN BYRUM, Lanham, Maryland, d. 2000

Due to aging and/or health problems among the Green, Hughes, or Starr families, who were riot survivors, I was never able to interview any of them. A relative, Patricia Williams, who was then a employee at the University of Wisconsin, provided me with information about her riot-connected relatives, many of whom went to Maryland after the riot. One, Charles Hughes, lives in Detroit, Michigan.

CELESTINE DANIELS, Tulare, California, b. May 15, 1902, d. 2001

On January 13, 1998, I had a delightful interview with Celestine Daniels, who shared the following information with me. At the time of the riot she was nineteen years old and lived in a rented house on the corner of Easton Avenue and Exeter Street, just east of the original Booker T. Washington High School. The house burned down. Her father owned eight store-front business in Mid-Greenwood, which included downstairs business offices and twenty-one upstairs rooms. There were no deaths in the family but much property loss. Mrs. Daniels spoke of how she saw black men, with their arms held high above their heads, being marched to Convention Hall on June 1, 1921. She said it still brought her grief all these years later just to remember

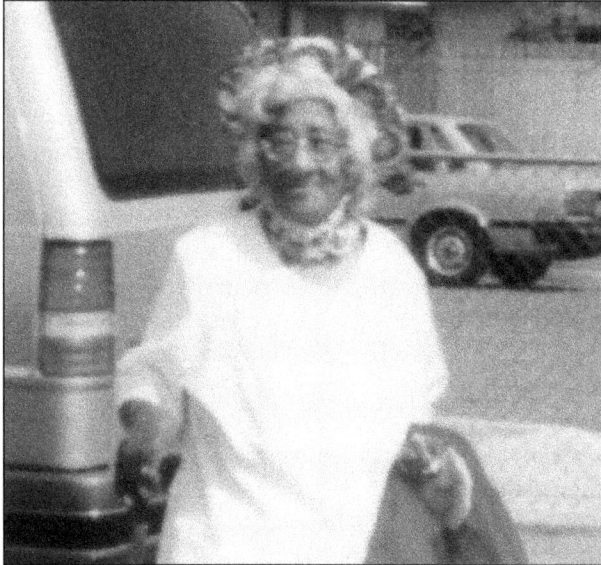

Celestine Daniels

that scene—old white men and women, young white men and women, and children shouting, jeering, throwing objects, and spitting on those men!

FLIPPER FAIRCHILD, Los Angeles, California, b. December 29, 1912, d. March 2000

When Flipper Fairchild's family noticed the "Last Call" for riot information in the *Los Angeles Times* in August or September of 2001, it was too late for an interview with Flipper Fairchild. He had died in March of 2000. His ninety-two-year-old widow, Yuri Fairchild, supplied me with basic information about her husband but said she had been so distraught since his death that she couldn't remember much. She did recall that her husband did speak of the riot, but she can't remember much of what he said.

HUBERT JEFFERSON GREEN,
Lanham, Maryland
Mr. Green was not able to be interviewed.

CLEO CHERRY HARDING, Tulsa, Oklahoma, b. July 19, 1916, d. September 16, 2001

What I remember most about Mrs. Cleo Cherry Harding is how much fun she had being interviewed and videotaped by Kavin Ross and me representing the Oklahoma Commission to Study the Tulsa Race Riot of 1921, and the two German newspaper correspondents she allowed us to bring along. Mrs. Harding was beauti-

ful in one of her "fancy dress outfits" complete with a saucy little hat. The newspaper men were absolutely smitten with her and called her "Queen Cleopatra" the rest of the day. They adored her house with its little nooks, crannies, and cupboards filled with dainty art glass, china, and pottery from the past. Nifty little lace dresser scarves, sofa arm covers, place mats, and tablecloths were everywhere. Dainty sheer curtains rustled in light breezes that day.

While Mrs. Harding's accounts of her riot experience did not add any startling new information about the riot, her quiet, reflective story, and her showing us some of her riot-connected memorabilia, did help us to better understand that event, which had such a profound effect on so many people so long ago and which still affects the Tulsa community.

She said that at the time of the riot, she lived with her parents at 713 E. Tecumseh Street in a home that they owned. They also owned a store. Mrs. Harding said that the Booker T. Washington Club House in Tulsa is located on the very site where their home stood. Because the reporters and I spent so much time looking at Mrs. Harding's lovely home and memorabilia, we had to cut short the interview and go to another scheduled interview. Mrs. Harding invited me to come again, and she promised to tell me more and to show me more. But that was a promise that she couldn't keep. I was so saddened when I read in the *Tulsa World* about her death in September of 2001. I will never forget how she looked that day we interviewed her, how she pranced around in her finery and took us on a tour of her house.

Cleo Harding

RUBYE KELLEY HENDERSON,
Tulsa, Oklahoma, d. 2001

Mrs. Rubye Kelley Henderson was a sweet, quiet little woman who agreed to an interview with me in 1998. At the time, she lived in a nursing home in south Tulsa. Most black Tulsans live in north Tulsa, and I had interviewed quite a few who lived in north Tulsa nursing homes. Mrs. Henderson was the first black riot survivor that I interviewed in the nursing home where she lived.

Ever since that interview, I meant to go visit that dear little lady again, not because I needed more riot information, but just to be a friendly face for her to see. We talked on the phone many times, but I was so busy with the riot interviews and riot research that I kept putting off a personal visit. Now it is too late! In March of 2001, Mrs. Henderson died.

IOLA STREETER JACKSON,
Tulsa, Oklahoma, b. 1905, d. 1998

Mrs. Iola Streeter Jackson answered that first call to come to the Mabel B. Little Heritage House to be interviewed by the riot Commission on April 16, 1999. She was quiet and reserved and kept apologizing for not having more vital, important, earth-shaking riot information. I told her that her just being there was vital and significant, for she was a living witness and that anything she shared with us was primary source material and infinitely more important than any secondary source, no matter what significant person or place it came from! She smiled, her sweet little face relaxed, and she gave me information. By the end of the year, she was dead. I am so glad she felt the need to come forward that day and share what she knew and had observed about that riot. I am glad that I convinced her of how important she was to the Tulsa community. I am just so sorry that she did not live to see a full recompense for her suffering.

ELWOOD LETT, Tulsa, Oklahoma,
b. December 16, 1919, d. 1999

Mr. Elwood Lett was one of the most colorful of the riot survivors and one of the most interviewed by the print and electronic media from all over the world. He was a favorite of us researchers and writers, and we played right into his hand. Because he knew he was a "national treasure," he called in his cards whenever he felt like it, and we came a-running at his beck and call!

We just absolutely adored him, and we wept and paid tributes to him when he died. One reason he was so widely interviewed is that he was one of the few living survivors who witnessed the death of a relative at the hand of a white mobster. He told the story many times about the death of his grandfather. I have seen the most in-control media persons wipe away tears when Elwood Lett told that story!

Mr. Elwood Lett was fascinated with the world and always had been. He showed me photographs of himself when he was a professional dancer in Los Angeles, California, when he was a handsome young man in his twenties. He had other photographs, printed articles, vintage fashions, and memories invaluable to researchers. Mr. Lett was as astute as an African vendor in getting his "merchandise" to the right "client." He knew how to bargain! Dr. Scott Ellsworth, the Tulsa-born and educated Oregon college professor who wrote the premier book about the Tulsa Race Riot, *Death in a Promised Land*, was a favorite of Mr. Lett.

Scott Ellsworth had the privilege of meeting Elwood Lett long before I knew Mr. Lett existed. But when Mr. Lett's path crossed mine after I was appointed to the Riot Commission, we instantly became good friends. He and Scott were bosom buddies. From Scott, he ordered hamburgers and milk shakes. He wanted me to drop everything and come when he had more riot information for me to come by and record. Also, he wondered if I would go by the post office and pick up some stamps for him or run some other minor errand for him. Scott and I never had to be prodded. We loved the man and would have done anything for him. But he always embellished his requests with a dire medical report. We were often told that this might be the last request we'd ever receive from him, for he was sure he wouldn't live until . . . Sometimes, he would actually give a date that would be his last day on earth. His faithful "servants," like Scott and me, often joked about this "crying wolf" syndrome. That is why we were so saddened when Elwood Lett died. How we wished it had been a "crying wolf" tactic, but it wasn't! That dear little man was gone forever from his beloved Greenwood District, where he lived out the remainder of his life. Whenever he beckoned, I ran to his little apartment on Newton Street, just a block off his beloved Greenwood Avenue. I am so glad that I did. The world is a more knowledgeable place today because Elwood Lett shared his life history with us.

MABEL BONNER LITTLE,
Tulsa, Oklahoma, d. 2000

Mrs. Mabel B. Little was the queen bee of riot survivors. She knew it, and she reveled in her status. After all, the Mabel B. Little Heritage House, right in the heart of Deep Greenwood in the former Black Wall Street of Tulsa, is named for her.

When Mrs. Little died in 2000, Mt. Zion Baptist Church, which was burned to its foundation during the Tulsa riot and later rebuilt, was packed with Tulsans of all races and religions who came to give their last homage to beloved pioneer Mabel B. Little.

Her minister, Dr. G. Calvin McCutchen, who came to Mt. Zion over forty years ago, said that Mrs. Little had planned her funeral many times but she kept coming back to him and demanding the program back! But that final plan of Mrs. Little was carried out at her funeral that day in 2000. I was one of the mourners there.

Before Dr. McCutchen's compelling eulogy, there were the usual proclamations and remarks. There were proclamations from the state and from the city. Then there were remarks from those who were closest to Mrs. Little in the past—her beloved nephew, Oliver Maurice Thompson, a retired Los Angeles Police Department officer, whom she helped raise when he was growing up in Tulsa. Then there was Clara Skillens, the loving caretaker of Mrs. Little in her final days, whose poignant remarks brought tears to the eyes of mourners.

On the way out, I overheard two women talking about Mrs. Little's influence on their lives. Their comments perfectly summarize the life and times of Mrs. Mabel B. Little. One women said to the other, "I admired and respected Mrs. Little, but we never got along very well. I had my way of doing things, and she had hers." The other lady replied, "Oh, you didn't get along with Mrs. Little. You just did what she said do!"

Mabel B. Little was loved in life, loved in death, and she will forever be loved in the collective memory of Tulsa!

RUBY McCORMICK, Tulsa, Oklahoma,
b. November 29, 1911, d. 1999

The survivor death that shocked me the most was that of Mrs. Ruby McCormick. At the first videotaping of riot testimony by Kavin Ross and me on April 16, 1999, at the Greenwood Cultural Center, Mrs. McCormick seemed to be in good health. In fact, she was bright and cheerful. A little over a month later, she was dead! She went into the hospital for routine eye surgery and died suddenly. I wish that I had had the time to do the follow-up interview that Mrs. McCormick and I planned to do in her home later. But neither she nor I knew that day that her time on earth was going to end so soon. Still, I am grateful for the brief testimony that she gave that day. Ruby McCormick is a part of the recorded collective memory of the Tulsa Race Riot of 1921.

Mabel B. Little

Ruby McCormick

AUGUSTA MANN, Tulsa, Oklahoma,
b. April 21, 1910, d. 2000

I first met Augusta Mann in 1994 when I began interviewing black pioneers in Tulsa to be featured in an oral history section of my second book, *They Came Searching: How Blacks Sought the Promised Land in Tulsa.* She was an animated little woman who flitted about her large, lovely home on Norfolk Avenue just up from the Greenwood Avenue and Pine area of north Tulsa,

Augusta Mann

where she lived with her husband, prominent Tulsa grocer M. M. Mann. She showed me Bibles, photo albums, old, yellowing news clippings, plaques and awards hanging from her walls, and other tangible evidence of the existence of the mighty Greenwood district, also known as Black Wall Street. Then she told me about the destruction of Black Wall Street on May 31, 1921, and June 1, 1921.

I interviewed Mrs. Mann a second time, in 1999, to gather information for the Riot Commission. She was much frailer, and quieter and more subdued in her new home, a nursing home, on East Virgin Avenue in north

Tulsa. I am glad that I had my notes and videotape from that first interview before her memory faded. There, in her home surrounded by her memorabilia of a lifetime, she poured out her story about Greenwood—all its travails and turmoil, plus all of its glory!

FRANCES ROSTON WALKER MILLER,
San Francisco, California, d. 1999
DAVID ROSTEN WALKER MILLER,
b. 1920, d. 2000

Mrs. Frances Roston Walker Miller and her infant son, David Roston, survived the Tulsa Race Riot of 1921. I interviewed David Roston once and gathered information about his mother and how they suffered during the riot. When Mrs. Roston Walker Miller died in San Francisco in 1999 and when David Roston died later in 2000, David's daughter, Netra Rosten-Warren of Las Vegas, Nevada, sent me obituary materials which helped me to flesh out the history of the Rosten Tulsa riot survivors.

EMMA B. TOOLE MONROE, Chicago, Illinois
(Stradford heir), d. 2000

Mrs. Emma B. Toole Monroe was the daughter of the famous Tulsa pioneer businessman J. B. Stradford, who owned the finest black hotel in Tulsa at the time of the Tulsa riot in 1921. Neither Mrs. Monroe nor her brother, John Anderson Toole of Chicago, were able to be interviewed. Their niece, the great great granddaughter of J. B. Stradford, Ann-Marie Usher, also of Chicago, served as spokesperson for the Stradford family. She was interviewed numerous times by this writer. (Her uncle John Anderson Toole lives with her.) Mrs. Usher graciously provided primary documents of her famous great great grandfather, J. B. Stradford, to the Riot Commission, including excerpts from his memoir and a handwritten account of his harrowing experience of being separated from his wife during the riot and fearing that she was dead! Mrs. Usher is presently at work on getting all of J. B. Stradford's writings published, and on her own personal book about the Stradford family and the effects the Tulsa Race Riot of 1921 upon them.

GEORGE DOUGLAS MONROE, Tulsa,
Oklahoma, b. May 27, 1916, d. August 23, 2001

George D. Monroe was one of the most popular of the riot survivors and was sought out for interviews by

George Douglas Monroe

almost every print and electronic media individual or organization that came to Tulsa to cover the Tulsa Race Riot of 1921. Although he was busy taking care of his beloved yard, vegetable garden, rental property, and, most important of all, restoring his "Pink House" Lounge, which he planned to reopen soon, he always stopped and obliged the media. He felt that it was his obligation to share his firsthand account of the riot with the world. He hoped lessons could be learned that could help prevent future atrocities. The reason people all over the world were so captivated by Mr. Monroe's story is that it chronicled how damaging the riot was to children. After wars, revolutions, riots, etc., many authors write specifically about the trauma to children caused by such events. Here is what George D. Monroe had to say about the riot:

"One memory that I just can't get out of my mind is the night of the Tulsa Race Riot of 1921, when I was five years old. When my mother looked out the window and saw white mobsters with lighted torches heading for our house, she yelled at my brothers and sisters, 'Get under the bed *now!*' The mobsters broke into our house and went straight to the curtains and set them on fire. When the mobsters were going over to set the curtains on fire, one of them stepped on my finger. I hadn't got as far under the bed as I should have. I was about to let out a scream, but my older sister, Lottie, put her hand over my mouth. Thank God she did. I shudder to think what that mob would have done to us if they had found us under that bed! That riot was so terrible—oh, the loss of life and property! Our family business, a skating rink in the Greenwood area, was totally destroyed, and my dad was never able to rebuild it. That just devastated him. After the riot, the only job he could get was as a janitor in a white theater. That riot destroyed so many promising lives. And it saddens me to see such resistance to reparations for riot victims. I know I will never live to see reparations. This city and state will never be ready to pay reparations to black people, not in my lifetime!"

George Monroe was right. He didn't live to receive reparations, or any of the voluntary monetary donations or in-kind services provided to riot survivors by the Tulsa community. I was at his funeral at St. Monica's Catholic Church in his beloved Greenwood area. As I said my farewell, I was saddened that this dear man carried the wounds of the riot to his grave and that justice had not come soon enough. I was also sorry that I would not ever get the chance to be at the reopening of his Pink House Lounge and hear George Monroe make music again. I had promised Mr. Monroe that I would be there. I would have, too. My friends know that I never break promises.

THEODORE O. PORTERFIELD,
Tulsa, Oklahoma, b. February 8, 1917, d. 2001

I had never heard of Theodore O. Porterfield, but on that first day of videotaping riot survivors at the Greenwood Cultural Center, on April 16, 1999, he was one of the first survivors to show up. What a joy it was for me to meet Mr. Porterfield. He enriched my life from that day forward until the day he died!

Painfully frail and thin, he was nevertheless full of zest for living. Our friendship was instant and took on an urgency that must have been compelled by the fact, not known to either one of us then, that it would be cut short so soon. But Mr. Porterfield and I crammed a lifetime of pleasant conversations and shared public events into the year and a half we had together as friends! He attended almost every riot-connected event from that April day, absent only during hospitalizations. At events, I would look out across the room and see those piercing brown eyes searching for me. I would go to him instantly. Because he was so frail, I would always go to the buffet lines and bring food to Mr. Porterfield's table. He had a voracious appetite for such a thin little man.

Theodore Porterfield

Sometimes, I had to go through the buffet line a second time for him.

Oh, how I miss Mr. Porterfield. Sometimes at riot meetings, programs, and events, I find myself looking out at the faces of riot survivors and almost instinctively look for those piercing brown eyes of Theodore Porterfield. But they are not there anymore. My heart grieves that Mr. Porterfield and eighty other riot survivors went to their graves without justice, without recompense for the sufferings that they and their families endured. That is why for three and a half years, with my loving family's permission, I put my personal life on hold and became an advocate for the riot survivors. I dedicated most hours of the day to research, recording, and writing on their behalf. It was so urgent to locate, find, and examine the "evidence of history." The Riot Commission did just that. Now we are waiting for the nation to "do the right thing" and provide justice for survivors and descendants of the Tulsa riot.

FRANCES BANKS PRICE, Chicago, Illinois,
b. October 5, 1913, d. December 2001

Frances Banks Price

CORNELIUS REYNOLDS, Tulsa, Oklahoma,
b. 1907, d. February 27, 2000

Late in 1999, I contacted Mr. Cornelius Reynolds for an interview about the Tulsa riot and he graciously agreed. But before I could get to Mr. Reynolds for that interview, he died in 2000. According to his only heir, Rosetta Daniels of Tulsa, with whom he lived, he had outlived four wives, the last of whom died in 1995. Mr. Reynolds' time came, too, on a cold February day in Tulsa.

LILLIE SKELTON RICE, Tulsa, Oklahoma, b. February 21, 1895, d. 1999

Mrs. Lillie Skelton Rice was one of the few centenarians among the riot survivors that I interviewed, and during her delightful interview she shared information about ordinary people and about powerful people, such as the presidents she remembers, about technological changes in America, her first sight of an airplane, the sinking of the *Titanic*, Halley's comet, the assassination of Martin Luther King, Jr., man's first walk on the moon, and many other things that happened in during her long, colorful life.

Lillie Skelton Rice

OLA SHAW, Tulsa, Oklahoma, b. September 24, 1905, d. 2000

Mrs. Shaw was unable to remember much about the riot. Her sons, Ronnie, Jodie, and Arnold Shaw, could not remember their mother talking much about the riot. When I asked survivors why they had not talked more with their children about the riot, most said they had two reasons: (1) They did not want to burden their offspring with the horrible details of the riot. (2) They did not want their children to harbor racial hatred in their hearts.

SAMUEL SIMS, Oklahoma City, Oklahoma, b. 1906, d. 1999

HERBERT SKELTON, Halstead, Kansas, d. 1999

LUEDA SMITH, Louisville, Kentucky, b. 1881, d. 1999

WILLIE SMITH, Tulsa, Oklahoma, b. March 5 (or 15), 1921, d. 2001

WILLIE DORFORD SMITH, SR., b. July 25, 1910, d. August 23, 2001

Willie Dorford Smith, Sr., a retired railroad porter, would never answer the telephone in his home. His loving wife, Delores, did all the talking for the household. Stressing the significance of the Riot Commission's work, I implored her to try to get him to talk to me. But he wouldn't budge. He told her he was old, hard of hearing, and tired, and he didn't have much faith that something would be done about the riot injustice anyway. After all, eighty years had passed and nothing had been done for survivors and descendants of survivors of that riot. And then one day, he was watching an Oklahoma Public Broadcasting System report about a recent Riot Commission meeting in which I was fearlessly defending reparations for survivors and descendants of the riot (Oklahoma Educational Television Authority, Channel 11). He told his wife to call me. He said to her, "That lady is so sincere. She is really trying to help us riot victims. Call her. Since I can't hear well, I'll tell my story to you and you tell it to her." And that is how I got the riot information from the reluctant Mr. Smith at last. Mrs. Smith said it was like a floodgate had opened. For the first time, Willie Dorford Smith talked about that riot, and the demons that had haunted him for years fled at last. His sweet little wife was elated, for even she had not been able, throughout the long years of their marriage, to get her husband to talk about that riot and to let it go. Here is what Willie Dorford Smith said about the Tulsa Race Riot of 1921:

"At the time of the riot, my family lived on top of Brickyard Hill (near present-day Oklahoma State University–Tulsa, at 700 North Greenwood Avenue). My parents, Robert and Josephine Bruner Smith, had moved to Tulsa from Wewoka, Oklahoma. When my mother left for work, May 31, 1921, we made an agreement to meet that evening at the Dreamland Theater. I was going by trolley car to spend the day in Sand

Springs with relatives. But when I came back by trolley car that evening, things were getting out of hand in Tulsa. In fact, the conductor on the trolley car told us that race tensions were so bad that evening that the trolley car couldn't go on to its normal stop at Greenwood Avenue and Archer Street. So I got off the trolley and walked east on Archer until I got to Greenwood. Sure enough, my mother was waiting for me in front of the Dreamland Theater. Things were so bad in Tulsa that my mother said we would not go home that evening to Brickyard Hill. We would go to Sand Springs and stay with our relatives. By then, there were no trolleys going to Sand Springs. So my mother and I started walking. We walked up by Dr. Bacoat's house.

Then we walked as far as the waterworks place, and a kind white man picked us up and gave us a ride to Sand Springs! We stayed in Sand Springs with our relatives for a few days. Then when the National Guard restored order in Tulsa, we returned home. When we were going to our home on Brickyard Hill, we were met by guards. They questioned us about where we were going and what did we want. They wouldn't let us return home then. They took us to the Ball Park. We didn't know it then, but we didn't have a house to return to. It had burned down in the riot. When we found that our house had burned down, we went back to Sand Springs and stayed with relatives. I never talked about that riot because I just wanted to forget it. I just didn't want to think about how it felt to be a ten-year-old boy wandering around, looking for his mother, having no home, staying in a detention center, and with relatives—just roaming around, lost, with everything I had known and loved burned up. I just wanted to forget about that riot!

WILLIS WEST, Tulsa, Oklahoma, d. 1998

JULIUS WILLIAMS, d. 1999

CHAPTER 7

Known Black Descendants of Deceased Survivors of the
Tulsa Race Riot of 1921 Speak Out

This was one of the most challenging chapters in the book. First, there was a larger category of persons than for any other group—more than 300, as of November 2003. As in the case of the 200 known living black riot survivors, the descendants had interesting family history and/or riot information. All descendants will be listed under the caption of their riot survivor ancestor, along with brief, biographical information. When available, more in-depth information provided by the descendants will be included.

The same procedure used in chapter 4 to whet the appetites of readers will be used in this chapter. The categories are the same. The compelling testimonies are likewise. The most interesting of all of the descendants interviewed was EDWARD LAWSON, who has homes on the East Coast and the West Coast. You might not recognize his name, but Mr. Lawson, known for his habit of walking daily in his California neighborhood, made history when his lawsuit (regarding his walking habit) ended up in the U.S. Supreme Court! Read his entire testimony to see why he filed his lawsuit, how it was settled, and what the unique Mr. Lawson is doing today.

Descendants' references to Tulsa's political, economic, and social phenomena at the time of the riot are similar to those of survivors of the riot.

Specific references that differed from those of survivors will be covered here:

Descendants Who Had Relatives Shot and Killed in the Riot

Descendant GERALDINE PERRYMAN-TEASE said her late mother, survivor ADDIE PERRYMAN-TEASE, had a brother, BOB PERRYMAN, who was shot and killed in the riot.

Descendants DR. D. GRANT WILLIAMS, St. Louis, Missouri, and his sister, DOROTHY WILLIAMS BRAMLETT, had both parents, FISHER JAMES WILLIAMS and DINAH FREEMAN WILLIAMS, and their grandparents, JOHN WILLIAMS AND WIFE in the Tulsa riot. The parents and grandmother survived; the grandfather did not. He was shot on June 1, 1921, and died of his wounds on June 21 at St. John's Hospital in the colored "ward" in the basement. In one of the first coverups of the riot, the actual cause of death—the gunshot wound—was omitted; instead, the cause of death was listed as asthma and syphillis!

Descendants JESSIE THOMPSON and ARTHUR JEFFERSON spoke of the shooting death of their uncle, survivor "SAUCER" GRAYSON. The nephews can find no relatives who remember the legal first name of this uncle. No one can remember him being called anything except "Uncle Saucer."

The Lynching

Descendants BERNICE LAWYER AND LORRAINE McFARLAND, of Los Angeles, California, remember hearing their mother, deceased riot survivor WILMA KIRKWOOD, tell of how she and her brother witnessed the lynching of a black man, a pregnant black woman, and the born-alive baby (by stomping) by mobsters during the riot.

The Riot: Shot and Wounded

Descendants DIANA LYNN SHELTON and SHIRLEY SHELTON of Oklahoma City, Oklahoma, remember that their grandmother, OLLIE STEELE, a Tulsa beauty shop owner at the time of the riot, was wounded by gunshots to both legs during the riot. She had to keep both legs wrapped in surgical bandages for the rest of her life, and she had to walk with a cane until her death in 1960 at age ninety. The quality of her life was destroyed by that riot!

Other Wounds

Descendant LINDA EDMONSON GRAVES said her dad's knees bothered him ever since the riot in 1921. Survivor LUTHER EDMONDSON damaged his knees permanently during the riot. He had no choice. With a rabid group of mobsters in hot pursuit of him that June day in 1921, he jumped into the Arkansas River and swam across, where he escaped to safety in the little town of Sand Springs. LINDA GRAVES remembers her father always massaging his damaged knees for the rest of his life.

The Riot: Missing, Presumed Dead

Descendant MARY A. WILSON of Englewood, Colorado, says her family grieved over her missing grandfather, DAN WILSON, ever since the riot. He was never heard from since they last saw him the first day of the Tulsa riot.

The Riot: the Beaten, Bruised, Burned, 'Buked, and Scorned

Some survivors of the riot told their descendants about beatings, burnings, crippled knees, and other physical pains. Others spoke of mental wounds. Specifically, they spoke of the cutting wounds caused by the verbal abuse of white mobsters, including hate-filled men, women, and even children. They specifically speak of the prolific use of the "N" word by jeering, cheering crowds of whites. "It was Nigger this, and Nigger that," they painfully recall. Some said that they had to fight for nearly a lifetime to overcome hatred for those white mobsters; others acknowledge that they have not yet reached full forgiveness! See the testimony of descendant DOROTHY JONES, about her survivor ancestors RICHARD and VIOLA HUGGINS, for a poignant example of verbal abuse.

The Riot: Other Harrowing Experiences

Some of the Tulsa riot escape stories rival those of the escapes of slaves in the U.S. before the Civil War. Running, forging rivers, sleeping in caves, woods, mine pits, hog pens, abandoned buildings, etc., they moved away from Tulsa to safety. Some hopped on freight trains and rode north. Descendant PEGGY ANN McRUFFIN MITCHELL says her parents, survivors JOHN B. McRUFFIN and HATTIE McRUFFIN, had an Underground Railway experience during their escape from the Tulsa riot. They were able to get on board a train bound for St. Louis. From there, they got aid and were able to move on to Detroit, Michigan.

References to Good White Samaritans

Descendant EMMA HERVEY spoke kindly of the Argue family, which hid her survivor parents, RICHARD TILLMAN and URSULINE RICHARDS TILLMAN, during the riot and after the riot until they could find another home. Her dad worked for Mr. Argue. Her mother often spoke of seeing numerous bodies of black riot victims piled like cord wood.

Descendant DONALD JOHN McGOWAN said that his father, survivor CLYDE WILLIAM McGOWAN said that a white delivery man who was delivering supplies to the McGowan store on June 1, 1921, saved the property from destruction by mobsters.

Descendant JOHN W. PATTON, Edmond, Oklahoma, and many other survivors and descendants remembered the kindness of Father Daniel P. Bradley, the priest of St. Monica's Church in the Greenwood District at the time of the riot. Father Daniel, a native of Philadelphia, Pennsylvania, left a legacy of commitment to the north Tulsa community when he died. At survivor GEORGE MONROE's funeral at St. Monica's in August 2001, I saw a tribute to that legacy—the beautiful commemorative wall in the church which is dedicated to the beloved Father Daniel.

Most Colorful Descendants

Descendant EDWARD LAWSON, Hollywood, California, and New York, New York, was perhaps the most colorful. See p. for more information on this heir of Survivors LONDY BOHANNON and TRAVELENE BOHANNON LAWSON.

The BELL family, Tulsa, Oklahoma, Cape Cod, Massachusetts, and the Maryland Shore area near Washington, D.C., were a close-knit, vibrant, fascinating bunch.

Descendants DR. D. GRANT WILLIAMS and his sister, DOROTHY WILLIAMS BRAMLETT, children of survivors FISHER JAMES WILLIAMS and DINAH FREEMAN WILLIAMS, were walking historical icons. Add STEPHANIE BRAMLETT, daughter of Dorothy, to the mix! She helped videographer James Kavin Ross and me with the videotaping of survivors.

Most Thorough Research by Descendants

The descendants of DR. SYLVESTER KIMBROUGH, a dentist in the Greenwood District at the time of the riot, did perhaps the most digging to get information about a famous riot survivor relative.

Most Meticulous, Detailed Documentation

Descendant LEONA JERRYE BRUNER ANTHONY of Marshall, Texas, sent more documentation to the Commission than any survivor or descendant. She sent original birth certificates, death certificates, marriage licenses, deeds to property owned by her survivor ancestors, employment records, and a plethora of other pertinent papers. I was on pins and needles until I made a dash to the downtown Tulsa Kinko's and made copies of those significant documents. I breathed a sigh of relief when I expressed the documents back to that dear lady!

Descendant MELVIN "TIP" JONES, Preston, Oklahoma, came in a close second to LEONA ANTHONY. He sent in original deeds to the property that he inherited, and other documentation. I knew that he was honest and that his story was true, for I grew up on a farm next to his childhood farm west of Preston. I also interviewed "TIP" JONES about his World War II experiences overseas, included in my book, *They Came Searching*.

Descendant ALLENE KNIGHT RAYFORD, Baton Rouge, Louisiana, a niece of survivor JUDGE AMOS T. HALL, sent a carefully drafted, impeccably typewritten letter to the Commission. Reading her letter was like reading a piece by a newspaper reporter.

Most Supportive Descendants: Letters, Telephone Calls, Attendance at Meetings, Riot-Related Events, Programs, Etc.

Descendant WILMA PRESLEY BELL was the descendant who kept in closest touch with me regarding riot updates and pertinent information. She also called sometimes just to offer gratitude for what the other commissioners and I were doing for the riot victims and descendants. I could also count on seeing her at programs, meetings, and other public gatherings relating to

civil and human rights. She was a jewel during this crucial mission!

The heirs of survivors WILLIAM WALLKER and LILLIE HOLDERNESS WALKER were right up there near WILMA PRESLEY BELL. At meetings and programs, I could almost always look out and see someone from the Walker family—usually granddaughters. Sometimes they would be joined by their survivor aunt and uncle from Kansas City, JOYCE WALKER HILL and SAMUEL WALKER. Once when I attended my Petit Family Reunion in Kansas City, Missouri, those two survivors came to my hotel room to meet with me. We had a wonderful time talking about the riot, taking still photographs, and being videotaped by my patient saint of a husband, Norman, who is often called upon to be "honorary documentary producer" at some of my "causes."

Descendant ALICE BOYD VAUGHN touched commissioners with her testimony regarding her mother, survivor GERTRUDE STAPLES TOWNSEND. She told of how her mother shared her riot information with her Sunday school pupils in her South Haven community in west Tulsa. She spread a message of love, repentance, and forgiveness.

Survivor PANSY TILLEY, Los Angeles, California, was the most supportive of the survivors in helping the Commission locate descendants of her deceased survivor relatives. She didn't leave a stone unturned until we had located the heirs of her riot victim relatives PEARL OLIVER and PARIS OLIVER!

Most Colorful Descendant Connections

Descendant RENE BEARD, Los Angeles, California, stated in his interview with me that he attended Mt. Vernon Junior High School in Los Angeles with a teenaged boy whose well-to-do father, an insurance agency owner, had just moved his family to L.A. from Louisiana. That young boy was none other than Johnnie Cochran, who is now a nationally known attorney!

Heirs of famous Tulsa riot survivor J. B. STRADFORD—ANN-MARIE USHER
Descendants of survivor ROBERT FAIRCHILD

Examples: Descendants Carrying on the Torch of Ancestors

The Stradford heirs.
SIMON BERRY, JR., who carried on the flying tradition of his famous father.

THELMA KINLAW GERMANY, who works at the Mabel B. Little Heritage House in the heart of Deep Greenwood, on a mission of preserving north Tulsa's glorious pioneer heritage.

The Sipuel heirs, HELEN LOIS SIPUEL HUGGINS and BRUCE FISHER

The Latimers.

The Dennies.

And many, many others too numerous to include here.

Unique Stories of Close Calls During the Riot: Saving Money!

Read the testimony of descendant SARAH CURVAY MAYSHAW and find out how a pair of muddy rubber boots that belonged to her father, survivor ARTHUR CHESTER CURVAY, became the "bank safe" that hid the family's life savings from mobsters who ransacked and looted the family home.

Descendants of survivor BERZELLE WILLIAMS HAWKINS talk of the money losses of their grandparents, ORLANDO WILLARD WILLIAMS, SR., and WILLIE ANDERSON WILLIAMS, during the Tulsa riot. ORLANDO SR. worked as a barber in Tulsa at the time and kept his cash in a trunk in his house. When mobsters burned down his home during the riot, the trunk, which held $1,000, burned up. But his wife, WILLIE ANDERSON WILLIAMS, had $1,000 on her person when they fled the riot. That sure came in handy after the riot, according to family lore.

Military/Pilots, Etc.

Some of the descendants of the survivors of the Tulsa Race Riot of 1921 recalled that their ancestors had served in the U.S. military. Some had ancestors who were pilots. Two of Tulsa's prominent, pioneering pilots, at this time were SIMON BERRY, SR. and JAMES LEE NORTHINGTON. See *They Came Searching*, for more information about those two colorful Tulsa pilots.

Most Touching Story to the Author

The "dead-baby-in-a-shoe box" story by survivor ROSA DAVIS SKINNER.

Dr. Clyde Snow, one of the foremost forensic experts in the U.S., was fascinated by the story of this lost newborn. In the final report of the Riot Commission, he speaks extensively about the search for information about the identity of the baby and the location of the remains of the child.

He thinks he found that baby!

Most Difficulty; Most Stress to the Author

1. Gathering information about a descendant who was incarcerated in a federal prison.

2. Treading the treacherous waters of family feuds—dealing with descendants who sought to self-judge relatives and to arbitrarily exclude "unworthy" heirs. I had to listen to many "He (or she) ain't no good" stories!

Descendant Families' Data: Numerical, Geographic, Social

Like riot survivors, descendants of riot victims live all over the United States, and one lives overseas, in Japan. Their political, economic, and social lives are as varied as those of riot survivors. Below, in alphabetical order and in their own words, are the stories that some of the descendants told about their notable riot survivor ancestors. Some of these testimonies, like those of survivors, are deep analytical probes into the psyche of the nation at the time of the Tulsa Race Riot of 1921. Others are poignant, personal accounts of the riot. All are fascinating and helpful historically.

Deceased Riot Victims and Their Descendants:

JOHNNY ADAMS; ELIZA ADAMS, riot victims.
Descendants:
Jessie Thompson, Montclair, California, grandson of
JOHNNY ADAMS and
son of **ELIZA ADAMS, deceased.**
Arthur Jefferson, Tulsa, Oklahoma, grandson; son

My mother, who was born in 1916, lived with her parents on Jasper Street in the Greenwood District at the time of the riot. My grandfather owned six or seven rent houses just off Greenwood Avenue. Everything that they owned was burned to the ground. When the mobsters first attacked, my relatives ran and hid in an old shed that was back of the area where their rent houses were—near an alley. They peeped through the cracks in the shed and saw the mobsters setting all their property on fire! They said the men were all heavily armed and that they were shooting everywhere. One of my uncles, "Saucer" Grayson, got shot and killed by the mobsters. To this day, none of us can recall Uncle Saucer's real name. All we ever knew was "Uncle

Saucer." But all our lives we heard about how Uncle Saucer got killed by a white mobster during the Tulsa Race Riot of 1921.

My Grayson relatives were Creek Indian blacks. The little all-black town of Grayson, Oklahoma, which is near Okmulgee, was named for my Grayson relatives.

Interview with Arthur Jefferson, July, 2001.

C. J. and LILLIAN ALEXANDER, riot victim
Descendants:
Juanita Alexander Lewis Hopkins,
Tulsa, Oklahoma, daughter.
C. J. ALEXANDER II.
C. J. Alexander III, son.
Lillian Alexander, daughter.

C.J. Alexander III and Lillian Alexander were raised by their aunt, Juanita Alexander Lewis Hopkins, one of Tulsa's most revered educators. At the time of the riot, their father, C. J. ALEXANDER II, was a six-month-old baby. The family lived in a home which they owned on Williams Street (which was later renamed).

RAY ALSUP, riot victim.
Johnetta Adams.

This was one of the hardest cases for the Riot Commission. But we persevered and, like good detectives, we followed leads until were located a survivor! The first big lead came from Gail Jackson, Oklahoma City, Oklahoma, who sent me an e-mail with information regarding descendant JOHNETTA ADAMS. She responded to a media appeal from the Survivors Committee of the Oklahoma Commission to Study the Tulsa Race Riot of 1921. Many descendants were located as a direct result of our national media blitz in search of survivors.

MARY FRANKLIN ANDERSON, riot victim.
Rhonda Anderson, daughter.
Robert Earl Anderson, son.
Dianne Anderson Steele, daughter.
Marietta Anderson Waiters, daughter.

Riot survivor HAZEL FRANKLIN HACKETT, Tuscaloosa, Alabama, provided the names of these four descendants. See Mrs. Hackett's testimony for information about this survivor family's history.

REVEREND JAMES P. AUTRY and
LAURA JEFFRIES AUTRY, riot victims.
Ruth E. Autry, Wichita, Kansas, daughter.
James Autry, Wichita, Kansas, son.
Elmer Autry, Compton, California, son.

JAMES P. AUTRY and LAURA JEFFRIES AUTRY had come to Tulsa from Holly Springs, Mississippi. At the time of the riot, REVEREND AUTRY was pastor of Holsey Chapel.

SIMON and SNORA AUSTIN, riot victims.
Aileen Joanne Coburn, Oklahoma City,
Oklahoma, daughter.
Leona McCain, Oklahoma City,
Oklahoma, daughter.

GENE AYERS and GRACE RUSSELL AYERS
(later Wimberly), riot victims.
Ramona Dinkins Wimberly, El Paso,
Texas, daughter.

Descendant Ramona Dinkins Wimberly said that at the time of the riot her father, GENE AYERS, owned a restaurant in the Greenwood District and that in addition to supplying Tulsans with good food, he supplied them with choc liquor. He was also a wrestler and a trainer of other wrestlers. One of his protegees, Ed "Stringer" Lewis, became a champion wrestler. Her mother, GRACE RUSSELL AYERS (later Wimberly), worked for a white lady in south Tulsa. It was there that the family hid during the riot.

FANNIE MAE BAGBY, riot victim.
Erline Crosslin, Kansas City, Missouri, daughter.
Billy Wayne Rucker, son.
J. C. Rucker, son.
Robert C. Rucker, son.
Rozella Turner, daughter.

DAVID BAILEY and CORA BAILEY, riot victims.
John Bailey, Oklahoma City, Oklahoma, nephew.

John Bailey, a retired Oklahoma City policeman, provided the information regarding his great uncle, DAVID BAILEY. David Bailey and his brother, John Bailey, are listed in the 1900 Texas census. David Bailey, CORA BAILEY, and their two children moved to Tulsa, Oklahoma, where they were living at the time of the riot. John Bailey, his wife Charlette, and their children

Corinne, Ammice, Amy, and Nancy, moved to Ponca City, Oklahoma.

PETER BAILEY, riot victim.
Roy Davis, son.

Roy Davis could not remember much that his father told him about the riot. He did recall that PETER BAILEY said that he owned a business which was located at Pine and Greenwood.

NICK BANKS, riot victim.
Nick A. Banks, Vancouver, Washington, son.
E. Bernice Banks Davis, Milwaukee, Oregon, daughter.
Audrey Banks Parsons, Milwaukee, Oregon, daughter.

The offspring of NICK BANKS try to keep in touch with their father's hometown of Tulsa, Oklahoma. They remember how he talked about Tulsa and about the riot of 1921. Audrey Banks Parsons came from Oregon and walked down Greenwood Avenue with this author. She tried to remember the things her father had said, and she tried to see the things that he had seen (not easy to do, since most of what Nick Banks had seen was burned to the ground during the riot). Audrey remembered her father telling his children that he was born in Muskogee, Oklahoma, and that when he was grown up, he moved to Tulsa to get a better job, that he owned a pool hall in the Greenwood District, and that he also worked as a chef at the Ketcham Hotel. He talked about the Small Hotel, and he talked about the riot. He said that riot was caused by jealous whites who couldn't stand the idea that blacks were so prosperous in Tulsa, Oklahoma!

MARY BEARD, riot victim (no children).
Raymond Beard, Sr., brother.

Raymond Beard, Sr., was very helpful to me in sorting out the genealogy of the Beard family. Through him, I learned much about MARY BEARD's nine siblings (Sarah Beard, Elijah Beard, Sr., Matthew Beard, Sr., Jacob Beard, James Beard, Curt Beard, Johnny Beard, Clemmie Beard, and Raymond Beard, Sr., himself).

MATTHEW BEARD, SR., riot victim;
deceased son Matthew Beard, Jr.

Rene Beard, Los Angeles, California, son of Matthew Beard, Jr., was the spokesperson for the Matthew Beard family. This was a difficult case study because Matthew Beard, Sr., had two wives and many children. When Rene Beard and I got through with all the "begats," a fascinating little "pearl of history" popped out. When Rene Beard was a student at Mt. Vernon Junior High School in Los Angeles, one of his classmates was a teenager whose father, a well-to-do insurance agency owner, had just moved his family to Los Angeles from Louisiana. That young student was none other than Johnnie Cochran, now a prominent attorney who is known all over the world!

DICK and IDA MAE BELL, riot victims.
Mary Bell Arrington, Lanham, Maryland, daughter.
R. G. Bell, Tulsa, Oklahoma, son.
Catherine Bell Snoddy, Lanham, Maryland, daughter.

Seated: Cathryn Bell Snoddy. Standing L-R: Mary Bell Arrington, Eddie Faye Gates, riot commissioner, during an interview in Lanham, MD October 31, 2000. The women are the children of Tulsa riot survivors J.D. and Ida Mae Bell

Survivor James D. Bell is a walking dictionary about many things—the Tulsa riot, the U.S. military, Tulsa's oil boom days, Oklahoma in general (where he has a home), and the Cape Cod region of Massachusetts (where he has another home and a plethora of other things!). But his sisters in Maryland, Mary Bell Arrington and Catherine Bell Snoddy, whom I met when I did research for the Commission in the Washington, D.C./Maryland area in 2000, added their views about Tulsa and the aftermath of that awful riot. Their brother, R. G. Bell, sent me the following letter:

Mrs. Gates. Commission:

This is a Documentary of the 1921 Infamous [sic] Race Riot Tulsa, Oklahoma.

My mother and father moved to Tulsa, Okla. From St. Louis, Missouri for the oil boom in 1918. They lived at 418 North Cincinnati Avenue. It was called Little Africa at the time. When the Race Riot started they went out the Santa Fe railroad tracks all the way to Mohawk Indian Nation Park. My mother was expectant with child. When they returned home Little Africa was destroyed. Ten days later the child was born—my older brother.

From R. G Bell

SIMON BERRY, SR., riot victim.
Simon Berry, Jr., Los Angeles, California, son.

CHARLES and LONDY BOHANNON, riot victims, and child, TRAVELENE BOHANNON
(later Lawson)
Naomi Lawson Brown, Colorado Springs, Colorado, Granddaughter; daughter.
Edward Lawson, Beverly Hills, California, Grandson; son.
Marcus Lawson, Buffalo, New York, grandson; son.
Margaret Ann Lawson, Buffalo, New York, granddaughter; daughter.
Palmer Lawson, Jr., Buffalo, New York, grandson; son.

As mentioned earlier in the introduction section, Edward Lawson is the most colorful of the Bohannon and Lawson descendants. Lawson, plaintiff in the landmark U.S. Supreme Court lawsuit regarding racial profiling, was a Californian who loved taking daily walks. But any policeman who got a glimpse of the walking man almost always stopped him. What aroused the suspicion of those California policemen was not the actions of the man, but the "look" of the man himself. For Lawson wore his hair in dreadlocks (a style not prevalent then as it is now) and he walked backwards! The U.S. Supreme Court, finding in favor of Lawson, stated that while the dress, hair style, and walking behavior of the plaintiff might be deemed "bizarre" by the ordinary citizen, they were not criminal.

Today, Lawson has homes in California and in New

L-R Sabryna-Joi King, Harriet Cotham, Kymberli-Joi King, and Wesley R. King. Mrs. Cotham is the niece of the late Simon Berry, Sr. The Kings in the photo are her children. They live in Chicago, IL

York City. He is founder of Pro Per Inc., a Beverly Hills, California activist support organization. He lectures frequently all over the nation about civil rights causes. He is also a film producer.

JAMES and JESSIE BREWER, riot victims.
Leona Jerrye Bruner Anthony, Marshall, Texas.
Clifton Joe Tipton, Tulsa, Oklahoma.

Leona Jerrye Bruner Anthony is the woman who sent the most materials to the Commission. In addition to supplying me with the blizzard of documentation, she called frequently to inquire about the work of the Commission, or just to send words of support and gratitude to the commission. Following are excerpts from the first letter she wrote to me:

Dear Mrs. Gates:

In the past, I sent you some documents re to my ancestors who resided in Tulsa, Okla. around in the same area which was attacked/raided etc. near and in the black community of Greenwood. If you have made copies please send my ref. papers back. These papers are the final papers for my historical files. However my daughter Sondia Fontenot, an Army Recruit out of Oklahoma City station, visited me recently. She brought me a tape which you are on talking about the 1921 Burning (of Tulsa). If you do have any information which you can make copies and send me, I would appreciate it. The Brewers, Johnsons, Tiptons, Martins, Millers, King and other allied families would like to know more about it. I'm sure if it wasn't tampered or burned, the census reports, tax records, housing authorities would know who lived in those 35 blocks of the burning. This was a massacre and more should be done for the peoples, and any still living today. More should be done.

Oprah Winfrey should be told, and a show and movie should be made for the world to see.

I was raised in the Greenwood District and walked the same paths—634 E. Jasper Street, and attended Charles S. Johnson Elementary School, and took the short cut across Coal Hill to get to school. My people are buried in Crown Hill Cemetery and some could be in the areas where the missing riot dead are buried. Let me know if I can be of help to you.

Sincerely,
Leona J. Anthony

BURNS, FULSOM, BROOKS, HARRIS, and HOWELL FAMILIES, riot victims.
Maximillian Howell, c/o of his mother, Ms. Johnson Howell, Topeka, Kansas

One day in 2000, I received a letter, neatly written in pencil on lined tablet paper, from a Ms. Johnson Howell. She was asking to have her son, Maximillian Howell, put on the descendants registry. She said that Max was a freshman student in the School of Engineering at Miama of Ohio college. She sincerely thanked me for my work on the Commission and asked me to send her pertinent information about how to get reparations for her son. But when I wrote to her for more information, I never heard from her again.

Her original claim seemed so sincere, I just could not drop her son's name from the registration list. (House Bill 1035 was very clear about how the Commission was to determine who was a bona fide survivor or descendant.) I still need a little more information about Maximillian Howell. But based on what was in that handwritten letter from his mother, the Survivors Committee of the Oklahoma Commission to Study the Tulsa Race Riot of 1921 decided to register Maximillian Howell. We thought that if there were doubts about the legitimacy of her son's eligibility, then the lawyers could handle that when the time came.

MATTIE PEARL CALHOUN; NAOMI FOSTER MOORE, deceased daughter of Calhoun, riot victims.
Wilbur Foster, Los Angeles, California, son.
Ronald Earl Moore, Springfield, Missouri, son.

ROBERT and JUANITA CARTER, riot victims.
Bernard Carter, Compton, California, son.
Eddie Hue Carter, Compton, California, son.
Robert Carter, Jr., Bakersfield, California, son.
Samuel Lee Carter, Bakersfield, California, son.
Bobbie Jean Carter Tennyson, Tulsa, Oklahoma, daughter.

Bobbie Jean Carter Tennyson of Tulsa helped me locate the numerous offspring of Robert Carter from his two marriages. I first met Bobbie at a Booker T. Washington (BTW) Alumni event at the Greenwood Cultural Center. I have never known a school with such loyal alumni. It seems like any day that one visits the Cultural Center, some BTW event is going on!

JOHNNYE MITCHELL CANNON, riot victim.
Mildred F. Wallace, Houston, Texas, daughter.
Johnnye L. Lawson, Houston, Texas, daughter.
Nathaniel C. Lawson, Houston, Texas, son.
Henry C. Cannon, Tulsa, Oklahoma, son.

Johnnye L. Lawson was the contact for the Cannon descendants. Below are poignant excerpts from a letter that Mrs. Lawson wrote to me:

Dear Mrs. Gates:

It was while reading my local newspaper that I became shockingly informed of the unconscionable acts that took place in my hometown of Tulsa. Subsequently, through the revelations of my 87-year-old aunt, Survivor Mildred Christopher, I discovered that my family was forced to flee their home to save their very lives. My aunt was just seven years old, my mother eight, and one of their young sisters was recovering from surgery at the time. The barbarity that ensued that day—the brazen shooting, looting, bombing and wretched torching resulted in the devastation of their entire neighborhood. My grandparents' home and its contents were consumed in the conflagration, and they were left with nothing but the clothes on their backs.

It is very painful and grievous to the soul to know that my mother, grandparents, aunts and other innocent citizens were subjected to such cruelty, callousness and inhumanity—and not by an invading force from another country but, rather, by one from their very own city. What a painful blight on the historic landscape of my hometown, compounded yet by years of failure to publically and officially acknowledge an occurrence of such gravity and magnitude.

My prayer is that each of us will take a moment to daily look within our hearts to contact that place of peace, harmony and goodwill resident within each of us. This place is God's gift to us for renewal and guidance, and communing there shows forth in our interactions with our fellow man.

May God's love, wisdom and strength direct you and the committee on which you serve.

Sincerely,
Johnnye L. Lawson

ARTHUR CHESTER and MATTIE OWENS CURVAY, riot victims.
Sarah Curvay Mayshaw, Tulsa, Oklahoma, daughter.

My father worked for the Union Depot Railroad Station on South Cincinnati at the time of the riot. On June 1, 1921, Dad was at work at the railroad station. Mother took his lunch to the station. Dad walked back to the corner with her. That area of the street is now named Martin Luther King, Jr. Drive. Mother was going to get a bus there from our house which was near the corner of Oklahoma Street and Greenwood Avenue,

next to the House of Resurrection Church. But the bus driver wouldn't take her there. Instead, he took her to the Convention Center on Brady Street, which is now referred to as "The Old Lady on Brady Street." It is where theatrical performances song concerts, lectures etc. are held.

The reason that bus driver wouldn't take his passengers on his normal route is because Greenwood was being burnt down! My mother worked as a domestic for a white woman named Mrs. Harris, who was in Arkansas at the time of the riot. But the son of that woman searched for us and found us. He took us to their home on Terwilliger Street in south Tulsa, where we stayed for a week.

Our home wasn't burned. So when the riot destruction was cleaned up, the few blacks whose homes had not been burned were allowed to return home. We found that while our home had not been burned, it had been ransacked, tore up, and looted. My dad didn't believe in banks. A pair of old rubber boots were his bank! The reason black men had rubber boots is because the streets in the Greenwood District weren't paved. And they got mighty muddy when it rained. Anyway, Dad had $300 stuffed in one of those old boots. When we got to our house, the first thing Dad did was shake that old boot, and out fell his $300. We sure rejoiced over that money!

We were so grateful that those mobsters hadn't touched those boots.

My dad retired in 1950 from his railroad job. I used to visit Dad at the lower level of the station where he worked. When I was a little girl, I referred to that beautiful Union station as "my Daddy's station"!

A. D. DAVIS, Sr., riot victim.
A. D. DAVIS, JR., son.
Ernest Davis, son.
Leon Davis, Tulsa, Oklahoma, son.
M. D. Davis, son.

A. D. Davis, Sr,. was one of Tulsa's first black policemen. He lived in an era when policemen and other public officials were given their jobs as "political plums" from grateful politicians they had supported. Though their employment was often interrupted when the "political bosses" ended their terms, these black officials are noted for their dedication and good service to the city at that time. I interviewed Leon Davis of Tulsa in 1994 about his famous father. Mr. Davis has moved away from Tulsa, and I was unable to locate a new address or phone number for him. I was unable to locate the other Davis sons. I am grateful that I did that interview in 1994. From that interview, I gathered firsthand information about the role of black policemen in pioneer Tulsa. Mr. Davis also gave me some documents relating to that era and a photo of Tulsa's black policemen then. I used that information in my second book *They Came Searching: How Blacks Sought the Promised Land in Tulsa*.

LUCINDA PITTMAN DAVIS, riot victim; Doris Patricia Presley, deceased daughter of Lucinda Pittman Davis. Jill Elizabeth Presley, Tulsa, Oklahoma, granddaughter; daughter. Lisa Presley, Tulsa, Oklahoma, granddaughter; daughter.

Survivor Lucinda Pittman Davis often talked to her children and grandchildren about the Tulsa riot. She was appalled that during the riot, Guards would not protect black people. Instead, she said, they concentrated on protecting white property. Instead of cordoning off Greenwood Avenue and keeping white mobsters out of the area, they devoted all their energy, time, men, and equipment to protecting white property—especially white businesses—across the tracks! She said troops were directed *away* from the area being bombed, looted, burned, and destroyed. They went toward South Cincinnati and over into the white district.

Mrs. Davis' children and grandchildren learned that a large number of Presley descendants first settled in the New Hope and Oktaha areas in Oklahoma. Then some of them came to Okmulgee and Tulsa, where they happened to have gotten caught in the Tulsa Race Riot of 1921.

LUTHER EDMONSON, riot victim. Linda Edmonson Graves, Tulsa, Oklahoma, daughter.

Below are excerpts from a letter that Linda Edmonson Graves wrote to me in which I first heard about her father's knees.

Dear Mrs. Eddie Faye Gates
Thank you so much for sending me your book, *They Came Searching*. It truly will always hold a special place in my heart forever, and will be passed down to my children to read and be proud of connection to such an awesome story.

I have been told so many times when I was a child how my Dad had swamed [sic] the Arkansas River to get away from a race riot. As a child, I remember asking my dad why was he always rubbing his knees. He told me that once he hurt his knees swimming across the Arkansas River. I asked him back why in the world would he swim across the Arkansas River and that is when he told me about the riot.

Riot survivor Ernestine Gibbs, whom I had called Aunt Ernestine all my life (I was grown when I learned she was not a blood relative but a dear friend of the family), would speak of the riot and tell of the friend (my dad) who knocked on her family's door the night of the riot to warn them of something going on downtown and he was said to have been very scared. That story always intrigued me because as a child, and even as an adult, I have never known my dad to be scared of anything and I mean *nothing*! But Aunt Ernestine would laugh and say that he was sure scared that night

So I learned from Dad and from Aunt Ernestine why my Dad was always rubbing his knees. Another thing that I remember from my Dad or others is that my Dad and his friend Archie Weathers were the only men in Tulsa that night that were brave enough to attempt that long gruesome swim across that river to safety and then go on into Sapulpa. I think that helped him to make him the strong, proud have-no-fear type of person that he was.

Enclosed is a check to cover the cost of the book, and thanks again so very much. I intend to read every word, and am looking forward to someday meeting you personally.

Sincerely,
Linda Carol Edmonson Graves

STANLEY FAIR, SR., riot victim.

Stanley Fair, Jr., Tulsa, Oklahoma, Jane Fair Pruett, Tulsa, Oklahoma, Janet Fair, Oklahoma City, Oklahoma, Brenda Fair Campbell, Tulsa, Oklahoma, Geraldine Fair Jessie, deceased: heirs one son and one daughter, Yvonne Fair Shaw, Tulsa, Oklahoma, children of Stanley Fair, Sr.

BUCK COLBERT FRANKLIN, riot victim. Dr. John Hope Franklin, Durham, North Carolina, son.

Dr. John Hope Franklin is one of the most prominent and well-known descendants of a Tulsa riot victim. He is so well known that I will not attempt to describe him here. Readers all over the world have read about him in the print media. He has also been well documented in the electronic media, where he has been the subject of national film productions.

HARRY GAMBLE, JR., riot victim.
Amy Gamble Eidson, Oklahoma City, Oklahoma, daughter.
Eva Gamble Morris, Lawton, Oklahoma, daughter.

LEWIS GOODSON, riot victim.
Margaret Thorpe, Tulsa, Oklahoma, granddaughter.
Rebecca Marks Jimerson, Tulsa, Oklahoma, granddaughter.
Judy Snelling, Tulsa, Oklahoma, granddaughter.
Earlene Marks, Tulsa, Oklahoma, granddaughter.
Pearl Burton, Houston, Texas, granddaughter.
Connie Goldsmith, Atlanta, Georgia, granddaughter.
Edward Thompson, Las Vegas, Nevada, grandson.

WILLIE JAMES GRAYSON and DORIS GRAYSON, riot victims.
Bobbie Jean Saulet, Kansas City, Missouri, daughter.
Dorothy Mae Brown, daughter.
Albert Grayson, son.

Bobbie Jean Saulet provided information regarding survivors Willie James Grayson and Doris Grayson. She said that they lived on North Lansing Street at the time of the riot and that the Grayson family owned a restaurant located near 18 North Greenwood Avenue called "The Eating Place." Willie James Grayson's mother, Hattie Grayson, who was born in 1880, provided most of the assets for the restaurant.

MARY ELLA GREEN, riot victim.
Mattie Davis Oliver, Tulsa, Oklahoma, daughter.

Mrs. Mattie Davis Oliver can't remember the exact address where her mother lived at the time of the riot but says that it was somewhere in the Greenwood District. Her mother and aunt lived together, and when the riot broke out, they fled to a little all-black town called Wybark, which was flourishing at that time. When they got to Muskogee, they met a group of blacks across the bridge over the Arkansas River. Police wouldn't let those blacks on the other side cross the river. They were trying to get to the Greenwood District in Tulsa so they could aid the besieged blacks there. But

the policemen did let the blacks who were fleeing from the riot in Tulsa cross the bridge.

Mrs. Oliver said that after the riot, people just "shut down" and did not talk about the riot. But she said that she did talk to her children about the riot. She said on Sundays, after dinner, she would tell them about it.

AMOS T. HALL, riot victim.
Jean Williams McGill, Tulsa, Oklahoma, niece.
Carolyn Williams Tolliver, Tulsa, Oklahoma, niece.

Relatives of the famous black Tulsa judge Amos T. Hall were a colorful lot! Nephew Bertram Williams, a survivor, told a spellbinding story of the riot and of its aftermath. See chapter 6.

MATTIE ELODIA HARRIS (LATER MOORE) and her daughter MERCEDES ADELE HARRIS, now deceased, riot victims.
Cheryl K. Simmons Ceaser, Tulsa, Oklahoma; Lemuel Jerry Harris; Lacy E. Murrell; H. Maurice Horn; Wilzette Faye Horn Holmes; Gaylen Ilene Simmons, children of Mercedes Adele Harris.

Cheryl K. Simmons Ceaser of Tulsa provided information to the Commission about the descendants of Survivor Mattie Elodia Harris (later Moore). We had many conversations trying to sort out this colorful family. I found that most of the descendants live right here in Tulsa!

ELIJAH and WILLIE HAWKINS, riot victims.

Registering descendants of riot victims Elijah Hawkins, his wife, Willie, and their son, Orlando Hawkins, Sr., was difficult. There were so many of them, and they lived everywhere! But the granddaughters of Elijah and Willie, Charlotte Williams of Washington, D.C., and the historian of the Hawkins family, Monyett Williams Ellington, of Washington, D.C., provided such excellent documentation and history that the job was successfully completed. In a thorough, most detailed letter from Charlotte Williams to the Riot Commission, some interesting historical information appeared. And below are the names of the heirs:

CLARENCE HAWKINS, JR., riot victim.
Jeanette Hawkins, Chicago, Illinois, daughter.

LULA HAWKINS, riot victim.
Olander Hawkins, Chicago, Illinois, son.

JOSEPH and MAMIE HENDERSON, riot victims.
Bobbye Louise Henderson Gilbert, Midland,
Texas, daughter.
Fannie Henderson Williams, Arlington,
Texas, daughter.

Ninety-six-year-old LeRoy Henderson of Pasadena, California, provided me with information about his two nieces, who are daughters of deceased riot victims Joseph and Mamie Henderson. Although Mr. Henderson was not in Tulsa at the time of the riot, a brother and sister (Mamie Henderson) were in the riot and told him all about it.

EMMA HERVEY, riot victim.
Naomi Nash Williams Wimberly, Tulsa,
Oklahoma, daughter.

Mrs. Naomi Wimberly says that her mother talked a bit about the riot, but when she did talk it was only to adults. The children were sent from the room. But her mother did tell the children of her great fear during the riot.

The Hervey family originally lived in Valiant, Oklahoma, which is near Hugo and Idabel, in southeast Oklahoma. Whites were especially vicious toward blacks in that part of Oklahoma. In fact, they had threatened to kill all blacks in the area. That is why my folks left that area and moved to Tulsa for safety and protection. Yet Tulsa is where they got caught in that awful riot.

In Tulsa, Dad worked for a white man who hid the family, including my grandmother, until it was safe to return to the Greenwood area. My mother said that she saw many dead blacks during and immediately after the riot. My mother was a good friend of Mrs. Mabel B. Little, a black Tulsa businesswoman who lost a lot of property during the riot. After the riot, we lived with Mrs. Little for a while.

ROBERT DANIEL HOLLOWAY, SR., riot victim.
Lena Mae Moore, Calumet City, Illinois, daughter.
Claudine Hunter, Emeryville, California, daughter.
Helen Dean, Washington, D.C., daughter.
Jane Holloway Chauteau, Richmond,
California, daughter.

Carla Lewis, Emeryville, California, granddaughter
(daughter of deceased Thelma Holloway Lewis).
Charles Lewis, Riverside, California, grandson.

At the time of the riot, Robert Daniel Holloway, Sr., lived at 1224 North Greenwood Avenue. His future second wife, Viola Margaret Goodlett, lived on North Frankfort Avenue. After the riot, they married and had six children.

RICHARD and VIOLA HUGGINS, riot victims;
their deceased daughter RUTH FOWLER MARTIN.
Dorothy Jones, Nancy Martin, Tulsa, Oklahoma,
Catherine Martin, Dallas, Texas, James Preston
Martin, Tulsa, Oklahoma, Felton Martin, Tulsa,
Oklahoma, Leslie Beard, Flint

Dorothy Jones of Tulsa provided the following information about the riot which had been told to her by her grandmother. Grandmother talked about how her family heard about the riot. She said blacks were running wildly down the streets—Greenwood and other nearby streets—trying to escape from the taunts and weapons of white mobsters. She said they joined the crowd. They ran and ran and ran. And they made it to safety from that vicious crowd of mobsters. When they returned, Greenwood looked like a war zone and people were just standing around in a daze talking about the riot, about how they had seen beatings, shootings, bombings, and even lynchings. Some of them had been beaten or wounded themselves. My grandmother never forgot that riot.

ELLA JOHNSON and CORA JACKSON,
riot victims.
Maxine Jackson Lacy, Tulsa, Oklahoma,
granddaughter of Ella Johnson and
daughter of Cora Jackson.

My grandmother was one of the original fourteen founders of Mt. Zion Baptist Church in the Greenwood District. She always talked about the sadness that the north Tulsa community felt over the burning down of their beautiful church, which they had just had renovated. (They later paid off every cent they owed on that renovation.) [Authors note: Mt. Zion Church was targeted because it was mistakenly thought to be a virtual arsenal for "militant colored men."]

ISAAC JOHNSON, riot victim.
Shirley Tyus, Conway, Arkansas, granddaughter.
Janice Lou Ross, Plumerville, Arkansas,
granddaughter.
Marilyn Kay Coley, Plumerville, Arkansas,
granddaughter.
Lena Mae Payne, Plumerville, Arkansas,
granddaughter.
Ronald Wayne Johnson, Little Rock, Arkansas,
grandson.

ROBERT FRANKLIN JOHNSON, riot victim.
Val Gene Johnson, Sr., Tulsa, Oklahoma, son.
Charlette Johnson Gibbs, daughter.

LEE JONES and STELLA JONES, riot victims.

Lee and Stella Jones lived in the 1400 block of North Kenosha at the time of the riot. Their home was badly burned. After the riot, they rebuilt. Both are dead now. When Stella died, she willed the property, equally, to an adopted son and a nephew, Melvin "Tip" Jones.

DR. SYLVESTER E. KIMBROUGH, riot victim.
Sharlie Kimbrough Daniels, niece.
Addie Kimbrough, Jr., nephew.
Nathaniel Kimbrough, nephew.
Wallace Kimbrough, nephew.
Jerry Jack Richardson, nephew.
Richard Richardson, nephew.

On a list of merchandise losses by Dun Company, published in Mary Elizabeth Jones Parrish's classic book *The Events of the Tulsa Disaster*, revised edition, Out on a Limb Press, Tulsa, Oklahoma, 1998, Parrish lists Kimbrough's business address as 206 North Greenwood Avenue.

Sharlie Kimbrough Daniels, Tulsa, Oklahoma, niece of Kimbrough, helped the author with the registration of Kimbrough descendants.

**EVANS KINLAW and
CALDONIA COLLINS KINLAW, riot victims.**
Thelma Kinlaw Germany, Tulsa, Oklahoma,
daughter.

At the time of the riot, the Kinlaws lived on Frankfort Avenue near Brickyard Hill, where the present Oklahoma State University–Tulsa is located.

Brickyard Hill was the site of much shooting and bombings during the riot.

Thelma Kinlaw Germany works near this historic area. From her desk in the Mabel B. Little Heritage House (named for Survivor Mabel B. Little), she can look out across the green grass, with the duck and geese pond to the left, and the OSU-Tulsa campus straight ahead to the area where her parents lived.

It is fitting and poetic that this riot descendant works in this area where her beloved pioneer Tulsa parents lived and loved—the revered and respected Greenwood District!

WILMA KIRKWOOD, riot victim.
Bernice Lawler, Los Angeles, California, daughter.
Lorraine McFarland, Los Angeles, California,
daughter.

Bernice Lawler and Lorraine McFarland remember their mother, who was the sister of riot survivors Lena Eloise Taylor Butler and Odessa Malone, telling them the chilling story of a lynching that she and her brother saw in Tulsa during the riot.

**JAMES K. KNIGHTEN and JULIA JACKSON
KNIGHTEN, riot victims.**
James Bernard Knighten, son.
Allene Knighten Rayford, Baton Rouge, Louisiana,
daughter.

Mrs. Allene Knighten Rayford, a niece of Judge Amos T. Hall, sent the Riot Commission a letter and a meticulously completed descendant's questionnaire. In her letter, Mrs. Rayford expressed hope that her response would be of help to the Commission. It was!

Not only did her information provide helpful, basic information about the people and places connected with the riot, but it also gave the commissioners a "feel" for the black community at the time of the riot—of what they valued and treasured as evidenced by what they had in their homes. Here is Mrs. Rayford's introductory letter:

Dear Mrs. Gates

I am enclosing herewith the completed information to the best of my ability which you have requested concerning the family losses incurred by my parents as a result of the Tulsa Riot of 1921.

In that my brother nor I was born at that time, we can only answer based upon our knowledge of what we grew up around. We were very keenly aware that my parents had lost everything in the riot, and that my Father, who was a builder, contractor and business man, had to start from scratch to rebuild a life for his family.

My brother, James Bernard Knighten, is seriously ill at this time and it has fallen to me to comply with your request as best I can.

The descriptions of ownership by my parents as described in this letter are those which I grew up around as a child. I sincerely hope my general appraisal of ownership values are in keeping with the economy of that era.

With sincere thanks,
Allene Knighten Rayford

OVID LACY, JR. , riot victim.
Ovid Lacy III, Kansas City, Missouri.
Robert Lacy, Kansas City, Missouri.

JAMES HAROLD LATIMER and JULIA LATIMER; William Shakespeare Latimer, Jayphee Clinton (J. C.) Latimer, Major Sylvester Latimer, Elihu Latimer, Fred Latimer, Sr., Patella Latimer (later Pegues), Thella Latimer, Ella Latimer (later Bradford), Maggie Latimer, Alice Latimer, children of James Harold and Julia Latimer
Rev. Bradford Bishop, son of
Ella Latimer Bradford, deceased.
Lisa Latimer, daughter of
Elihu Latimer, Sr., deceased.
Jayphee Clinton (J. C.) Latimer, Jr., son of Jayphee Clinton (J. C.) Latimer, Sr., deceased.
Caesar C. Latimer, son of
Major Sylvester Latimer, deceased.
Julius Pegues, son of
Patella Latimer Pegues, deceased.
Daughter of Julia Latimer Warren, deceased.
Daughter of Rita Latimer Wright, deceased.
Caesar Latimer, son.

That Latimer family is one of Tulsa's most prominent pioneer families.

WILLIE LEWIS, riot victim.
Jimmie Lewis, Joe Lewis, Lorraine Lewis, and Della Morgan, living children of Willie Lewis.

Deceased children of Willie Lewis who have offspring (heirs): John Wesley Lewis, two daughters; Glen Lewis, two daughters, one son; Oscar Lewis.

JOE LOCKARD and RINA HAWKINS LOCKARD, riot victims.

Cortez Lockard, Japan, Son
Edward Lockard, Chicago, Illinois, son.
Ernest Lockard, Detroit, Michigan, son.
Frank Lockard, Tulsa, Oklahoma, son.
Jessie Mae Lockard, Detroit, Michigan, daughter.
Oscar Lockard, Detroit, Michigan, son.
Selma Lockard, Tulsa, Oklahoma, daughter.
Children of deceased daughter Pearlie Mae Lockard.

Gloria Watts of Eufaula, Oklahoma, relative of Oklahoma's U.S. Representative J. C. Watts, Jr., provided the Riot Commission with information on their riot survivor relatives, Joe Lockard and Rina Hawkins Lockard.

CARRIE B. McDONALD, riot victim.
Carrie M. McDonald Strother, Kansas City, Missouri, adopted daughter.

Carrie M. McDonald Strother sent the following letter to the Commission:

February 10, 2000
Mr. Bob L. Blackburn, Chair
1921 Tulsa Race Riot Commission
2100 N. Lincoln Blvd.
Oklahoma City, OK 73105

Dear Mr. Blackburn:

I am so pleased with the extensive work that you and the Commission are doing to bring about justice in what can be described as one of America's greatest tragedies.

My aunt and foster mother, Carrie B. McDonald, was a business woman in the Greenwood area of Tulsa at the time of the 1921 riot. For all of my years until she and her sister died, I had heard them speak of this devastating atrocity. Yet, in all my years of schooling, even in my studies of Black History, I had never heard mention of the 1921 riot. I remember trying to find mention of it in the encyclopedia when I was a teen. I downplayed the magnitude of the incident since I never even met anyone else that had lived through the experience. Finally, several years ago I stumbled across a documentary about it on public television. I was fascinated to finally discover that it really had happened, just like the stories I had been told repeatedly. Shortly after that program aired I attended a book signing by Ron Wallace, who was in Kansas City promoting his book, *Black Wall Street*. I had an opportunity to introduce myself and speak with him briefly about Tulsa and the riot.

Our family left Tulsa in 1944 and I have visited several times as an adult, but was not interested in finding out any of this information until it became real to me that the Tulsa Race Riot really happened. I had the opportunity to visit two years ago and walked along the area where they had their businesses. I went into the Cultural Center and saw pictorial accountings of the event. What an impact all of that had upon me. I saw the memoriam to the people who had lost businesses in the riot. (I became sad when I discovered that my aunt was not even remembered in that tribute.)

When I went back to my hotel room, I sat for a long time just staring into space. Suddenly from deep within my spirit there came a fountain of tears that began to pour uncontrollably from my eyes. Where had all this pain been stored? I realized that I was crying for my "mother" who had lost everything that she had worked so diligently to accomplish. It was the release of the anguish that I never saw her exhibit. She lost everything but her dignity and her ability to keep smiling through adversity.

I am amazed that a person could lose so much and not become embittered by it all.

My mind wandered back to the times when she would tell how she had owned a boarding house/hotel, a restaurant and a grocery store in the Greenwood area. She would tell about the men from the Brickyard that ate at her restaurant and the railroad men that had rooms in her boarding house. She would tell about the soft leather sofas and chairs and the marble topped mahogany library tables that she had in her reading room that was looted or burned in the riot. She told of how they took her wardrobe trunks with fine silk lingerie trimmed with lace as "deep as your hand." After the riot, some of her belongings were seen in the window of a downtown pawn shop. She would go on to say that at one time she was "rolling in dough" until the riot took everything from her. She tried to start over but things were never the same. She struggled through the depression years and finally closed for good about 1934.

My goal now is to see that her name not be forgotten. She was a young (32 year old) woman with remarkable business acumen. It is said that she was able to deal with the toughest of white businessmen when seeking the most for a dollar.

In a 60 Minutes II segment recently, I heard Mr. Don Ross say what my aunts said so often—that they "won the riot." I know that they won, because they endured. Like Mr. Ross, I too am angry. I am bitter when I think that a person, who once dared to believe in the American dream, was rudely awakened by the travesty of racial hatred. She did win because she did not die with a broken spirit. I, too, am angry, Mr. Ross, very angry. Anger is the legacy that was left to me.

America! Oklahoma! Tulsa! What shall you render for this great travesty? You told her to pull herself up by her bootstraps and like a thief in the night, you stole her boots. It is time to pay up!
Sincerely,
Carrie M. Strother

REVEREND A. L. McGLORIE and LUCINDA McGLORIE, riot victims.
Martha McGlorie Swindall,
Tulsa, Oklahoma, daughter.

CLYDE WILLIAM McGOWAN, riot victim.
Donald John McGowan, Tulsa, Oklahoma, son.

At the time of the Tulsa riot, I had a lot of relatives in the riot—my grandfather, who owned a house and a grocery store on Newton, and another one on Pine Place, my uncle Samuel McGowan, who owned a large store, and other relatives too numerous to name, including my cousin, riot survivor Juanita McGowan Burnett. My parents lived at 1303 North Madison Place at the time in a home owned by my grandfather. The house had been built by a builder named Mr. Gary.

During the mob violence, my parents, Mr. Nichols (who was the father-in-law of the barber Mr. Tecumseh, who owns Tee's Barber Shop on Greenwood Avenue presently), and others escaped the mob by running to Crosby farms and hiding out. That is in the area near the present Booker T. Washington High School. In 1921, it was wilderness-like farm area. While they were hiding out, mobsters tried to burn down our grandfather's fine merchandise store, but white sales delivery men (called drummers) stayed at that store throughout the riot and would not let them touch that store. [Author's note: See chapter 4 interview with Juanita Delores McGowan Burnett for more details about the McGowan family and the Tulsa riot.]

VERA C. MARSHALL McGOWAN, riot victim.
Lorenzo Carlos Vann, Tulsa, Oklahoma, son.

Lorenzo Carlos Vann is a member of the North Tulsa Historical Society and enlightens club members with wonderful oral history and empirical documentation about his colorful ancestors. Of Creek/African heritage, his ancestors were among the original settlers in Oklahoma and owned much of the oil-rich land which was later "redistributed" (stolen, according to Oklahoma historian Angie Debo and others) during the Dawes Act era.

At the time of the riot, Mr. Vann's mother was married to one of the famous McGowan Greenwood area merchants, Euell McGowan. After the riot, she and Euell divorced and she married Rufus Cooley Vann and had ten children—nine boys and one girl.

Lorenzo Vann's father, Cooley, was quite an interesting figure. He rode fourteen years with the notorious Oklahoma outlaw Cherokee Bill, who was hanged for his dastardly deeds.

Lorenzo Vann grew up hearing the fascinating history of his ancestors. From his mother he heard details of the riot. That is how he says he knows which blacks killed the most whites during the riot—Seymour Williams, Cecil Hall (father of Judge Amos T. Hall), Horace "Peg Leg" Taylor, and an Okmulgee-born man whose name he can't remember. He does remember that the man lived on Peoria Avenue and claimed to be an original member of the Dalton gang. Readers who live in the Tulsa area, come to our North Tulsa Historical Society meetings. We meet the third Monday of each month, 6:30 p.m., at Rudisill North Regional Library, 1520 North Hartford Avenue (just past Greenwood and Pine, where most of the riot activity occurred in 1921). Lorenzo Vann is one of our most faithful members. You will be entertained by him, and you will learn much history from him!

WEBBER McGOWAN, riot victim.
Mary Huddleston, Los Angeles, California,
granddaughter.

WALLACE McLEOD, riot victim.
Audele McLeod Beeks, St. Louis, Missouri,
daughter.
Felecia McLeod Johnson,
Los Angeles, California, daughter.
Wallace McLeod, Jr., Tulsa, Oklahoma, son.
Patricia McLeod Stephenson,
Kansas City, Missouri, daughter.

The McLeod family was a captivating family to interview. Usually one sibling is the historian of a family, but in this case all of the McLeods had interesting stories to tell. A composite account of the family's riot recollections follows:

At the time of the riot, the family lived in a home that they owned at 301 North Elgin Street. Their father, Wallace McLeod, was captured, tied up, and taken to the Convention Center. The home was burned down, and after the riot a new home was built at 302 North Frankfort Avenue.

The McLeod offspring spoke fondly of the Tulsa of their childhood. Among their playmates and classmates remembered were Tuleta Duncan Shawnee, George Monroe, Kinney Booker, and their cousin survivor Wilhelmina Guess Howell. Schools and teachers mentioned and fondly remembered (not necessarily listed in order here) were Dunbar Elementary School, Carver Junior High School, Booker T. Washington High School; Cynthia A. Bankhead, Emma Adams, Mildred P. Williams.

The mother of the McLeod descendants, Bessie Audele Beatty McLeod, was remembered as a very spiritual-minded individual who was one of the first black Christian Scientists in Tulsa. They aren't sure just how their mother got interested in Christian Science, but she did, and even in segregated Oklahoma at that time, she was determined to go to the white branch church, First Church of Christ, Scientist, in downtown Tulsa. Blacks were allowed to come in, but they had to sit in the back of the church behind ropes. Black Tulsans didn't like the idea of having to sit behind the ropes, so they started meeting in the McLeod home, not as an official church, but just as a little study society. Among those who came were Mrs. Opaline Armstrong Bradley, an outstanding music teacher at Carver, Mrs. Juanita Foshee, a Mrs. McKeever, and two sisters, Blanche and Helen. Later, a branch church, Fifth Church of Christ, Scientist, was built by these early black Tulsans. Wallace McLeod helped the members secure the building, and he helped them find the native rock to build the beautiful little church on North Peoria. (The little church was among the many buildings torn down in 2000 to make room for the expansion of North Peoria Avenue.)

Bessie McLeod was very fond of some of the white members she had met at the downtown church, and she called upon one of the white Christian Science practitioners from the church when she needed prayerful support in dealing with a problem. Audele McLeod Beeks said that with the help of that practitioner, she was healed permanently of asthma, which had plagued her early childhood years.

JOHN B. and HATTIE JOHNSON McRUFFIN,
riot victims.
Peggy Ann McRuffin Mitchell,
Dallas, Texas, daughter.

Peggy Mitchell's questionnaire was thorough and typed. Her mother had been born in Tulsa in 1894 and her father in Terrell, Texas, in 1895. She doesn't recall the exact address of the rent house in which they lived at the time of the riot but said that it was somewhere in the Greenwood area.

Her mother spoke often of their losses. She said they lost everything they owned in the riot—jewelry, clothes, including a fur coat, furniture—just everything! They escaped with the help of some people and an underground railroad (a network of supportive people). They were able to get to St. Louis, Missouri, and then on to Detroit, Michigan.

MILLINGTON MINNER, riot victim.
Sally Jean Minner Matson, Chicago, Illinois.

Sally Jean Minner Matson couldn't remember much about what she had been told about the Tulsa riot by her late parents. She did remember that her father, Millington Minner, was nine years old at the time and that the Minner family owned property in Tulsa. She said that the property was stolen from the family by a rich white man in Tulsa. There was a Boswell, Oklahoma, and a catfish farm connection to the property loss (via a lawyer?). She did give names of some of the whites connected with the property loss, but they will not be listed here, since proper research and analysis has not been done on the subject. Though the details of the loss are sketchy, the bottom line is that the property that this once prosperous family once owned was lost.

OSBORNE MONROE, riot victim;
LOTTIE MONROE, child riot victim.
Audrey Taylor, Tulsa, Oklahoma.

Audrey Taylor is the daughter of Osborne Monroe's deceased daughter Lottie Monroe Tyree. Her uncle, survivor George Monroe, who died in August 2001, was one of the most popular of the riot survivors and appeared in the print and electronic media at local, state, national, and international levels more than perhaps any other survivor.

LEROY MUSGROVE and
NETTIE MAY MUSGROVE
Betty Musgrove Cocas, Denver, Colorado, daughter.
Robert Musgrove, son.

At the time of the riot Leroy and Nettie May Musgrove lived in a home that they owned at 760 E. Queen Street in the Greenwood District. They often

talked of the great fear that washed over them as they fled the murderous mobs of Tulsa that June day in 1921.

JAMES NAILS, SR., riot victim.
Claxton Nails, Tulsa, Oklahoma, son.

Claxton Nails is the son of James Nails, Sr., and the nephew of Henry Nails, who were prominent Tulsa businessmen at the time of the riot.

OSCAR NASH and MOLLIE OLIVER NASH,
riot victims.

The deceased son of Oscar and Mollie Oliver Nash left nine children. Their names and addresses were unavailable at press time.

PEARL OLIVER, her son PARIS OLIVER,
riot victims.

The Oliver descendants are:
  Mary Jo Williams, Topeka, Kansas.
  Patsy R. Robinson, San Diego, California.
  Donald C. Wharry, Brooklyn Park, Minnesota.
  Evelyn L. Cross, Topeka, Kansas.
  Kenneth W. Chambers, Kansas City, Missouri.

MYRTLE FIELDS PARKER, riot victim.
Irma Anthony, Tulsa, Oklahoma, granddaughter.
Leontyne Thomas Harrell, Oakland, California, granddaughter.
Jerry Fields Thomas, Oklahoma City, Oklahoma, grandson.
Edsel Thomas III, great grandson.
Carmen Thomas, Chicago, Illinois, great granddaughter.
Linda Thomas, Chicago, Illinois, great granddaughter.

STEVE and MARY LUE HICKS PARKER,
riot victims
Lavada Louise Parker Osborne, El Cerrito, California, daughter.

Mrs. Lavada Parker Osborne provided the following information about her parents:

At the time of the riot, my parents lived at 1439 N. Iroquois Street. They had come to Tulsa from Wilmot, Arkansas. They owned their three-bedroom brick home and also a grocery store and a restaurant. They were picked up by Guardsmen and taken to the Stockade during the riot. My mother was thirty-nine years old when I was born and she had no other children. She never would talk to me about the riot. She thought I was "nervous and temperamental." But she DID talk to my friend Annese Barber, who now live in Chicago. So that is how I learned about the riot.

I have strong connections to Tulsa. I graduated from Booker T. Washington High School in 1951. I am a classmate of Senator Maxine Horner (who co-sponsored HB 1035, which created the Oklahoma Commission to Study the Tulsa Race Riot of 1921).

CALVIN PATTON and WILLIE THOMPSON PATTON, riot victims.

John W. Patton, nephew, provided the following information about Tulsa's early history:

I am the nephew of Calvin and Willie Thompson, who were in the Tulsa Race Riot of 1921. I was born and raised in Tulsa. I had a rough beginning in life. When I was one year old, my mother died. When I was five years old, my father died of a heart attack. I was raised by my aunt in Tulsa, America Pitts. I had another aunt in Tulsa, Cleo Jordan, who lived near Berry Park. I had a brother who was reared by our uncle, Dr. R. C. Patton, a dentist in Boley, Oklahoma. Well, that brother died when he was nineteen!

Although I have a lot of sad memories connected to Tulsa and to Boley, such as being an orphan and losing my older brother, I have some pleasant memories, too. The happiest and best memories that I have are connected to St. Monica's Catholic Church, which was (and still is) in the Greenwood District. Father Daniel P. Bradley, a native of Philadelphia, Pennsylvania, who was the priest, was my favorite. Oh, he was a jewel of a man and was so loved by the black community. In fact, he fought with the blacks against mobsters on Brickyard Hill during the riot. There is a plaque on the wall of St. Monica's which was dedicated to Father Daniel, as we always called him. Another thing that I remember about St. Monica's church back then is that the church had a black housekeeper, Miss Bernice. She was well liked by the church members. I remember she was a light-skinned black woman and that she left Tulsa, went to California, and married the black comedian known as Step-In Fetchit.

In 1942, I graduated from Booker T. Washington High School, and later I joined the Navy. I was a minesweeper and spent most of my duty in the U.S.

[AUTHOR'S NOTE: St. Monica's Catholic Church is still a respected institution in the North Tulsa community. The priest today is Father Desmond Okpogba, who is from Africa. I met him for the first time when I attended survivor George Monroe's funeral there in August 2001. Before all the mourners arrived for the funeral, Father Okpogba asked some of Mr. Monroe's classmates and fellow survivors if they wanted to speak during the services. John Melvin Alexander and James D. Bell spoke. He asked me if I wanted to speak on behalf of the Riot Commission, but I declined. I thought this was the survivors' day and I would take "a back seat" to them.

Since I got to the funeral early, I went down to the front and looked at that tribute wall to Father Daniel. Though I never met the man personally, I feel a connection to him, and I have love and respect for him for all the good things he did for black people in Tulsa when it was not "politically correct" to do so. For instance, he got white wealthy Tulsans to become "sponsors" for north Tulsa black youth, such as the orphaned John Patton. Sponsors provided sports equipment, uniforms, transportation, etc. for these youth. Mr. Patton remembers that Father Daniel got one of the wealthiest men in Tulsa to be his (Patton's) sponsor—none other than Mr. Harry Sinclair, the oil baron. John Patton said not only did Mr. Sinclair do the normal "sponsor things," he also had the hollow-legged teenaged John Patton to his home for dinner once a week! He also bought shoes and clothes for the young man.

According to John Patton, Father Daniel was transferred from Tulsa to Providence, Rhode Island. But his memory still lingers on in Tulsa. I felt such a connection to that kind man that day just before George Monroe's funeral. Now Father Daniel is forever a part of my memory, too!

MARY PAYNE, riot victim.
Leroy Kirk, Jr., Tulsa, Oklahoma, son.
Mae Etta Kirk Reynolds, Tulsa, Oklahoma, daughter.

At the time of the Tulsa riot, Mary Payne was a student at Booker T. Washington High School and lived with her sister Georgia Payne.

ADDIE PERRYMAN-TEASE, riot victim.
Geraldine Tease, daughter.

Mrs. Geraldine Tease was born in Boley, Oklahoma, but has lived in Tulsa for the past sixty years. She remembers her mother, Addie Perryman-Tease, talking about the riot, about how her brother, Bob Perryman, was killed by the mobsters. According to Geraldine Tease, her mother and her mother's sisters, Eva Perryman-Grace and Rose Perryman, talked about the terrible things that happened during the riot until the day they died.

JOHN SMITH and JOSEPHINE DAVIS PRESLEY and RAYMOND and HARRIET MAY ROSS PRESLEY, riot victims.
Wilma Presley Bell, Tulsa, Oklahoma, Granddaughter; daughter.
Maybelline Presley Hooks, Tulsa, Oklahoma, granddaughter; daughter.
Mildred Presley Kavanaugh, Palmdale, California, granddaughter; daughter.
Betty Presley McMillan, Los Angeles, California, granddaughter; daughter.
Elizabeth Presley Monday, North Carolina, granddaughter; daughter.
Joyce Marie Presley, Tulsa, Oklahoma, granddaughter; daughter.
Raymond Presley, Tulsa, Oklahoma, grandson; son.
Ronald Dean Presley, Muskogee, Oklahoma, grandson; son.

Wilma Presley Bell, daughter of deceased riot survivors Raymond and Harriet May Ross Presley

Every family has a "resident genealogist" and passionate defender of the family's rights and place in history. (Sometimes this position is self-designated; sometimes it is family-ordained). The passionate, zealous, and dedicated spokesperson for the Presley family was Wilma Presley Bell. In addition to being a wonderful genealogist for her family, she is a persistent and loyal pursuer of rights for all Tulsans. Her advocacy, especially on behalf of those who have not always been the recipients of equal justice in the city, has been helpful in bridging the gap between promises made and promises kept toward black Tulsans. Like the Raphael Walker descendants, Wilma Presley Bell attends most riot-related programs and events, calls frequently to get updates on the latest riot information available, and is anxiously awaiting the dispensation of justice, at last, for survivors and descendants of deceased riot survivors. Thank you, Wilma Presley Bell. Whenever I felt overwhelmed by the pressures and duties of riot commission work, or when I felt frustrated by denials and deadlocks connected to the work, I looked out and saw you. Your persistence, determination, and burning desire to see justice done rejuvenated and sustained me. You were an angel sent from God. Your presence was more effective than you will ever know!

RUTH FAIRCHILD PRICE, riot victim.
Floyd Price, Tulsa, Oklahoma, son.
Carolyn Price Johnson, Plano, Texas, daughter.

HOWARD L. RODGERS and IDA RODGERS, riot victims.
Howard Leroy Dennie, Tulsa, Oklahoma, grandson.
Lawrence Herman Dennie, Tulsa, Oklahoma, grandson.
Alfreda O. Dennie Franklin, Kansas City, Missouri, granddaughter.
Norma Jean Dennie Leshie, Tulsa, Oklahoma, granddaughter.
Frank Eugene Rogers, Tulsa, Oklahoma, grandson.
Ida Louise Dennie Willis, Tulsa, Oklahoma, granddaughter.
Edna Earyle Dennie Works, Tulsa, Oklahoma, granddaughter.

The Rodgers descendants are among Tulsa's most prominent citizens.

REVEREND TRAVIS B. SIPUEL and MARTHA BELL SMITH SIPUEL, riot victims.
Helen M. Sipuel Huggins, Oklahoma City, Oklahoma.

According to his daughter, Helen M. Sipuel, her father was born in the Deep South in 1877 and her mother was born in Dermott, Arkansas, in 1897. They moved to Tulsa in 1918 and rented a house in the Greenwood District which they furnished comfortably. The value of the house was between $8,000 and $11,000.

For more information on the colorful, dynamic Sipuel family, see the autobiography of Helen Sipuel Huggins' sister, Dr. Ada Lois Sipuel Fisher, who was the plaintiff in the landmark U.S. Supreme Court case *Sipuel v. University of Oklahoma*, a case that led to the desegregation of Oklahoma's institutions of higher learning. The book, entitled *A Matter of Black and White*, was published by the University of Oklahoma Press, Norman, Oklahoma. In the book, Ada Lois Sipuel Fisher tells the captivating story of her ancestors, beginning with her grandmother. She says, "Our grandmother, Lucinda, was a dark-skinned slave, while our grandfather, Cap'n Smith, was the white (Irish descent) slave owner. All seven of my mother's brothers and sisters were fair and were deemed white at the first physical impression."

Mrs. Huggins is doing further research in the Tulsa area to find out more about her parents' riot experiences and about their religious experiences in Tulsa.

ROSA DAVIS SKINNER, riot victim.
Fred Davis, Tulsa, Oklahoma, son.
Mildred Louise Davis Scott, Detroit, Michigan, daughter.
Theresa Davis Scott, Tulsa, Oklahoma, daughter.
Sandra Jean Davis Landrum, Tulsa, Oklahoma, daughter.
James Thomas Davis, Eddie Maurice Davis, Etoyce Marie Davis, children of Elmer Lee Davis, deceased son of Rosa Davis Skinner.
Deborah Powell and Sandra Elaine Taylor, daughters of Lulu Sue Davis Taylor, deceased daughter of Rosa Davis Skinner.
Phillip Davis, Byron Davis, Jerry Davis, Bob Davis, Bill Davis, Gerald Davis, Harold Davis, children of James Harold Davis, deceased son of Rosa Davis Skinner.
Fountaine Hayden, child of Rosalind Marie Davis, deceased daughter of Rosa Davis Skinner.

Rosa Davis Skinner

Mike Wilkerson, producer of the documentary film about the Tulsa Race Riot of 1921, *The Tulsa Lynching: A Hidden Story*, which aired on Cinemax television and was nominated for two Emmy awards in 2000, asked me to pick the most touching riot story that I heard when I interviewed all the riot survivors. I had heard numerous stories that moved me to tears, but the one story that tugged at my motherly heart the most was Rosa Davis Skinner's little-dead-baby- in-the-shoe-box story. Mrs. Skinner told me this story just after she had celebrated her ninety-eighth birthday. She was so joyful that day when I went to her home in the historic Brady Heights district on North Denver Avenue (now on the national Historic Register because it was once where Tulsa's first rich oil barons lived, before and immediately after the riot). She received so many birthday cards, including one from President Bill Clinton, that she had them hanging on a rope that was strung around all four walls in her living room! But when I left, Mrs. Davis was not joyful anymore; she was weeping, once again, for a little dead newborn baby that was lost in the riot.

I couldn't for the life of me find the name of the Davis' neighbors who lost the baby. I was so captivated by the story that Mrs. Davis was telling me that I didn't interrupt to ask then. Later, after Mrs. Davis died, I asked her children who the neighbors were and they didn't know. Neither could Dr. Clyde Snow, the forensic expert to the Riot Commission, find out the name of the family, even though he tried hard because the story of that little baby captivated him, too. He did find the coroner's report and the story of how the baby had been found. Here is what Mrs. Skinner told me about that little boy:

"On the night of May 31, 1921, the dear neighbor family of ours had suffered a great tragedy. Earlier that night the wife had delivered a stillborn baby boy. Because it was so late, the husband put the little baby in a shoe box and told his grieving wife that he would take the child to the morgue the next day. [Dr. Snow found the account of that baby in the morgue records that he examined on behalf of the Riot Commission. From information in the morgue records, including quotes made by the man who brought in the little corpse, Dr. Snow has concluded, that in all likelihood the man was a mobster who responded to a touch of decency still left in his heart.]

"Well, that riot broke out that night and we had to run for our lives from those hate-filled mobsters. Honey, we didn't even have time to get dressed. We were runnin' in our nightgowns and we were barefoot. Well, this neighbor family had to flee fast, too. But the wife took time to grab that shoe box with their little dead baby in it. Well, during all that runnin' and pushin' and shovin', the wife dropped that little shoe box. She got down on her hands and knees and tried to find her baby. But she couldn't! Her husband just dragged her away so they wouldn't get killed by the mobs.

"I can still hear her cry ringing in my ears to this day, 'My baby, my baby, I've got to find my baby.' But she never did find that baby! I have blotted most of the memories of that riot from my mind. I just forced myself not to dwell on them. But one memory that I never could blot out was the memory of the loss of that child. Not a day goes by that I don't think about that baby and I say to myself, sometimes out loud, 'I wonder what happened to that po' little baby.'"

MR. (first name unknown) SMALL and EVA SMALL, riot victims.
Jo Ann Ewing, Aurora, Colorado.
Wanda Ewing Pope, Accra, Ghana, West Africa.
Robert Ewing, Oakland, California.
Bill Ewing, Louisville, Colorado.

The Smalls were among Tulsa's wealthiest black families at the time of the Tulsa riot. The Small Hotel, located at the corner of Archer Street and Greenwood Avenue, catered to the needs of elite visiting blacks in Tulsa from pre-riot days until the 1950s. Visiting black dignitaries had no other choice except all-black hotels in the Greenwood area due, to Oklahoma's rigid racial segregation laws.

WILLIS SMITH and MAGGIE SMITH SMITH (Maiden Name was Smith), riot victims.
Rosie Lee Smith Jackson, Tulsa, Oklahoma, daughter.
Fred Smith, Tulsa, Oklahoma, son.
Fannie Smith Verner, Tulsa, Oklahoma, daughter.
Erma Smith Thompson, Montclair, California, daughter.

The author first learned about this charming family and their riot history when she was talking about the Tulsa Race Riot of 1921 at a book signing at Black Images Bazaar and Book Store in Dallas, Texas, in 2000, which was hosted by the Dallas branch of the reparations coalition, NCOBRA. Mrs. Rosa Lee Smith Jackson was visiting her daughter and family in Dallas and just happened to drop by the book store that day. I am so glad that she did. As a result of that happenstance visit, I was able to get that family in the Commission's report.

L-R Riot Commissioner Eddie Faye Gates, guest of the Africans and African Americans for Enslavement Reparations, Black Images Book Bazaar, Dallas, Texas, March 19, 2000. Rosie Lee Smith Jackson of Tulsa, visiting a daughter in Dallas, happened to come in the book store. She is the sister of a Tulsa riot survivor, and daughter of deceased riot survivors.

MARVIN SPEARS and MINNIE SPEARS, riot victims.
Delores Spears Herrington, daughter.
Shirley Spears Ridley, Chicago, Illinois, daughter.

WILLIE STAPLES and GERTRUDE STAPLES
(Later Townsend), riot victims.
Oscar Boyd, Tulsa, Oklahoma, grandson; son.
Alice Boyd Vaughn, Tulsa, Oklahoma,
granddaughter; daughter.

At the time of the riot, nineteen-year-old Gertrude Staples (later Townsend) lived with her grandparents Mr. and Mrs. Willie Staples. They lived in a home on Elgin Street near the old Booker T. Washington High School. The home burned to the ground during the riot. After the riot, Gertrude Staples Boyd Townsend lived in the South Haven community in west Tulsa, where she was a popular Sunday school teacher. She often taught her students about the Tulsa Race Riot of 1921. She warned them about the dangers of holding hatred in the heart for anyone. She stressed that they love all mankind regardless of race, wealth, or position in society. She stressed love, repentance, and forgiveness!

OLLIE STEELE, riot victim.
Diana Lynn Shelton, Oklahoma City, Oklahoma, granddaughter.
Shirley Shelton, Oklahoma city, Oklahoma, granddaughter.

Ollie Steele's granddaughters are her legal heirs, but they are young so I went to Ollie Steele's nephew, who is approaching eighty years, for riot information. And boy, did I get an earful! Here is what Moses Wood of Los Angeles, California (a native of Perry, Oklahoma) told me:

"My daddy, G.W.S. Wood, a Depew, Oklahoma, preacher, was the brother of Ollie Steele. At the time of the riot, Aunt Ollie owned a beauty shop in Tulsa. She was fifty-one years old at the time. She was born in 1870. She said it was terrible when the white mobs came through Greenwood. She said they were heavily armed. She said fleeing blacks had one gun and whites had a gun factory! She said the whites just came through in droves and they blocked off exits so the blacks couldn't escape. She said she saw with her own eyes 'white mobsters shooting and killing fleeing blacks just like shooting fish in a barrel. It was a damn slaughter!' Aunt Ollie herself was shot. She was shot in both of her legs. After the riot, she kept both legs always wrapped in surgical wrap, and she walked with a cane until she died in 1960 at age ninety.

What made Aunt Ollie even madder was that she said she actually saw Guardsmen join in with the mobsters! Just thinking about the riot disturbed Aunt Ollie so that she rarely elaborated about it. She especially wanted to protect children—her children and all children. She didn't want them burdened with hatreds. She didn't want them consumed with plans for retaliation. She said that would be a battle that they couldn't win.

"After the riot, Aunt Ollie and many other black Tulsans came back to a burned-out Greenwood. But other black riot victims came to Cushing, Oklahoma and other small towns. They feared Tulsa. It was not until the late 1930s and early '40s that some of these people trusted Tulsa enough to return to it."

ELLEN URSULINE RICHARDSON TILLMAN,
riot victim.
Mary Priscilla Parker Harrison, Tulsa, Oklahoma, daughter.

Mary Priscilla Parker Harrison remembers that her mother, Ellen Ursuline Richards Tillman, said that her family was originally from Fort Smith, Arkansas, but they had moved to Kansas City, Missouri, seeking a better life. They had come to Tulsa, Oklahoma, after the oil boom, thinking that this would be an even better place for blacks to make a good living. Her mother worked for white folks. She remembers that her mother mentioned an Argue family, and she assumes that she worked for this family, which helped the Harrison family during the riot and after the riot.

Mrs. Harrison said that her mother never talked about the riot.

ANNA TOLBERT, riot victim.
Marguerite Hudspeth Bagby, Tulsa, Oklahoma, daughter.

Anna Tolbert was born December 3, 1889, in Mississippi. She lived in a rented house in the Greenwood District at the time of the Tulsa riot. She died in 1985 at the age of eighty-six.

ANNA TYSON and MATTIE KING (later
Mitchell), her daughter.
Pat Galbraith Moore, Tulsa, Oklahoma, Daughter of
Anna B. King Hurd, daughter of Mattie King
Mitchell, deceased.

Pat G. Moore is a Tulsa icon. The noted pianist/singer, a member the Oklahoma Jazz Hall of Fame, is one of Tulsa's most talented musicians. Her performances are always crowd-pleasers! Pat Moore is among a long line of descendants of strong Tulsa pioneers who are carrying on the tradition of excellence in the Greenwood District of Tulsa, Oklahoma.

HOSEA O. VADEN and LIDA AGNETTA VADEN, riot victims.
Maxine Jessie Vaden, Tulsa, Oklahoma, daughter.
Joyce Vaden Ramsey, Tulsa, Oklahoma, daughter.

The daughters of Hosea Vaden, riot survivor and owner of one of Greenwood's most popular businesses, Vaden's Pool Hall, love to talk about their famous father and the celebrities who visited his pool hall when they were in Tulsa.

GUY VANN and IDA WHITMIRE VANN, riot victims.
Euna Vann Smith, Tulsa, Oklahoma, daughter.

At the time of the Tulsa riot, the Guy Vanns lived in the 600 block of North Marshall in what was known as the Greenwood District.

RAPHAEL WALKER, child riot victim, son of WILLIAM WALKER, riot victim.
Hakeem Carr, Los Angeles, California and Holly Carr, Los Angeles, children of Raphael Walker's deceased daughter Edwina Walker Carr.
Marcia Walker Puckett, Chicago, Illinois, daughter.
William D. Walker, Tulsa, Oklahoma, son.
Olene Walker Washington, Tulsa, Oklahoma, daughter.
Shirley Ann Walker Williams, Tulsa, Oklahoma, daughter.
Karen Foster, Los Angeles, California, and Keli West, Los Angeles, California, daughters of Faye Walker, deceased daughter of Raphael Walker.

The Walker family was one of the most supportive of families toward the Riot Commission. At riot programs, events, meetings, etc., I would always scan the audience for "my Walker bunch." I was never disappointed. Someone in the Walker clan was always there. Even when I went to my paternal family reunion (the Petit family from Lott—near Waco—Texas) in 1999 in Kansas City, Missouri, some Walkers came to my hotel room to be interviewed and to take pictures.

Children of deceased riot survivors William and Lillie Holderness Walker.

L-R. Olene Walker Washington and Shirley Walker Williams, Tulsa, granddaughter of William and Lillie Holderness Walker, deceased riot survivors.

L-R. Jariud and Jajuan Shelton, 7 months, great grandchildren.

Toni Shelton, age 18 months, Tulsa, great grandchild of William and Lillie Holderness Walker, deceased Tulsa riot victims

RILEY WALKER, SR. and ESSIE MATTHEWS WALKER, riot victims.
Riley Walker, Jr., Oakland, California, son.
Denette Maria Walker, Tulsa, Oklahoma, daughter.
Frank Walker, Sr., Inglewood, California, son.
Harvey Leon Walker, Sr., Seattle, Washington, son.
Harry Daniel Walker, Tulsa, Oklahoma, son.

Daniel Walker Bitson, Jr., David Harold Bitson, Pamela Bitson, Paula Bitson, Michael Bitson, children of Imogene Jean Bitson, deceased daughter of Riley Walker, Sr.

Leroy Walker, Owasso, Oklahoma, son of Patricia Ann Walker, Tulsa, Oklahoma, deceased daughter of Riley Walker, Sr.

Keith Hamilton, Richmond, California, Jarred Hamilton, Sherrie Hamilton, Nora Hamilton Parker, Tulsa, Oklahoma, Price Hamilton, Atlanta, Georgia, Rene Hamilton Traylor, Tulsa, Oklahoma, and Coleen Hamilton Vann, children of Ethel Mae Walker Hamilton, deceased daughter of Riley Walker, Sr.

Carl Walker, Jr., Fullerton, California, Sandra K. Walker Gibson, Los Angeles, children of Carl Walker, Sr., deceased son of Riley Walker, Sr.

The Riley Walker, Sr., heir questionnaires had me pulling out my hair! Some of them inadvertently ended up in the William Walker questionnaires. But after frantic calls to Riley Walker, Sr., relatives I think everything was straightened out. If not, errors will be corrected in the next edition of this book.

Frank Walker, Sr., of Inglewood, California, was very helpful in providing information regarding the Riley Walker, Sr., Tulsa riot victims. He said that at the time of the riot, his parents were living at 423 East Latimer Court in the Greenwood District. They had come to Tulsa from Texas. He said their house burned down in the riot. The mother, Essie Matthews Walker, worked as the cleaning lady at a mortuary. She was at work when the riot broke out, and she had to stay at that mortuary for a week after the riot! She never talked to us children much about the riot. In later years, she explained that the reason she hadn't talked about it was because she didn't want us to be prejudiced.

DR. CHARLES WICKHAM, riot victim.
Jimmie Wickham, daughter.

Jimmie Wickham says that at the time of the riot, her father, and his first wife, lived across the street from Mt. Zion Baptist Church in the Deep Greenwood area of Tulsa. She said he had a lovely two-story home. His clinic was in the downstairs part of the home. She said the home/clinic building was burned to the ground in the riot.

After the riot, Dr. Wickham (and his relative Dr. Todd) moved from Tulsa to Oklahoma City. Soon after, his wife died. He later met and married Jimmie Wickham's mother. Dr. Wickham was also active in the Knights of Pythias organization. He was Grand Pythias in Oklahoma City. He lived across the street from Calvary Baptist Church in Oklahoma City, which was located on Second Street, off Walnut. In Oklahoma City, Dr. Wickham built a new house and clinic.

DELTESSA STARR WILLIAMS, riot victim.
Dianne Williams Beavers, granddaughter.
Patricia Williams, granddaughter.

Patricia Williams, who was then employed at the University of Wisconsin in Madison, contacted me soon after the Riot Commission was formed to tell me about her grandmother, Deltessa Starr Williams, who was a riot survivor. Mrs. Williams died in October 1994, so Patricia and I missed the opportunity to probe her grandmother's mind about the riot. But based on what Patricia told me, and the documentation she provided, her grandmother's name was added to the survivors' registry.

FISHER JAMES WILLIAMS and DINAH FREEMAN WILLIAMS, riot victims.
Dorothy Williams Bramlett, Tulsa, Oklahoma, daughter.
Dr. D. F. Grant Williams, St. Louis, Missouri, son.

This family was one of the most interesting that I met during my work on behalf of the Riot Commission. In my interview with Dorothy Williams Bramlett, I found that her grandfather, John Williams, had been born in North Carolina but his family moved to Texas when he was seven years old. John grew up in Hubbard City, Texas, which is near Houston. As a teenager, he was waterboy on cattle drives from Texas to Oklahoma.

At the time of the riot, Fisher Williams and Dinah Freeman Williams were buying a home on Cameron Street, just off Brady Avenue, which is near Greenwood. Dorothy Williams Bramlett carries on the pioneer legacy of hard work and adventure that was begun by her dynamic ancestors. She is an activist in the Tulsa community and is especially vocal on education issues.

Dr. Grant Williams, a professor of urban studies at Washington University in St. Louis, Missouri, was one of the most intellectually astute and dedicated researchers I met during the study of the Tulsa Race Riot of 1921. He did much research in Tulsa on the riot and attended many Riot Commission meetings. His scholarly report was part of the resources in the bibliography materials listed in the final report that the Commission submitted to the governor of Oklahoma, the Oklahoma legislature, and the mayor of Tulsa on February 28, 2001. The paper, entitled "Economic Dualism, Institutional Failure, and Racial Violence in a Resource Boom Town: A Reexamination of the Tulsa Riot of 1921," was submitted to the *Journal of Urban History* in 2001 for publication. Dr. Williams returned to the U.S. at the end of 2001 from an extended urban study program in Paris, France.

Stephanie Bramlett, daughter of Dorothy Williams Bramlett, carries on that strong Williams legacy. She became a Riot Commission volunteer and provided valuable services to the Commission. She assisted Kavin

Ross with the videotaping of survivors, and she was always available to assist with presentations—lectures, plays, meetings, programs, etc.—at the Greenwood Cultural Center.

JOHN WESLEY and LOULA WILLIAMS; William Danforth Williams, child survivor, son, riot victims.
Anita Williams Christopher, granddaughter, daughter.
David O. Williams, grandson, son.

Anita Williams Christopher and David O. Williams, along with the J. B. Stradford heirs, the Andrew Jackson Smitherman heirs, and a handful of others, are among the heirs of the most prosperous of the victims of the Tulsa riot—those who owned the most property, property that everyone in Tulsa, black and white, knew about and that was admired and respected, or hated and envied, by those races respectively. John Wesley and Loula Williams owned the Dreamland Theater on Greenwood Avenue, and also a confectionary which Loula ran while John Wesley ran the popular theater.

In her book *The Event of the Tulsa Disaster*, first published privately by Mary Elizabeth Jones Parrish in 1921, Mrs. Parrish describes the Williams Building as being located in the "Williams Building No, 2, a 2-Story Brick, 129-133."

Mary Elizabeth Jones Parrish, the only eyewitness professional black journalist to write about the riot, had been fascinated by Tulsa since girlhood. She had always heard her relatives talk of the teeming city. She first saw it for herself in 1918 after she came from her journalism job in Chicago, Illinois, to McAlester, Oklahoma, not too far from Tulsa, to help her siblings care for their seriously ill mother. When their mother died six months later, she returned to her job in Chicago. But Tulsa was a magnet that pulled her back. Chicago's loss was Tulsa's gain. Unfortunately for Mrs. Parrish, the Williamses, and other riot victims, their businesses would be destroyed—ransacked, looted, and/or burned to the ground by white mobsters and strafed from the air by whites (wealthy businessmen and others). Parrish's book has been invaluable to historians, authors, and others in providing primary source materials about the riot.

Primary source information about the Williams family's prominent Dreamland Theater is also found in the Redfearn Case lawsuit document.

Mary Elizabeth Jones Parrish, only professional journalist to witness, and write a book, about the Tulsa riot.

Clarence Love, nephew by marriage of Mary Elizabeth Jones Parrish, had his famous aunt's book reprinted in 1998.

LOUVENIA WILLIAMS and her son, TOM SWIFT HAMEL, riot victims.
Mildred Marian Hamel Miller, Austin, Texas.

Mrs. Mildred Miller's daughter, LaDawna Miller of Austin, Texas, contacted the Riot Commission and provided the following information:

"My great grandmother, Louvenia Williams, and several of her relatives, lived in a rented house near Haskell and Jasper Streets in the Greenwood area at the time of the riot. I have heard many stories about the riot from my mother and her other relatives who lived through the riot. My mother remembers the riot well and would like for you to call her so she can share her stories with you."

DAN WILSON and VIOLET DIXON WILSON, riot victims.
Mary A. Wilson, Englewood, Colorado, Bertha Wilson and Elizabeth Wilson, granddaughters of Dan Wilson and daughters of Richard Wilson, deceased son of Dan Wilson

Mary A. Wilson says that her father, Richard E. Wilson, told and retold the story of his father's disappearance during the Tulsa Race Riot of 1921 so many times that she knows it by heart. He said that his dad, Dan Wilson, had some business to take care of in Tulsa. So at about sundown on May 31, 1921, he and his wife, Violet, headed for Tulsa. Richard, who was sixteen at the time, says his parents took a horse and buggy for the trip and that they stayed at a minister's house when they got to Tulsa, and that there was another lady staying there (perhaps someone who was fleeing from the riot). They were told that there was race trouble in Tulsa and that the minister's wife was gone. She was taking children to the country to get them away from the dangers in Tulsa.

Richard Wilson said that is the last information he has concerning his father, for the next day, he vanished without a trace. His family has never heard a word about him since that day. The family has been consumed by agony, grief, and doubts about their beloved patriarch for eight decades now. They had hoped that the Riot Commission would uncover some information about the missing Dan Wilson. But that was not to be. So Dan is among those whose final place on earth will probably never be known. His family wonders if he is among the riot dead seen floating in the Arkansas River, or in abandoned mine pits, city incinerators in west Tulsa, the earth under brickyards, department stores, or highways, in mass graves in a downtown cemetery, or in cemeteries in other parts of Tulsa, including the area that was once wooded farmland but is now affluent southeast Tulsa. It is hard on the remaining descendants not to know what happened to their beloved ancestor.

TISHIE WRIGHT, riot victim.
Della Shelton Jackson, Oklahoma City, Oklahoma,
Johnny Shelton, Los Angeles, California,
Faye May, Edmond, Oklahoma,
Betty Anderson, Edmond, Oklahoma,
Mamie Shelton, Los Angeles, California,
Billy Shelton, Oklahoma City, Oklahoma,
Margaret Lee, Oklahoma City, Oklahoma,
children of Della Oliver Wright, deceased daughter of Pearl Oliver, riot victim.
Ruby Spears is the deceased daughter of Della Oliver Wright and left two heirs, sons Raphael Spears of El Segundo, California, and Raoul Spears of Gardena, California.

Tishie Wright had been meaning to visit her cousin Pearl Oliver in Tulsa for some time. But she always regretted the time she chose to make that visit, May 31, 1921, for she got caught in the Tulsa Race Riot of 1921! According to Tishie Wright's heirs, "Cousin Pearl lived in a house that she owned on Greenwood Avenue. She also owned a beauty shop and some other buildings. Grandma Tishie always wished that she had made that visit earlier."

Special Category: Victims Not in Tulsa on the Days of the Riot. Victims Had Fled Vandalism of Their Home and Business and Threats on Their Lives Just Before the Riot Broke Out. Home and Store Were Burned Down:

BERNICE BURNETT WHEAT, Austin, Texas, b. January 5, 1908

Chapter 8
Claims of White Victims of the Tulsa Race Riot of 1921

City of Tulsa minutes from 1921 to 1926 (most of them in the first couple of years after the riot) and Tulsa County minutes show that most white claims for riot damages and/or losses were routinely paid upon filing. This was not the case with black claimants. Their cases were routinely marked, "Application Not Accepted." A few cases were accepted, but a look at the minutes later would show, "Request Denied." Two court cases were filed against the City of Tulsa by prominent black Tulsa businessmen, William Walker and Sam Mackey (his wife, Lucy, was also listed as plaintiff).

The Mackey case was dismissed on May 31, 1937. A look at the signature of one of the City of Tulsa attorneys in the case was revealing to some of us riot commissioners. That same name, Harry Halley, is on one of the Ku Klux Klan rolls in the Special Collections of McFarlin Library at the University of Tulsa. A number of Tulsa's attorneys and judges were card-carrying Ku Klux Klansmen at the time of the riot, and even more were after the riot. Many other Tulsans had a Klan mentality.

At least two whites did not receive compensation for their losses and contacted the Riot Commission. Grace Woodall Culp, of Sarasota, Florida, age eighty-four in 2000, had her daughter, Charlene M. Knop, of Charlotte, North Carolina, write the following to the commission:

"Her name at the time of riot, 1921, was Grace Fremont Woodall. Her birthday is 2/11/16. She was born in Flagstaff, Arizona, to Leonard John Woodall and Carrie Lydian Gilman Woodall. Her mother died during the riots. Her father was either a policeman or fireman. His brother was also one or the other (as I understand it the forces were combined at that time).

"I will try to get more information from my mother (although she can become somewhat hysterical when talking about this). My understanding has always been: The four sisters hid under the bed in the front bedroom with the mother when shooting erupted in their area. My grandfather had already been called out. My grandmother was about 6 months pregnant at the time. According to my mother's oldest sister (now deceased— Ollie Myrtle), my grandmother was wounded by a ricocheting bullet and started labor. By the time my grandfather was able to get to the house to check on everyone, my grandmother was almost dead from blood loss and a miscarriage. He took my grandmother outside to see the sunset (her dying wish), and that was when the girls saw bodies in the front yard and almost everything around them burned. My grandmother is buried in Rose Hill Cemetery. This is the story my mother has told my entire life (52 years) and two of her sisters always confirmed. My grandfather later remarried a lady named Nell Coleman who had two sons. They divorced about 1934 or 35 and he again remarried. He retired from the fire department. He died in 1959."

In an interview that I had with Mrs. Knop after her letter had been received, she added that her mother's body was kept in their home for one week to prevent her from being buried with blacks. She said her grandfather had put the body in the coolest place in the house. She sadly related that her grandfather was "taken in" by the Ku Klux Klan. At first he was reluctant to join, but the Klan convinced him that it was necessary in order to protect his motherless girls.

The other white riot claim came from Leo David Marks.

"My name at the time of the riot, 1921: Leo David Markovitz. Family name legally changed Oct. 21, 1942, in Tulsa County District Court to Marks by my father, Sam Marks.

"Date of Birth: Nov. 4, 1915

"Place of Birth: Omaha, Nebraska.

"Address at time of riot: On North Detroit Ave. Home information not moot. It was not damaged. This information concerns my father's neighborhood grocery which was looted and destroyed by fire set by rioters early in the morning of June 1. The grocery was located on a side street east of Detroit Ave., the west edge of what was considered the Greater Greenwood area, and just north of the Katy railroad tracks. The side street no longer exists because of Interstate 244.

"As a child of five, I recall my father coming home from the store crying that he had pleaded with the rioters, but they wouldn't listen. 'You can see I'm not black.' I remember he said he told them, 'Why are you doing this to me?' Their reply, he said, was, 'You're a Jew, and you do business with blacks, that's why.' It was true. He always said his best-paying customers were blacks, including a municipal Judge. I also recall riding my trike on the sidewalk outside our house the day of the riot, until my mother snatched me inside, while she watched men in khaki uniforms with guns and rifles drawn and bugles sounding, marching up Detroit Ave. toward Standpipe Hill where some blacks were said to be entrenched.

"I grew up in Tulsa, and went to Central High and the University of Oklahoma. I am a combat veteran of World War II, and my father and mother's sole survivor. He did Sept. 22, 1971, and my mother died Aug. 24, 1980. They moved to Kansas City, Mo. from Tulsa in 1966.

"Estimated total loss of property in the race riot? I would estimate it at about $100,000, including the structure, a standup cooler and other equipment, furnishings and contents. What few personal records survived the years don't show any compensation for the loss, or any mention of riot insurance, if indeed it was even offered at the time. Neither have I turned up my father's personal account of the riot itself, or estimation of damage. He might have filed a claim with the Tulsa City Commission, but there's no evidence of that in my possession. Perhaps the commission or the Oklahoma Historical Society has a record of such action. If so, it would probably be filed under his previous name, Sam Markovitz.

"Any consideration in this matter would be appreciated."

These two claims were included in the official listing of claimants in the final registry of riot survivors, descendants, widows, spouses, and others who felt that they had legitimate claims for damages incurred in the Tulsa Race Riot of 1921. The said list was sent by Fed-Ex before the deadline of October 1, 2001.

Chapter 9

White Accounts of the Tulsa Race Riot of 1921

My heart overflowed with love and gratitude at the out-pouring of love, good will, best wishes, and tangible help that was given to Tulsa's riot victims, descendants of riot victims, the Riot Commission, and to the north Tulsa community in general from some members of the white community. Despite disapproval, and sometimes warn-ings, from their relatives, friends, co-workers, bosses, the media, and their political, economic, and social organi-zations, they came forward, took the heat, and con-tributed to the mission of uncovering the long-sup-pressed story of the riot. Bypassing the kill-the- messen-ger syndrome, they jumped in and contributed to the success of the Commission's research, writing, and com-pilation of the final report.

There are four verses in the Bible where Jesus en-courages people to do more for their fellow man. He notes that people are often willing to help "their own," their immediate family and closest friends, but he com-pels them to go the extra mile and to help those in need who are not close family or close friends. He said, " And if ye do good to them which do good to you, what thank have ye? for sinners also lend to sinners, to receive as much again. But love your enemies, and do good, and lend, hoping for nothing again; and your reward shall be great, and ye shall be the children of the Highest: for he is kind unto the unthankful and to the evil. Be ye there-fore merciful, as your Father also is merciful" (Luke: 33-36). This chapter is about those good white Samaritans, "the children of the Highest," who went the extra mile, who came forth and helped their fellow man who was not family nor close friends—black Tulsans who were af-fected by the Tulsa Race Riot of 1921. Note: A few of the witnesses asked that their identities be kept confi-dential. Those requests were honored.

I: In Their Own Words: Stories Told by White Eyewitnesses Themselves: Primary Sources

ANONYMOUS MALE:

This man called the Riot Commission to share what he saw when he worked for Manhattan Construction Company when Tulsa's present Civic Center at 400 South Denver Avenue was being built. He said that the Civic Center was built right over an old Indian cemetery which closed in 1906 when there was no more room for burials. He estimates that over 1,000 graves were un-covered, and he said that he and other workers boxed up forty-one boxes of remains. He wonders where they were taken. He wonders where the funeral records for that cemetery are located. He says he has done a lot of searching regarding those remains but fears that the records were probably destroyed, as many other records relating to the riot were. He still worries about "those bones we unearthed that day." He worries about the re-mains that were not boxed. He thinks many of them were just left where they were and that they are buried forever underneath the Civic Center. He heard that some remains were buried in a triangle where the pres-ent Hodges Coal Storage area is located, at Eleventh Street and Peoria Avenue. This thoughtful and caring man just can't rest in peace until he finds out that those people whose remains were disturbed during the con-struction of the Tulsa Civic Center rest in peace.

ANONYMOUS MALE:

This gentleman called the Riot Commission to give information about the role of the Ku Klux Klan before, during, and after the riot of 1921. He had noted that the media in Tulsa, and some whites, seemed reluctant to admit to a Klan presence in Tulsa until the late 1920s. This man, whose grandfather had been a policeman in the early 1920s, told of where evidence was found which showed clearly a Klan presence in Tulsa before the riot. Some leaders of Tulsa were active, card-carrying Klansmen, including some who were in the police force (Examination of Klan rolls at the University of Tulsa's McFarlin Library by the Oklahoma Commission studying the Tulsa riot certainly does corroborate this. On rolls there, 1928-1932, I found the names of Tulsa leaders including a mayor, numerous attorneys, judges, policemen, teachers, boy scout leaders, businessmen, preachers, the grandfather of at least one state legislator, and many others.)

RUTH SIGLER AVERY:

A long-time member of the Tulsa Historical Society, and a persistent, scholarly historian who has researched and written about the Tulsa riot for seven decades, shared the following eyewitness account:

"The night that the Tulsa riot broke out, May 31, 1921, my Catholic school in downtown Tulsa was having a school program. I was on stage and had just held up my doll, Rosemary, for the audience to see, and I was reciting my poem.

"I was wearing a beautiful white dress and I had been warned not to get it soiled because the dress had to be dry cleaned. But right in the middle of my presentation, someone ran into the school and shouted that a riot was on and that we had to get out of town. I was hustled offstage by my parents.

"During our harried flight out of the downtown area to our home at 206 E. Eighth Street, a block east of Central High School, I saw sights that no child's eye should see. We came home by trolley car and, being a curious child, I peered out the windows. I saw an old black man who was releasing some cows dropped by a bullet. A little boy who was with him ran into the road and joined other fleeing blacks. And then, disaster struck. Mobsters shot out the windows of the trolley car! Shattered glass fell all over passengers. Trolley officials shouted for us to lie flat on the trolley floor and to use our hands to protect our heads. Although glass was all over my head—my hair was just full of glass—I wasn't concerned about that. I was concerned with two things—keeping my precious white dress clean and protecting my doll, Rosemary. I did protect Rosemary, but I couldn't keep my white dress clean. The person next to me on the trolley had been wounded and he bled all over my new white dress. I was just petrified that my parents would be upset with me for letting that beautiful dress get soiled. (But they weren't, to my relief).

"On June 1, 1921, things had gotten worse and like many others, we fled Tulsa. That was the worst day of my life. I saw sights that traumatized me and that haunt me to this day. I saw two large trucks filled with dead black bodies. On top of one truck was a little boy about my age (7). The truck hit a bump and the boy's head flopped over. His eyes were wide open and his mouth was opened wide, as if he had just let out a death scream. He was barefoot and he was wearing blue pants and a plaid shirt. The sight of that little boy is engraved in my mind. It will be with me until I die. I also remember a woman whose leg kept flopping over the side of the truck bumper. I can't get the picture of those trucks with those black bodies out of my mind. I was a sheltered child. I had not even seen a dead animal before, let alone a truckload of dead humans!

"On this escape from Tulsa, we witnessed a miraculous escape by a poor black man. My dad was driving us to Sand Springs where we would be safe with family. We looked out the car window and saw an old black man crawling on his stomach. Dad stopped and picked up the man. We learned that he had survived by crawling on his stomach two miles down a water line. The mobsters couldn't see him. Thank God, my dad did see him. Dad just stopped the car, got out, and ran over and took that poor man out of the water line. When we got to safety in Sand Springs, Dad told the poor, muddy man to take a good hot bath. Then he fed him a chicken dinner. The man stayed two days with our family. Then Dad took him to the Red Cross Center."

Ruth Avery, historian at First Wednesday Reading Club, Tulsa.

AUTHOR'S NOTE: The father of Ruth Sigler Avery was C. C. Sigler. When C. C. was born, his parents gave him only initials for his first name. They decided that when he was old enough, and had learned something about the world, he could choose his own name. When C. C. was twelve years old, he picked his name—Christopher Columbus!

CLYDE EDDY:

Mr. Eddy became a favorite of the Commission and of the media. He frequently described how he, a cousin, and several little playmates saw piano boxes filled with black bodies buried at Oak Lawn Cemetery at Eleventh Street and Peoria Avenue in June of 1921. See numerous videotapes, news articles, and the Riot Commission Report for more details.

MORRIS B. FELL:

Morris Fell called the Commission to tell of how he was an eyewitness to the shooting of blacks in the 200 block of East Independence Street during the riot, and how his father, Jacob Fell, took black workers from his plant to safety in Coweta, Oklahoma, during the peak of the riot. His memory of that day is as clear today as it was then when he was a bright-eyed six-year-old.

Mr. Fell said that his father, who owned Bradford Pipe and Supply Company at 115 North Detroit Avenue, was very concerned about the safety of his black employees. So he went into the besieged black neighborhood and on two different occasions brought a carload of black people to safety to an oil lease that he owned near the edge of Coweta, Oklahoma. There was a little vacant house on the oil lease land and that is where he hid his black employees. Morris Fell can't remember the names of all of the black workers that his father saved, but he does remember one married couple, Willie and Mae. Here is what Mr. Fell remembers about that day:

"My sister and I were visiting an aunt and uncle who lived in the 200 block of East Independence Street when the riot began. Their house was on a hill and we could look down and see the mob terror. We could see the fires and hear the shooting. While we were looking out at all the commotion, a bullet came through a window and broke a water bottle. We all ducked down and laid on the floor then! Then my dad came for us. And that is when he went to the homes of his black employees and took them to safety. To hide the fact that he was carrying blacks away to safety, he took me along with him. He thought authorities wouldn't be suspicious of him if he had me beside him in the car. So that is how I got a good look at that riot. To hide the blacks, dad had them lie down on the floor and seats of the two cars carrying them and he covered them with blankets. That worked.

Authorities never suspected that we were taking black refugees out of Tulsa to safety. But that is exactly what we were doing! My mother and sister stayed home. But I got to be a witness during that riot. I got to see shootings, and burnings, and all sorts of terrible things. When the riot was over, I got to see the ruins of my father's business, which was totally destroyed by the mobsters. I have always been proud of what my father did. He was a lovely man. He was such a fine gentleman."

ROBERT FISHER:

Robert Fisher was an eight-year-old boy when he saw Guards marching blacks to "refugee camps" down the street which later became part of old Highway Route 66. The guards were marching the black people to Carbondale in West Tulsa (on the other side of South Haven). He described these camps to riot commissioners.

TOM GAGE:

Tom Gage was six years old when the riot broke out. His dad put him on his shoulders, so he could look at the fighting on Standpipe Hill in north Tulsa. He still has this picture in his head of five houses in a row—all on fire. He can still hear the noises of animals in distress. He says he heard howling dogs, snarling cats, squealing pigs, low-moaning cows. Humans and animals were in deep distress that day.

Mr. Gage said that after they looked at the burning for a while, his dad took him to a drug store downtown, and then to Guinn's Grocery Store. He said that on that day of the riot, and the following day, white men were just milling around aimlessly. Those not participating in the melee just stood around looking.

WILSON GLASS:

The late Wilson Glass, a former Tulsa County Assessor, was a delightful man that I often saw at my church, First Church of Christ, Scientist, Tulsa. He knew of my work on the Riot Commission, and one day he just poured out his heart to me about what he knew about the riot. And he knew plenty, for his father was Merritt Julius Glass, who was chair of the Tulsa Real Estate Exchange! In an hour-long followup interview, Wilson Glass provided me with valuable firsthand information about his famous father, his pioneer mother, a journal-listed Christian Science practitioner who lived to be ninety-one, and the bustling city of Tulsa that achieved so much by the 1920s and suffered so much in the awful riot of 1921.

ROBERT CLARK FRAYSER:

I interviewed Mr. Frayser in 1994 and included his poignant vignette in my second book, *They Came Searching*. The Frayser family lived in Vinita, Oklahoma, and befriended blacks who came to their town before, during, and after the riot. Some came by car down the highway that later became known as Route 66; others walked the nearly fifty miles from Tulsa. Robert Frayser never forgot the sight of the ragged group of riot refugees. He recalled that "These wandering people were just walking—past Chelsea and other little towns and right into Vinita. They had sacks on their backs and babes in their arms, and little children holding on to their hands. Some of them showed up in our back yard, and Mattie, our maid whom we all just adored, was known as a great organizer and she just took over. She had some refugees cut wood for fire, and others draw water from our well, and still others setting up makeshift shelter for the homeless people. She put some of the women to work shelling peas and cooking for the crowd, or just doing whatever needed to be done. I was always glad that we helped those poor refugees who had lost everything they owned in that riot."

MYLES JOHNSON:

Myles Johnson of Washington, D.C., sent the Riot Commission a letter explaining why he was contacting the Commission and twenty pages from a family history that he published several years ago. The excerpts cover the experiences of his grandfather, B. F. JOHNSON, who was in Tulsa doing business on May 31, 1921, and got caught in the worst race riot in U.S. history! Myles Johnson said that "While it sheds no new light on those horrible events, it does provide one eyewitness' reaction. Even a conservative Virginia racist man was horrified by what he saw."

That account of the "Virginia racist man" is powerful and corroborates the accounts made by many other witnesses of the brutality that occurred during the riot.

O. W. LLOYD

O. W. Lloyd is the late father of Jim Lloyd, who was one of the commissioners on the Oklahoma Commission to Study the Tulsa Race Riot of 1921. During the riot, O. W. Lloyd was a taxi driver in Tulsa and drove visiting oilmen, businessmen, and others all over Tulsa, including the Greenwood District. This kind, sensitive man loved people and was quite distraught by the riot. He collected every newspaper account of the riot that he could get his hands on and

carefully put them into his own personal archive. His son, Jim, a lawyer who lives in Tulsa and practices law in Sand Springs, inherited his father's loving nature. With his own money, Jim made copies of every one of his father's newspapers and gave a set of them to each riot commissioner. He also went to Tuskegee University in Alabama and added copies of newspapers to his riot collection of papers. Tuskegee University has the largest collection of newspapers covering the riot in the U.S.

JEANNIE NORMAN:

This lady from Langley, Oklahoma, called the Commission to share information about the Grove, Oklahoma, area and about riot refugees.

HAZEL LEIGH WHITNEY PARCEL:

Hazel Parcel is a sweet little housewife who lives in Wichita, Kansas. She, too, answered my appeal in the *Tulsa World*. During that first interview, I learned some interesting things about Mrs. Parcel's family and about the riot in general. I learned that she was an eight-year-old school girl at Lincoln Elementary School in Tulsa when the riot broke out and that she and her mother lived with her grandparents, J. W. and Etta M. Whitney. Her grandfather was the City of Tulsa Street Commissioner and her grandmother was Etta Whitney, who considered herself "quite a poet."

Mrs. Parcel sent me a packet of supporting documents and other information. Included in the packet were some of Etta Whitney's poems! After reading Mrs. Whitney's poems, I decided that she right. She *was* a good poet!

It was good to get "insider" information about one of Tulsa's white city leaders during the riot period. And the icing on the cake was becoming friends with Mrs. Parcel.

PHILIP RHEES:

Philip Rhees is still another person who answered my appeal in the *Tulsa World* for white eyewitnesses to the Tulsa Race Riot of 1921. We hit it off immediately and are the best of buddies to this day. His accounts of his actions as an eight- year-old on the second day of the riot are among my absolute favorites:

"Two things happened during that riot that sure made me mad. First, I had been playing in my front yard at 720 South Elgin Street, where my parents and us five kids lived. It was a lovely little house and I lived a peaceful, carefree life. My parents were loving people who had come to Oklahoma from Pennsylvania via

Good White Samaritan Philip Rhees, age 8.

Good White Samaritan Philip Rhees, today.

Ohio. First they lived in Morris. Then they came to Tulsa, where Dad was superintendent of the Prairie Oil and Gas Company. Mother stayed home and cared for us children. Dad hired a black maid named Cora to help my mother. She was a wonderful woman and was just loved by our family. In fact, she was just one of the family! My parents had none of the prejudices toward other races like so many Oklahomans had at that time. They treated all people with dignity and respect. Perhaps that is why I got so mad when I saw those Guards marching those black men down our street on the way to McNulty Park that day. Well, I got mad enough to do something about it. I got my B-B gun and went under the front porch, which had lattice work around it, about thirty to fifty feet of lattice. I stuck my gun through the lattice holes and popped those Guards in their backs as they marched by! They didn't know what was popping them in their backs. They'd stop, look around, and, seeing nothing, they'd march on. Then I would pop them again! I thought they were just a bunch of 'bad guys' for treating those black people like that.

"Now the other thing that made me mad was something that I couldn't do anything about. I just had to let time take its course. On the day of the riot, I went to get a haircut at my neighborhood barbershop. There was still some riot activity going on. One barber told the barber who was cutting my hair to "Hurry up and finish cutting that kid's hair so we can get our guns and go down to Midland Valley and shoot some niggers." I don't know whether they went and shot any black people or not, but I do know that my barber hurried up. He just botched up my hair! Whether they shot any black people or not, I don't know. I do know that they left the barbershop with that intent."

Others besides me are fascinated with Philip Rhees. Mike Wilkerson, owner of Barristers' Studio in Tulsa called me one day after he had just finished reading about Philip in *They Came Searching*. Mr. Wilkerson said that he just *had* to feature Philip in the documentary film that he was making about the Tulsa riot for Cinemax Television. I made the necessary arrangements, and Philip is just wonderful in the film. Wilkerson also wanted to feature Rep. Don Ross, whose idea resulted in the creation of the Oklahoma Commission to Study the Tulsa Race Riot of 1921, and me. We dutifully obliged Mike. That documentary film, *The Tulsa Lynching of 1921: A Hidden Story*, is my favorite of all Tulsa riot-related films. It was nominated for two Emmys in 2001.

MERLE DWIGHT ROBERTS:

The late Merle Dwight Roberts lived in a beautiful residential care home, Goshen, in Mounds, Oklahoma. He called the Commission because he had "something to get off his chest." This author and Kim Johnson of the Rudisill North Regional Library took a camcorder and went to interview Mr. Roberts. He was delightful (as was the meal we shared with Mr. Roberts thanks to the generosity of the care facility's operator, Gladys Lytle). What Merle Dwight Roberts wanted to "get off his chest" was a riot memory that had haunted him all his life. He thought that if he shared that memory with me, he could put it to rest. What haunted him so, all those years, was a sight he saw when he was a little boy during the riot. His dad was carrying him somewhere in Tulsa (perhaps to safety) and they passed a utility pole. Hanging from the pole was the body of a black riot victim. I don't know if telling me the story helped Mr. Roberts in purging that picture from his mind. I do hope so. Less than a year after that interview, Mr. Roberts died. I hope that he is at peace at last.

Merle Dwight Roberts who, as a small child in 1921, was so traumatized by the sight of a black man hanging from a lamp pole during the riot that it bothered him all his life. Months after being interviewed by Commissioner Gates, he died.

REVEREND RAYFORD WALLACE:

Reverend Rayford Wallace pastored a small United Methodist Church on the west side of Tulsa from 1978 to 1981. In that church was an elderly gentleman who had been in the National Guard at the time and was one of the Guardsmen dispatched to the riot area in 1921. Rev. Wallace said he had two reoccurring conversations with that member of his congregation which went along these lines:

"Every time I mentioned the commandment, 'You shall not kill!' he would collar me after the service to explain to me that that meant murder, not killing in the line of duty as a soldier. He did this so regularly that I concluded that it was not me he was trying to convince: it was himself.

"More than once he told me of his involvement in the riot as a Guardsman. More than once he said to me, 'You'd be walking down the street and see someone—you know, Niggers—come from behind a corner. You'd shoot and they'd go back behind the corner. You wouldn't know if you had hit them or not.' He used the word 'Nigger' hesitantly—as if he didn't want to but thought that I might not understand who he was talking about if he didn't. And I apologize to my black neighbors for quoting it here.

"My memory of these reoccurring conversations leaves me with two mental images: One is of National Guardsmen patrolling the streets in the riot area and shooting, at least shooting at, blacks on sight. The other is of one of those then young Guardsmen struggling in his twilight years to maintain his belief that those possible killings were justified and not a violation of the sixth commandment—wrestling with his conscience over half a century later."

II: Stories Told by Offspring, Other Relatives, Friends and Acquaintances of White Riot Eyewitnesses: Secondary Sources

LARRY ABBOUD:

Larry Abboud of Sand Springs, Oklahoma, called Reuben Gant at the Greenwood Chamber of Commerce in north Tulsa. Reuben Gant called me. Mr. Abboud was upset about an old black cemetery, the Haynes Plantation Cemetery, which was unkempt—the fence was down, some tombstones had toppled, water from years of rain had washed away much soil, leaving some graves eroded, and cattle were walking over graves. The road leading to the cemetery was an overgrown wilderness, and families with relatives buried there could not get to the cemetery to take care of the graves (a violation of Oklahoma law). Among those buried in that cemetery were at least one decorated Korean War soldier and many black pioneers, some who had come to Oklahoma long before statehood, and, according to the testimony of some witnesses, victims of the Tulsa Race Riot of 1921. I brought this issue up at the next North Tulsa Historical Society meeting and the organization created a "Restoration of Black Cemeteries in Northeastern Oklahoma" project. Bob Littlejohn and I attended the next Sand Springs City

Council meeting, and I was put on the agenda and allowed to speak about the cemetery and about Oklahoma law. Also attending that meeting was Dick Warner of the Tulsa Historical Society. Dick and I were interviewed by reporters from the *Sand Springs Leader* and the *Tulsa World*. Things are better at the cemetery now, thanks to the concern of Larry Abboud.

ANONYMOUS MALE:

This white male came to the *Oklahoma Eagle* with his riot story. The *Eagle* referred him to me. He said that his father had a black friend named Taylor who was in the riot. He said that his late father often talked about what Mr. Taylor told him about the riot. He said that Mr. Taylor always wept when he talked of the riot. Mr. Taylor stated that he saw horse-drawn carts taking stacked black bodies to the Newblock Park incinerator. He said the incinerator was located in a low area near a levy. Mr. Taylor also said some black bodies were taken to Dawson Road and buried there.

ANONYMOUS MALE:

This anonymous white male wanted to share information about how the Tulsa Police Department had many policemen and officers, including the chief of detectives, who were Ku Klux Klansmen. This man was a neighbor of the policeman who was secretary/treasurer of the Tulsa Ku Klux Klan and often played with the policeman's daughter.

ANONYMOUS MALE:

This man who contacted the Riot Commission said that his dad died over forty years ago and that he died an unhappy man. He had been sad ever since the Tulsa Race Riot of 1921. The things he witnessed, and did under protest because he was ordered to, haunted him for the rest of his life. The anonymous source said that his father drank a lot after the riot and often sat and talked and cried about the riot. The son of the unhappy riot participant had this to say about his father:

"At the time of the riot, Dad worked at a concrete company that later became the major concrete company in Tulsa, McMichael Concrete Company. During the riot, Dad said he helped load the bodies of dead blacks, and groaning wounded blacks, onto the company trucks, where they were taken to a strip mine pit near Pine and Dawson Road and buried. After the riot, Dad once took me to that pit area. He pointed to it and said, 'Son, that was a bad place in 1921.' Then he sat down and cried about what had happened to black peo-

ple then. He had some black friends that he worked with—Fred Isom and Arthur Kellam. He had a good white friend, Clyde Turner, who owned an auto store in west Tulsa next to Elmo Cline's grocery store in the 2400 block of Southwest Boulevard. I would often ride with Dad in his pickup truck. I would lie in the truck while Dad talked to his buddies. I saw that my dad was a sad man. He remained sad over that riot and he carried the shame of burying those bodies to his grave!"

DAVID BROWN:

David Brown called to share some riot information regarding his grandparents, Albert Oscar Brown and Hazel Bell Miller Brown, who died in the 1980s. According to Mr. Brown, "my grandmother, who was away from home, was the first in the family to hear the first shots fired in the riot. She went home and took cover. But things continued to get worse, and the black people began to flee. Grandma said, 'People just went nuts—black and whites just went nuts!' Later, Grandma said she saw bodies stacked up like cord wood and she said there was a horrible smell in the air—the smell of burning flesh—for days after the riot.

"Grandpa was in the cleanup detail after the riot. He worked in the Low Water Dam area where Estill Park is now—the Sand Springs area north of the Arkansas River. He saw some riot dead buried in Oak Lawn Cemetery at Eleventh Street and Peoria Avenue. He saw riot victims being 'quick-limed.'"

Mr. Brown said that his great grandmother, who witnessed the riot, wrote a letter to his uncle Earl in which she vividly described the riot. Mr. Brown's cousin, Lita, now has the letter. Mr. Brown will try to get a copy of the letter made for the Riot Commission.

Graves of two black riot victims, 1921, Oak Lawn Cemetery, Tulsa.

LEE CHAPMAN:

A quiet, sensitive, dedicated activist who works for peace and justice in the world, Lee Chapman always looks for opportunities to further the cause of justice. Recently when he went on a trip to California, he came by to get books and articles to take with him to give to activist author Ishmael Reed with whom he had a meeting scheduled in Oakland. He also took Reed a copy of the Oklahoma Commission to Study the Tulsa Race Riot report. Lee works in a book store in mid-Tulsa and just before he left my house, he left a book from the store that he thought I would want to read. He was right! The book was *Patrick J. Hurley: An American, A Biography* by Don Lohbeck, Henry Regnery Company, Chicago, Illinois, 1957. The book is signed: "To Alfred E. Aaronson, with highest esteem, William S. Bailey," and is dated January 1960. Patrick Hurley was a controversial character in Tulsa's history. To some Tulsans, he was Tulsa's version of Wyatt Earp and the hero who almost singlehandedly put down the rioters during the Tulsa Race Riot of 1921. To President Hoover, who sent the a letter to author Don Lohbeck at his Santa Fe, New Mexico, home, he was an astute statesman. But to some other Tulsans, notably black Tulsans, Hurley was a blowhard and a bigot.

BARBARA COOK:

I interviewed Barbara Cook, a teacher at Francis Scott Key Elementary School in Tulsa, after her ex-husband Nuel Holmes, a Holway Company engineer who is a fellow member of First Church of Christ Scientist, Tulsa, told me about Barbara's Tulsa pioneer family.

Barbara Cook's grandfather, known as "Doc" Ellis, was a Tulsa pharmacist. At the time of the riot he had a wife and four little girls ages eleven, three (Barbara's mother), two, and one. Doc was a good friend to many members of the Tulsa Police Department. Upon hearing about the commotion down at the courthouse, he piled his wife and little girls into his new-fangled open touring car and went down there. He left the wife and children in the car while he went in to talk to his police friends. While he was talking to his friends, the confrontation between a white man and a former World War I black soldier, in uniform, over the black man's gun took place. A shot was fired; the riot was on!

A friend of Doc's, a white man who had come down to the tense courthouse area to observe the history-making event, saw the woman and children sitting right in the middle of a race riot. With a few choice words for

Doc, he jumped in the car, which had its engine still running, and drove the woman and children to safety.

Before the interview, Barbara had talked to an elderly relative who was in the riot. That eyewitness recalled seeing blacks marched to detention centers. She remembered that some of her friends and relatives employed blacks and that white employers could go down to the detention centers, call out the names of their black employees, and have them released to them.

JOHN COUEY:

John Couey, a thirty-two-year City of Tulsa employee, was featured in an August 2001 issue of the *City News Monthly* newsletter. He spoke of his family's link with Tulsa's history. His great aunt, BETTY ELDRIDGE, was featured in the documentary film, *The Tulsa Lynching of 1921: A Hidden Story*.

In the film, Betty Eldridge described how from her front porch she could see fires on Greenwood Avenue and the crosses burning on Reservoir Hill during the riot.

MIKE DUFFY:

Mike Duffy, an Emmy-award-winning journalist, worked for the *Oklahoma Eagle* when the Riot Commission first began its work in 1997. Before he took another job, he wrote numerous articles about the riot, and he forwarded some information to the Commission that a source, who desired to remain anonymous, had shared with him.

That source's information was helpful in that it was another corroboration of testimony that black riot victims had been buried, by the truckloads, in a strip mine pit near Pine Street and Dawson Road.

TROY DUNLAP:

Troy Dunlap, a real estate developer, also shared information regarding the Pine Street and Dawson Road burial site for riot victims.

BETTY FAULKNER:

Betty Faulkner of Prue, Oklahoma, is a former reporter for the *Hominy News*, Hominy, Oklahoma. Her area of expertise is cemeteries. She shared vital information with the Commission regarding black burial sites in northeastern Oklahoma in general, and areas where black riot victims might be buried. She gave detailed descriptions of various cemeteries and clear, concise directions of where the cemeteries are located, right down to which fence to cross and which muddy roads to avoid!

GLORIA GUTUERRES LOUGH:

I first met Gloria Gutuerres Lough when I was the keynote speaker at a Black Heritage Program February 29, 2000, which was jointly sponsored by the U.S. Army Corps of Engineers and the Internal Revenue Service.

This was a joyous day for me (I am always exuberant when I speak before a receptive audience). It was an especially good day for the Internal Revenue Service people, too, who remarked that they seldom have "joyous meetings" with people!

The day was made more special for me when Gloria Guterres Lough came up to the podium to speak to me after my speech was finished. She told me a story about her grandmother. I nearly jumped off the platform when it dawned on me who her grandmother was. She was none other than the Mexican woman who became a folk legend and a hero in the Greenwood District because she saved the lives of two little black boys who were targeted by a low-flying airplane during the peak of the riot. Her story had been found by Dr. Scott Ellsworth, who presented it, along with other eyewitness accounts of the riot, to the Riot Commission at one of its meetings. Mrs. Lough and I hugged each other and expressed gratitude for her brave grandmother, who risked her life to save those two little boys that day. The grandmother said that those white men in that airplane seemed to take special pleasure in shooting at and tormenting those terrified boys. With motherly instinct, Mrs. Gutuerres' grandmother ran to the boys and sheltered them with her own body. The men in the plane, noting her lighter complexion, shouted a warning to her: "Get away from those little Niggers or you'll get shot too!" But she wouldn't let go of those little boys, and the men wouldn't shoot at the boys any more for fear of harming her.

MARY ANN HAYES:

Mrs. Hayes was born and raised in Pawhuska, Oklahoma. She now lives in Skiatook, Oklahoma. Her area of concern was cemeteries. She has much history about the Pawhuska Cemetery. She thinks highly of the Crowner family, a black family that has relatives buried there. She called the Riot Commission because of her love, respect, and concern for the dead. She supported us in our efforts to locate the riot dead and to establish a memorial in their honor where there could be closure to the riot era, when black riot victims were not given normal, proper burials that are the standard in civilized societies. The State of Oklahoma did appropriate money for such a memorial. Mrs. Hayes and many others welcome that government action and await the day

when the memorial to the riot dead is complete. May all riot dead then rest in peace!

CHESLEY C. HERNDON, JR.

Chesley C. Herndon, Jr., an Oklahoma City, Oklahoma, geologist, sent a single-spaced, four-page letter to the Riot Commission which was absolutely fascinating. He included historical background about the Tulsa Race Riot of 1921, details of his family's Tulsa history, and a blow-by-blow account of what each family member (he was not yet born) was doing at the time of the riot. That letter should be the introduction to a book, for it made me want to know more about the Chesley C. Herndon, Sr., family. Just from those four pages, I felt the love, respect, spirituality, and tenderness of that family. And some black survivors of that riot owe their lives to that loving family.

GARY HIMES:

Gary Himes has a book store, Himes Books, Inc., at Fifteenth and Lewis. Dr. Scott Ellsworth, historian/advisor to the Riot Commission, introduced me to Himes. Book stores are among my favorite places in the world. When I am finished with this book, I'll spend more time in Himes' store!

ROBERT HOWER:

Bob Hower, grandson of the revered Maurice Willows, director of the American Red Cross during the

Maurice Willows, American Red Cross Director, Tulsa, after the riot His riot report of Dec., 1921 is a major riot primary source.

Bob Hower, former television anchor, who had the book of his grandfather Maurice Willows reprinted.

riot, was a favorite with riot commissioners. He has recently reprinted his grandfather's excellent book, *Angels of Mercy*. The new book, entitled *1921 Tulsa Race Riot, America's Deadliest: Angels of Mercy,* is a major primary source document for the Riot Commission.

JOYCE KILGORE:

Joyce Kilgore called me one day and said she had an old newspaper that she wished to give to me. That paper, a 1913 issue of the *Tulsa Star*, published by Andrew Jackson (A. J.) Smitherman, was absolutely spellbinding. I read it from first page to final page, gingerly handling the brown, delicate pages. Joyce's husband was a nephew of white pawnshop owner Dick Bardon, who did a lot of business with the black community during the 1920s. He treated everyone fairly and was respected in both the black and white communities.

I met Joyce and her husband at the ninetieth birthday party of riot survivor Mrs. Eldoris Mae Ector McCondichie, which was held at First Baptist Church in north Tulsa in September of 2001. She, her husband, and I sat at the same table. And I was so glad to tell

Dick Bardon's nephew how many of the riot survivors and their descendants spoke so highly of his uncle and the many kindnesses he had always shown toward black Tulsans before, during, and after the riot.

JESSIE McNATT:

Jessie McNatt, a Burns Security Guard at the City of Tulsa, called me with information that his father had shared with him about the Tulsa riot. His father, Paul Buster McNatt, of Scottish descent, was born in 1906. His mother was a Native American who was born in Henryetta, Oklahoma. They had come to Tulsa in 1919 or 1920 to make some money. He said the night of the riot, his dad and some of his drinking buddies had been running around all over north Tulsa, mainly hitting the bars, which were called "choc joints" in those days. His father said that he and his buddies got caught in the area where the rioting occurred and that they personally saw some of the commotion. He said they saw a pit with bodies laid out beside the Convention site, now called the Brady Theater. Some men were busy digging a pit. He said nineteen bodies were put into it.

In 1924, renovation began at the old Convention building, and it was finished in 1925, according to Paul Buster McNatt. Mr. McNatt told his son that those nineteen bodies were covered over by the new construction.

It is not known how Paul B. McNatt was so certain of the exact number of black dead he saw that day at the Brady Convention site. Did he count them? Since Mr. McNatt died in 1982 and was buried in Hanna, Oklahoma, we will never know the answer to that question.

ROBERT D. NORRIS:

Robert D. Norris has done much historical research and writing about riots in general, and about the Tulsa Race Riot of 1921, specifically. He was very generous in sharing his findings with members of the Riot Commission. I am especially grateful to him for all the sociological data that he shared with me. This material helped me to probe, and ultimately understand, the deep, complex aspects of mob behavior.

The most significant thing that Robert Norris shared with the Commission was the African Blood Brotherhood materials that he had sent to the downtown Tulsa library.

STEPHEN NEITZKE:

Stephen Neitzke is a Tulsa white male who is consumed with desire to see a just world for people of all races, ethnicity, class, etc. I first met him at the main Tulsa City-County Library in downtown Tulsa, where he was checking out books and I was trying to retrieve a utility bill I had absentmindedly dropped in the book drop receptacle instead of in the utility receptacle next to it. We had a good laugh about that. Then we got serious because we are both serious, determined individuals when it comes to justice and equality. Stephen's mission is to reform society via his "Citizens Concerned Over Racism" organization. This organization wants a constitutional amendment to be passed which would prohibit the government from funding any study, any time, any era, where racial bias is involved, especially racial bias in which government is involved.

MIKE NOMURA:

Mike Nomura was so touched by the information he learned about the Tulsa Race Riot of 1921 that he wanted to do something. He called Rep. Don Ross at the state capitol in 2001. Ross told him he could join the Oklahoma Commission to Study the Tulsa Race Riot of 1921 Commemoration Society. He did. He helped to plan the activities for the June 3, 2001, commemoration event, which was one of the finest events ever held in the Greenwood District!

WILLIAM M. (BILL) O'BRIEN:

Bill O'Brien, longtime Tulsa historian, is the son of Gerald F. O'Brien, who was a Tulsa judge known for his fairness to blacks during the 1920s. In fact, according to his son he saved the life of a black civil rights lawyer who had been targeted by the Ku Klux Klan.

Bill O'Brien's main historical focus is the Civil War, but his interest was piqued by the Tulsa riot and he has done much research and writing on that subject. From all his research about the Tulsa riot, he has written a book entitled "Tulsa Race War, May 31 and June 1, 1921," Who Speaks for Us? The Responsible Citizens of Tulsa in 1921." He gave a copy of the book manuscript to each member of the Commission. His extensive research and writings about the riot in general, and specifically about Ku Klux Klan activity in Oklahoma, were very helpful. (Note that Mr. O'Brien does not call the 1921 event a "riot." He says that is a misnomer. He says the event was a "race war").

AL PRICE:

I met Al Price when I spoke at his church, Kirk of the Hills Presbyterian Church, in south Tulsa in 1998. Al and I hit it off right away and a few days after my talk, a huge envelope arrived at my house containing a personal letter to me, photographs of Al in his WWII uniform, photographs of weapons, and battle scenery from Normandy, Belgium and Germany, and a copy of the March 20, 1998 "Pentagram" newsletter which featured an article about 11 black soldiers who were massacred on a frigid December day in 1944 in Germany. (Al is on a crusade to see that those 11 men get the National Medal of Honor award due to each of them).

Also in the envelope were a 1,000 mark Reichbanknote, a copy of a letter from a WWII German soldier, Siegfried Mai of Mellenbach, Germany, who had answered a German newspaper's appeal from American soldiers who wanted to hear from German soldiers who had fought in Normandy in 1944, a copy of a touching soldier's poem, "The Night Before Christmas," written by Al, the names and addresses of two people with Holocaust information—Mrs. Lucie L. Liebman of El Paso, Texas and Mr. Curtis Whiteway of Marshfield, Vermont. Mr. Whiteway was with the 99th Infantry Division in WWII and fought in the same Battle of the Bulge area as did Al.

Finally, in that envelope were a photograph of an older Al Price, attired in a red, white, and blue shirt with stars on it, dancing on stage with Broadway dancer Gregory Hines, two self-addressed envelopes, and an appeal for me to keep in touch—to call so we could have some "skull talks." Al is a delightful, sharing, caring man and we do have those "skull talks" every now and then! In one of those "skull talks," I learned that Al took up tap dancing, with lessons, when he was 70 years old! His latest dance episode was tap dancing at the annual Central High School, Tulsa, School Daze Program in 2001. One of his favorite movies is "Taps" which starred Sammy Davis, Jr. and Gregory Hines.

Al Price can never stop thinking about the Battle of the Bulge, and other battles which he fought during WWII. He has been back to the site of that battle several times, has interviewed many participants who fought in that battle including former enemy, German soldiers who are now friends and many experts on war. He knows the geography of the The Bulge battle site as well as he knows Tulsa's geography. The men's stories of the battle are engraved in his heart. He has been putting all those bits and pieces together since the war years and now he is finally ready to write a book about the battle. He already has his title—"Blood in the Snow." I can hardly wait for that book! No one is more qualified to write a book on that subject than Al Price. He's "been there and done that." He can spout off the top of his head, without any reference to his extensive notes, who was in the Battle of the Bulge, the exact area where they fought, how they fought, what weapons, vehicles, and machinery they used, and any other circumstance, however minute, about that battle. Al believes that battle was perhaps the most significant single battle in U.S. history, not just because he was there, but because he believes that battle made a believer of the world's nations. Before that battle, American troops were viewed as spoiled, pampered, "soft" troops. After that battle, Al Price said the world knew better. People knew that properly trained, highly disciplined American troops, fighting for the freedoms they loved and enjoyed, were unbeatable.

I am so glad I met Al Price that day at Kirk of the Hills Church. My life has been so enriched by this wonderful man. What a walking military encyclopedia he is! I anxiously await his book.

TONY PRINGER:

Tony Pringer is the grandson of the late Herbert and Molly Johnson. Pringer, a writer himself, answered my article in the *Tulsa World* appealing for eyewitness or secondary accounts of the riot. Tony later told my husband, Norman, that when he answered that appeal, he didn't know he would be bonding to me for the rest of our lives! (Norman confirmed that a response to me inevitably leads to lifelong bonding.)

I learned some fascinating things about the Johnsons from their devoted grandson. I learned how different views on race conflicted families in the 1920s, just as philosophies had divided families during the Civil War in the U.S. For instance, Herbert Johnson, southern born, was a racist, according to his grandson. Molly, born in the North, vicariously suffered right along with black Tulsans who lived in an unequal, racially segregated society in Tulsa during the 1920s. Never were their philosophical differences so evident than on June 1, 1921.

On that worst day of the riot, Herbert Johnson, fire chief at the North Denver Boulevard Fire Station, shut down the station, went home, got his gun, and left with some of his like-minded buddies and went out to "shoot some Niggers!" One of his hapless buddies missed out on "the fun" because he accidentally shot himself in the foot and had to hobble home to recover. Meanwhile Molly, who was sweeping off her porch, saw Guardsmen marching blacks down her street on the way to the Brady Convention site for internment. Molly recognized nine black maids among the detainees. They had

Card-carrying Ku Klux Klansman, Denver Blvd. Fire Chief Herbert Johnson.

Sweet, gentle Good White Samaritan Molly Johnson, wife of Herbert Johnson, who went out to "shoot niggers" while Molly hid nine black maids in their basement during the Tulsa riot.

often walked past her house on their way home from the Denver Boulevard mansions (near downtown Tulsa), and she had spoken to them and sometimes gave them lemonade. This day Molly marched right up to those Guardsmen, shook her broom at them, and demanded that they release those nine maids to her, for she knew them personally and could vouch for them. The startled guards released the ladies to broom-wielding Molly!

Molly hid those nine maids in her basement and went upstairs to bake one of her legendary cakes for them. Later, while the cake was being devoured by the grateful ladies, Herbert came home for more ammunition, smelled the cake, and looked everywhere for it. Molly convinced him that she had not baked a cake that day. Poor Herbert was absolutely stumped, for his nose told him that there was cake in the house somewhere.

FLOYANNE GRIFFIN RADZINSKI:

Floyanne Radzinski was a little fireball of a woman. I first met her when my church, First Church of Christ, Scientist, Tulsa, worked with other Christian Science churches in Tulsa to sponsor a booth at the Annual Women's Show, held at the Tulsa Fairgrounds each February. That little woman whipped us volunteers into shape, and our booth has become an annual favorite. Floyanne took her job seriously.

Floyanne Radzinski read about the Tulsa Race Riot of 1921 in the *Tulsa World*. Since her family was one of the pioneer white families that lived near the Greenwood District, she thought I might be interested in some of her family history and artifacts. She was right! I was fascinated with her story of her pioneer family and with the copies of numerous family documents that she made and gave to the Riot Commission! She sent biographical information, deeds to family property, photographs, and a history of the first Christian Science church in Tulsa. Her family's home on Archer Street, right across from Greenwood Avenue, was the site of some of the first Christian Science "services" in Tulsa.

The Tulsa Christian Science community, as well as anyone else who knew Floyanne Radzinski, was saddened by her sudden death in February 2001.

STEPHEN K. ROSE:

Stephen Rose was one of my history students at Edison High School in south Tulsa. He responded to a request for riot information by writing me a letter regarding his grandparents, who lived in Tulsa at the time of the riot.

Stephen wrote that "My grandfather, E. A. Rose, was employed by Carter Oil Co. Which was later purchased by Haliburton Oil Co. (Duncan, OK).

"He and his wife lived in Turley, and on June 1, 1921, their son, my father (Elton A. Rose) was born. His (the father's) path to get the Dr. for the birth was thru Greenwood to downtown and back."

Stephen said that for many years, he heard his grandfather tell stories about the riot. He said that many bodies were loaded on flatbed type trucks and taken to the open pit mines between Catoosa and Claremore. I never doubted this information and always assumed it to be common knowledge!

Steven still wonders about his grandfather's riot story. In discussing his agonizing over the pictures the story conjured up in his mind, he said, "Pondering Grandfather's story, I made many guesses as to his knowledge of this event. Could his position with Carter Oil allow him access to that type of truck, and was that location easy to get to from north Tulsa? I still have many questions and only wild guesses on my part."

MICHELLE SIMPSON:

Michelle Simpson gave the following information to the Riot Commission: "My grandfather, Pat Adams, was a Tulsa Deputy Sheriff who drove dump trucks for Jack McMichael Construction Company in 1921. The company eventually became Mid-Continent Concrete Company. Grandpa said that 12-15 trucks took black bodies to a strip pit near Pine Street and Dawson Road and buried them on the east side of the strip."

JACKIE SMITH:

One day in 1999, Jackie Smith, wife of a white activist lawyer in Little Rock, Arkansas, contacted Dr. Bob Blackburn at the Oklahoma Historical Society in Oklahoma City and told him about her grandfather, Harvey Ernest Mullenax, witnessing the Tulsa Race Riot of 1921. He put her in touch with me. We talked, and soon she sent me an 8 x 10 photograph of her grandparents, photographs of her family, and the following story of her grandfather's riot experience. Jackie explained that it was her husband, Mike, who first saw articles about the riot in the *Arkansas Democrat-Gazette* and soon both became captivated by the Tulsa riot stories. Jackie listened to some audiotapes her grandmother made of her grandfather's riot experience, and from the information contained in the tapes, and from the memories she had from personally hearing her grandpa's story, she sent me the following:

A young Harvey Ernest Mullenax and young wife, 1919; A Good White Samaritan to blacks during the burning of Greenwood.

Harvey Ernest Mullenax, born May 15, 1899, shown shortly before his death.

The Mullenax family lived in Tilden, Illinois, in the early 1900s but left there because there was so much racism in the town. Blacks could not spend the night in the town. But the Mullenax family sometimes let blacks stay in their barn if they got caught after dark in Tilden. There were similar "sunset" laws in Oklahoma, but the Mullenax family didn't know that. So the family came to Oklahoma expecting the booming oil town to be more open and receptive to all people. Little did they know that they would be caught in the worst race riot in the history of the nation.

When Ernest Mullenax and some of his friends learned that black Tulsans were being besieged by white mobs, they went out to see if they could help the black people. Being white, they had easy access into the Greenwood District. They were presumed to be white mobsters. But Mr. Mullenax and his friends were Good White Samaritans and they went in to save blacks. Blacks were not very cooperative with them, for they feared that they were mobsters bent on doing them harm. In fact, Mr. Mullenax told his family of the difficulty that he had in convincing one black fellow that he was a Good Samaritan. He ran into a burning house on Greenwood Avenue and pulled one black man outside to safety. But the terrified man thought that Mr. Mullenax, a twenty-two-year-old white man, was a mobster and he fled back into the burning house. Harvey Mullenax went back into that burning house, found the terrified man hiding under a bed, and pulled him to safety again. This time, "through God's help," he was able to convince the man he meant him no harm, and he and his friends took that man to a safe place.

After the riot, the Mullenax family moved to Kansas City, Missouri, where Ernest and his brother, Jack, ran a plaster business. Jackie says that her grandfather, and her great uncle, Jack, hired mostly blacks and Mexicans to work in their business because they knew how badly mistreated those groups were in American society.

Jackie Smith still corresponds with me, still sends photographs, and like her gentle, loving grandfather she champions causes that benefit Americans of all races and ethnicity.

MABLE SWINNEY:

Mable Swinney, daughter of the late James Leonard Swinney, founder of Swinney's Hardware Store located on South Lewis Avenue in the historic Whittier Square District of Tulsa, gave important information to the Riot Commission. I was led to interview Mrs. Swinney because of a chance meeting with her nephew, Mike Brandt, grandson of James L. Swinney.

James Leonard Swinney and his family first lived on a farm in Lenepah, Oklahoma. Later they settled in Tulsa, where Swinney founded his hardware store, which was an icon in the pioneer Tulsa community. Among Swinney's many loyal customers were many blacks. They were drawn to Swinney's because of the kindness and fairness of Mr. Swinney, but most of all by the fact that he let them buy on credit! For his kindnesses toward blacks, James Swinney was threatened by whites. But he kept right on being kind and fair to all people.

The Swinney Hardware Store is one of the original Mom and Pop stores still hanging on in Tulsa. It can't compete, in volume, with Home Depot and Lowe's, but it still has its loyal customers who are willing to pay a bit more for the special goods and services that they get at Swinney's Hardware. James Swinney would be proud that his legacy lives on in Tulsa!

ELIZABETH (BETTY) DAVIS TROWER,
Austin, Texas:

Elizabeth Trower called and gave information about the riot which she had heard from her stepfather. Mrs. Trower, a graduate of Tulsa's Central High School, class of 1957, said that her stepfather was five years old when the riot broke out in Tulsa and that he was absolutely terrified. He had a great fear of black people, for he was raised by relatives who hated black people. Their hate-filled indoctrination was so strong and effective that he later became a Klansman.

A former brother-in-law of Mrs. Trower (whose name she kept confidential), worked for the Tulsa Police Department in the 1960s. He told family members that police officers were taught about what happened during the 1921 race riot and they were to keep information about the riot concealed!

III: Whites Who Shared Similar Stories of Trauma

DIANNA SMITH,
"Surviving the Battle of Britain during World War II"

Dianna Smith is one of the most sincere, dedicated, hard-working persons that I have ever met. She joined the Tulsa Reparations Coalition because she felt a deep connection to riot victims due to similar experiences with war and terrorism—she survived the Battle of Britain during World War II!

She deeply respected the Riot Commission for what it was doing to enlighten people all over world about the causes, effects, and dangers of war and terrorism. She was especially supportive of those of us commissioners who were avid supporters of reparations. At meetings and programs relating to the riot, I could almost always look out into the audience and see Dianna and her friend Geraldine Washington cheering us on! She volunteered to help the commission by sharing some of her extensive research and writings on the sub-

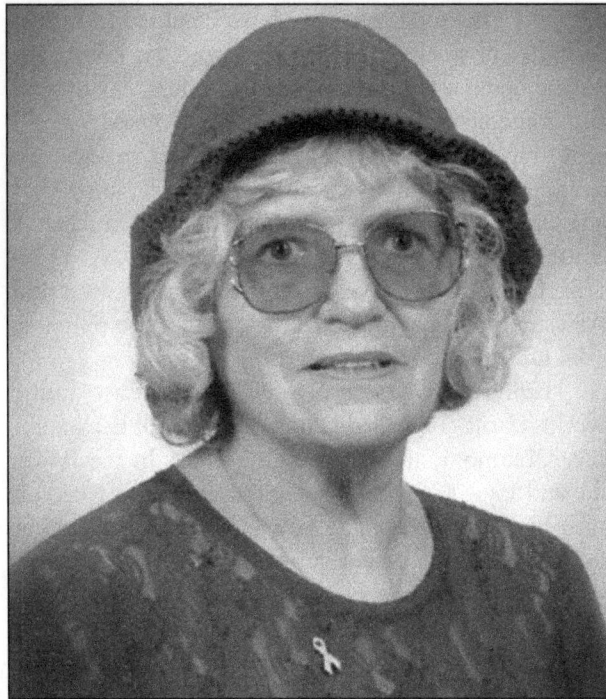

Dianna Smith, Good White Samaritan, who shared her Battle of Britain near-death experience with riot survivors and commissioners.

ject. She spent hours in libraries researching, and her carefully handwritten notes were extremely valuable to the Commission.

Dianna's inspiration comes from the book of Joel in the Bible, Chapter 1, verses 2 and 3:

> Tell ye your children of it,
> and let your children tell
> their children, and their
> children another generation.

Dianna said she is also inspired by a quote of the late black author James Baldwin, who warned, "You cannot fix what you will not face." All of her life Dianna Smith has been trying to get mankind to face its problems and fix them. She has been telling children and adults for generations about her experiences during the Battle of Britain. Here are excerpts of what she wrote to the Riot Commission:

"When German pilots mercilessly bombed the United Kingdom of Great Britain around the clock for three weeks straight in 1938 during World War II was one of the worst periods in British history! And I lived through it! The German pilots flew planes that dropped cluster bombs, and the area where we lived in London was especially hard hit. On the day that our house was hit, the German pilots dropped two bombs right in succession. The first bomb narrowly missed our house; the second bomb was a direct hit on our house. My mother and grandmother were killed instantly. My sister and I were trapped under a mass of debris—we were buried alive! In fact, our house was such a mangled mess that officials put yellow tape around the house and left a written message which said, 'NO RESCUE—NO POSSIBILITY OF SURVIVORS HERE!' But my sister and I did survive. Someone heard our cries and we were dug from underneath all that debris."

Having survived that near-death experience during World War II compelled Dianna to work all her life for peace, harmony, and justice in the world. In the 1960s, she and some of her political science friends worked on such issues at the Foreign Policy Research Institute at the University of Pennsylvania. She has also done extensive research on Japanese atrocities during World War II, on Russian violations of human rights, and on the Jewish Holocaust. Her most recent research has been on reparation movements all over the world. Thank you, Dianna Smith, for your lifelong commitment to all mankind. Thank you for sharing your vital information with the Oklahoma Commission to Study the Tulsa Race Riot of 1921.

IV: Conclusion

This was one of the most difficult sections in the book to write. I wanted to mention every single act of kindness toward the Greenwood community during the Commission research period, 1997-2001, and the acts that continue to occur to this day. If any act or event was left out of this section, it is purely coincidental and inadvertent.

V: Speaking Engagements

Whenever the call came for a speaker, or for a panel of speakers, to enlighten some audience about the experiences of Tulsa's black pioneers, and, especially about the Tulsa Race Riot of 1921, the need was always met. One of us local black authors, researchers, or other experts in specific fields would speak; sometimes five or six of us would serve on a panel. Whatever the need, it was always met! Some of the events, at local, state, national and international levels, in which speakers went forth like "babes in the wilderness" to spread the word about the riot were as follows:

Business / Business-Connected Organizations:

LOCAL:

International Association of Administrative Professionals Banquet, October 10, 2000

Business & Professional Women's Clubs: Various programs, 1994-present

Metropolitan Tulsa Urban League Events: Annual banquets, tours for visiting groups, annual Youth Awards/Celebration programs, "Do the Right Thing," annual Martin Luther King, Jr. Commemoration breakfasts, various workshops and seminars throughout the years

African-American Women in Business Conference, Los Angeles, California, held in Tulsa, Oklahoma, August 21-24, 2001

NATIONAL:

Association of Black Engineers, Lawrence Livermore National Laboratory, Livermore, California, July 2000. Videotape and speech, "The Tulsa Race Riot of 1921," by Eddie Faye Gates

Cultural Organizations:

LOCAL:

Greenwood Cultural Center (GCC): The Greenwood Cultural Center, located at 322 North Greenwood Avenue in the historic "Deep Greenwood" district, is the site of many, perhaps most, black political, economic, and social events held in Tulsa. Among the numerous events held here are the Oklahoma Jazz Hall of Fame banquets, North Tulsa Heritage Foundation Annual Image Awards banquets, North Tulsa Heritage Foundation Annual Sophisticated, Sassy Seniors Fashion Shows, North Tulsa Heritage Foundation Annual Youth Talent Shows, and many other programs too numerous to mention.

Various local, state, national, and international organizations hold events in the Cultural Center throughout the year, such as annual Tulsa Charms western-themed dinner/dance fundraisers, Jewish Foundation events such as annual host events for exchange students from Israel, writers workshops sponsored by various organizations, and many others. In addition, some other events at the Greenwood Cultural Center include:

Tours of the GCC:
• Mable B. Little Heritage House
• Oklahoma Jazz Hall of Fame

• Daily Tours—Rep. Don Ross' Permanent Exhibit, "From Ruins to Renaissance: The Photographic Exhibit of the Tulsa Race of 1921;"

Walking Tours:
• Black Wall Street Memorial down to Deep Greenwood
• Various after-school educational programs
• Various summer school educational/cultural programs
• Various national events such as the visit of Attallah Shabazz, daughter of the late Malcolm X, on February 29, 1999, for the unveiling of the 33 cent Malcolm X stamp, and a workshop/panel discussion with Useni Perkins, Drama Department chair, Chicago State University, a riot commissioner and a riot survivor on April 27, 2001. The award-winning play *If We Must Die* was performed the same night in the Oklahoma State University auditorium, which is adjacent to the Greenwood Cultural Center

Educational Institutions/Organizations:

Tulsans have voracious appetites for speakers, especially authors. Throughout the year, writers, speakers from a number of political, economic, and social organizations, private individuals who have had some interesting experiences, public individuals who have interesting histories, or "bad guys or bad gals" who have strayed but want to tell others how to avoid their plight are out speaking. Nowhere is the demand for speakers greater than in the education field. Tulsa Public Schools' seventy-seven institutions need speakers, Tulsa's private schools need speakers, and on some days, so it seems, everyone needs a speaker! January, February, and May are the busiest months because of Martin Luther King, Jr. activities, Presidents' Day, Black History Month, and commencements. Tulsa's newspapers and monthly magazines have excellent listings of upcoming events, and Tulsa's speakers usually have sizeable, cordial, receptive audiences. With all the focus on the Tulsa Race Riot of 1921 the past three and a half years, "riot speakers" are the hottest commodity in Tulsa. Tulsa's published black authors, such as Dorothy DeWitty, Arthur Farakhan, Hannibal Johnson, Eddie Madison, Clifton Taulbert, and I can hardly keep up with the demand for speakers. Sometimes the "Big Guns" are brought in, some of them Tulsa Greenwood expatriates like published authors Dr. John Hope Franklin, Dr. Julia Hare, Dr. Nathan Hare, and other celebrities like former Tulsans Gayle Greer Morgan and actress Alfre Woodard. White riot authors who reside in Tulsa also speak frequently. They can be seen at book signings or before various receptive audiences. Later came riot books by other white authors, such as Tim Madigan, Al Brophy, Jim Hirsch, and many others (see Bibliography). Among those seen speaking during the "riot study era" were Dr. Scott Ellsworth, Bill and Ethel Blair, Bob Hower, Bill O'Brien, Robert Norris, and the late Ruth Sigler Avery, who generously shared with others her seven decades of riot information.

Fiction writers got caught up in the race riot era too. Coming out during the riot study period were two critically acclaimed novels, *Magic City* by Jewel Parker Rhodes, a black professor at Arizona State University, and *Fire in Beulah,* by Rilla Askew, an Oklahoman who now lives in New York.

Following are some specific examples of sharing of the riot experience with educational institutions and organizations:

LOCAL:
BOOKER T. WASHINGTON HIGH SCHOOL (BTW), Tulsa—numerous talks to classes, but the stellar BTW event was the Prom of 1999, in which ninety-four-year-old riot survivor Veneice Dunn Sims was named honorary Prom Queen. This event made up for the Prom that she missed in 1921 because of the riot.

TULSA PUBLIC SCHOOLS—Numerous workshops, seminars, lectures, etc., for faculty, and annual bus tours to all-black towns.

PRIVATE SCHOOLS—Guest lectures and workshops on the issues of race, revolution, riots, reform. Schools included Cascia Hall, Monte Cassino, Victory Christian School, Riverfield Country Day School, and others.

Annual Tulsa Alliance of Black School Educators (TABSE) Awards Programs.

LOCAL COLLEGES—Langston University-Tulsa, Northeastern University-Tulsa, University of Oklahoma, Oklahoma State University-Tulsa, Oral Roberts University, the University of Tulsa, and Tulsa Community College hold a variety of cultural diversity events throughout the year, and during Black History Month, a variety of programs about race, ethnicity, and culture are presented.

The University of Tulsa hosts a number of events yearly that draw large crowds. Among these are the annual Hardman/Nimrod Literary Awards, political programs featuring renowned national and international speakers, annual Alumni Association events and banquets, Phi Beta Kappa inductions, local programs such as the Law Forum on Reparations for Tulsa riot victims, and many, many other outstanding programs throughout each year.

A fascinating local event with educational, historical, and cultural tones was the one-hundredth birthday celebration of Jobie Elizabeth Holderness, widow of the brave Tulsa riot victim Len Holderness, who was one of the defenders of Mt. Zion Baptist Church from invading mobsters.

STATE:

Conners State College, Warner, Oklahoma Black History Month programs, some dealing with the Tulsa Race Riot of 1921.

Langston University-Langston, Oklahoma, Panel discussion, February 2001, dealing with the Tulsa Race Riot of 1921, featuring two commissioners from the Oklahoma Commission to Study the Tulsa Race Riot of 1921 and a professor from Tulsa Community College.

OKLAHOMA STATE UNIVERSITY-OKMULGEE, Annual Black History Month programs. Some have dealt with the Tulsa Race Riot of 1921.

OKLAHOMA STATE UNIVERSITY-STILLWATER, numerous Black History Month events.

OKLAHOMA STATE UNIVERSITY-TULSA, Annual Black History Month programs. Key speakers such as Tony Brown of *Tony Brown's Journal*, musicians such as the GAP Band, diversity workshops, storytelling workshops, book signings, and many other outstanding programs.

SAPULPA, OKLAHOMA, HIGH SCHOOL, Black History Month speeches.

NATIONAL:

Annual National Association of Black School Educators (NABSE) awards held in various cities in the U.S.

PRINCIPIA COLLEGE, Elsah, Illinois: Black History Month events, 1998 and 2000, relating to the black experience in America, including Tulsa race relations and the Tulsa Race Riot of 1921.

UNIVERSITY OF TOLEDO, Toledo, Ohio, February 15, 2001: Black History Month program "The Black Experience in America, Including The Tulsa Race Riot of 1921." Guest classroom lecturer and keynote evening speaker was a commissioner from the Oklahoma Commission to Study the Tulsa Race Riot of 1921.

UNIVERSITY OF BUFFALO, Buffalo New York,

Eddie Faye Gates, student, American Gathering of Holocaust Survivors Summer Study Program for American Educators, between two Israeli soldiers keeping the peace at Mt. Scopus, Old City, Jerusalem, Israel, July, 1991.

Eddie Faye Gates, Summer Study Program student, besides two Arabs in the Carlton Hotel, Nahariya, Israel, July 19, 1991.

Eddie Faye Gates, Summer Study program student, sitting on the railroad tracks that ended near the crematorium at the Auschwitz Concentration Camp, Poland

Gas ovens, Auschwitz Concentration Camp, Poland.

Uncrowned Queens Program, November 6-8, 2003.
INTERNATIONAL:

In the last decade, educators from all over the U.S. have been awarded fellowships to attend the annual Holocaust Summer Study Seminars in Poland and Israel. Each year, a Tulsan is usually among the group chosen from a large number of entries. They develop curriculum and and ensure that Holocaust education is taught in their school districts.

Fellowship to study in Japan.

Various annual trips, all over the world, taken by educators and student groups.

Tulsa Community College (TCC) International College Abroad Summer Study Program in Ghana, West Africa, March 2001. Twenty persons participated in the program. Among those attending were two commissioners from the Oklahoma Commission to Study the Tulsa Race Riot of 1921. Dr. Vivian Clark-Adams and me.

VI: Faith Communities

Oklahoma has a reputation for being the Bible Belt of the nation. Among the first settlers in Oklahoma were "men of the cloth" who came after the explorers of all races, Indians, cowboys, ranchers, farmers, and oil men converged upon the territory. They set about their self-imposed task of taming the "wild and wooly" area—Indian Territory and Oklahoma Territory—that became the state of Oklahoma in 1907. Tulsa's faith community still works hard to bring out the best, spiritually and practically, in the city. An article in the *Tulsa World* about a huge interfaith meeting in Tulsa recently speaks of this commitment.

Below is a list of various faith communities and their actions on behalf of Tulsa's Greenwood District:
LOCAL:

All Souls Unitarian Church, Reverend Marlin Lavanhar, Pastor

Ba'hai Faith Community

B'nai Emunah Synagogue, Rabbi Marc Fitzerman

Boston Avenue Methodist Church, Reverend Mouzon Biggs, Jr,. Pastor

Christ Temple AME Church, Reverend William Johnson, Pastor

Christ Temple CME Church, Reverend Stacy Cole, Pastor

Church of the Restoration, Reverend Gerald Davis, Pastor

Claremore, Oklahoma Church, Reverend Glen Shaffer, Pastor

Community of Hope, United Church of Christ, Reverend Leslie Penrose, Pastor

Fellowship Christian Church, Reverend Russell Bennett, Pastor

First Baptist Church of North Tulsa, Reverend Dr. J.W. Johnson, Sr., Pastor, until 2000; Reverend T.J. Buxton, Pastor, 2002-present

First Presbyterian Church, Reverend Doctor James D. Miller, Pastor

Grace Lutheran Church, Reverend James R. Haner, Pastor

Greater Mount Rose Baptist Church, Reverend Dr. Andrew Phillips, Pastor

Greenwood Christian Center, Pastors Gary and Debbie McIntosh

Higher Dimensions Church, Reverend Carlton Pearson, Pastor and Bishop of the Azusa Inter-denominational Fellowship

International Gospel Center, Pastor Chyanna Mull-Anthony

Islamic Center of North Tulsa, Iman Arthur Farakhan

Islamic Society of Tulsa, spokesman Mujeeb Cheema

Kirk of the Hills Presbyterian Church, Reverend Tom Gray, Senior Pastor, Reverend Wayne Hardy, Assistant Pastor

Mt. Zion Baptist Church, Reverend Dr. G. Calvin McCutchen, Pastor

St. Andrews Baptist Church, Reverend Dr. Bertrand M. Bailey, Sr., Pastor

St. Anthony's Orthodox Catholic Church, Father George Eber, Priest

St. Augustine Catholic Church, Father Desmond Okpogba, Priest

St. John Baptist Church, Reverend Cleon Ratliff, Pastor

St. Monica's Catholic Church, Father Desmond Okpogba, Priest

Shiloh Baptist Church, Reverend Melvin Bailey, Pastor

Temple Israel Synagogue, Rabbi Charles Sherman

Tulsa Metropolitan Ministry, Stephen Cranford, Executive Director

Vernon AME Church, Reverend Dr. Isaac Hudson, Pastor

VII: Literary Institutions/Organizations

Tulsa is noted for its love of literature and draws authors to the city on many occasions.

Among the national authors who have spoken in Tulsa since the riot/justice/equality focus are: Dr. Ivan van Sertima, Dr. Nathan Hare, Dr. Julia Hare, L. B. Ransom, Tina McElroy, Walter Mosely, Maya Angelou, Tony Brown, Jewel Parker Rhodes, Dr. Scott Momaday, Earl Hamner, Peter Burchard, Dr. Scott Ellsworth, Rilla Askew, Barbara Bush, and Sister Helen Prejean.

LOCAL:
TULSA CITY-COUNTY LIBRARY SYSTEM:
Downtown Central Library:
Rudisill North Regional Library in North Tulsa:

STATE:
OKLAHOMA CITY LIBRARY SYSTEM: Excellent black experience–type programs throughout the year and especially during January and February. Tulsa guest speakers have spoken in Oklahoma City libraries regarding black literature and the black experience in northeastern Oklahoma. The Tulsa Race Riot of 1921 is always a popular topic.

VIII: Historical Institutions/Organizations

LOCAL:
NORTH TULSA HISTORICAL SOCIETY:
The North Tulsa Historical Society is an organization of mainly north Tulsans whose mission is "To commemorate the contributions and achievements of black Americans from their ancestors' beginnings in Africa, through the early migrations out of Africa, the African explorations in the Americas before the European explorations, the slavery/Civil War/Reconstruction Eras, the Post-Reconstruction Era, through present civil rights movements; to purge inaccuracies, downright myths, stereotypes, misconceptions, and lies from the record, and to set the record straight with the empirical truths available from past and present impeccable empirical sources." Members are inspired by the following poem, written by Langston Hughes:

But someday somebody'll
Stand up and talk about me,
And write about me—
Black and beautiful . . .
I reckon it'll be
Me myself!
Yes, it'll be me.

Meetings are held the third Monday of the month, except for January and February, at 6:30 P.M. in the Rudisill North Regional Library, 1520 North Hartford Street, Tulsa. Members represent occupations such as doctors, lawyers, historians, authors, teachers from kindergarten teachers to college professors, librarians, business entreprenuers, geologists, engineers, journalists, undertakers, and college students.

In addition to monthly meetings, members engage in constant research, writing, and speaking locally, statewide, nationwide, and internationally. Some members are published authors, while others have unpublished manuscripts or other writings in progress for future publication. The organization also co-sponsors, with the Tulsa City-County Library System, an annual All Black Towns Bus Tour, and with the *Oklahoma Eagle* newspaper, a forum project.

TULSA AFRICAN ANCESTRAL SOCIETY:
"Black Holocaust Memorial for the Victims of the 1921 Race Riot," May 28, 2000, Chief Egbe Fegunjobi, President.

NIGERIAN SOCIETY OF TULSA: Annual cultural program/banquet, Greenwood Cultural Center.

TULSA HISTORICAL SOCIETY: A major source for information on the history of Oklahoma. Many photographs and books about Oklahomans of all races come from this organization.

STATE:
OKLAHOMA HISTORICAL SOCIETY: A major source of information about the state of Oklahoma. Organization is widely used by historians, authors, educators, researchers, and visitors from all over the world.

The organization also has excellent museum displays, meeting rooms, and traveling displays, including exhibits about black experience.

OKLAHOMA EDUCATIONAL TELEVISION AUTHORITY

MELVIN B. TOLSON MUSUEUM, LANGSTON, OKLAHOMA

Black Liberated Arts, Inc., OKLAHOMA CITY, OKLAHOMA, is the Oklahoma City equivalent of the Greenwood Cultural Center in Tulsa. Anita G. Arnold, director, has brought tour groups to Tulsa.

NATIONAL:

National Archives, Washington, D.C.
Library of Congress, Washington, D.C.
Smithsonian Institution, Washington, D.C.
Washington, D.C., Public Library (Capital District)
Spigarn Research Center, Howard University, Washington, D.C.

INTERNATIONAL:

W.E.B. Dubois Memorial and Museum, Accra, Ghana, West Africa
Kwame Nkrumah Memorial and Museum, Accra, Ghana, West Africa
Ashante National Village/Museum Center, Kumasi, Ghana, West Africa
Kakun National Rain Forest Park, Kumasi, Ghana, West Africa

IX: Donations: Artistic, Literary, Historical, Photographic, Media, Musical, Dramatic, and Others

PHOTOGRAPHS:

LOCAL:

MATTHEW ELLIOTT, Tulsa, Oklahoma
SHIRLEY HOWELL
PAT LUCY, Tulsa, Oklahoma
GEORGE LeRICHE, Tulsa, Oklahoma

George LeRiche, who works for the local electric utility company (earlier known as Public Service Company of Oklahoma, and now as American Electric Power Company) came upon two photographs of the Tulsa Race Riot which he shared with the Riot Commission. The pictures were chilling in that they showed downed electric lines and black riot victims being marched, right in the midst of that ravaged area, to detention centers in the Convention Center area.

STATE:

OKLAHOMA HISTORICAL SOCIETY

NATIONAL:

MARILYN BRETT, New York, New York

Marilyn Brett, a white woman in New York, sent photographs to Rudisill North Regional Library in North Tulsa that belonged to her father, who lived in Tulsa at the time of the Tulsa riot. Kim Johnson, director of the African-American Resource Center at the library, shared the photos with the Riot Commission.

JACKIE SMITH, Little Rock, Arkansas

Jackie Smith, wife of a Little Rock, Arkansas, attorney who has long been interested in civil rights, sent an 8 x 10 photograph of her grandparents.

BOOKS, PAMPHLETS, MAPS, IN-KIND SERVICES, ETC.

LOCAL:

DUDLEY THOMAS, Tulsa, Oklahoma
JAMES AND ETHEL BLAIR, Tulsa, Oklahoma

STATE:

BOB BLACKBURN, RODGER HARRIS, and BRUCE FISHER of the Oklahoma Historical Society, Oklahoma City, Oklahoma, were most helpful. They aided researchers and writers in their search for sources; they provided exhibits and speakers for all areas of the state; and they were always "on call" to answer questions about the history of all Oklahomans.

NATIONAL:

SONYA D. SWINTON, Washington, D.C., federal employee, sister of a Tulsan who is an avid follower of Tulsa Race Riot of 1921, helped a riot commissioner with the gathering of primary source information in the Library of Congress, the National Archives, the Smithsonian Institution, the downtown public library, and Howard University.

ARTISTIC CREATIONS:

LOCAL:

THE ENOCH P. WATERS COLLECTION OF AFRICAN ARTIFACTS AND MEMORABILIA, Greenwood Cultural Center. This exhibit was donated by the late Tulsa Race Riot 1921 survivor George Douglas Monroe. Enoch P. Waters, longtime editor of the prominent black newspaper *The Chicago Defender,* was married to Monroe's sister, Regina. Waters began collecting in Africa during World War II and continued for more than forty years. Enoch Waters was also the author of *The American Diary,* a compilation of personal experiences. The couple were often guests of celebrities, such as President and Mrs. John F. Kennedy at a reception in 1963. Waters died in 1988. Later, after the death of Mrs. Waters, the collection went to Tulsans George D. and Martha Monroe.

DON THOMPSON AND EDDIE FAYE GATES, Tulsa Black Settlers Exhibit (photographs and biograpical texts) on permanent display at Oklahoma State University, Tulsa, Oklahoma, B.S. Roberts Room.

DRAMATIC CREATIONS:

LOCAL:

TRIQUETA GROUP, Tulsa, Oklahoma, play *Song of Greenwood,* written, produced, directed, and choreographed by Tim Long and Jerome Johnson, natives of Okmulgee, Oklahoma. Second play, *Roofless,* in progress.

NATIONAL:

ROBERT BENEDETTI, Hollywood, California, wrote script entitled "Death on Black Wall Street," in 2001, which is based on events described in *Miz Lucy's Cookies: And Other Links in My Black Family Support System,* Coman and Associates, Tulsa, Oklahoma, 1996, and *They Came Searching: How Blacks Sought the Promised Land in Tulsa,* Eakin Press, Austin, Texas, 1997, both written by Eddie Faye Gates. Script is presently being considered as a play and/or a film.

Useni Perkins, Chicago playwright, standing: 3rd from left, in Tulsa for the debut of his play, "If We Must Die." A contemporary response to the riot seven decades ago.

CHICAGO STATE UNIVERSITY, Chicago, Illinois, play *If We Must Die,* written by Chicago State University drama professor Useni Perkins, presented by actors from the university's drama department and from other departments at the university. Play premiered in Chicago in 2001 and was repeated in Tulsa at Oklahoma State University, Tulsa, Oklahoma, on April 27, 2001, and in Chicago again in October of 2001.

GEORGIA ENGEL, Hollywood, California, actress, was in Tulsa in 2001 when she starred in the female version of the play *The Odd Couple.* She purchased a book about Tulsa's black experience.

LITERARY CREATIONS:

LOCAL:

Play, *Riot on Greenwood,* based on the book *They Came Searching: How Blacks Sought the Promised Land in Tulsa,* by Eddie Faye Gates, by playwright Rodney Clark, Tulsa Community College Theatre Professor/Dean, in progress.

STATE:

CAROLE ELLIS, Bristow, Oklahoma, poem.

NATIONAL:

HARRY POIRIER, South Royalton, Vermont, two poems, one about Dr. Martin Luther King, Jr., and one about the Tulsa Race Riot of 1921. Copies made and distributed to commissioners and others at a commission meeting in Tulsa.

MAPS:

LOCAL: JIM AND ETHEL BLAIR.

OAKLEY DEISENROTH AND THE SANBORN MAPS, 1913 to 1930: Oakley Deisenroth, now in his thirties, was one of my most studious and devoted high school history students. He loves collecting historical items and knows that I love collecting them too. He keeps me informed about great finds in Tulsa. One day he summoned me to the Tulsa Fairgrounds Flea Market, where I bought five large, leatherbound Sanborn maps. The "cream of the crop" in that collection is the map that shows the streets of the Greenwood District before the Tulsa Race Riot of 1921. Thanks, dear Oakley!

KAVIN ROSS also summons me to flea markets and yard sales where both of us often find great "riot collectibles." My latest find, thanks to Kavin calling me to the Admiral Flea Market, is a sheet of stationery of the United Confederate Veterans, dated 1918, summoning participants to a twenty-eighth annual reunion in Tulsa, September 24-27, 1918. At the top of the document are key local leaders, such as W. Tate Brady and Merritt J. Glass.

MEDIA: ELECTRONIC—Videotapes, Television

LOCAL:

Radio and television stations were generous in supplying the riot commission with copies of tapes that the stations had made of commission meetings, interviews, and other riot-related events.

INDIVIDUALS:

RESHA GRANT, both a journalist and a videographer, wrote numerous news articles about the riot for *The Oklahoma Eagle* in the first year of Riot Commission research. She also undertook the task of privately producing a documentary film about the riot.

SUSAN SMITH, a University of Tulsa television production instructor, along with a student from Israel, Ziona Menor, uncovered so much information about the Tulsa riot that they decided to produce a film documentary.

J. KAVIN ROSS, videographer for the Oklahoma Riot Commission, produced some of the most stunning videos about the riot. Excerpts from some of his tapes were shown on local, state, and national television shows including *60 Minutes II, Tony Brown's Journal,* Tom Joyner's live radio show broadcast from Tulsa. Entire productions made by Ross were shown nationally.

STATE:

Print and electronic journalists from all over the state came to commission meetings, and they wrote prolifically about the riot and aired numerous hours of riot stories throughout the entire four-year period of riot research.

NATIONAL:

National print and electronic media converged on Tulsa during the riot research period, 1997-2001, and made the Tulsa Race Riot of 1921 known all over the globe. See chapter 10 for specifics.

MUSEUMS:

Local museums held specific Africa-oriented pro-grams, between the riot research period, 1997, and the post-commission research period. Some examples were:

LOCAL:

GILCREASE MUSEUM:

"Celebration and Vision: The Hewitt. Collectiion of African-American Art," with Mrs. Vivian Hewitt, New York, New York, as special guest of honor, January 19, 2002.

PHILBROOK MUSEUM:

"A Personal Journey: Central African Art from the Lawrence Gussman Collection, February 10-April 7, 2002.

IDA DENNIE WILLIS MUSEUM OF MINIATURES, TOYS, AND DOLLS:

Numerous African-oriented programs with outstanding national guest speakers such as Floyd Bell, world-famous doll-maker.

MUSICAL CREATIONS

LOCAL:

The Tulsa community possesses a unique, talented pool of local musicians, among them EARL CLARK.

A group of young rap musicians formed a group called MED-U-NETAR. They wrote a song about the riot called "Taking Back Greenwood."

Various state individuals and groups visit Tulsa throughout the year, and especially during annual Juneteenth celebrations, jazz festivals, blues festivals, and other annual events held in the Greenwood District.

NATIONAL:

There is always a national presence in the Greenwood District. On any given day, foreign visitors can be seen touring the Greenwood Cultural Center or attending annual spectacular events, especially the Tulsa Global Alliance Organization visitors who are often given guided tours by Tulsa authors Hannibal Johnson and me.

KATHLEEN SALISBURY, a professional singer in Hollywood, California, did not come to Tulsa, but she mailed to the Riot Commission an audiotape of a song that she wrote and recorded about the riot. Ms. Salisbury, a graduate student in French literature at UCLA, was inspired to write this song by an article she read about the riot in the *Los Angeles Times* October 23, 1999.

INTERNATIONAL:

Visitors to the Greenwood District throughout the year include tourists, speakers, and artists from all over the world. Among the international visitors to area was a musical group from Israel that performed in the Greenwood Cultural Center.

OTHER:

Organizations and Individuals That Had Programs in the Greenwood District And/or Recognized Riot Survivors, 1997-2002:

American Red Cross
Booker T. Washington Alumni Association
North Tulsa Business & Professional Women's Club
Rotary Clubs of Tulsa
United Nations Association of Eastern Oklahoma
Women in Communications
National Organization for Victims Assistance (NOVA) (Keynote speakers, 1996, Attorney General Janet Reno, attorney Christopher Darden)
Leadership Tulsa
Leadership Oklahoma
Retired Senior Volunteers Program (RSVP)
Rosa Parks, the Rosa and Raymond Parks Institute for Self-Development, Detroit, Michigan
Oasis Project, Black-Jewish Relations
Global Alliance of Tulsa

OTHER:

Individual Acts and Events Related to Riot Survivors:

CATHERINE AUGUSTE:

One day I received a telephone call from a sensitive, caring young woman name Catherine Auguste. Deeply religious, she had been touched by the story being told in the 1990s about the Tulsa Race Riot of 1921. The Carribean native, who first came to Tulsa to study at Oral Roberts University, felt she had been called by God to do something for riot victims. We had several strategy meetings, and she began to work on finding out just what her riot effort should be. Her work is still in progress, and I know that one day it will be complete, for it is God-ordained!

SEAN WILSON:

On another day, I received a call from another sensitive, caring young woman, Tulsa artist Sean Wilson. Sean knew exactly what she wanted to do: (1) spearhead a drive to replace the magnificent pipe organ at Mt. Zion which burned up in the Tulsa riot and (2) prepare for a Purification-by-Fire Ceremony on Greenwood Avenue. Ms. Wilson met with local officials regarding the ceremony and ran into difficulties because of the

fire part of the ceremony. But Sean Wilson is not a person who gives up easily. I know that someday Tulsa will have that Purification-by-Fire Ceremony!

JIM SLOAN:

I first met Jim Sloan when he joined United Nations Association of Eastern Oklahoma, which is a grassroots organizations that supports the national United Nations. An avid treasure hunter and history lover like me, he often shows me some of his finds, gives me some (perfume bottles, etc.), and sells me some, such as the object that he found in the ground near Paradise Baptist Church in north Tulsa where much riot activity took place.

X: MONETARY DONATIONS

The following monetary donations to the Oklahoma Commission to Study the Tulsa Race Riot of 1921 to be distributed to riot victims were received between 1997 and 2002:

Received and distributed:
1. Mike Wilkerson, Barristers Studios,
   Tulsa, Oklahoma, $10,000
2. Audrey Earnhart, Ohio donor $200
3. Anonymous donor $50

Received and distributed:
1. Tulsa Metropolitan Chamber of Commerce
2. Tulsa Metropolitan Ministry Fund
   Foundation
   (donations from private sources and from
   other sources) $28,000

XI: IN-KIND SERVICES

Many individuals and organizations, frustrated by the delays of city, county, state, and national entities to help survivors and descendants of the Tulsa Race Riot of 1921, banded together to "just do something now!" The CHURCH OF THE RESTORATION, an interracial church located on North Greenwood, was among the first to act. On board the reparations movement from day one in 1997, church members founded the TULSA REPARATIONS COALITION in 2001. Dr. Vivian Clark-Adams and I were the two riot commissioners who joined the coalition. The work of the coalition will be covered in chapter 10, where the Riot Commission is examined in depth.

In-kind services, in the early stages of riot commission research, included help of all kind from the the

GREENWOOD CULTURAL CENTER and the NORTH TULSA HERITAGE FOUNDATION. Helping to get volunteers to transport elderly survivors to the center for interviews and to other riot-related events in Tulsa and in Oklahoma City were the most appreciated services of all from those two agencies, along with clerical help from FRANCES FLEMING, who typed most of the riot survivors records kept in the center's computer. Actually, everyone at the Cultural Center bent over backward to help the Riot Commission, the survivors and descendants, and visitors to the center for riot-related information research or for attendance at the myriad events and programs relating to the riot. Thanks, FAI WALKER, FRANCES JORDAN, CINDY DRIVER, MECHELLE BROWN, and all the support personnel at the center!

One of the latest in-kind endeavors to help Tulsa's elderly race riot survivors grew from the joint efforts of groups that were already working individually to aid the survivors. Christal Jordan-Mims and the the Women of Tomorrow leadership group created a program to provide consistent, permanent contact with survivors of Tulsa's riot of 1921. They meet at the Greenwood Cultural Center. Fai Walker, director of the center, loved their idea. Across town in south Tulsa, Bill Major, director of Tulsa Senior Services organization, was already providing services to needy elders, including some who were riot survivors. In downtown Tulsa, Steve Cranford, director of the Tulsa Metropolitan Ministry, was working on a program for in-kind support to Tulsa's riot victims.

On a bright, sunshiny day in November, a meeting was held in the Tulsa Senior Services building, and people representing all kinds of organizations from all over the city came to a kickoff meeting for a massive in-kind project to support Tulsa's riot survivors.

In attendance at that meeting, in addition to Fai Walker, Bill Major, Steve Cranford, and Christal Jordan-Mims, were personnel from Bill Major's Tulsa Senior Services, including Nora Burns, Margaret Love, Wilma Harding, Kathy Polleschultz, Connie Fox, Lena Bennett, and Diane Asher. Also present were Joanna Davis of the University of Tulsa legal clinic, Galen Lassiter of Crossroads Hospice, and me, Eddie Faye Gates, representing the Oklahoma Commission to Study the Tulsa Race Riot of 1921.

The following agencies/individuals were absent due to prior commitments but are dedicated to this project: Dr. Lawrence A. Reed, Westview Medical Clinic, Dr.

Nancy Feldman, retired University of Tulsa Sociology professor, Stephanie Dillard, Wild Oats, and Talva Lacey.

At this meeting, goals were defined, tasks assigned, guidelines and timelines set, and work begun on immediate, pressing needs of survivors. Work continues daily, and each day we get telephone calls from survivors needing help or from grateful survivors calling just to say thanks.

THE NORTH TULSA HISTORICAL SOCIETY's research, writing, and publishing in newspapers, magazines, and books, plus the organization's photographs, videotapes, and films about the riot, which were generously shared with the commission, provided impeccable documents and documentation to the Riot Commission.

YVONNE BURNS volunteered her paralegal services to the commission.

KEITH JIMERSON and KIMBERLY JOHNSON of the Rudisill North Regional Library, located just off Greenwood Avenue, provided invaluable services to the Riot Commission. The commission was always notified promptly about new donations of photographs, videotapes, films, and other riot-related memorabilia to the library. At monthly meetings of the advisory committee to the library, I was always given an opportunity to provide updates on the riot, as were Sen. Maxine Horner and Rep. Don Ross, who were also members of the advisory board and attended meetings when they were not in legislative session in Oklahoma City or at other engagements.

But the "mother of all in-kind services," at the local level, was the creation of the "Writing the Final Chapter 1921 Survivor Project." On December 4, 2001, individuals and representatives of local agencies met at Tulsa Senior Services headquarters to discuss ways to help survivors now while legal, culpable entities were still debating about how they would address the issue of survivors and reparations.

XII: Miscellaneous: Other Events from Family Reunions to Cemeteries and Everything Else in Between!

The Greenwood District is never quiet or deserted. It still draws people from all other the world, some coming for historical events, some for musical events, some for class reunions, family reunions, or funerals.

Today, many events are interracial. However, some things still remain distinctly black and white because they are vestiges of the past, of the old days when the races were separated by law. So Booker T. Washington

High School reunions, which include classes before the 1960s, are all black, and those who visit graves of their relatives who died before the '60s visit black cemeteries.

It seems that on any given day, some Booker T. Washington class is having a reunion in the Greenwood Cultural Center! And black families have a tradition of holding family reunions. Some families which held reunions in recent years were:

THE GUYTON/BAGBY FAMILY (Preston, Okmulgee, Tulsa roots)

THE POWELL/POINTER FAMILY (Preston, Okmulgee, Beggs, Tulsa roots)

THE MILLER/POWELL FAMILY (Preston, Okmulgee, Beggs, Tulsa roots)

THE (BLACK) PERRYMAN FAMILY (Alabama, Mississippi roots)

THE EUGENE HARRIS FAMILY

THE PETIT/WASHINGTON FAMILY

THE WILBUR NORTHINGTON FAMILY

CHAPTER 10

The Oklahoma Commission to Study the Tulsa Race Riot of 1921, 1997–2001

I will not re-create the wheel in this chapter covering the Oklahoma Commission to Study the Tulsa Race Riot of 1921, for the full commission report is readily available to internet subscribers and printed copies can be viewed in libraries. Copies have even made it to flea markets! Recently, when I shopped at my favorite Tulsa flea market (on Admiral Boulevard near Memorial Avenue), the manager of the booth where I often find great historical treasures, such as vital historical documents that corroborate Ku Klux Klan activity in Oklahoma, whispered that he had something I would surely want. It was a copy of the commission report. I turned to the page where commissioner biographies were written and showed him mine. I explained that this report was indeed "a find" but that as a commissioner, I was given one of the first copies of the report at the February 28, 2001, meeting at the State Capitol in Oklahoma City, where our report was presented to Governor Frank Keating, Oklahoma state legislators, Tulsa mayor M. Susan Savage, and Tulsa city councilors. One of my favorite flea market stories about authors' valuable (at least to them) works ending up in flea markets is about one of my fellow Tulsa author friends. At the book signing for her first book, which was widely acclaimed and reprinted numerous times, she had carefully composed a touching tribute to her beloved grandmother. Well, years later, she found that book, with its touching tribute, in an Oklahoma flea market! She, of course, retrieved the priceless book. When she questioned her grandmother about the book, the grandmother said nonchalantly that she knew all the stuff that was written in the book, so she gave it to the flea market so someone else could learn about it!

So, for the full nitty-gritty details of the who, what, where, when, why, and how of the commission, go to the full report. I will focus on the behind-the-scenes details of the commission, on the emotional, psychological, and sociological aspects of the study.

I will begin by telling about how grateful the Tulsa black community was to Rep. Don Ross, Democrat, District 73, Tulsa, and Sen. Maxine Horner, Democrat, District 11, Tulsa, for co- sponsoring House Bill 1035, which created the commission. Those two, and the other three members of the Black Caucus of the Oklahoma Legislature, were the driving force behind the resolution that created the law establishing the commission. But that vocal caucus, as dedicated as it was, couldn't have gotten that bill through on its own. Tribute must also be paid to the entire state legislature. The majority of its members sensed the importance of addressing justice and religious/moral issues, and they recognized how significant such a study was to the black people of Tulsa. They knew about the need for acknowledgment, repentance, reconciliation, and closure in dealing with past injustices. They knew about such movements worldwide. And so, with this law, they opened up their state's history to the world—sort of the opening up of a can of worms! But they did it, and for that act of courage, I thank the legislature. In my summation of the Riot Commission, you will see that I was not pleased with all the responses of the legislature to the commission's recommendations—especially regarding reparations for survivors and descendants of survivors—but for tackling the issue of the riot head-on, I give the legislature praise.

Actually, the Riot Commission study had its beginning in the fertile mind of Rep. Don Ross, who as a fifteen-year-old student at Tulsa's Booker T. Washington High School in 1956, first heard about the riot in the history class taught by the revered W. D. Williams.

Once planted, this kernel was destined to blossom, full-bloom, when the time was right. Known for his pit-bull tenacity in the pursuit of equality and justice for all people, Ross did not rest until the facts were made known to the world. He knew that there would be denial, delayed acknowledgments, anger, frustration, and conflict let loose as a result of this study, yet he doggedly pursued it.

Rep. Don Ross, Dr. John Hope Franklin, and two Oklahoma legislative assistants at riot commission meeting, Greenwood Cultural Center, Tulsa.

Ross himself had been in denial as a fifteen-year-old when he first heard Mr. Williams' accounts of the riot. It was only after the teacher brought to school bulging scrapbooks and photograph albums containing eyewitness documentation of the riot that the skeptical student was convinced. He made a pledge in his heart that someday the whole city, state, nation, and world would know about this riot too. Thank you, Don Ross, for making that promise of yours a reality!

Now let me tell you about how riot commissioners felt about the Riot Commission. I believe that every single commissioner took his or her appointment to this commission seriously. I have served on numerous boards, authorities, commissions, etc. at local, state, national, and even a couple at the international level, but I consider this appointment to the Commission by Mayor Susan Savage to be the Holy Grail of my volunteer service. Here is a broad, general, bare-bones basic

Dr. Scott Ellsworth and Dr. John Hope Franklin at a riot commission meeting.

Riot Survivors at June 4, 2001 Tulsa Race Riot, 1921 Commemoration Program, Mt. Zion Baptist Church, Tulsa.

L. to R. Ruth Sigler Avery, noted Tulsa Race Riot, 1921 historian, talking to riot survivors Ernestine Gibbs and George D. Monroe.

look at the Oklahoma Commission to Study the Tulsa Race Riot of 1921. The entire commission report can be downloaded from the internet, and the Tulsa Reparations Coalition mass-produced copies, at cost, for only $12 each, which can be purchased from the Church of the Restoration in Tulsa, Oklahoma. So here is a capsule look at the Riot Commission study.

THE LAW THAT CREATED THE TULSA RACE RIOT, 1921 COMMISSION:

HB1035 was an excellent bill—clear, concise, detailed, focused. Because of that, the task of commissioners was made easier. See page 1 of Riot Commission Report, February 28, 2001 for specific details of the law.

COMMISSIONERS:
See Danney Goble's warmly personal descriptions of riot commissioners, pp. 2-3 of Riot Commission Report.

COMMISSION ADVISORS:
Dr. John Hope Franklin
Dr. Scott Ellsworth
See p. 3 of Riot Commission Report.

COMMISSION CONSULTANTS:
See pp. 3-4 of Riot Commission Report.

TASK:
See pp. 4-6 of Riot Commission Report.

RESEARCH:
Over three and a half years of research and the examination of over 20,000 documents.
See index of Riot Commission Report, p. 5.

MEETINGS:
The meetings of the commission, held quarterly at the beginning of our research in 1997 and then escalating to monthly meetings, and even to special called meetings near the end, were always vibrant, exciting, and well attended, especially when the national and international media were on hand. When the *Sixty Minutes* crew from New York descended upon North Tulsa in 1999, there was standing-room-only at the riot commission meeting!

As much as it meant to commissioners to have their hard work appreciated by the national media, riot experts, consultants, historians, etc., whose faces we recognized at our meetings, nothing warmed our hearts more, or stirred us to work harder, than the loving, beaming faces of the survivors themselves or their devoted descendants. They were the reason the commission had been formed, and they were the reason for our hard work. They kept us motivated; just the sight of them rejuvenated us!

During most of our commission meetings between 1997 and 2001, and at some of the meetings of the Tulsa Reparations Coalition, which was formed after the Riot Commission completed its work in February 2001, a face we could count on seeing was that of Genevieve Tillman Jackson, along with her constant companion/supporter,

Riot commission meeting

her look-alike daughter, longtime Tulsa community activist Karen Jackson Simpson. They could hold their own with anyone, friend or foe alike! Information that Karen had from her experiences at the University of Tulsa, where she was once employed, and her extensive background of

Riot commission meeting.

legal research came in handy during some stages of commission research, and later at Tulsa Reparations Coalition meetings. She is on a first-name basis with many nationally known lawyers. Her no-nonsense, "cut to the chase" approach gained the attention of survivors, commissioners, and the media.

In some of the newspaper accounts of our Riot Commission meetings, and in some of the other research and writings now out about the riot, scholars, historians, and authors often concentrated more on divisiveness between commission members rather than on the content of our research. Though we were a racially and geographically diverse group of people, and though we had legitimate cultural differences and experiences which contributed to our world-views, we were thoughtful of each other and carried out our research in an atmosphere as harmonious as could be under the circumstances. There was no bitterness or hate between any of the commissioners. In fact, one day after an especially difficult commission meeting when we were discussing the issue of reparations, one of the most conservative members of the commission, one of the white legislators, came over to me and said, "I love you, little lady. We may differ in our opinions regarding the riot and in the ways we believe best for dealing with riot issues, but I am sincere in my efforts and I know you are sincere in yours." We hugged each other and I replied, "I love you too, and I know that what you just said is true."

Given the seriousness of the issue of race in any culture or nation, it is no wonder that some committee meetings were tense. Race is the most divisive of all issues. Yet, black commissioners did not come to the table with axes to grind, with agendas to promote individual causes, or with overblown egos and desires to grandstand.

We did come to the table as a marginalized group

whose history had been neglected in the nation, with the knowledge that this riot was an event that happened to our culture, and for Tulsa commissioners, in our community. We did intend to use this opportunity wisely to fulfill our state-mandated task of leaving a record of the events of the riot that would clear up misconceptions, and that would lead to long-overdue reconciliation and healing.

So if there was too much "contentious dialogue" or "excessive divisiveness" at commission meetings for some participants and observers, perhaps the following information about the controversial issues that generated such dialogue will clarify what the debate was about and why it was significant. The issues that generated the most debate at commission meetings were: (1) the reparations issue, (2) the role of the Ku Klux Klan in Oklahoma, in general, and in Tulsa, specifically, before, during, and after the Tulsa Race Riot of 1921, (3) the role of airplanes and/or a conspiracy in the destruction of the Greenwood District in the riot, and (4) the role of black primary sources before, during, and after the Tulsa Race Riot of 1921.

Some of our extensive research for riot information (the examination of over 20,000 documents) cleared up questions, but some questions will probably never be answered. I will conclude this chapter by giving some input on the "contentious dialogue" that occurred over the four above-listed issues:

REPARATIONS:

It is the nature of the human being to want to be loved, respected, treated with dignity, and to be seen in "a good light." Also, human beings tend to be protective of their individual resources, as well as of the collective resources of their nations. So there is usually a natural resistance to dispensing monetary reimbursements from individual pocketbooks and from the collective tills of nations. That is a given, but there seems to be more resistance to reparations when the receiving subjects are "subgroups" in the nations doing the dispensing. Dr. Vivian Clark-Adams and I took a lot of flack because we were assumed to be too aggressive, too strident, too obsessed, and "militant." We didn't consider ourselves to be any of those. We considered ourselves educated, assertive, articulate women who were making a strong case for reparations for a deserving group of people.

All of us commissioners knew that reparations was a touchy issue, and we worked hard to learn as much about the subject as we could. We thoroughly did our research, reading, researching in libraries, museums, and archives, viewing videotapes and films, interviewing people, and speaking individually and on panels, all over the nation (and in Africa). We looked up definitions of reparation and restitution. We compared and contrasted reparation examples in history and found a wide range of views on the subject. In addition to studying the materials that we found ourselves, we studied the materials that our legal consultants and scholars provided for us. Al Brophy's legal materials grounded us in the legal aspects of reparations, and we drank in Dr. Ed Linenthal's speech before the committee about dealing with massacres, riots, and reconciliation and healing.

Among some of the local programs on the topic of race, reconciliation, and reparations that some commissioner attended were:

1. The University of Tulsa's American Inns of Court, Council Oak Inn Tulsa Race Riot Part II Program: "Fashioning a Remedy," in which lawyers presented pro and con arguments regarding reparations.

2. National Conference Dialogue programs on "Race and Reconciliation."

3. Oklahoma State University-Tulsa programs on "Racial Profiling."

4. The Metropolitan Tulsa Urban League program "Reframing the Dialogue on Race."

Dr. Vivian Clark-Adams and I also served on reparations panels at Tulsa Community College, Langston University, Oklahoma State University-Tulsa, Southwest Missouri State University, Springfield, Missouri, and the State University of New York, New Paltz.

Some of us commissioners, and others connected with the riot commission, also spoke individually at programs relating to the riot. Rep. Don Ross was a favorite with survivor audiences all over the nation, especially at large black churches in urban areas such as Chicago. I also was guest lecturer in classes at the University of Toledo and speaker at the evening Black History Program. Dr. Clark-Adams and I also fielded reparations questions on the Tulsa Community College Summer Study Program in Accra, Ghana, West Africa in March of 2001.

There seemed to be a national and world hunger for racial healing and reconciliation the last few years. As a result of the media descent upon Tulsa for riot and reparations information, and of my travels, I now have a deeper understanding of the reparations issue. I have found that there is a wide range of views regarding reparations. Some people, and culpable entities, believe in a total, sincere commitment to genuine reparations by in-

dividuals and nations if there is ever to be a repairing of damages caused by past violent and tragic behaviors and incidents; others believe that "a dash of cash" and mumbled apologies suffice. The fear that support of reparations implied an acceptance of personal responsibility for past wrongdoing causes many to shy away from advocating reparations.

Reparations is a serious issue that must be faced if there is ever to be peace, harmony, healing, and reconciliation on the planet earth.

THE ROLE OF THE KU KLUX KLAN:

There was a lot of bickering and nitpicking between commissioners and others over what constituted a Klansman and over exactly what role the Klan played in the Tulsa Race Riot of 1921. Some people, mainly some whites, supported the theory that the Tulsa riot was a "white ruffian" riot devised and carried out by that group without the knowledge and consent of the leadership of Tulsa or Tulsa's "good and decent" citizens; others (mainly blacks) felt that evidence showed the leadership showed not only prior knowledge but that the leadership—and others of the elite class—participated in the riot. While there was never a clear consensus between all, there is evidence of many shades of gray when it comes to an assessment of the role of the Ku Klux Klan. It is obvious that the Klan was a secret organization and did not leave records about for easy observation; on the other hand, Klansmen (by the way the Klan included women, who often brought their children along on marches) were not ashamed of their philosophy and the organization. In fact, in a *Tulsa World* article, Tulsa Klansmen boasted that their membership would soon surpass Dallas, Texas' membership numbers! Newspaper articles show the Klan presence in Tulsa before the riot. My examination of the Ku Klux Klan rolls at the University of Tulsa's Special Collection at McFarlin Library provided information that clearly showed that a number of Tulsa's leadership—doctors, lawyers and judges, teachers and preachers, businessmen and bankers, as well as musicians, entertainers, undertakers, brick masons, garbage men, farmers and working class persons supported the Klan.

While it is true that Tulsa's Klan rolls expanded after the riot, that is no solace. In my opinion, it is worse to be a member of the KKK after the terrible destruction of the Tulsa Race Riot of 1921. Before the riot, one might claim ignorance about what race, religious, and class hatred could cause. They could try to make a case that the Klan was an organization that tried to protect women, children, and families. After that riot, no think-ing person could claim ignorance about what organiza-tions such as the Klan stood for. (See chapter 3 regard-ing conspiracy, the Real Estate Board, etc.)

The Role of Airplanes in the Destruction of the Greenwood District and/or a Conspiracy

For a long time, Tulsa has lived under the stigma that it was the only American city to be bombed by its own military. The Riot Commission was able to refute that charge. Dick Warner of the Tulsa Historical Society did extensive research on the airplane subject. Other military experts also provided information and materials for the commission. By examining records, Warner was able to establish approximately how many airplanes were in Tulsa at the time of the riot, who owned them, and who flew them.

At the same time, the commission was able to re-fute the theory of some (mainly whites) that no air-planes dropped anything during the riot. According to the evidence airplanes did drop something on Greenwood. But what they dropped were not World War I-type military bombs. The commission report refers to the items dropped as "incendiary devices." Regarding the conspiracy theory and the role of the leadership in the "bombing" of Tulsa's black community, black commissioners and the black community in gen-eral firmly believe that there was collusion between leaders and mobsters during the riot, especially assaults that resulted from devices dropped from the air. The bottom line is that "poor white ruffians" don't own air-planes and don't have the luxury of paying for, flying les-sons! So figure this out for yourself!

The Role of Black Primary Sources Before, During, and After the Tulsa Race Riot of 1921

If I had to categorize the contentious issues in order of seriousness, the role of black primary sources would be the number-one issue! But as mentioned in earlier chapters, it was not racial animosity that caused this contention. Rather, it was just a classic example of how race impacts society and how cultural differences, his-tory, and the sociological and psychological needs of in-dividuals are such powerful factors in human relation-ships. All of us mortals see things through the lenses of our own culture. And the culture that had told the his-tory of our nation, and western civilization, was the pre-dominant white culture; naturally, people of that cul-

ture, that race, would be more comfortable with their sources and skeptical of the unknown. Actually, there was no need to be skeptical. Black resources, written by the people most familiar with the Tulsa Race Riot of 1921, the people who lived through it, and those who came to the aid of the afflicted survivors of the ordeal, proved to be quite credible, quite reliable, and helped tremendously in documenting and validating the events that occurred in Tulsa in 1921.

Naturally, black commissioners, as well as some white commissioners who had a strong background in civil rights issues and much knowledge of the Black Experience in America, people like Jim Lloyd, Bob Blackburn, and Pete Churchwell, took a strong interest in the black source materials too, much of it newly found. (Some of the black documentation source mate-rials came from my research in Washington, D.C., and Maryland in late October and early November 2000.) Any commissioner who came across black resource ma-terials, or any other material that might be helpful in the commission study, gladly shared all such informa-tion with the entire commission.

It was a powerful experience to actually see, touch, and feel those fragile documents dealing with one of the most stress-filled periods in U.S. history, the era of lynchings, race massacres, riots, etc. Pulling up infor-mation on the internet or reading about history in li-braries is no match for the hands-on handling of histor-ical documents! I would spend the whole day pulling down documents from the shelves, reading and copying significant information for the commission. At night, I would organize my findings and write summaries to share with the commission of what I had found.

Among the documents that I examined in Washington and in Maryland were :

1. African Blood Brotherhood (ABB) materials dat-ing back to the founding of the organization and espe-cially the materials pertaining to the Tulsa Race Riot of 1921 (original constitution, goals, letters, and other correspondence from all over the world, newspaper ar-ticles, etc.).

2. National Association of Colored Peoples (NAACP) materials—historical records, minutes, corre-spondence, etc. about the organization and its leaders.

3. Urban League materials—historical records, minutes, correspondence, etc. about the organization and its leaders

4. The National Negro Business League—historical records, correspondence, including that from founder

Booker T. Washington of Tuskegee Institute, Tuskegee, Alabama.

5. The Liberty League—historical records and correspondence.

6. American Labor Year Book documents.

7. Miscellaneous documents and materials related to the 1920s era, such as documents from insurance companies that had a history of dealing with blacks at that time, companies such as the Modern Woodmen of America.

The documents that fascinated me the most during this research in the nation's capital were those of the African Blood Brotherhood, an organization founded in desperation in New York City. It was a self-help organization that was determined to protect black citizens in the U.S. who were so neglected by their own local, state, and national governments. Leaders of the national organization traveled all over the U.S. counseling and organizing local chapters. On more than one occasion, leaders had visited Oklahoma. A poignant letter, dated May 23, 1921, from Muskogee, Oklahoma in the ABB collections shows what the racial climate was like in Oklahoma, at that date. W. R. Smith lived at 641 North Third Street, Muskogee, at the time. He wrote the letter on company stationery—W. R. Smith-J. F. Thompson Manufacturing Confectioners, 223 South Second Street, Muskogee, Oklahoma, Telephone 4830.

In that handwritten letter, Mr. Smith pours out his heart and appeals to the organization for help:

"We are appealing to you for aid in matter of lands allotted to the Freedmen of Okla. (Negroes of Indian blood) who have been victims of the white man's exploitations and vicious conversions of land-minors and wards whose Guardians have sold lands of value and squandered the money. The courts indorse [sic] such activities."

Letters such as this, and others from Tulsa, Oklahoma, regarding the intolerable racial climate in Oklahoma at the time, brought members of the ABB to Tulsa before and after the riot. (Some black survivors say that a few got caught in Tulsa at the time of the riot.)

Another document that I found during my Capital Area research fascinated me. It was an 8x14-inch flyer written by a spunky black woman who haf lived in Tulsa, Indian Territory before statehood. At the top of this flyer, dated August 21, 1910, in bold, enlarged black lettering, is this caption: "Notice to the World at Large"! The bottom of the flyer is signed "MRS. CARRIE B. PECK, Grand Supreme Evangelist."

In between that flyer caption and Mrs. Peck's sig-nature at the bottom is a powerful history lesson. Unlike some blacks in America, Mrs. Peck didn't petition black leaders and black organizations for help. She petitioned God! She speaks on behalf of a "God-ordained" organization, the Noble and Grand Loyal and Royal Etheopians [sic]. In that flyer, she states their goals, which she lists as "to take up the work of all unfinished business that may come up."

The old business that she addressed in this flyer were:

1. Africans brought to America as slaves.

2. The disgrace of slavery in America.

3. The failure of government to protect black people in America.

4. God, the only protector of black people in America.

The new business that she discussed was the grandfather clause that had been one of the first laws adopted into the Constitution of Oklahoma after statehood in 1907. Mrs. Peck bitterly condemns the grandfather clause, but she vows to carry on the fight for equality for black people in Oklahoma. She pleads with no man for aid. She put her faith in God as the only leader and defender for black people in Oklahoma.

There was fear and suspicion on the part of whites toward black organizations and black leaders in the 1920s. Some people say that there always has been such fear and suspicion between various racial, ethnic, religious, political, economic, social, cultural, and geographic groups, and that there always will be. Patterns of history certainly do seem to show this. A modern example is the present Middle East conflict which is having world ramifications today.

In cases of conflict, one of the first acts on the part of people and nations is to discredit the individual, group, or nation under suspicion. That certainly happened during the 1920s. No group in America came under more suspicion. And even in the era of the Riot Commission study, we had to fight that battle again about credibility and validity. After thoroughly examining the black documents and resources, and using the standards of historiography in which we had been trained (four of the black commissioners were trained historians, all with at least master's degrees and two with doctorate degrees), we found the black documents just as credible as white documents. We rejected the kill-the-messenger tactics of some would-be detractors. Such tactics were used in the 1920s (playing the "Communist" card); in the 1960s when the "Communist" card was used to try to discredit Martin Luther King, Jr.; and today during the Middle East crisis.

We found black leaders and organizations in the 1920s just as credible as their white counterparts. Their goals seemed reasonable and not revolutionary. They were simply seeking their constitutional rights in their own nation. They were aware of world movements at that time to keep black people in subordinate positions. The fear of blacks being lured into the Communist Party is often overplayed. A look at the historical record shows that the Communist Party has had less success with black people in America and world-wide than with any other race or group. The Communist philosophy does not appeal that much to oppressed peoples. Capitalism can hold its own. Black people then and now just want their rights, and their share of the dream, in their democratic, capitalistic nations.

Some of the white commissioners also were trained historians, or were lawyers and businessmen who had dealings with all races and classes of people. Some of them felt as we black commissioners did about the black resources; I hope that those who had reservations will read this and will see that it was not compromising to consider those black sources as credible and those leaders as seekers of freedom and justice like American patriots who fought in the Revolutionary War.

So those were some of the touchy issues the commission dealt with. One of the most stressful times for the commission was the period just before our commission meeting in Oklahoma City in February 4, 2000. The commission had been at work for two and a half years, we were due to report to officials the status of our report at that date, and there was no written report from our scholars! (There was a glitch in communication regarding the written report. Neither the scholars nor the commission had clear-cut guidelines on this issue.) So the week before the deadline, some of the riot subcommittee members met daily, being careful that our numbers would not go over the limit and break the open-meeting law, to draft some kind of report. The night before the commission meeting, we worked into the wee hours of the morning; Dr. Vivian-Clark Adams, one of the younger members of the commission, worked all night at her computer putting the finishing touches to "The Preliminary Report of The Oklahoma Commission to Study the Tulsa Race Riot of 1921." The Investigative Subcommittee that prepared the report consisted of riot commissioners Dr. Vivian Clark-Adams, Pete Churchwell, Jim Lloyd, and me. I have read some disparaging remarks about the preliminary report in some media accounts, and in some of the new books out about the riot, but I am proud of that report. I think that it was well written and that it accurately reflects the documentation and analysis of our riot research at that time. See chapter 3 for complete details of the preliminary report.

FINAL REPORT:

Since some of us had been through the trial-by-fire experience of preparing the preliminary report of the riot commission, we felt that the researching, discussing, editing, modifying, and adding input for Danney Goble, who was to write the final report of the commission, would not be too traumatic. We were wrong! Writing that preliminary report was a piece of cake in comparison to bringing the final report to fruition. But, on the other hand, the sense of making history lifted our spirits, and we "waded into the water" and began our final tasks. In fact, I really enjoyed this stage in our commission work. Years of effort were coming to an end. We were winnowing through our research, separating the chaff from the wheat, and doing our part in the preparation of a document that we believed would bring about reconciliation and healing. I think that period was our finest hour during the whole process.

KEY DOCUMENTATION:

See each chapter for listings of key primary and secondary sources that helped in the preparation of the final report.

KEY FINDINGS OF THE RIOT FINAL REPORT:
See full report.

AFTERMATH: UNEXPECTED EFFECTS:

1. Worldwide Focus on Tulsa and the riot: recognitions, apologies, tributes, plays, poems, songs, monetary contributions to survivors.

2. Outpouring of love, respect, and appreciation to the 167 living black survivors, who became media celebrities; respect and interest in the spouses of deceased riot victims, and in the numerous descendants of Tulsa riot victims.

3. The sincere respect and appreciation, from locally to internationally for the riot commissioners for their hard work and their final report documenting the Tulsa race riot.

4. The hunger and thirst, from local to international levels, for information about the Tulsa Race Riot of 1921.

5. National print and electronic media focus on Tulsa and the resulting free public relations boost for the city (newspapers, TV, radio programs, magazines, web links, et al!).

6. Riot-focused healing and reconciliation programs all over the nation, sponsored by political, economic, and social organizations, schools, churches, and entertainment organizations, etc.

In conclusion, all the team members of the Oklahoma Commission to Study the Tulsa Race Riot of 1921 took their duties seriously. We studied hard, we thought hard, and we came to what we thought were the best conclusions possible based on the evidence that we found.

Read what Danney Goble wrote about the work of the commission. Pull the Final Report of the Oklahoma Commission to Study the Tulsa of the Tulsa Race Riot of 1921 up on your web site. Or better yet, buy your own copy of the report. The Tulsa Reparations Coalition printed copies of the study and sells them at cost. They can be ordered from:

The Church of the Restoration
1314 North Greenwood Ave.
Tulsa, OK 74120

$12 plus $2 mailing fee

I think Danney Goble did a good job writing the final report. He was at first overwhelmed by the mountains of documents delivered to him at commission meetings (I was one of the main pack rats who dropped off loads of materials)! But he listened carefully at meetings, and he plowed through the documents and materials we commissioners gave him, materials that schol-

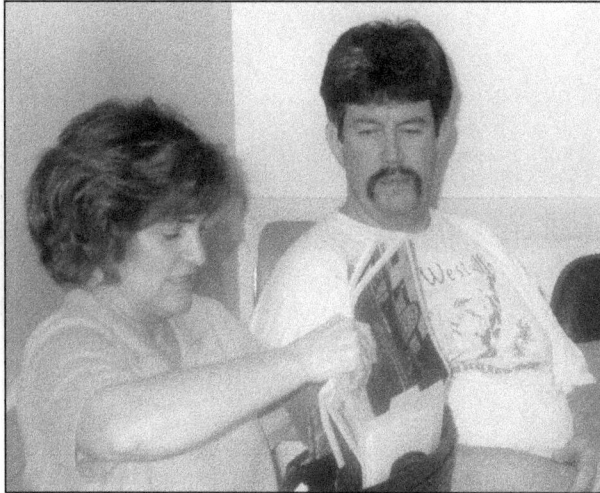

Rose Kennedy and Ken Hollis of the Tulsa Reparations Coalition.

Tulsa Reparations Coalition members, Eddie Faye Gates, and Dr. Kimberly Ellis, Purdue University, discuss plans for reparations movement.

Mark Stodghill, TRC Chair, Center for Racial Justice, Tulsa branch.

Africans & African Americans for Enslavement Reparations (AAAER) present a chapter notebook for Tulsa riot commissioner Eddie Faye Gates to take back to Tulsa. Black Images Book Bazaar, Dallas, Texas, March 19, 2000.

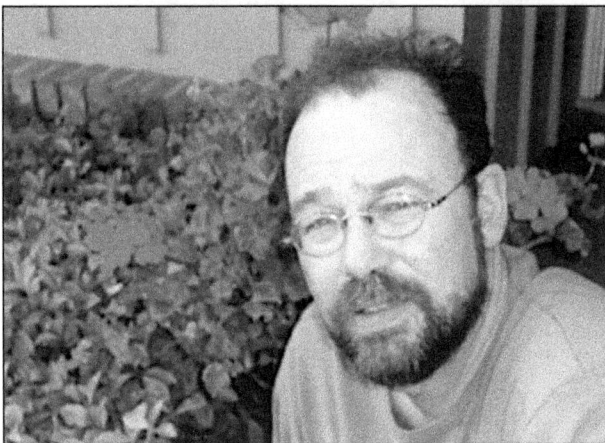

Deep Greenwood today, overlooking the downtown area.

Mabel B. Little Heritage House in the Greenwood Cultural Center area.

Greenwood Cultural Center Building

Greenwood Area—Oklahoma State University.

ars, advisors, consultants, lawmakers, experts, and interested citizens gave to him, and the mounds of materials he himself had accumulated during all his years of research and writing. He made revisions and corrections after every meeting, and when he had done all he could do with the information that he had about the Tulsa Race Riot of 1921, he sent his manuscript to press. Danney, you did a good job!

We all did the best that we could do. I feel that the Oklahoma Commission to Study the Tulsa Race Riot of 1921 was God-ordained. It was time for justice; it was time for reconciliation and racial healing. Thank you, God, for allowing me to be part of that great mission.

The Black Wall Street Memorial in the Greenwood Cultural Center area.

CHAPTER 11

Lessons to Be Learned from the Tulsa Race Riot of 1921

An observation of domestic terrorism manifested as lynchings, massacres, riots, and revolutions in the past, and global terrorism of the present being manifested as broad, blatant attacks on world nations such as the September 11, 2001, attack on the United States, clearly show that mankind has plenty of lessons to learn before there can be peace and harmony in individual nations and in the world.

There is an obvious gap between professed high religious ideals in nations, and professed high principles of government in nations. Most nations have religious traditions that stress good character and good conduct. Most nations have such codes of behavior written in sacred books. Most nations have good codes of government written also in great documents—charters, constitutions, etc. Yet the world seems adrift in conflict, disharmony, war. What lessons are there still left for mankind to learn?

One would have to have been living in outer space not to have been bombarded with information about present conflict in the Middle East and about its ramifications. From the vast body of information that has poured forth, it seems that the lessons we most need to learn are these:

BASIC HISTORICAL FACTS ABOUT WORLDWIDE CONFLICTS

1. Most present conflicts are rooted in old hurts.
2. There are two sides to every conflict between two individuals or two nations.
3. Each side in a conflict (individual or nation) holds firm beliefs that injustices have been perpetrated against them, and perceived injustices are often as harmful to peace efforts as real ones.

4. All individuals and nations long for a safe and secure homeland where people may pursue peace, prosperity, freedom, justice, and happiness.
5. According to history, the main deterrents to world peace are hypocrisy, greed, arrogance, and violence in individuals and nations.
6. Most conflicts in history have been tribal, racial, ethnic, or land conflicts.
7. Might does not make right! Sheer brute force may seem to end conflict, but it does not heal the conflict at its roots; conflict will surely resurface again unless fairness and justice are involved in the settlement of the conflict.

Now that some of the basic causes of conflicts in the history of the world have been listed, here are some suggestions that are presently being cited as necessary for the true healing of conflicts.

BASIC SOLUTIONS FOR THE HEALING OF CONFLICTS

1. The parties in conflict must move from the denial stage regarding the conflict.
2. The parties in conflict must advance to the acknowledgment stage in the conflict. This has not happened in the Middle East conflict, where there must be an acknowledgment of two things: (1) the intense need for a homeland for Jews emerging from Holocaust-torn Europe after World War II; (2) that there were some basic flaws in the UN resolution that created the Jewish State in 1948. Ramifications from that resolution, created mainly by England and other Western European powers with a history of imperialism, are still felt by Arab peoples in the Middle East to this day.

3. Avoidance of inflammatory speech that inflames or accelerates conflicts.

4. Sincere, true dialogue on conflict. This can not be overstated. Oppressed black Americans, who struggled for civil rights before the 1960s revolution ushered in a new era of equality and justice, did not resort to violence and war in their search. They were able to "hang in for the long haul" because they had hope. Without dialogue and hope, people often resort to violent, unacceptable behavior such as murder and suicide.

Some people and organizations have expressed deep regrets that the U.S. and Israel did not participate in the UN Conference on Racism in Durban, South Africa, in 2001. Some experts infer that the nations boycotting the conference may have had a role in provoking the September 11 terrorist attacks.

5. Have realistic expectations. Don't expect instant solutions for old conflicts.

Hindsight is always better than foresight when one is espousing solutions to problems. Looking at these lessons of history, each of us can do something to help heal conflict in the world today. We can pray daily to keep our thoughts spiritually pure and uplifted as we strive to have a just, safe world for ourselves; we can also pray for that for all peoples of the world. We can live up to our highest political principles, and we can work with our local, state, and federal governments to provide a free, equal, and just society for all citizens. We can also work with organizations that are dedicated to promoting those principles on a global level. In other words, in the words of Martin Luther King, Jr., we can "Walk the walk, not just talk the talk." There is evidence that people all over the world are doing just that! People are bonding with each other more; they are participating more in dialogue via forums, lectures, speeches, etc.; they are contributing more to charities that help people all over the world; there has been an increase in church attendance after September 11. People are praying more for themselves and for the world.

Epilogue

Bonding with the Motherland: My First Trip to Africa

I feel that my life has come full circle. I have gone from my first baby thoughts about geographic origins, culture, and family which I learned as a five-year-old sitting cross-legged on the floor of one of the numerous sharecropper's houses of my childhood to setting foot on African soil for the first time March 25, 2001. What an emotional, spiritual event that was! I will never forget that day!

I was already an experienced world traveler. I had been to Europe three times (twice as a military-dependent wife, and once on a Holocaust Summer Study fellowship program for American teachers), to the Middle East once (to Israel for the continuation of the Holocaust Summer Study program), and to the Caribbean twice (on Carnival ship cruises all over the area), but there was an aching void in my heart. Like Alex Haley, who wrote the classic book, *Roots*, I longed to set foot in Mother Africa.

When I stepped off that plane onto African soil for the first time, felt the moist, warm heat on my body, smelled the flowers, looked at the palm trees around the airport, I felt a deep, spiritual connection to the land. What was I looking for here? I was looking for information about the land of my ancestors. I wanted to see what they had seen, smell what they had smelled, touch what they had touched. I was hungering and thirsting for more knowledge, wisdom, understanding about this land of my people. And I found what I was looking for.

PEOPLE:

Actually, the bonding-with-the-motherland syndrome kicked in even before I got on the plane to Africa. I saw a level of African (black) autonomy that I had never seen before. I saw black people in total control of Ghana Airlines at John F. Kennedy International Airport! It is not often that black Americans see black people in total control of large institutions, organizations, or anything, especially those of us from states where we are a numerical minority, such as Oklahoma. I had seen glimpses of black autonomy when I visited Detroit, Michigan, and Atlanta, Georgia. But never before had I been in the presence of black people with so much power and authority. It was an empowering moment for me to hear the description of the airplane, the flight itinerary, and introduction of the crew and staff, all done by black folks! And when the crisply attired, articulate, efficient flight crew appeared, it was a sight many of us black Americans had never seen before. I will never forget Captain Asamwa, who flew that huge DC-111 aircraft from New York to Accra, or Captain Qua Kan, who flew a similar aircraft back from Ghana to New York. Before the plane took off, we were told that there were 302 passengers aboard. In the "sea of humanity" on that plane, I noted that only two were white. (The two white passengers seemed very at ease and must have had a lot of experience in being a minority).

One of the insidious effects of racism is that it distorts history so that people are often kept ignorant of the good deeds and accomplishments of some population groups. This is especially true in nations with a legacy of slavery. With their hidden agenda of perpetuation of the status quo—white supremacy—the imperial powers of Europe, and later the Americas, distorted African history. The effects of those thoughts and actions of the past have a direct effect upon present world conditions. All over the world, nations are dealing with residual effects of long-range, deep-seated problems such as racism, unjust land distributions with inevitable subsequent economic problems, religious and cultural intolerance, and other problems.

Other passengers slept through the night as we crossed the Atlantic, but I was too excited to sleep (as was one other female passenger). We both wrote feverishly in our journals. I paper-clipped off three sections for my notes: (1) People (2) Places (3) Events. All night long on that flight to Africa, I wrote down what I was looking for and why this search was so important.

Once in Africa, I searched the faces of Africans that I encountered everywhere. I was fascinated with the people. I looked at body builds to see who looked like my paternal Petit ancestors, who were slaves on a plantation near Waco, Texas, or like my maternal Minter ancestors, who were slaves on a Sulphur Springs, Texas, plantation near Dallas. My Petit ancestors were mostly tall and muscular, with large feet, as were some of the Minter males. But my grandmother Retter Hardeman Minter came from a family of dainty little women who had small feet (she wore size five shoes). I did not see any Africans in Ghana as tall and muscular as the males in my family. I did see many women who reminded me of dainty little dark-skinned Grandmother Minter.

I looked at colorfully attired Africans streaming out of villages into teeming market centers, some of them to sell, some of them to buy, and I wondered if my African ancestors might have come along that very route before the diaspora to America. That is what separates the experience of many African-Americans from the experience of other immigrants to America. As captives, our ancestors were plucked unexpectedly from their homeland and did not have the luxury of bringing to America precious mementoes of their motherland to tide them over in their adjustment to the new world as immigrants did. As a historian, I have done much research on immigration and migration. I have deep respect, appreciation, and love for the people who migrated from all over the world to carve out new lives in the Americas. The women, especially, fascinate me. It was they who packed beloved artifacts and mementoes into trunks to bring across the ocean. It was they who kept their native language, religion, customs, and culture alive for their children. These immigrant women, carrying on the ancient tradition of women-as-civilizers, must be given their due respect.

Likewise, African-American women of slave descent deserve special recognition. They fulfilled their roles as women civilizers under the most trying circumstances. Not only did their capture prevent them from bringing mementoes of their homeland to the Americas, slave masters tried to purge even thoughts of Africa from their minds! But those wonderful women shared their culture with their descendants through their memories of their homeland. Thus, an African subculture evolved in the Americas in which the art, music, literature, dance, fashion, hair styles, and other traditions of Africa were passed on to Americans of African origin. Alex Haley was able to trace his ancestors back to Gambia in West Africa because his Tennessee grandmother remembered a few words that her Africa-born father had taught her.

I observed the mental characteristics of West Africans, especially noting their alertness (sometimes bordering on aggressiveness as they sought to do business with tourists whose economic output was so desperately needed). Many myths about Africans, and people of African descent, were put to rest when we American student/tourists saw the African people and culture with our own eyes. Nowhere did we observe the slow, shuffling, docile, happy-go-lucky figure so often depicted in American history. Instead, we saw agile, quick-moving people seriously going about their daily business.

Of course, the Africans that our study group grew to know best were those connected with this Tulsa Community College Summer Study tour—George (Yaw) Ohene Asante, tour director, Ishmael Kwame Ofori Akrofi, professional tour guide, Francis, bus driver, and Kwame, a young man hired to look after George Asante's three-year-old son Richard, whose mother was back in the U.S.

George Asante, a native of Ghana, is a member of an African royal family. He lived in Washington, D.C., for thirty years where he worked in a U.S. government job. Ishmael Akrofi took his job seriously, as did other guides who spoke to our group. Knowing of the distortion of African history worldwide, African tour guides are vigilant in their professional, self-proclaimed duty to set the record straight regarding African history.

I found the tour guides extremely qualified, articulate, and efficient in sharing the history of their continent with us eager students. I found that the first inhabitants of Ghana came from Nigeria, where they had been engaged in such turmoils and wars that they voluntary left to find a more peaceful place to live. The place they found was Ghana. Because they came in by ocean like droves of ants, they were called "Ga" people, for "ga" means ant in the Ghanaian language. To learn more about the languages and tribes of West Africa, I stocked up on books about language and culture in the region.

Here is a bit of information about the Tulsa Community College Summer Study in Africa program:

PLACES:

ACCRA

I was spellbound by many of the places that I saw in Africa. No place was more exciting than teeming Accra, the capital of Ghana. Its streets, open markets, historical buildings, private housing reflecting both European and African influences, museums, memorials, businesses, restaurants, hotels, soccer stadiums, and other structures were fascinating. I especially enjoyed our tours at the Kwame Nkrumah Memorial and the W.E.B. Du Bois Memorial and Museum.

The Kwame Nkrumah Memorial contains some poignant, powerful, historically significant artifacts ranging from childhood memorabilia of Nkrumah, to his artifacts from his re-created college dormitory room at Lincoln University in Pennsylvania, to key documents, papers, books, letters, and photographs chronicling his presidency in the first nation to be freed from European colonialism (in 1957). Finally, the memorial contains mementoes relating to his death, including the first coffin in which he was buried. (He was disinterred from his first burial place in Accra and is now buried in his native village.)

The W.E.B. DuBois Memorial and Museum was especially touching to me, for I knew the story of why Dr. DuBois had come to Ghana to found the first International Museum of Black Inventors, and why his magnificent life collection of memorabilia was on African soil and not on his native American soil. It was because of his total rejection of prejudice, discrimination, and racism that had been so prevalent in the America in which he had been born and in which he had lived his whole life. Feeling that America would never be "America to me," as so eloquently stated in a Langston Hughes poem, he reluctantly, and finally, rejected the U.S. In 1963, Ghana became his home.

My husband, Norman, an electrical engineer, was naturally fascinated by the Black Inventors Museum and spent most of his time in there. Being a history major and an English minor, I wore myself to a frazzle trying to see every historical thing, as well as every literary object in the museum! The vintage clothing exhibit of DuBois and his wife, as well as period clothing from other donors, was exquisite. An unprecedented "literary moment" for me was having my photograph taken with the DuBois Museum guide, Dr. DuBois'

main biographer, Dr. Daniel Agbeyebiawo. We were both holding a corner of a first-edition copy of Dr. DuBois' most famous book, *The Souls of Black Folk!*

Icing on the cake for us American study-program participants was hearing a lecture on Pan-Africanism by a University of Ghana, Legon, professor. The lecture had to be held outside in the courtyard behind the museum, not by design but because the electricity tripped off inside the museum at the exact time the lecture was to start (a typical experience for us in museums, restaurants, and even in four- and five-star hotels)! (Hundred-degree weather, in the most humid conditions most of us Americans had ever experienced, was one of the negative aspects of our stay in Africa. The other was our difficulty in adjusting to the very different cuisine.) The lecture was one of the most profound that we black Americans had ever heard. To hear this history of Africa of the past, its struggles for unification in the present, and its hopes and dreams for a prosperous, harmonious, peaceful future moved us to tears. To hear this history told by a black African expert was just too good to be true. We thought that we must be dreaming!

The other negative experience I had at the DuBois museum is that right in the middle of the passionate lecture by the University of Ghana professor, I felt a burning sensation on my left ankle. I looked down and found that a little red African ant had declared war on me. This foreigner was the victor, for I pinched that little ant to death! We had been warned about mosquitos and told to bring repellants. I had enough mosquito repellant to protect the entire study group.

CAPE COAST CASTLES

The highlight of my Africa trip, and for most, if not all of my fellow study participants, was the visit to two slave castles in the Cape Coast region of Ghana.

The region is gorgeous—white sandy beaches, blue-tinted Atlantic Ocean, the tallest palm trees that I have ever seen, coconuts everywhere, and bustling, friendly African people going about their daily routines despite curious, questioning tourists. It is hard to imagine that this area was once the scene of the brutal slave trade, but it was. I bought a little book at Elmina Castle, the first slave castle that we visited, and it helped me to grasp the deep complexities of the European and American slave trade. The book, *Forts and Castles in Ghana*, Albert van Dantzig, Sedco Publishing Limited, Accra, Ghana, 1980, is only ninety-six pages long. Yet it tells a fascinating story about the history of Ghana. When the Europeans first explored the region, then called the Guinea Coast, they found so much gold that they renamed the area the Gold Coast. When Europeans shifted to the capture, exportation, and marketing of humans from Africa, they renamed the area the Slave Coast.

The two slave castles that we visited took us, vicariously, to that awful period in history. First, we visited Elmina Castle, which was first a Portuguese slave port in the fifteenth century. It was captured by the Dutch in the seventeenth century. Next we visited Cape Coast Castle, which has had a confusing history, with much wrangling between the Dutch, Swedish, and Danish explorers. But it was the British who became the rulers of the Cape Coast region and ruled there in the eighteenth and nineteenth centuries.

ELMINA CASTLE

Of the two castles we toured, Elmina Castle had the deepest effect on us. It is huge and had such a history during the slave trade era. In fact, near the end of the year 2001, the castle was featured in a television documentary that was viewed all over the U.S. Those of us who had been on the Ghana study tour identified with those weeping persons we saw on television who were telling about their experiences and emotions during the castle tour. We knew from our experiences exactly what they were talking about. We felt the same gut-wrenching emotions as we stood in the slave port courtyard, looked at its water cistern, stationary guns, cannon balls, and peepholes. We felt even more despair as we looked up to where the tour guide pointed—up to the balcony where the Dutch colonial governor of the area stood as he watched naked African slaves brought from their dungeons and paraded before him so he could

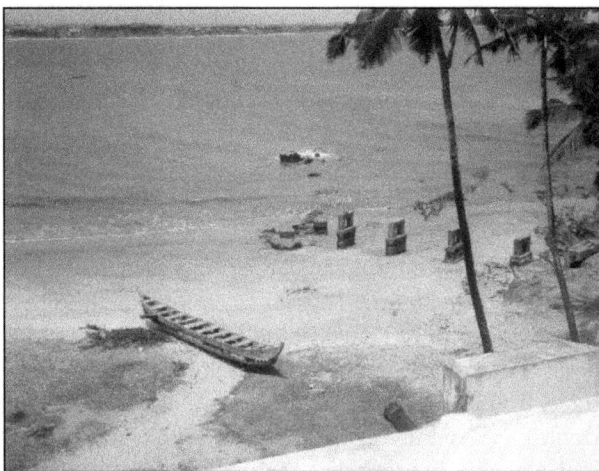

Beach in front of ELMINA SLAVE CASTLE, Elmina, Ghana, West Africa, March 2001.

make his choice for his night bed partner. (We later toured the living quarters, then elegant, where the governor resided.) We wept again as we toured the male slave holding cells, especially the one where "troublesome" males were locked in and starved to death.

Right next to where the Dutch governor stood while selecting his sex partners was a huge sign over the entryway leading to the church. We felt intense anger at this blatant example of sheer hypocrisy!

CAPE COAST CASTLE

The Cape Coast castle area was even more beautiful than Elmina. The beaches were more accessible to our hotel rooms, and we did more "beach bonding" here than we did at Elmina. The tour guide had told us that 60 percent of all black Americans who were descendants of slaves had ancestors who came from Ghana's two slave ports, Elmina and Cape Coast. The other major slave port in West Africa was in the Senegal and Gambia region (from which Alex Haley's ancestors came).

Since I had no knowledge of exactly where that first African ancestor in the Petit or Minter family came from, I chose Elmina and Cape Coast as the probable sites of my ancestors' homeland before the slave diaspora. If that can never be empirically proved, I am content to have those two places as at least symbolic and generic locations of my African roots. Early one morning, I went down to the Cape Coast beach alone. I had brought two little jars from the U.S. with me, and I began to fill the jars with the powdery white sand. But I was interrupted in my sacred "bonding with the motherland" moment by an early-morning vendor, a teenaged boy named Michael. He snatched the jar from my hand and began to fill it with sand. But I snatched it back and explained why only I should fill that jar with sand from the beach that my African ancestors might have trod centuries ago. He understood and left me to my "bonding." But when I finished filling the jars and began picking up seashells to fill another jar that I had brought from the States, he and another teenaged boy joined me, and I gladly accepted their help. I have never seen seashells so delicate and shaped like those (spirals, etc.). Norman joined me and took pictures of the African teenagers and me gathering seashells. Before Michael left, he gave me a large, beautiful pink sea shell because he said I reminded him of his mother (which I am sure I did not). The next day, I went to the beach early again and there was Michael. He had a hard-luck story to tell me. He said that, sadly, he must ask payment for the sea shell he had given me the previous day. I gave him the equivalent of $5 in Cedis and learned another lesson about African vendors! But I will always be grateful to him for understanding the emotional significance of my bonding experience. And he probably needed that $5 more than I did.

UNIVERSITY OF GHANA AT LEGON

On our way to Kumasi and the Ashanti region of Ghana, we stopped by the University of Ghana at Legon. In many ways, the university looked like a typical Historic Black College (HBC) like Tuskegee Institute in Alabama, where my husband, Norman, and I met in the 1950s.

But in many ways, it was different—the scorching heat and humidity, the food, buildings, dorms, etc. The book store is where we felt most at home. We went wild buying books, maps, posters, pens, and everything "African" that we could find!

We also had the pleasant experience of meeting an exchange summer student from Tulsa, a blonde, fair-skinned young woman who had attended the same Tulsa high school, Edison High, where I had taught history for twenty-two years! She was from an Oregon university. She had heard us mention Tulsa in our conversation and came right over and made herself at home with us. When I returned to Tulsa, I called her parents. The father answered the phone, and he excitedly yelled for his wife to get on the phone quick! She asked the usual "mother questions." How did she look? Was she happy? Was she healthy? Had she been using proper amounts of suntan lotion? I informed the parents that their daughter had a bout of malaria when she first got to Ghana but had fully recovered. I explained that she looked fine—in fact, she was radiant. She had no sunburn, and she seemed extemely happy. I was pleased to talk to those parents. I am just like that mother. I want to know at all times that "my babies," now in their thirties and forties, are all right!

KUMASI

Kumasi was one of the most exciting regions we visited. It was so different from the coastal region in the Accra capital area of Ghana. This was to the east and north, and we noted the changing geography and the different tribes of Africans we were now seeing. We saw more cattle, more industry, and the "mother of all markets," the grand Kumasi Market, which is so big and prosperous that vendors come not only from all over Ghana to market their goods, but from surrounding

countries. Our study tour group was the delight of market vendors that day. Goods ranged from the finest African carvings, fabrics, jewelry, furnishings, and musical instruments to live chickens and pygmy goats for evening dinners! The sights, colors, noise, and high-velocity atmosphere of the market were intoxicating. One articulate African woman who spoke perfect English, attired in the brightest-colored dress that I saw during my Africa trip, wanted to hire herself out to me as my private tour guide for the day. I explained that I did not need her help, as a guide led our college study group. Still, she was not convinced that I did not need

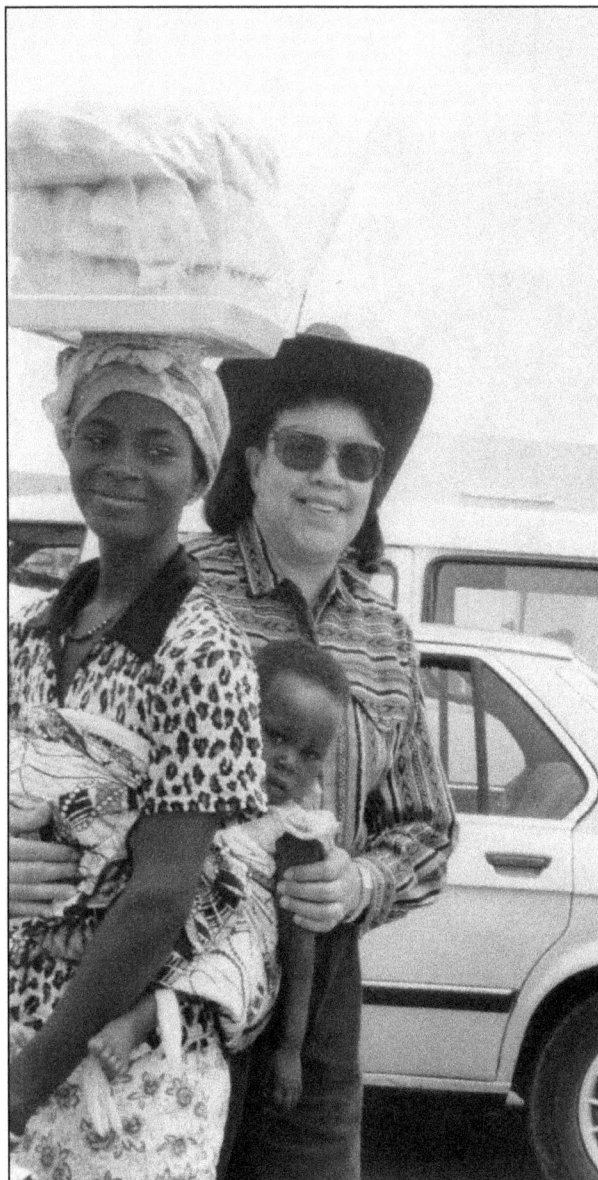

African mother and child, Kumasi, Ghana, West Africa, March 2001.

LA-PALM ROYAL BEACH HOTEL, *Gift Shops, Coffee shops overlooking the Atlantic Ocean, Accra, Ghana, West Africa, March 2001.*

LA-PALM ROYAL BEACH HOTEL, *Accra, Ghana, West Africa, March 2001.*

her as a personal guide, and she continued to follow me, insisting that she could do more than that guide could do. Only when I went to board the bus did the woman give up.

Another unforgettable experience was our visit to the Ashanti region in the Kumasi region. This was where Ghana's ancient kings lived. We had a grand tour of the Ashanti King's Castle. (We had to leave all cameras and camcorders on the bus. Absolutely no photographs or recordings were allowed. Security and restrictions were tighter in this area than they had been when I was a summer Holocaust fellowship student in Israel in 1991!) Once we were cleared, we entered the King's Castle and had a marvelous tour. Our tour guide was Dr. Osaei Kwadwo, who has authored two books about Asante history. I bought both of his books (and he bought both of mine). He signed my books, "Best wishes to a fellow author." My husband and I stocked up on goods from the Ashanti region in the Kumasi district—kente cloth and various kente cloth items, carvings, gold jewelry, animal print backpacks, Africa keychains, desk sets, maps, posters, books, and the cutest little African outfit for our four-year-old grandson Kendrik Jerome Gates.

The little two-piece suit and the little fez hat, outgrown by Kendrik, adorn the walls of one of our bedrooms and bring back pleasant memories of Africa every time I look at them.

The final exciting experience for our tour group in the Kumasi region was our visit to the Kakun National Rain Forest Park, which has a connection with the U.S. Department of Interior. The major attraction for tourists who visit the park is the rope bridge over the 120-foot gorge in the park. Young brave souls, as well as some older brave souls who were visiting the park that day, crossed the bridge one at a time. It took one hour to cross. I do not like heights and chose to sit out this "travel moment" opportunity. My brave husband, a former military man, fears nothing and would have gone. But being the gentleman that he is, he chose to stay with me. We killed time by taking pictures of lizards (one ran over my foot), weaver birds, and crocodiles. We also bought more souvenirs at the park gift shop. When the group got back, we heard all about the shaky rope bridge. Luckily, they did not see any snakes, and no monkeys dropped down out of trees onto them as they had been cautioned about from tour guides who prepared them for the trip.

Each member of our group received a copy of a master videotape of the entire summer study program made by Carl Adams, husband of Dr. Vivian Clark-Adams, one of the co-directors of the TCC study program. So even though Norman and I sat out the "rope-bridge experience," we can see from the tapes what it was like. Viewing that tape made me glad that I chose to stay behind that day.

EVENTS:

GIRLS' RITE OF PASSAGE CEREMONY—ACCRA

One of the most interesting events that happened while we were in the Accra region in March 2001, was the annual presentation of a girls' rite of passage ceremony. The local community was most gracious to the TCC group and allowed our members to view this usually private ceremony, which is taken very seriously. Women, in their finest Sunday-go-meeting clothes, come together to share the history of their culture with young women who will be charged with preserving, cultivating, and passing on that culture to future generations. These lessons are taught through music, dance, and poetry. Men stand in the background, and when the ceremony is over, they come forth and there is much joviality among all. Carl Adams took powerful photographs during the ceremony and immediately after. One of my favorite pictures is that of a little baby boy strapped to his mother's back. During all that singing, dancing, chanting, poetry reading, etc., the baby slept soundly!

AFRICAN DANCE—CAPE COAST

One night when we went to dinner at the Coconut Grove Hotel in Cape Coast, Ghana, we had a surprise waiting for us. The hotel had brought in an African dance troupe—about twelve of the most agile young men and women I have ever seen. These dancers had neck and shoulder moves that I didn't know humans

African dance group, Coconut Grove Hotel, Cape Coast, Ghana, West Africa, March 2001.

could make! Their dance attire was beautiful, their faces shone with excitement and joy, and their movements defied science and anatomy. We were caught up in the hypnotic music and dance. So when the troupe invited our group to join them on the dance floor, most of us went, even if just for a quick photo opportunity. Vivian Clark-Adams and I surprised ourselves by dancing longer than we thought we could. One woman in our tour group, Patricia Peterson of the D.C. area, was young enough, talented enough, and in good enough shape to dance the entire duration of the performance (about two hours)! Another young woman, Michelle Jackson of Tulsa, danced a long time too. Though Vivian and I don't expect any casting calls as a result of our "African dance experience," we had fun, and when we show our Africa videotapes, our friends and co-workers get a kick out of seeing us "dancing up a storm in the Motherland."

OPEN MARKET SHOPPING

No matter where I travel, and no matter what fascinating historical sites I visit, shopping is always on my agenda too. Africa is a shopper's paradise. There are vendors selling goods everywhere. Vendors are very assertive (sometimes aggressive), but the extreme poverty that we saw and the intense desire of the people to provide goods and services to improve their livelihood made us very receptive them. We even bonded with some of them—like the eight vendor brothers who seemed to camp outside the Gates' chalet at the La-Palm Hotel and who delivered goods to our hotel room at all hours of the day or night. One brother provided wood carvings, and another provided fashions like the exquisite three-piece wrap outfit that I bought to wear on special occasions. Still another brother did artwork, and another provided transportation—a taxi which carted the brothers to whatever region our tour bus took daily. All the brothers had specific duties, and they were all serious about their business, which was sell goods to the Americans whether the Americans needed them or not. After listening to one or all eight of the brothers, most customers were convinced they did need those African items!

Vendors knew our schedule better than we did (insider information from relatives) and often honked and waved at us as they sped on to be in the next town to greet us with goods when we stepped off the bus! Hotel and restaurants hired security guards who literally beat persistent vendors off their premises, but security guards and billy clubs are no match for a determined African vendor. One vendor, who sported a saucy beret, had a gold tooth, and rode a motorcycle to our various scheduled events, became our favorite. We nicknamed him "Superfly." No matter where we went in Africa during our study tour, we could count on seeing him.

ELEMENTARY AND SECONDARY SCHOOL EVENTS

We loved meeting schoolchildren, for children are the greatest icebreakers in the world. The children were just beautiful in their crisp school uniforms. We tried not to spoil them with gifts, money, and snacks. Officials feared that some students would become so enamored with tourists that they would neglect their school work, or maybe even drop out of school to chase after "the American dream."

None of us members of the TCC College overseas study group ever missed an opportunity to stop and talk to the children. Some, like Darrell of San Francisco, California, created their own opportunities. Darrell would get up early so that he could walk to the nearest elementary school. Wherever we toured, he made it a point to find and talk to educators. He would tell us how he would share the information he gained in Africa with the California youth with whom he worked.

CONCLUSIONS:

Study tours such as ours are wonderful. Knowledge gained, memories made, and pictures recorded for posterity will last forever. The predeparture orientation classes given by the TCC tour directors were excellent and very helpful to us, but nothing can really prepare one for the cultural changes inevitable in international travel. The heat and humidity were the most difficult conditions for me to adjust to. My $75 hairdo vanished the minute I stepped off the plane. The hair trials of

African-American women are legendary. In Africa, our "American hair" (actually a complex composition bearing traits of our African and European ancestors) was ever a source of concern. We women spent every night trying to get it presentable for the next day!

The pest problems that we had been warned of never gave us much trouble. Proper use of repellants kept us safe. Sunburn was not a problem, either. Lathering on the lotion and wearing hats and long-sleeved clothes kept safe, even those with sensitive skin and who are prone to sunburn.

Sanitation was a problem for us. Developing countries do not have the luxury of plenty of water and clean sanitation facilities. We just did like we were told to do in those orientation classes—we made do with what we had and we respected the land, the culture, and the people despite our lack of the amenities that we were accustomed to. Travelers to Africa should pay close attention to the list of items they are told to bring. We followed directions and had a surplus of bottled water, travel toilet paper, and handi-wipes.

But by far the most difficult thing for me was adjusting to the food. I didn't realize how "Americanized" I am when it comes to food. I take for granted the vast array of restaurants of all types—from the elegant and expensive to fast food places in the United States. I love them all! I found no equivalent in Africa. We took most of our meals in the hotels where we stayed, and all the meals we had in Africa (southern coastal region or western and northern regions) were almost identical. For eight days in a row, we basically had the same "Ghanaian favorite meal"—fish, usually whole with the eyes still in place, which tasted like American carp, two to three kinds of rice, fresh vegetable salad, yam balls, and fried plaintains. I know that the cooks put a lot of effort into preparing our food. Sometimes, we were taken into the kitchen to see preparations. I really did try to develop a taste for the African food, but eight days just wasn't enough time to get used to the differences. I found the food too hot and spicy.

Evidently, dessert is not that important in African cuisine, for we seldom had dessert. Exceptions were mango ice cream and pineapple upside-down cake, which were served in the homes of two African ladies who lived in elegant, upper-middle-class homes in Accra. Both hostesses served our group in elegant courtyards.

The hotel breakfasts were very good. We had some of the best fresh-squeezed tropical fruit juices that I have ever tasted. The fresh fruit was great also. Chefs made omelets on request and brought them to our tables. The pancakes and pastries were supreme. But there was no bacon, and the sausages were mostly starch fillers which Americans did not reorder after the first time. There was a meat dish at breakfast which Americans usually skipped. It was a beef stew. We also skipped the huge pan of baked beans. Those dishes reflect Africa's tradition of providing hearty breakfasts for African workers who often left the breakfast table to go to mines for long, bone-breaking work.

Upon our return to Tulsa, some of our tour members, including me, suffered exhaustion, sleep deprivation, and "food deprivation disorders." My food problem was soon overcome after I sent my grown son to bring me a "prescription" from Long John Silver's restaurant and from Braum's. After I downed a hearty helping of fried shrimp, french fries, onion rings, vegetable salad, and the largest strawberry milk shake that Braum's offers, I was well on my way to recovery!

Perhaps with more time, I could have learned to like the African cuisine. Still, the study program in Africa was a marvelous experience. I highly recommend such trips for all who want to connect to and bond with Africa. You'll never forget your experience there!

Bibliography

BOOKS

Askew, Rilla, *Fire in Beulah*, Penguin Putnam Inc., New York, New York, 2001

Baker, T. Lindsay and Julie P., *The WPA Oklahoma Slave Narratives*, University of Oklahoma Press, Norman, Oklahoma, 1996

Burton, Art, *Black, Red, and Deadly*, Eakin Press, Austin, Texas, 1991

Debo, Angie, *And Still the Waters Run*, Princeton University Press, Princeton, New Jersey, 1940

Ellsworth, Scott, *Death in The Promised Land*, Louisiana State University Press, Baton Rouge, Louisiana, 1982

Gates, Eddie Faye, *They Came Searching*, Eakin Press, 1997

Hower, Bob, *Tulsa Race Riot "America's Deadliest"*, Homestead Press, Tulsa, Oklahoma, 1993

Johnson, Hannibal B., *Black Wall Street*, Eakin Press, 1998

Lee, Victoria, *"Movers and Shakers"*, A Touch of Heart Publishing, Tulsa, 1997

Rhodes, Jewell Parker, *Magic City*, HarperCollins Publishers Inc., New York, 1997

Vaughn-Roberson, Courtney Ann and Glen, *City in the Osage Hills*, Pruett Publishing Co., Boulder, Colorado, 1984

Weygand, Sammy, *Color Blind*, Color Blind Productions, Claremore, Oklahoma 1994

MAGAZINES

Amundson, Heidi, *Writer lives ideals she teaches to others*, Alumni Review, University of North Dakota, Grand Forks, North Dakota, May/June 1999

Atkinson, Pat, *Lighting the Way*, TulsaPeople, Langdon Publishing, Tulsa, Oklahoma, January 2001

Bachhofer, Aaron, *Strange Bedfellows*, Chronicles of Oklahoma, Oklahoma Historical Society, Oklahoma City, Oklahoma, Fall 1999

Basore, Brian and Pierce, Barbara, *Oklahoma Cemeteries A Bibliography*, Oklahoma City Historical Society, Oklahoma City, 1993

Beach, Christopher, *To Finally Bring About Race Riot Healing*, Community Spirit, Equipment Publications, Inc., Tulsa, June 2000

Bennett, Lerone Jr., *10 biggest lies about black americans*, Ebony, Johnson Publishing Company, Chicago, Illinois, May 2001

Bewley, Nell Hart, *Toys of Christmas Past*, Tulsa Cityscape, J3 Publications, Tulsa, December 2001

Butler, Atiya, *Reading the Black Experience*, American Legacy, Forbes, Inc., New York, New York, Fall 1997

Carter, Kent, *Tams Bixby Doing Government Business in The Gilded Age*, Chronicles of Oklahoma, Winter 2000/01

Chappell, Kevin, *How Black Inventors Changed America*, Ebony, February 1997

Cleghorn, Reese, *Martin Luther King Apostle of Crisis*, The Saturday Evening Post, The Curtis Publishing Co., Philadelphia, Pennsylvania, June 1963

Colley, David, *The Red Ball Express*, American Legacy, Spring 2001

Commander, Tulsa Post, *African Blood Brotherhood, The Tulsa Riot*, The Crusader, Cyril Y. Briggs, New York, New York, July, 1921

Franklin, John Hope & Ellsworth, Scott, editors, *The Tulsa Race Riot of 1921: A Historical and Scientific Report*, Duke University, Durham, North Carolina, June 2000

Gates, Eddie Faye, *Good News/Bad News: Black History Month*, Oklahoma Family Magazine, Schuman Publishing Co., Tulsa, February 1998

Goodwin, Alquita, senior editor, *Greenwood: A historical perspective*, Oklahoma Eagle Publishing Company, Tulsa, 1989

Henderson, Gina, and Johnson, Marlene L., *Black Wall Street*, emerge, BET Group Publishers, Washington, District of Columbia, February 2000

Jackson, Ken and Angie, *Bountiful Browsing*, TulsaPeople, March 1999

Jessup, Michael M., *Consorting with Blood and Violence*, Chronicles of Oklahoma, Fall 2000

Johnson, Roy S., *Going Home*, Fortune, Time Inc., July 1999

Johnson, Roy S., *Going Home*, Your Company, Time Inc. Publishing, New York, July/August 1999

Judt, Tony, *Writing History, Facts Optional*, Alumni Newsletter, U.S. Holocaust Memorial Museum, Washington, Winter 2000/01

King, Casey, and Osborne, Linda Barrett, *Oh, Freedom!*, American Legacy, Fall 1997

Levin, Shachar, *Antisemitism Then and Now*, Yad Vashem, Jerusalem, February 2001

Lewallen, Robert D., *Let The People Rule*, Chronicles of Oklahoma, Fall 1995

Lipstadt, *My Fight for Truth and Justice*, Alumni Newsletter, Winter 2000/01

Lowitt, Richard, *Dear Miss Debo: The Correspondence of E.E. Dale and Angie Debo*, Chronicles of Oklahoma, Winter 1999-2000

Madar, Orit Ohayon, *A Family Legacy*, Yad Vashem, February 2001

McKnight, Dr. Mamie, editor, *African American Families and Settlements of Dallas: On the Inside looking out*, Black Dallas Remembered, Inc., Dallas, Texas, May 1990

Mundende, D. Chongo, *The Undesirable Oklahomans*, Chronicles of Oklahoma, Fall 1998

Paldiel, Dr. Mordecai, *A Nondescript Bicycle*, Yad Vashem, February 2001

Parks, Gordon, *The Cycle of Despair*, Life, Time Inc., March 1968

Ruffin, Kimberly N., facilitator, *100 Years of African American Literature and Letters*, Black Issues Book Review, Cox, Matthews & Associates, Fairfax, Virginia, November-December 1999

Satterwhite, Aisha, *Oklahoma's Promised Land*, American Legacy, Summer 2000

Schickel, Richard, *Into the Arms of Strangers*, Alumni Newsletter, Winter 2000/01

Shippey, Kim, *The Healing of America*, Christian Science Sentinel, Boston, Massachusetts, November 1998

Shippey, Kim, *Polishing Rough Diamonds in Oklahoma*, Christian Science Sentinel, December 1998

St. Jean, Wendy, *You Have the Land. I Have the Cattle*, Chronicles of Oklahoma, Summer 2000

Thomas, Dudley, *Greenwood Avenue*, Greenwood Chamber of Commerce, Tulsa August 1999

Unknown, *Panel on 1921 Tulsa Race Riot Urges Reparations For Victims*, Jet, A Johnson Publication, Chicago, Illinois, February 2000

Unknown, *Black's White*, Time, Time Inc., January 1938

Unknown, *Charity Begins At Home*, Oklahoma Magazine, Schuman Publishing Co., December 2001

Unknown, *Living History*, Oklahoma Today, Oklahoma Tourism and Recreation Department, Oklahoma City, July/August 2001

Unknown, *Newsmaker Awards*, TulsaPeople, May 2000

Unknown, *Reflections on a Legacy*, The Oklahoma Eagle, January 2000

Unknown, Tulsa Historical Society "Tulsa Hall of Fame 1999", TulsaPeople, September 1999

Waller, Barrett, *The Brady District Tulsa's Urban Village*, TulsaPeople, July 2001

Waller, Bill, *Greenwood Tomorrow*, TulsaPeople, September 2000

Walton, John Brooks, *Lost Mansions of Tulsa*, TulsaPeople, December 2000

Walton, John Brooks, *Tulsa's Castle*, TulsaPeople, August 2000

Westerbeck, Colin, *Chicago Art Institute Pays $185,000 for Douglass Portrait*, Ebony, February 1997

Wheeler, Ed, *The Disaster of the 1921 Race Riot*, Impact, June-July 1971

Wickett, Murray R, *The Fear of "Negro Domination"*, Chronicles of Oklahoma, Spring 2000

Woodard, Alfre, *Family Ties*, ExcellStyle, Tulsa, May-June 1999

Yacovone, Donald, *I am a soldier now*, American Legacy, Fall 1977

Addendum

Johnnie Cochran reading Eakin Press books by E. F. Gates

A lawsuit was filed in United States District Court in Tulsa, Oklahoma on February 24, 2003, on behalf of plaintiffs and descendants of 1921 Tulsa riot victims

Conveners (attorneys) for the lawsuit were Johnnie Cochran, Willie E. Gary, Charles Ogletree, Dennis Sweet III, Randall Robinson, Adjoa A. Aiyetoro, Michelle A. Roberts, Eric Miller, Michael D. Hausfeld, Suzette M. Malveaux, Rose Sanders, *aka* Faye Ora Rose Toure, Lorenzo Williams, J.L. Chestnut, Jr., Joseph M. Sellers, Tricia Purks Hoffler, James O. Goodwin, Leslie Mansfield, Jim Lloyd, Sharon Cole Jones

Al Brophy, Professor, University of Alabama School of Law, Consultant, Historian to the lawsuit team

Paul Finkelman, Tulsa, Oklahoma, Consultant

Eddie Faye Gates, Riot Commission Member, 1997-2001, and Mark Stodghill, Member, Tulsa Reparations Coalition, President, Center for Racial Justice (CFRJ), Tulsa, were appointed Co-Liason Persons between the "Legal Dream Team" attorneys, whose headquarters are in Boston, Massachusetts, and the plaintiffs and survivors in the lawsuit, who live all over the United States (and one in Paris, France)

Paul Ellis, Attorney, Pittsburgh, Pennsylvania, Consultant to the Tulsa Reparations Coalition and the Center for Racial Justice, Tulsa

About the Author

Eddie Faye Gates was born in Preston, Oklahoma, and was an honors student at Tuskegee Institute in Alabama for three years. She later attended Texas Southern University in Houston, Texas, and the University of Maryland's Overseas College at Burtonwood Royal Air Force Base in Warrington, England. She graduated magna cum laude from the University of North Dakota in 1968, and received a master of arts degree, with honors, from the University of Tulsa in 1974.

Mrs. Gates was a military dependent wife from 1954 to 1968 and lived on air bases all over the U.S. and in Europe. She moved to Tulsa in 1968 and taught history at Edison High School for twenty-two years, and was curriculum coordinator, social studies K-12, Tulsa public schools from 1990-1992. She retired in 1992 and is now the published author of two books, *Miz Lucy's Cookies: And Other Links in My Black Family Support System,* Coman & Associates, Tulsa, Oklahoma, 1996; and *They Came Searching: How Blacks Sought the Promised Land in Tulsa,* Eakin Press, Austin, Texas, 1997.

Mrs. Gates is a community activist and has served on various boards, commissions, and councils of organizations dedicated to the uplifting of all mankind, such as Advisory Council, National Conference, United Nations Association/USA, New York, New York; Oklahoma Commission to Study the Tulsa Race Riot, 1921; The Oklahoma Historical Society, Oklahoma City, Oklahoma; Oklahoma Educational Television Authority, Oklahoma City, Oklahoma; and Tulsa Human Rights Commission (chair for two terms). Mrs. Gates has received numerous honors, including recently being inducted into the University of Tulsa's Phi Beta Kappa Organization, the nation's oldest and most prestigious honors organization, founded on December 5, 1776, at the College of William and Mary in Williamsburg, Virginia.

Mrs. Gates is also active in her church, First Church of Christ, Scientist, Tulsa, and served as first reader of Third Church of Christ, Scientist, Tulsa, 1975–1978. The joy of her life is traveling with her husband, Norman, a retired United States Air Force major, to visit the couple's five grown children, seven grandchildren, and two step grandchildren.

Cover Artist

Norman Gates, Jr., graphic artist, Dallas, Texas. Mr. Gates studied art at Tulsa Junior College, the University of Tulsa, and North Texas State University. He won the Doel Reed Art Award for a pen and pencil drawing that was exhibited at Tulsa Junior College, and the Alexandre Hogue Award at the University of Tulsa for a drawing that was exhibited at the university. He was also the recipient of an Alumni Art Trust Scholarship at the University of Tulsa.

Index

Davis, E. Bernice Banks, 131
Davis, Elmer Lee, 145
Davis, Ernest, 134
Davis, Etoyce Marie, 145
Davis, Fred, 145
Davis, Gerald, 145
Davis, Harold, 145
Davis, James Harold, 145
Davis, James Thomas, 145
Davis, Jerry, 145
Davis, Joanna, 179
Davis, LaVerne Cooksey, 65-66
Davis, Leon, 134-135
Davis, Lucinda Pittman, 135
Davis, M. D., 134
Davis, Phillip, 145
Davis, Rosalind Marie, 145
Davis, Roy, 131
Davis, Sammy, Jr., 165
Dawson, Willie Williams Pannell, 99
de Tocqueville, Alexis, 11
Dean, Helen, 137
Debo, Angie, 140
Deisenroth, Oakley, 176
Dennie, Alfred Stanley, 22
Dennie, Howard Leroy, 144
Dennie, Lawrence Herman, 144
Desvignes, Russell, 92
DeWitty, Dorothy, 7, 171
Dillard, Stephanie, 179
Dozier, Richard, 38
Dozier-Walton, Carol, 38
Driver, Cindy, 179
DuBois, W.E.B., 89, 90, 195
Duffy, Mike, 162
Duncan, Carrie, 95
Duncan, James L., 95
Dunham, Katherine, 89
Dunlap, Troy, 162
Dunn, Arthur Fritz, 96
Dunn, Georgia, 74
Dunn, Hattie Lilly, 47, 60, 66, 115
Dunn, Lillian Anderson, 96
Dunn, Nina, 7, 10
Dupree, Adonia, 67
Durant, Glovenia, 66
Durant, James, 47, 66-67
Durant, Will, 41
Dysart, Willie, 58

Earnhart, Audrey, 178
Earven, Edward, 46
Ector, Harriet, 85
Ector, Howard, 85
Eddy, Clyde, 157
Edison, Thomas, 57

Edmondson, Luther, 127, 135
Edwards, Corine, 58
Eidson, Amy Gamble, 136
Eldredge, Betty, 162
Ellington, Monyett Williams, 136
Elliott, Matthew, 175
Ellis, "Doc," 162
Ellis, Carole, 176
Ellis, Kimberly, 189
Ellis, Paul, 205
Ellsworth, Scott, 7, 8, 10, 19, 33, 163,
    171, 174, 182, 183
Emery, Robert J., 4
Engel, Georgia, 176
Everett, Reuben, 117
Ewing, Bill, 146
Ewing, Jo Ann, 146
Ewing, Robert, 146

Fahnstock, V., 67
Fair, Janet, 135
Fair, Stanley, Jr., 135
Fair, Stanley, Sr., 135
Fairchild, Flipper, 118
Fairchild, Florence, 113
Fairchild, Robert, 77, 113, 128
Fairchild, Ruth, 77
Fairchild, Yuri, 118
Farakhan, Arthur, 7, 171
Faulkner, Betty, 162
Fegunjobi, Egbe, 174
Feldman, Nancy, 179
Fell, Jacob, 157
Fell, Morris B., 157
Figures, Lucille B. Buchanan, 49, 67
Finkelman, Paul, 205
Fisher, Ada Lois Sipuel, 145
Fisher, Bruce, 129, 175
Fisher, Robert, 157
Fleming, Frances, 116, 179
Fletcher, Daddy, 74
Flurry, Edward, 15, 16
Flurry, Fannie Jackson, 15, 16
Flurry, Jessie, 15, 16
Flurry, Virginia, 15
Flurry, William, 15
Fontenot, Sondia, 133
Forrest, Nathan Bedford, 8
Foshee, Juanita, 141
Foster, Karen, 148
Foster, Wilbur, 133
Foushee, Helen, 77
Fox, Connie, 179
Franklin, Alfreda O. Dennie, 144
Franklin, Anna, 77
Franklin, Archie Jackson, 67-68, 94

Franklin, B. C., 35, 37, 43, 90, 92, 135
Franklin, Frances, 71, 72
Franklin, Jackson Washington, 71, 71
Franklin, Jimmie Lilly, 47, 60, 68, 115
Franklin, John Hope, 11, 19, 35, 60,
    77, 135, 171, 182, 183
Frayser, Robert Clar, 158

Gage, Tom, 157
Gamble, Harry, Jr., 136
Gambrel, Joan Hill, 68
Gant, Reuben, 160
Garvey, Marcus, 16
Gary, Mr., 140
Gary, Willie E., 205
Gates, Bertha Jean Owens Gates, 58
Gates, Henry Louis, 11
Gates, Kendrik Jerome, 198
Germany, Thelma Kinlaw, 129, 138
Gibbs, Charlette Johnson, 138
Gibbs, Ernestine, 42, 44, 69-70, 183
Gibbs, Harold, 70
Gibbs, Lodious, 70
Gibbs, Minnie, 70
Gibson, Walker, 149
Gilliam, Theressa Cornella
    McNeal, 47, 50, 57, 70, 115
Glass, Merritt J., 35, 157, 177
Glass, Wilson, 157
Glover, Johnnie, 58
Goble, Danney, 30, 183, 188, 189-190
Goldsmith, Connie, 136
Goodkid, Mr., 75
Goodlett, Viola Margaret, 137
Goodson, Lewis, 136
Goodwin, Edwin L., 20, 113
Goodwin, James H., 42, 88, 113
Goodwin, James O., 20, 113, 205
Gordon, Dorothy L., 20
Grady, Adell Hopskins Arteberry, 70
Grant, Resha, 177
Graves, Linda Edmonson, 127, 135
Grays, Ben Franklin, 70-71
Grays, Leon, 50, 70-71
Grayson, Albert, 136
Grayson, Cenia Simmons, 58
Grayson, Doris, 136
Grayson, Hattie, 136
Grayson, John L, 58
Grayson, "Saucer," 126, 129
Grayson, Willie James, 136
Green, Hubert Jefferson, 118
Green, Mary Ella, 136
Green, Mr., 99
Guess, H. A., 43, 79, 91, 78, 104
Guess, James, 78

Gurley, O. W., 24, 42, 88
Gustafson, John, 24, 33
Guyton, Bertha Hopskins, 71

Hackett, Hazel Franklin, 45, 49, 67, 71-72, 130
Hadden, Eddie Renord, 68
Hairston, Anita, 62
Hairston, Birdie, 62
Hairston, Everette, 62
Hale, Hannah, 105
Hale, Henry, 105
Haley, Alex, 194, 196
Hall, Amos T., 20, 43, 108, 128, 136, 138, 141
Hall, Cecil, 108, 141
Hall, Mildred Johnson, 46, 72-73
Halley, Harry, 104, 153
Halliburton, Rudy, 7
Hamel, Tom Swift, 151
Hamilton, Alice Moore Wiley, 73
Hamilton, Ethel Mae Walker, 149
Hamilton, Jarred, 149
Hamilton, Keith, 149
Hamilton, Milton, 73
Hamilton, Price, 149
Hamilton, Sherrie, 149
Hamner, Earl, 174
Hampton, Nell Hamilton, 73
Harding, Cleo Cherry, 118
Harding, Warren G., 32
Harding, Wilma, 179
Hardy, J. E., 91
Hare, Julia, 171, 174
Hare, Nathan, 171, 174
Harrell, Leontyne Thomas, 142
Harris, Jesse, 38
Harris, Lemuel Jerry, 136
Harris, Louis, 83
Harris, Mary Priscilla Parker, 147
Harris, Mattie Elodia, 136
Harris, Mercedes Adele, 136
Harris, Mrs., 134
Harris, Rodger, 175
Harrison, Richard B., 89
Hatcher, Augustus, 46, 73
Hatcher, Leroy Leon, 46, 73-74
Hatcher, Lois Muster, 73
Hausfeld, Michael D., 205
Hawkins, Berzelle Williams, 129
Hawkins, Clarence, Jr., 136
Hawkins, Elijah, 136
Hawkins, Jeanette, 136
Hawkins, Lula, 137
Hawkins, Orlando, Sr., 136, 1367
Hawkins, Willie, 136

Hayden, Fountaine, 145
Hayes, Mary Ann, 163
Hayes, Rutherford B., 18
Haynes, Madeleine, 45-46, 74-75
Henderson, Joseph, 137
Henderson, Mamie, 137
Henderson, Rubye Kelley, 119
Henry, Lula Row, 85
Henry, William, 85
Herndon, Chesley C., 163
Herrington, Delores Spears, 146
Hervey, Emma, 127, 137
Hewitt, Vivian, 177
Hill, James "Bottlehead," 48, 75
Hill, Joyce Walker, 45, 76, 103, 104, 128
Hill, Sarah Stamps, 75
Himes, Gary, 163
Hines, Gregory, 165
Hirsch, James, 7, 41, 171
Hoffler, Tricia Purks, 205
Holderness, Jobie Elizabeth, 113, 172
Holderness, Lynn, 113
Hollis, Ken, 189
Holloway, Robert Daniel, Jr., 77
Holloway, Robert Daniel, Sr., 77, 137
Holloway, Roberta Smith, 77
Holmes, Nuel, 162
Holmes, Wilzette Faye Horn, 136
Hood, Muzzy, 72
Hooker, Anita J., 62, 77
Hooker, Olivia, 47, 77, 78
Hooker, Samuel D., 42, 62, 77, 91
Hooker, Samuel, Jr., 78
Hooks, Maybelline Presley, 144
Hoover, Herbert, 17
Hopkins, Juanita Alexander Lewis, 20, 130
Horn, H. Maurice, 136
Horner, Maxine, 38, 71, 143, 179, 181
Houston, Merton, 26
Howard, Louvenia Flurry Bivens, 15
Howell, Johnson, 133
Howell, Maximillian, 133
Howell, Shirley, 175
Howell, Wilhelmina Guess, 43, 78-79, 141
Hower, Robert, 163, 171
Huddleston, John, 73
Huddleston, Mary, 141
Huggins, Helen, 129, 145
Huggins, Richard, 127, 137
Huggins, Viola, 127, 137
Hughes, Charles, 79, 117
Hughes, Horace, 77
Hughes, Langston, 174
Humphrey, David, 64

Humphrey, Hattie, 64
Hunter, Claudine, 137
Hurd, Anna B. King, 147
Hurd, Myrtle Wells, 79

Ingram, Vera, 45, 79
Isom, Fred, 161

Jackson, A. C., 42, 43, 72, 78, 86, 89, 94-95
Jackson, Cora, 137
Jackson, Della Shelton, 152
Jackson, Douglas, 111
Jackson, Eunice Cloman, 47, 76, 79-80
Jackson, Gail, 130
Jackson, Genevieve Tillman, 49, 50, 80
Jackson, Iola Streeter, 119
Jackson, Michelle, 199
Jackson, Oda Winn, 15, 16
Jackson, Rosie Lee Smith, 146
Jackson, Samuel Malone, 47, 80
Jackson, Willie Bell, 81, 101
Jarrett, Hobart, 47, 81
Jarrett, Wilson, 21, 42, 110
Jefferson, Arthur, 126, 130
Jeffries, George, 106
Jessie, Geraldine Fair, 135
Jimerson, Keith, 77, 179
Jimerson, Rebecca Marks, 136
Johnson, Artie Lacy, 59, 83
Johnson, B. F., 158
Johnson, Calvin, 64
Johnson, Carolyn Price, 144
Johnson, Edith G., 20
Johnson, Ella, 137
Johnson, Felecia McLeod, 141
Johnson, George, 72, 73
Johnson, Hannibal, 7, 10, 23, 171
Johnson, Herbert, 166, 167
Johnson, Isaac, 138
Johnson, James Weldon, 10
Johnson, Jerome, 176
Johnson, Katie Lee Staples, 73
Johnson, Kimberly, 160, 175, 179
Johnson, Lula Belle, 83
Johnson, Molly, 166-167
Johnson, Myles, 158
Johnson, Ovide, 83
Johnson, Robert E., 83
Johnson, Robert Franklin, 138
Johnson, Ronald Wayne, 138
Johnson, Val Gene, Sr., 138
Johnson, Verdell, 77

May, Faye, 152
Mayshaw, Sarah Curvay, 129, 134
McArthur, Douglas, 60
McCain, Leona, 130
McClure, Roanna Henry, 85
McCondichie, Eldoris Mae Ector, 4, 46, 44, 48, 50, 60, 85-87, 164
McCormick, Ruby, 120
McCullough, Sheriff, 33
McCullough, Willard M., 24
McCutchen, G. Calvin, 49, 72, 120
McDonald, Carrie B., 42, 139
McElroy, Tina, 174
McFarland, Lorraine, 87, 126, 138
McGill, Jean Williams, 20, 136
McGlorie, A. L., 140
McGlorie, Ucinda, 140
McGowan, Adelle, 67
McGowan, Clyde, 94, 127, 140
McGowan, Donald, 94, 127, 140
McGowan, Euell, 141
McGowan, Samuel, 42, 52, 67, 140
McGowan, Vera C. Marshall, 140
McGowan, Webber, 141
McKeever, Mrs., 141
McLeod, Bessie Audele Beatty, 141
McLeod, Wallace, 141
McMillan, Betty Presley, 144
McMullen, Sandy, 96
McNatt, Jessie, 164
McNatt, Paul Buster, 164
McNeal, Annie, 42, 57, 70
McRuffin, Hattie Johnson, 141
McRuffin, John B., 141
McVeigh, Timothy, 19
Means, Willie Musgrove, 90
Menor, Ziona, 177
Miler, Eric, 205
Miller, David Rosten Walker, 121
Miller, Frances Roston Walker, 121
Miller, LaDawna, 151
Miller, Robert Ryal, 5
Minner, Millington, 142
Minter, Clifton, 18
Minter, James Matthew, 18, 19
Minter, Orion, 18
Minter, Retter Hardeman, 18, 19, 194
Mitchell, "Dad," 77
Mitchell, Barbara Ann Taylor, 83
Mitchell, Dale, 83
Mitchell, James, 62
Mitchell, Jessie Cunliff, 62
Mitchell, Mattie King, 147
Mitchell, Peggy Ann McRuffin, 127, 141
Mitchell, Thelma Ford, 50, 90
Mitchell, William Willis, 44, 83

Momaday, Scott, 174
Monday, Elizabeth Presley, 144
Monroe, Dorothy, 91
Monroe, Emma B. Toole, 121
Monroe, George, 50, 60, 75, 91, 98, 121-123, 127, 141, 142, 143, 175, 176, 183
Monroe, Lottie, 122, 142
Monroe, Martha, 176
Monroe, Osborne, 42, 142
Monroe, Thomas I., 55
Moore, Lena Mae, 137
Moore, Naomi Foster, 133
Moore, Pat Galbraith, 147-148
Moore, Ronald Earl, 133
Moran, Edna McLeod, 90
Moran, Ishmael S., 49, 90
Moran, Julius, 90
Morgan, Della, 139
Morgan, Gayle Greer, 171
Morris, Eva Gamble, 136
Mosely, Walter, 174
Motley, Dr., 73
Mullenax, Harvey Ernest, 167, 168
Mullenax, Jack, 168
Murray, Maggie, 84
Murrell, Lacy E., 136
Musgrove, Leroy, 142
Musgrove, Nettie May, 142
Musgrove, Robert, 142
Myrdal, Gunnar, 11
Myrtle, Ollie, 153

Nails, Claxton, 142
Nails, Henry, 42, 142
Nails, James, 21, 42
Nails, James, Sr., 142
Napier, Fannie, 92
Napier, James, 92
Nash, Mollie Oliver, 142
Nash, Oscar, 142
Nash, Ruth Dean, 46, 91
Neal, Mrs., 75
Neal, Simeon L., 49, 91
Neitzke, Stephen, 164-165
Newberry, Isom, 94
Newkirk, Almadge, 43, 48, 91-92
Newkirk, Amos, 91
Nichols, Mr., 140
Nichols, Reverend, 64
Nkrumah, Kwame, 195
Nomura, Mike, 165
Norman, Jeannie, 158
Norris, Robert, 8, 9, 30, 164, 171
Northington, James Lee, 22, 129

O'Brien, Gerald F., 165
O'Brien, William, 8, 9, 30, 165, 171
Oakley, Harold, 15
Oakley, Irene Winn, 15
Ogletree, Charles, 205
Okpogba, Desmond, 143
Oliphant, Judge, 89
Oliver, Mattie Davis, 136
Oliver, Myrtle Napier, 92
Oliver, Paris, 128, 142
Oliver, Pearl, 49, 128, 142, 152
Osborne, Lavada Louise Parker, 142-143

Page, Geraldien McCoy, 92
Page, Sarah, 23, 36, 97, 110-111
Parcel, Hazel Leigh Whitney, 158
Parker, Helen Washington, 92, 105
Parker, Mary Lue Hicks, 142
Parker, Mrs., 55
Parker, Myrtle Fields, 142
Parker, Nora Hamilton, 149
Parker, Steve, 142
Parks, Rosa, 178
Parrish, Mary Elizabeth Jones, 7, 9, 10, 150, 151
Parry, Juanita Maxine Scott, 92
Parsons, Audrey Banks, 131
Partee, Mrs., 42
Pate, Mr., 62
Patterson, Ida Burns, 92
Patton, Calvin, 143
Patton, John W., 127, 143
Patton, R. C., 143
Patton, Willie Thompson, 143
Payne, Frank, 85
Payne, Freddie, 93, 95
Payne, Georgia, 143
Payne, Katie, 85
Payne, Lena Mae, 138
Payne, Louvenia, 85
Payne, Mary, 114, 143
Pearce, Betty, 79
Peck, Carrie B., 187
Pegues, Julius, 139
Perkins, Sandra L. Bell, 116
Perkins, Useni, 80, 176
Perry Juanita Maxine Scott, 95
Perryman, Bob, 126, 144
Perryman, Rose, 144
Perryman-Grace, Eva, 144
Perryman-Tease, Addie, 126, 143-144
Perryman-Tease, Geraldine, 126
Persons, Carrie, 77
Peterson, Patricia, 199
Petit, Joseph, 17, 18